ALSO BY ANDREW J. NATHAN

Modern China, 1840–1972: An Introduction to
 Sources and Research Aids (1973)

Peking Politics, 1918–1923: Factionalism and
 the Failure of Constitutionalism (1976)

Popular Culture in Late Imperial China (co-edited
 with David Johnson and Evelyn S. Rawski, 1985)

Human Rights in Contemporary China (with
 R. Randle Edwards and Louis Henkin, 1986)

CHINESE DEMOCRACY

CHINESE DEMOCRACY

ANDREW J. NATHAN

UNIVERSITY OF CALIFORNIA PRESS
Berkeley   Los Angeles

First Paperback Edition 1986
University of California Press
Berkeley   Los Angeles

Published by arrangement with Alfred A. Knopf, Inc.

Grateful acknowledgment is made to the following for permission
to reprint from previously published materials:

Columbia University Press: condensed version of two chapters
from *Human Rights in Contemporary China* by Andrew Nathan,
R. Randle Edwards, and Louis Henkin. Copyright © 1985 by
Columbia University Press. By permission.

University of California Press: condensed version of "The
Beginnings of Mass Culture: Journalism and Fiction in the Late
Ch'ing and Beyond," from *Popular Culture in Late Imperial China*,
David Johnson, Andrew Nathan, and Evelyn Rawski, eds.,
University of California Press.

Library of Congress Cataloging in Publication Data

Nathan, Andrew J. (Andrew James)
    Chinese democracy.
    Bibliography: p.   Includes index.
    1. Political participation—China—History.
2. Political rights—China—History.   3. China—Politics
and government—20th century.   I. Title.
JQ1516.N38   1986   323'.042'0951   86-11305
ISBN 0-520-05933-6 (pbk. : alk. paper)

Printed in the United States of America
    2   3   4   5   6   7   8   9   0

CONTENTS

ACKNOWLEDGMENTS

It is presumptuous for a non-Chinese to write on a subject as broad as democracy in China, but those inside China who could do the job better do not have the freedom of inquiry it requires. Fortunately, I have had the help of many Chinese. Some talked with me informally and some granted interviews for the media portion of the study. At each meeting I was reminded of the difficulty of generalizing about a subject as complex as China, but also of how important it is for both Westerners and Chinese to think about the issues of power and freedom there. My first expression of gratitude is to my informants, although they remain nameless.

For financial support since 1973, I wish to thank the John Simon Guggenheim Memorial Foundation; the Joint Committee on Contemporary China of the American Council of Learned Societies and the Social Science Research Council; the Luce Fund for Asian Studies of the Henry Luce Foundation; and the East Asian Institute of Columbia University.

For comments and suggestions, I am grateful to members of the Workshop on Communications and Publics, the Modern China Seminar, and the Seminar on Neo-Confucianism, all at Columbia; to members of my classes there; and to participants at other gatherings at which parts of the book were presented as papers, as specified in the source notes. I also wish to thank Richard Bernstein, Thomas P. Bernstein, Chang P'eng-yuan, Chou Yang-shan, Wm. Theodore de Bary, R. Randle Edwards, Fu Po-shek, Gong Xiang-rui, Charles W. Hayford, Louis Henkin, Huan Guocang, Steven I. Levine, Leo Ou-fan Lee, Liang Heng, Perry Link, David Mamo, Thomas A. Metzger, Barrett L. McCormick, William L. Parish, James Polachek, Mary Rankin, Stanley Rosen, James D. Seymour, Anne Thurston, Tu Nien-chung, Sondra Venable, Andrew Walder, Ralph Wang, Claude Widor, Roxane Witke, and Zhang Eping. I received materials or assistance from some of them and also from John Burns, Jocelyn Charles, Leonard L. Chu, Madelyn Ross, Robert Weick, and others who cannot be named.

I am not a believer in the kind of analysis of other societies that tries to avoid value issues on the grounds that different societies' values are not the same. Discussing another society's values seriously is a sign of respect, not cultural arrogance. Not to do so means either pretending that differences do not exist or—disrespectfully to our own values—acting as if we do not consider them important. Here we have the freedom and facilities to think about subjects that are important everywhere. For encouraging me to do so, I want to thank my wife, Roxane Witke, and my father, Paul S. Nathan.

ANDREW J. NATHAN
January 1985

Note on Romanization

I have used the pinyin system, except for a few place and personal names that are well known in other forms.

A.J.N.

PREFACE

We live in the age of democracy. Military and one-party regimes hold plebiscites and elections to show that they rule by consent. The few remaining monarchs claim to exist only to serve the interests of their people. Yet, however governments may strive to look as similar as possible, at root they are profoundly different. Only by comparing one another's versions of democracy can we see what kind of sense each set of values makes in theory and what it leads to in practice. We must get behind the international façade of verbal similarity if we wish to understand more fully where we and other cultures fundamentally agree and disagree. Such inquiry also allows us to reconsider what is distinctive about our own values and whether we still believe in them. For these purposes, this book explores the meaning of democracy in China—a nation that considers itself and is widely viewed as a model of democracy—viewing it implicitly against the contrasting background of American ideas.

Seen in a world perspective, the American version of democracy is more unusual than the Chinese. Our emphasis on individual rights, our tolerance for the expression of conflict and antagonism in politics, our acknowledgment that the political process can legitimately be used by individuals and groups to try to force the state to serve their selfish interests, and our system of judicial review are among the ways in which our system differs from most others in the world. The Chinese system, by contrast, belongs to a large family of socialist and other states that share a philosophy of politics as a realm of harmony rather than antagonism between the citizen and the state, of one-party leadership, of the supremacy of the public interest over citizens' rights, and of the power of the state to make any laws it deems necessary without judicial contradiction. Such states consider their systems superior to the "bourgeois democracies" of the West. They aim, in the words of Chinese leader Deng Xiaoping, to create "a democracy which is at a higher level and more substantial than that of the capitalist countries."

At the same time, Chinese democracy is not just a copy of a socialist type. The Chinese have aspired to democracy as they understood it for a hundred years, have claimed to have it for seventy, and for the last thirty-five years have lived in one of the most participatory societies in history. Marxism has been interpreted in China in ways that are compatible with a century-old tradition of democratic thought. Part of this book is devoted to exploring that tradition.

The beginning of Chinese democracy can be dated, as nearly as any such large event can be, to the year 1895. Until then Chinese politics had been closed to people outside the bureaucracy. Memorials aimed at influencing policy flowed through a system of official posts to the court of Peking. The emperor went through piles of documents each day, marking his comments in vermilion ink. His decisions were put into the form of edicts, recopied, registered, and sent back to the bureaucracy through the posts. Normally only high-ranking officials could memorialize, and then only on matters that directly concerned them.

At times of crisis, the opportunity for political participation might be extended temporarily to lower officials and out-of-office literati. The emperor could choose to "widen the road for speech," signaling that regular officials were permitted to send their views on matters outside their jurisdictions, while lower officials who ordinarily had no right to memorialize could submit their opinions through the men in higher positions. The lower literati typically took advantage of the opportunity to denounce the emperor's advisors with unrestrained vituperation. Referring to their views as "pure opinion," they exchanged letters and poems to whip up one another's indignation. But, as illustrated by the early careers of Kang Youwei and Liang Qichao, two of the last of the literati opinion-makers (see Chapter 3), their hope of exerting influence still lay with the emperor. After he had heard enough, the ruler signaled the closing of "the road for speech" by punishing a few memorialists for being too outspoken in their sentiments.

It was not until 1895 that significant numbers of people outside the bureaucracy began to claim a regular right to influence government policies and personnel. In that year, China signed a disastrous peace treaty with Japan. The war and negotiations stimulated the demand for news on the part of students, merchants, and other educated citizens outside the literati, and created the conviction that the nation's survival could no longer be left in the hands of officialdom. Changes in society, thought, and politics accelerated rapidly. The Chinese sent study delegations and students abroad, built railways and telegraph lines, cleaned and lighted the cities, put up modern buildings, reformed the educational system and the army, and created a system of local elections and assemblies. To foreign observers China suddenly seemed modern.

Political debate was directed increasingly toward the newly emerging public, whose size I estimate to have been two to four million persons in the late Qing (Ch'ing) period (see Chapter 7). Any and all ideologies and institutions were up for discussion. The terms for "sovereignty," "citizen," "constitution," and "democracy" entered daily usage along with hundreds of other new terms. A politician could exert influence now not just by competing for the emperor's ear but by arousing public opinion so as to force his hand. Reformers and revolutionaries founded scores of newspapers and magazines. Although they were printed mostly in a few cities, they were circulated to towns and villages all over the country. Politicians began to write in a new style. The language of politics became simplified and stirring. Detail was sacrificed for vision, prudence for polemic. Public discourse came to be dominated by propaganda and has continued to be ever since.

After 1912, when China became a republic, virtually all politically aware Chinese agreed that China must be in some sense democratic. But political thinkers disagreed on what this meant in terms of the actual rights and powers of the people. In Europe, the rising middle classes established their right to a voice in government by wielding financial and political power. But when the concept of democracy came to China it was presented as an ornament of modernity and an asset for rulers, a principle whose desirability had already been settled in the West. Instead of new classes fighting for power, the authorities at each stage of China's twentieth-century development seemed to concede to public opinion a role that it was not really prepared to exercise. The public had more nominal power than actual influence.

Every constitution after the fall of the Qing in 1911 recognized the people as sovereign. Warlords and dictators justified their actions in terms of a putative public demand that was often created at considerable expense by their own agents. At the same time rulers tried to limit any real public interference in their exercise of power. In 1895 the court suppressed study societies and sent the publishers of reform newspapers fleeing to the provinces. In 1905, when merchants conducted a nationwide anti-American boycott to protest restrictive U.S. immigration laws, the government discouraged the movement as illegitimate and dangerous. In 1906 the court announced its intention to grant a constitution and convene a national assembly, but it banned the movement that sprang up a few years later to petition for a speedup of the process. In 1911 the dynasty was overthrown by a coalition of popular forces, but elements of the old bureaucratic elite clung to control of government. The Constitutions of 1912 and 1923 limited the electorate to a small proportion of the population and restricted the powers of Parliament.

Chinese historians conventionally recognize the May Fourth movement of 1919 as marking the dominance of democratic forces in the Chinese revolution. Constitutions from 1931 on did away with property restrictions on the electorate. Political documents were written increasingly in the vernacular rather than in the classical language. Ideologies of mass politics—communism and nationalism—dominated public debate. Students, merchants, factory workers, and eventually peasants were mobilized into politics.

Yet men in authority continued to defeat attempts by elements of the public to exert real influence in government. Both the Guomindang (Kuomintang), which ruled from 1927 to 1949, and the Chinese Communist Party were centralized and disciplined Leninist-style parties. Both allowed other small parties to exist but prevented them from becoming rivals for power; discouraged the existence of any interest groups except those they established themselves; controlled the press through legal restrictions, cooptation, intimidation, and direct management; and established systems of government that made the executive branch an instrument of the party and gave the executive control over the judiciary and independence from the legislature. Both viewed democracy as a means to national wealth and power rather than a method of public control of government. Both appealed to China's backwardness as a justification for dictatorship—a dictatorship, they said, that was in the people's interests.

There were reformers inside each party and critics outside who said that democracy's benefits could be realized only if the people were given power. But because of China's extended crisis of national survival, this tradition of criticism was always weak. Under Mao, it seemed to come to an end. Although Mao still spoke about democracy, it was one in which the masses kept watch over the bureaucracy under the monocratic guidance of the national leader. Power was tightly concentrated in the leader's circle, while all aspects of life were controlled by vast bureaucracies of economic management, police surveillance, political supervision, and propaganda. Unlike the Soviet Union and Eastern Europe, China had no visible movement of dissent. There was no sign that the issue of diffusing power was still of interest to Chinese.

In 1976, Mao died and his closest followers were arrested. Power was soon taken by Deng Xiaoping, someone Mao had once denounced as a "capitalist-roader." The party announced a far-reaching decision to correct all the miscarriages of justice that had occurred in campaigns from the land reform through the Cultural Revolution. It decreed changes in the organization of rural communes, educational institutions, factories, and courts. Within a few years the party would publish a reevaluation of the historical role and legacy of Mao, conduct new elections for local people's congresses, and adopt new party and state constitutions. Chinese knew that the political orthodoxy of their system was Marxism-Leninism–Mao Zedong Thought, but they also knew that communism had been interpreted in strikingly democratic ways in

Yugoslavia, and that Poland was experimenting with coexistence between an independent trade union and a ruling communist party. For many Chinese, these years held the hope of epochal change.

In 1978 a small democratic movement reopened the old question of how a powerful government might be reconciled with the exercise of influence from below. In contrast to the late Qing, there was now a strong state led by a communist party. The activists were students and factory workers rather than young literati; they put up wall posters and sold mimeographed journals instead of submitting memorials; and they wrote as Marxists rather than Confucians. But the questions the democrats were asking were a hundred years old—why the country was backward, how the rulers could tap the people's energy to invigorate the state, and how popular participation could be reconciled with strong authority. Even their language was often the same as that of the late Qing reformers. The significance of their debates with the party and among themselves can be understood only in historical perspective.

Chinese democracy is too vast a theme for chronological treatment. I have moved back and forth among selected historical and contemporary episodes in an effort to identify the dominant tradition of Chinese democratic thought and the major controversies within it. (The Chronology that follows this Preface lists the major events I refer to.) The book starts with, and returns to, the democracy movement of recent years, not only because it is dramatic and close to our time but because it encapsulates the major issues that Chinese democrats have raised throughout the century; and dwells on the official reforms, because they demonstrate the purposes and limits of orthodox Chinese democracy in theory and practice. Several chapters reach back to the late nineteenth century and beyond, to place the ideas of both the movement and the regime in historical context. Other chapters describe the history and current role of the press, which for eighty years has been the strongest and most consistent link between the Chinese citizen and the state. In the early years of the century the press was the chief instrument for mobilizing citizens to action; now the media transmit government policy and articulate popular demands. For the average citizen the most vividly present fact of Chinese democracy is the domination of public life by propaganda.

Only a minority among the democracy activists challenged the party's theory of natural harmony between rulers and ruled. Their argument—that a competitive party system and an independent press are necessary to allow the people to control the rulers—is essential to democratic thinking in the pluralist West but has rarely been made in China. In discovering how this theory has fared in the debates within China, we in the West may learn something about our own values as well.

CHRONOLOGY

1895   China's peace treaty with Japan and scholars' protest in Peking: beginning of the era of democratic politics.

1898   Kang Youwei and Liang Qichao flee China after the failure of the Hundred Days of Reform.

1903   Liang Qichao's trip to America.

1911   Overthrow of the Qing dynasty; the next year, China becomes a republic.

1919   May Fourth demonstration in Peking.

1921   Founding of the Chinese Communist Party.

1927   Beginning of Guomindang rule.

1937   Full-scale Japanese invasion of China.

1949   Establishment of the People's Republic of China.

1957   Hundred Flowers movement and Anti-Rightist campaign.

1966   Start of the Cultural Revolution.

1976   *April 5:* Tiananmen Square incident.
          September 9: Death of Mao Zedong.

1978   *Fall:* Intense activity at Democracy Wall.
          December: Third Plenum of the Eleventh Central Committee marks the rise to power of Deng Xiaoping.

1979   *January:* Petitioners' demonstration in Peking.
          March: Deng Xiaoping articulates the "four basic principles"; arrest of Wei Jingsheng.

1980   High point of Deng's political reforms (Gengshen Reforms). Elections for county people's congresses.

1981   Document No. 7 refines propaganda policy. Arrest of most remaining democracy activists.

CHINESE DEMOCRACY

1

THE DEMOCRACY
MOVEMENT

On an October day in 1978 a group of young Chinese appeared in the center of Peking in an alley next to the building housing the offices of the party newspaper, the *People's Daily*. They unrolled a series of large posters and pasted them to a wall. White-uniformed public security officers looked on as a crowd gathered, knowing that recent government policy allowed citizens to post personal complaints and suggestions.

The posters contained a suite of poems dedicated to the "God of Fire" and written in a sentimental, Whitmanesque style long popular in China. They described a monstrous idol forcing himself on the Chinese people:

> *I lie among people.*
> *I separate these people from the others*
> *So that they are constantly guarding against others. . . .*
> *They want to push me down, destroy me*
> *Because my body blocks their view,*
> *Blocks them from the world outside their own little yards.*

And they spoke of a long "war of spiritual enslavement."

> *The war goes on in everyone's facial expression.*
> *The war is waged by numerous high-pitched loudspeakers.*
> *The war is waged in every pair of fearful, shifting eyes.*

This was a war of political surveillance and mutual propaganda that every Chinese had had to endure in the late years of Mao's rule. But now the poet was optimistic. He saw torches

Moving at the edge of the sky far, far away,
Swinging on the expansiveness of the sky of dark blue.
A shining troop, a silently flowing river of fire.

The torches heralded "a world ruled by light and warmth." They would thaw the frozen world of the past, open hearts, melt suspicions, and reconcile enemies. "O torch," said the poet,

You extend a thousand shining hands,
Open up ten thousand shining throats.
Awaken the great road, awaken the square,
Awaken all members of this whole generation.

This "Song of the Torch" was annotated: "13 August 1969, 10:00 A.M., Thinking in doubt; 15 August 1969, Written in streaming tears." The author, Huang Xiang, was a worker at a knitting mill in a southwestern provincial capital, Guiyang, about 1,500 miles from Peking by train. Like millions of other educated young Chinese he had been "sent down" from school to the factory after the army broke up the Red Guards in 1968. There he started to write poems and recite them at meetings of the group of friends who later called themselves the "Enlightenment Society." After the police raided his home to search for manuscripts, he started to wrap his works in sheets of plastic and seal them inside homemade candles.

The Enlightenment group's discussions dwelled on the question that has obsessed Chinese political thinkers for the last hundred years: "What are the basic reasons our nation has made progress so slowly?" For centuries the Chinese believed that theirs was the world's most advanced civilization. But the Opium War and later humiliations forced a change of perception. Chinese came to see their country as the poverty-stricken, militarily vulnerable, despised "sick man of Asia." In 1949 Mao declared that the Chinese people had finally "stood up." And China was indeed richer and stronger in 1978 than in the nineteenth century. But the pace of progress had been disappointing. Housing averaged less than four square meters per person in the cities; cotton cloth, grain, cooking oil, and other goods were still rationed after thirty years of "socialist construction." Radios, watches, and cameras were luxury items, and those produced in China were prone to break down. TV sets were a rarity. It was unusual for an ordinary person to make a telephone call. Peasants still did most of their hauling by human-drawn cart.

Like their question, the Enlightenment group's answer to the riddle of backwardness was of nearly a century's standing:

The history of China seems very complex but in fact is very simple. . . .
Our history has been dominated mainly by Qin Shi Huang's totalitari-

anism. [Qin Shi Huang was the dynastic founder who unified China in 221 B.C. and cemented his rule by "burning the books and burying the scholars."] After he translated the theory of extreme autocracy into absolute administrative orders and laws, the broad masses lost all their freedom of action and their right to express their ideas. . . . From the day of their birth they had to submit to restrictions by the emperor or the gods and devils and thus became slaves without human dignity or human rights.

Being slaves, the people were ignorant and passive. "Autocracy refuses to give people the right to think, while fetishes forbid people to advance any scientific hypothesis." The emperors preferred to keep the masses stupid rather than to mobilize their productive energies. The 1911 republican revolution "overthrew the emperor as a person only, but the concept of emperors remained in people's minds."

This is the reason why China is behind other countries today. In order that it may become strong, it must first of all give up autocracy and fetishes; secondly, it must have a stable democratic government; and thirdly, it must fully mobilize the enthusiasm and wisdom of every member of the society. This is the recipe for curing the Chinese nation of its age-old sickness.

What the Enlightenment group understood by "democracy" was shaped by descriptions of the Paris Commune in Marx's *The Civil War in France* and Lenin's *State and Revolution*, pamphlets Mao had required all Chinese to study during the Cultural Revolution. Marx described how revolutionary Paris was governed from March to May 1871 by a working council, "executive and legislative at the same time," whose members were elected by universal suffrage, bound by the formal instructions of constituents, and subject to recall at any time. In this way, Marx said, government's "legitimate functions were wrested from an authority [officialdom] usurping pre-eminence over society itself and restored to the responsible agents of society [elected delegates]," so that "public functions ceased to be private property" of bureaucrats. By contrast, in China in 1978 all officials were appointed from above—including those in ostensibly elected positions, since only one candidate was put forward for each post. They enjoyed lifetime tenure and privileges of office, and acted like masters rather than servants of society. The Enlightenment group believed that the persistence of such "feudal" and "autocratic" practices and "backward ideology" was the root of China's weakness.

The example of the United States proved to them that a true democratic system "is always linked with a high degree of development of material and spiritual civilization." Democracy, symbolized by the fire in Huang Xiang's poems, was the key to development because it would melt down the idol that imposed alienation on the people.

> The fire will enable people completely to shake off brutality and hatred, and there will be no quarrel among them. They will share the same views and principles and have identical ideals. In lofty and harmonious unity they will produce, live, think, invent, pioneer, and explore together. With these dynamic forces they will enrich their social life and cultivate their big earth.

By the fall of 1978, the course of events in Peking seemed to have brought near the day of the democratic torch. The twice-purged "revisionist" and "capitalist-roader" Deng Xiaoping had returned to office in July 1977 as vice-premier and party vice-chairman. A month later the Eleventh Central Committee convened. More than half of its 201 members were people who, like Deng, had been purged in the Cultural Revolution and later restored to office, in contrast to the preceding Central Committee, dominated by persons like Party Chairman Hua Guofeng who had risen to prominence in the Cultural Revolution. The same preponderance of "veteran cadres" over "cultural revolutionaries" was discernible in the new Politburo and its Standing Committee, the party's real ruling bodies. Deng's consolidation of power was to continue over the next several years. In December 1978 the Eleventh Central Committee's Third Plenum elected additional Deng followers to the Politburo; at the Fifth Plenum in February 1980 four of Deng's opponents resigned from the Politburo and two of his allies were raised to the Standing Committee; and in 1980 and 1981 Deng's two chief allies, Zhao Ziyang and Hu Yaobang, replaced Hua Guofeng in his twin posts of premier and party chairman, respectively.

Deng's ascendancy was reflected in the actions of government and in propaganda in the official press. In February 1978 a new constitution was adopted which spoke of popular supervision of government and guaranteed

> freedom of speech, correspondence, the press, demonstration and the freedom to strike, and . . . the right to "speak out freely, air their views fully, hold great debates and write big-character posters."

The party newspapers revived their pre–Cultural Revolution letters to the editor columns and used them, together with investigative reports, to expose lower- and middle-level bureaucrats who abused their powers. The papers said such "bureaucratism" could be corrected only by protecting people's democratic rights to criticize cadres (the Chinese term for officials at all levels). In May, the two major party papers published a commentary entitled

"Practice Is the Sole Criterion of Truth" that called into question the ideological standard of strict adherence to Mao's words. In June, Deng told a conference of armed forces political officers that the correct way to apply ideology was not to "copy straight from Marx, Lenin and Chairman Mao" but to "seek truth from facts." He thus applied an ancient philosophical phrase referring to painstaking textual analysis to argue that as conditions changed one could try new policies, even if they were not described in the works of Mao. Mao was even brought in to testify posthumously against himself: the party newspaper printed for the first time a 1962 speech in which he had stressed his own fallibility.

The challenge facing the Deng group was to repudiate all that had been done in Mao's name during the Cultural Revolution without discrediting the monopolistic structure of power that had enabled him to do these things. They had to separate the party from twenty years' deeds of the man who had led it, while leaving the party dictatorship intact. The new head of the party Organization Department, Deng's follower Hu Yaobang, launched a massive rehabilitation campaign, which was to continue for more than five years, to review and correct the cases of those who had been persecuted, convicted, labeled, or otherwise penalized since the beginning of the regime. This included more than twenty million who had been labeled "landlords, rich peasants, counterrevolutionaries, or bad elements" in the early 1950s; another half-million or more persons labeled "rightists" in 1957, together with several million rural residents labeled "anti-socialist elements" in the early 1960s; three million cadres who had been implicated in "unjust and erroneous cases" in the Cultural Revolution; and over 300,000 who had been wrongly convicted of crimes, mostly counterrevolutionary, during the Cultural Revolution. Together with their families, the affected numbered one hundred million, or one-tenth of China's population, Hu later told a group of Yugoslav journalists.

For the reformers, the danger was that they might lose control of the rehabilitation process. The public signals of change notified millions of desperate people that their grievances were ripe for resolution. Beginning shortly after Mao's death and increasing in number throughout 1977 and 1978, personal written appeals began to appear in Peking's Tiananmen Square, at the base of the cenotaph to the revolutionary martyrs and on the wooden fences around the construction site of the Mao Zedong mausoleum. As the political atmosphere signaled in the press grew increasingly permissive, the wall posters turned to more general though still safe subjects, such as praise of the deceased Premier Zhou Enlai on the anniversary of his birth.

Peking has always been a political city. In the old, central part of town, life takes place in courtyards screened from the lanes by gray walls. Families sharing a courtyard watch one another jealously, quarrel, or endure. At Peking's center is the Forbidden City, walled in red. Its eastern portion consists of formal halls and palaces which are open to the public as a museum, but the section to the west is the retreat of the nation's political leaders. This Zhongnanhai (Central and Southern Lakes) is a vast park built by various dynasties for boating and feasting. Now it houses the top Politburo officials and the offices of the party Central Committee and the State Council. No building affords a view of its interior. Rumors say its residents have sometimes poisoned one another's food and put microphones in one another's walls. The petitioner for justice can get only as far as the outer gate.

Running from west to east in front of Zhongnanhai's gate and through Tiananmen Square is the six-lane Changan Avenue (Avenue of Perpetual Peace). Peking was laid out by the Mongols and developed by the Ming dynasty (1368–1644) on a north-south axis so that the emperor's authority could radiate from the Three Great Halls of the Forbidden City through the Gate of Heavenly Peace to the nation beyond. In front of this gate the communists cleared a square of nearly a hundred acres. They built the Great Hall of the People on one side, two history museums on the other, and a memorial stele to the heroes of the revolution at its center. In 1977 the Chairman Mao Memorial Hall was erected in the square's southern half.

A few blocks east of Tiananmen Square, Changan Avenue intersects Wangfujing, the street of Peking's main department store and (in 1978) the offices of the *People's Daily*. In the other direction Changan Avenue runs past a series of government offices, including the telegraph administration with its clock tower, and then about a mile from the square intersects with Xidan Road, another busy shopping street.

This rectangle two miles from east to west and half a mile deep is the heart of public Peking. It encompasses the old and new centers of national and municipal power, large open spaces of ceremonial and symbolic import, tourist attractions for Chinese and foreigners alike, and two busy shopping districts. The whole central area is served by bus lines from the outer districts, satellite towns, and agricultural suburbs beyond.

In modern times the high gates and public squares became gathering points for mass demonstrations that might cow or celebrate a government, depending on who controlled them, or serve one political faction against another. In 1895 thousands of scholars met at a building on the site that would later become Tiananmen Square to present a petition protesting the terms of the peace agreement with Japan. Their act launched China's democratic era, for they followed it by establishing study societies and newspapers that aimed to exert a continuous influence on government policy. The famous May Fourth demonstration in 1919 assembled here before the Gate of Heavenly Peace; Chinese communist historians call this incident the beginning of the "new democratic revolution"—the era which brought their party to power.

In 1935 the December 9 demonstration against Japanese aggression paraded past the gate. Many of the participants were to be among the rulers of China after 1949. On October 1, 1949, Mao climbed the gate to declare the founding of the People's Republic. In August 1966 he reviewed a million-strong rally of Red Guards there before turning them loose on his party colleagues throughout the capital and across the country.

In 1978, as for hundreds of years in the past, Peking was the company town of a huge bureaucratic empire. Perhaps as many as half of its residents were government employees or their family members, all vitally concerned with the political fortunes of the top leaders and well connected to the rumor network. Another large group were factory workers, a well-educated and politically conscious stratum—and particularly so in Peking, where many younger workers are the middle-school-educated offspring of factory workers or government employees, who took factory jobs in the 1960s and 1970s because there were no universities to attend or technical jobs to move into. Peking's population also includes tens of thousands of middle-school and college students, among them those of the elite Peking and Qinghua universities. And, as the post of most of the foreign correspondents and diplomats admitted to the country, Peking was the best place in China for demonstrators to catch the world's eye.

In November 1978, a series of events spurred the poster-writers and petitioners gathered in Peking to more daring. Secretly, but perhaps known to many who had connections in the party, a central work conference convened on November 10 to prepare for the upcoming Third Plenum of the Eleventh Central Committee. Crucial policy and personnel decisions would be made at this meeting, establishing the predominance of Deng Xiaoping in the party. In the eyes of victims of the Cultural Revolution like the poet Huang Xiang, Deng's victory in the internal political struggle was crucial both to their personal hopes and to the prospects of the nation. Wrote one of Huang's group:

> Putting heaven and earth in order, opening the doors, establishing order, discipline, and great democracy, Vice Premier Deng is open-minded, humble, and honored by the entire world. His greatness, beauty, and success in seizing the seat of government are hailed in the north and the south. . . . [Under him] the nation will be rich and strong, and the economy will be pushed ahead.

Huang and people like him had thus come to Peking not only to appeal their personal cases but to support Deng at a crucial moment in his fight to reform and democratize the communist system. "If anyone interferes with and harasses our aboveboard and legitimate actions and obstructs the pace of great socialist democracy," wrote Huang's group, "we will criticize, expose, and bring accusations against him in accordance with the party and government constitutions."

The spark that ignited the democracy movement was the reversal of the official condemnation of the Tiananmen Square incident of April 5, 1976. That incident had been the climax of several days when tens of thousands of Peking's citizens turned out in the square carrying wreaths, memorial photographs, and posters to mourn the recently deceased Premier Zhou Enlai. In speeches and poems, the demonstrators criticized Mao and his closest collaborators in much the same terms that Huang was simultaneously using in his poems in Guiyang. On the fifth, the demonstration was violently broken up by police and militia under the authority of the mayor of Peking, Wu De. The Politburo promptly blamed Deng Xiaoping for the disturbances and dropped him from all his party and government posts. Now that Deng was back in office, the history of the incident was rewritten. From May 1978 onwards, without public announcement, the Peking Public Security Bureau "rechecked" the cases of 388 people it had arrested at the time of the incident, and reversed their convictions as counterrevolutionaries. The "reversal of verdict" on the Tiananmen Square incident was formally announced on November 15.

Extending a hundred yards or so along the north side of Changan Avenue, between the telegraph tower and the Xidan intersection, is a gray wall seven or eight feet high, set well back from the street, that belongs to no government office. It fronts on an athletic field and a bus stop. Because it was the closest large wall to Tiananmen Square, people had been pasting posters there for some time and by late 1978 had started calling it "Democracy Wall." On the first weekend after the Peking municipal government vindicated those convicted in the Tiananmen Square incident, hundreds of factory workers, students, junior officials, and out-of-town visitors gathered at the wall to post, read, copy, and discuss political posters. The crowds grew during the week.

On the following Saturday, November 25, the discussions assumed an organized form. According to a participant, the organizers (whose identities are unknown) announced three purposes of the discussions:

1 To put into practice the "freedom of assembly and expression" which the Constitution confers on the citizenry.

2 To ascertain the cause and origin of the "Gang of Four's" accession to power, to demand socialist mass democracy, and gradually to realize the principles of the Paris Commune under conditions of stability and unity.

3 To eliminate superstition and emancipate people's thinking, so as to sweep away ideological obstacles to the realization of the Four Modernizations [of agriculture, industry, science and technology, and national defense] and thus to play the role of pioneers in science and democracy.

Many gave speeches while the crowd shouted its comments. One speaker complained of the rising price of dumplings. Another advocated independent legislative, executive, and judicial organs and a system of checks and balances, and objected to the Maoist anthem, "The East Is Red," because it referred to a "deliverer." A third commented that the Cultural Revolution had been "like a hurricane which swept away all dirty mud patches, but the pity was that the dirtiest things happened to be right at the center of it!" This "Democracy Forum" was the first in a series that lasted several nights.

Two days later, when the crowd of about ten thousand grew too large for the sidewalk of Changan Avenue, the organizers decided to move to Tiananmen Square. The participants formed ranks of ten to fifteen people each. One marcher recalled:

Some in the ranks ... linked their hands, and some took the lead in shouting the slogans "We demand democracy!" and "We demand freedom!" Thus they proceeded through Changan Avenue to meet one another before the monument [to the heroes of the revolution, in the center of the square]. Several hundred of them sat in the center of the square. Another several hundred stood around them in an outer circle or climbed to sit on the rails of the monument. Those who were even farther stood on their bicycles.

The speakers shouted into microphones against the chilly wind:

"I came here after eight hours of work and after I finished washing my baby's diapers [laughter], and I am going to return to the office and work hard too! We must do well with our Four Modernizations."

"We have no particular ambitions. We are common people. . . . But we want to be common people who are free and happy!" [Cheers.]

"We are not afraid of death! The blood of the martyrs of April 5 has already been shed here!" [Pointing to the platform of the monument.]

"We must uphold the party! But we must also supervise the party! And make it the public servant of the people!"

The crowd at Democracy Wall was young, educated, and well informed about political conflicts in the party. When an American journalist who was going to see Deng Xiaoping dropped by, he was told to ask Deng, "When will the new policy on Liu Shaoqi (Liu Shao-ch'i) be put into effect? When is the new policy on Peng Dehuai (P'eng Te-huai) going to be put into effect?" Liu was the head of state who had been toppled during the Cultural Revolution; Peng was the minister of defense purged in 1959 for criticizing Mao. The crowd seemed to know that at the secret central work conference Deng Xiaoping was recommending the posthumous rehabilitation of these two men. But in the event, some leaders opposed the move as too dangerous to Mao's prestige, and the plan was tabled for the time being.

Inside information was also reflected in the crowd's selection of political villains and the way it exposed them. They most hated Wu De, who had been mayor of Peking when the Tiananmen Square incident occurred. Peking is a special municipality, administratively on the same level as a province, and because it is the national capital its mayor outranks most provincial governors and often sits on the Politburo. One measure of Wu De's unusual status had been that he controlled the city's public security forces and militia without interference from the Ministry of Public Security. His tape-recorded voice, ordering the Tiananmen demonstrators to disperse, had been broadcast on April 5, 1976, just before the police and militia moved on the crowd. Many now blamed Wu for scars borne since then. Although Wu had been replaced as mayor in October, he was still in the Politburo.

A satiric wall poster in the form of a soliloquy punned on Wu's name, which is homophonous with "no morals" (*wu de*):

> I have lived in Peking for more than ten years, but I have "no morals" nor good conduct. . . . Some people say I am a "laughing tiger, ruthless and inhuman." . . . Nothing but vicious slander! . . . I have always been merciful. . . . Why, when Tiananmen was washed in blood on April 5, I did not touch one gun or one cannon.

The demonstrators exposed Wu's past. A subordinate of his who headed the Peking Public Security Bureau in 1976 had committed suicide in 1977, "for his guilty conscience," the demonstrators alleged. Still earlier, Wu had been a protégé of Kang Sheng, the hated secret police chief and *éminence grise* of the Cultural Revolution. Wu was also linked to Wang Dongxing, sinister commander of Mao's palace guard and leader of the orthodox Maoist faction, himself criticized by the crowd for building an expensive mansion within the walls of Zhongnanhai.

Party Chairman Hua Guofeng was vulnerable to many of the same charges, yet he remained almost untouched in the posters and speeches of 1978. He too was a beneficiary of the Cultural Revolution and of Kang

Sheng's sponsorship, and he had been minister of public security at the time of the Tiananmen Square incident. Yet his name came up mostly in favorable and ritual contexts, such as the "correct decisions of the Central Committee headed by Chairman Hua." The demonstrators' restraint matched Deng Xiaoping's in inner party councils; Hua was not to be demoted until 1981.

But Mao could be discussed. "Did Chairman Mao commit any error? Can the masses of people discuss his merits and shortcomings?" a poster asked. The writer pointed out that neither Lin Biao nor Jiang Qing (Chiang Ch'ing, of the "Gang of Four") could have risen to power without Mao's backing. Unless Mao's last years are scientifically reevaluated, another writer proposed, his "mistakes will become a mental burden on our minds . . . and an excuse for enemies to attack us." A third writer called up the image of the feeble Mao in his book-lined study familiar to Americans from photographs of his meetings with Nixon and Kissinger:

With the personal background of a small producer, an inward-looking gaze, too many ancient books, and plenty of flattering voices in his ears, he was now unable to see the rapid development of science abroad and unable to hear the people's urgent appeals.

The question of Mao in turn implied the even larger question of reform of China's political system.

However great and wise a leader might be, he certainly cannot be immune from making mistakes. Several thousand years of feudal history and over a hundred years of the people's dauntless struggles have taught us one truth: we must place our hope in a healthy, effective, scientific and democratic system, so that both the common people and the public servants they elect are bound by this system and strive for the well-being of the people in accordance with this system.

"Comrades," said another writer, "the proletariat has to safeguard itself against its own deputies and officials, or in other words, people have to safeguard themselves against their leaders. Do you feel surprised when you hear this? But this was how Engels summed up the experiences of the Paris Commune" (in his preface to The Civil War in France). This echoed Huang Xiang's views about the political roots of China's backwardness: "if the mind is fettered by the 'Gang of Four's' taboos, obsessed with idolatry and full of worries, such a spiritual state cannot be conducive to the accomplishment of the Four Modernizations."

Statements like "Chairman Mao was no god!" made front pages around the world, yet in this and many other views the demonstrators were only a step ahead of the Central Committee. It was not long before Peng Dehuai, Liu Shaoqi, and others were rehabilitated. Wu De and Wang Dongxing fell from the Politburo in February 1980. Kang Sheng was denounced in a series of secret speeches and finally condemned as a criminal in the "Gang of Four" trial and posthumously expelled from the Communist Party. That the Cultural Revolution had been a disaster became official doctrine on the thirtieth anniversary of the People's Republic of China in 1979. The implications of that position for Mao's historical role were openly accepted in 1981. (Deng had already said in 1978 that Mao was 70 percent good and 30 percent bad, a position not substantially altered later.) On the question of the democratic system, a series of reforms was introduced in 1979 and afterwards that I will discuss in Chapter 4.

But not all the posters of late 1978 and early 1979 stayed within bounds that would later be validated by the party. One called for premarital sex, saying that repression had increased the rate of sex crimes and worked against the development of socialism. There were two open letters to President Carter; one warmly praised American democracy, while the other actually asked Carter to intervene on behalf of any Chinese citizen arrested for exercising the right of free speech. (The notion of any sort of foreign intervention is offensive to most Chinese.) An organization called the China Human Rights League issued a "Nineteen-Point Declaration" that among other startling suggestions called for the removal of Mao's sarcophagus from Tiananmen Square and détente between China and the Soviet Union. After China launched its "defensive counterattack" on Vietnam in February 1979, a poster went up ridiculing "a big country like China" for "striking a little childlike Vietnam."

More deeply offensive to the party leaders was a broad attack on the government that was posted on December 5. Its sarcasm did not spare even Deng Xiaoping, the hero of most of the demonstrators.

> After the arrest of the "Gang of Four," people hoped eagerly for the reestablishment of the great banner of Vice-Premier Deng who might "restore capitalism" [as he was accused during the Cultural Revolution of wanting to do]. Finally Vice Premier Deng returned to his leading post in the Central Committee. How excited people were, how inspired, how . . . But regrettably the old political system so hated by the people was not changed, the democracy and freedom they hoped for could not even be mentioned, there was no improvement in people's living conditions, and the wage "hike" [of some 15 percent in urban wages, announced in 1977] was far from matching the soaring inflation.

These were among the opening lines of "The Fifth Modernization" by Wei Jingsheng, who was to become the most famous victim of the government's crackdown on dissent. After Wei, other democrats would also challenge the legitimacy of party dictatorship, although they did so, unlike him, on Marxist grounds. I will describe in Chapter 5 the ideas of these Marxist pluralists and explain why their writings finally made the democracy movement intolerable to the regime.

In December and January mimeographed publications began to be displayed on the wall; copies of them were sold at times posted in advance. (One journal published an apology after its representatives failed to show up at the announced time, leaving several hundred people standing in the cold for nearly an hour.) Prices were usually five to twenty cents (Chinese) per copy. Some magazines charged special prices of fifty cents or one yuan (Chinese dollar) per issue for foreigners. Some offered mail subscriptions.

Several magazines had approached printing shops, only to be told that outside jobs could not be accepted without the permission of the authorities. At least one editor tried to borrow a Chinese typewriter from a foreign journalist. Such typewriters are not widely available in China, and among the unofficial periodicals I have seen, only one had typewriter-cut stencils. All the others were cut by hand with steel styluses in long hours of tedious labor, with neat characters placed as close together as possible to save space.

Chinese mimeograph machines are not the rotary type familiar in America. They are hinged devices, consisting of an upper frame in which the wax master is held and a lower frame into which a stack of paper is placed. The master is lowered and pressed with an inked roller, which is re-inked after every tenth or so impression. After each pressing the frame is lifted to retrieve the printed sheet. Such machines were available in state-run stationery shops for under a hundred Chinese dollars, but in principle they could be sold only to offices and schools. To buy large quantities of stencils, ink, and paper a citizen was supposed to show a requisition from his or her unit. Otherwise, quantities had to be assembled from a number of small purchases made at different shops. Even then, materials were often unavailable. One journal printed an issue with red ink because it could not get black.

Considering the inconvenience of obtaining materials and the tedium of copying, printing, and collating the magazines (typically ten to forty pages), the small staffs who devoted long evening and weekend hours in their own or their parents' crowded apartments were fortunate to be able to publish five hundred or so copies of a single issue per month. The Chinese government later implied that publishing magazines was a nice way to make money. It is true that *April Fifth Forum* reported a 370-yuan profit (somewhat over U.S. $200) on sales after nearly a year of operation, and tried to pay taxes on it, but this included no recompense for hundreds of hours of labor and barely matched the 364 yuan in start-up capital originally contributed by the founders to buy materials.

The periodicals called themselves "people's publications," implying that they were not official like all the other publications in China, and yet not "dissident" or "underground." They saw themselves as analogous to legitimate "people's" organizations encouraged by the government in some years past, such as locally financed schools. (Of course the government had had particular reasons for promoting such schools: they removed an item of expense from the state budget in stringent times. There was no similar advantage in the people's periodicals.) Each journal published its editor's name and address, not only to allow subscribers and writers to get in touch but to demonstrate its aboveboard nature to the authorities. *April Fifth Forum* sent copies of each issue to Chairman Hua, Vice Premier Deng, Mayor Lin Hujia of Peking, and various libraries. Several journals even asked the government to provide financial support, printing facilities, and access to news events.

The journals wanted to register with the authorities, but no one knew how. Several magazines published appeals asking how to register and pay taxes, but received no answer. It was not until November 1979 that the Standing Committee of the National People's Congress announced that laws and decrees adopted since 1949 remained valid until replaced by new laws and decrees. This meant that regulations for printing and publishing enterprises that had been promulgated in 1952 were still in effect. But their requirements could not be met in 1978. The regulations said that each publication must have the guarantee of two private shops, entities that had disappeared in 1956. They ruled out private mimeographing, requiring printing to be done at "fixed premises and installations," which were now all government-controlled and had already denied their services to the unofficial magazines. And they required registration with the local industrial and commercial federation, an organ that no longer existed. None of the people's publications was able to register despite persistent attempts, and this fact was eventually used to close them down.

Huang Xiang's group seems to have been the first to come out with a mimeographed publication. *Enlightenment* No. 1 was dated October 11, 1978, with a second printing dated October 24. Thirty-nine pages long, it carried the complete texts of the "God of Fire" poems together with a foreword and epilogue. No. 2 came out as the Democracy Wall events were reaching their height, on November 24. It enthusiastically welcomed "the great ideological revolutionary movement to distinguish truth from falsehood now sweeping the country" and announced the formal founding of the Enlightenment Society by eight persons in Peking. Most of its fifty-one pages were devoted to an exegesis of the "God of Fire" poems by Huang Xiang's close friend Li Jiahua. Issue No. 3 of January 1, 1979, carried the organization's provisional draft program of twelve articles and contained a long essay, "On Human Rights," by Lu Mang, which was issued as a separate pamphlet a week later.

The opportunity to publish brought disagreements in the group to the surface. On February 27 a number of Enlightenment Society members back home in Guiyang announced that they were splitting to form the Thaw Society, charging Huang Xiang with being too "conservative."

> The Thaw Society is a newborn organization that has outgrown the Enlightenment Society. It will shoulder the historic task which the Enlightenment Society is unwilling or unable to shoulder.

The group distributed in Guiyang and Peking a mimeographed "Manifesto" that hailed Rousseau's ideas on human rights, Sun Yat-sen's on democracy, the Christian spirit of peace, forbearance, and universal love, and two-party competition between the Chinese Communists and their civil war enemy, the Nationalist Party.

The second periodical to appear was *April Fifth Paper*, dated November 26, 1978. The founders felt it was "inconvenient for the people to spend a lot of time before that cold Democracy Wall conducting discussions and pasting up and reading big-character posters." A newspaper could serve the democratic movement more effectively than posters. The two staff members soon joined with two others who ran a journal called *Democratic Forum* to form *April Fifth Forum*. The leading figure was Xu Wenli, a thirty-six-year-old army veteran, son of a Red Army doctor and great-grandson of an official of the imperial regime, now working in Peking as an electrician. The magazine's office was a space some five yards square in Xu's two-room apartment, which he shared with his wife and seven-year-old daughter. "The equipment was simple," a Western visitor wrote:

> a desk, a pair of easy-chairs, a reading alcove with the latest papers, a cupboard with books and study materials, a bed, and—under the bed packed in boxes—the printing plant [a mimeograph machine]. Everywhere were piles of the most disparate papers and periodicals as well as bundles of freshly-printed copies of *April Fifth Forum*.

The staff eventually grew to about twenty, mostly factory workers and teachers ranging in age from twenty-two to thirty-six, and including Communist Party and Communist Youth League members. In the early months each staff member had to donate one yuan or 1 percent of his or her monthly salary (i.e., about sixty U.S. cents) to cover expenses, as well as work evenings until midnight or later putting each issue together.

Unlike *Enlightenment, April Fifth Forum* emphasized loyalty to Marxism and the party but believed the party was split between "reformers" (Deng and his faction) and "conservatives" (rigid Maoists), a political situation that they said had repeated itself over and over in China since the late nineteenth century, when the reformers Kang Youwei and Liang Qichao tried to modernize the country during the Hundred Days of Reform. In backing the "Practice Group," as it called Deng's faction, *April Fifth* tried to make constructive suggestions, such as that measures be taken to ameliorate Peking's industrial smog and that Democracy Walls be set up in front of the offices of provincial governments throughout China. Its pages occasionally reflected access to inside information about the reform faction's thinking, as when it pointed to the need for a public trial of the Gang of Four before this had become official policy, or advocated the posthumous rehabilitation of a victim of the Cultural Revolution, Yu Luoke, whose public exoneration did not come until more than a year later.

While denying that Western democracy and culture were desirable models, *April Fifth* ridiculed the conservatives' xenophobia. Long hair and tight-hipped, broad-ankled trousers are enduring fashions in Hong Kong, and for some reason these are among the cultural imports most deeply irritating to conservative Chinese. *April Fifth*'s solution was "Anti–Bell-Bottom Trousers," which they touted with sly humor as completely shapeless:

> They are suitable for fat and skinny people of either sex and any age with any physical shape. There is no difference between the front and the back. They are dark in color, dignified in appearance, and can be used in all four seasons by all members of the family.

The item contained puns on several twentieth-century reactionary slogans, such as "national essence," "restoration of the past," and "revival."

With its issue No. 10 (June 1979), *April Fifth Forum* entered a new phase. This book-length volume of 121 closely copied pages sold for the relatively high price of 1.20 yuan. It consisted of a provocative theoretical essay entitled "On the Proletarian Democratic Revolution" which argued that a "bureaucratic monopoly privileged class" wielding economic and coercive power might block China's progress to communism. Only a "proletarian democratic revolution" could prevent this, and such a revolution would install, among other things, a two-party system. While *April Fifth Forum* had previously argued that the people should supervise the party to prevent its becoming corrupted by power, such a comprehensive argument showing such deep mistrust of the party and suggesting such a radical solution was new to its pages. The author, Chen Erjin, was a newcomer too: a coal mine statistician from Yunnan, he had written the book in 1974–76 and had come to Peking in late 1978 or early 1979. Not only did the *Forum* editors find his essay a step in the right direction, as they stated in their preface to issue No. 10, but they were sufficiently persuaded to repeat its key points in many articles in succeeding issues of the journal.

On January 8, 1979, *Peking Spring* made its appearance. It stood for the same goals as the other journals—democracy and science, political reform, economic modernization. The first issue stated:

> To be rich and powerful, China must be built into a modern socialist power. This is the ideal long dreamed of by the Chinese people. However, to stride toward this great ideal, we must break down modern feudalism and modern superstition, and gradually acquire socialist democracy and modern science.

Like *April Fifth Forum, Peking Spring* saw itself on the side of the reformist faction. In its third issue it announced that it sought the following kinds of material:

1 Propaganda for and discussions of the communiqué of the Third Plenum [the crucial December 1978 meeting where Deng's line was adopted].

2 Criticism of "superstitious worship of an individual" and of the "whatever faction" [leaders who believed that whatever Mao said must be followed]. . . .

The flavor of insiderism was even stronger in *Peking Spring*'s pages than in those of *April Fifth*. The articles were full of current and historical information about political figures the editors supported or opposed, which must have been drawn from intraparty documents and reminiscences of older cadres. The journal called for the rehabilitation of "Comrade Shaoqi" (Liu Shaoqi) and reported the whereabouts of his widow before word of her appeared in the official press. It reviewed Peng Dehuai's career as "conscience of the Chinese revolution" and reprinted his 1959 letter of criticism that had caused Mao to purge him. There was an eyewitness account of the return of former mayor Peng Zhen to Peking and a call for him to be assigned to work in the legal field, where in fact he soon turned up in a leading role. The magazine published a supportive biography of the elderly economic planner Chen Yun, who soon reemerged in power, and puffed Deng Xiaoping's rising follower Hu Yaobang as a "hero in destroying 'modern superstition.'" On the negative side, *Peking Spring* exposed the late secret police chief, Kang Sheng, providing information not previously known in the West and at that time not publicly revealed in China, and criticized Wang Dongxing for allegedly building himself a mansion in Zhongnanhai.

Aside from the top leaders, the magazine defended a number of dissidents. "Li Yizhe" was a writing group, three of whose members had been imprisoned for putting up a critical poster in Canton in 1974. *Peking Spring* published the article "Li Yizhe Is Innocent" shortly before the three authors were released and exonerated. The journal advocated official recognition for an "underground" novel (circulated only in handwritten copies) called *The Second Handshake*, which was later officially approved and published. It exposed new details about the case of Zhang Zhixin, a party member who had been tortured and executed in 1975 for refusing to recant her criticisms of Chairman Mao.

Many of *Peking Spring*'s editors had participated in the April Fifth demonstration. Two, Han Zhixiong and Wang Juntao, were imprisoned in 1976 but just before the reversal of verdict on the April Fifth incident, were elevated to membership and alternateship respectively in the Central Committee of the Communist Youth League, along with a third *Spring* editor. A fourth was a party member. It must have been through them that the journal got some of its political information. Such respectability also helped persuade printers at the Foreign Languages Press to print one issue in a run of ten thousand. All the others, however, were mimeographed in small runs.

Peking Spring apparently believed that the municipal party committee and public security departments were still strongholds of Wu De's followers, although he was no longer mayor. Reporting the 1977 arrest and beatings of some "honest and righteous comrades" by the police, the journal stated:

> People of good will may perhaps not believe that in Peking where Chairman Hua and the CCP Central Committee are located, atrocities of this kind are rampant. Now that Wu De has been transferred away, will these conditions continue to exist?

They printed several hair-raising articles about the police, including one called "Trampled" that described the torture of a Peking worker who had participated in the April Fifth incident. The police officer who had interrogated Han Zhixiong in 1976 was quoted as threatening to "clear up accounts" with him now for the way Han had blackened his name after the reversal of verdict. (This officer, Ma Danian, was still in charge of suppressing dissidents as late as 1979. Another people's journal reported in September 1979 that Ma had led a search of a staff member's house.) *Peking Spring* also published pointed news items (e.g., "Destitute Petitioner Forced to Sell Cotton Padded Quilt"), fables (Western and Chinese), articles of political theory, literary criticism, poetry, and fiction. .

Spring's most thought-provoking item, which I will discuss further in Chapter 5, was a short story, "A Tragedy That Might Happen in the Year 2000." It imagined a coup d'état in which followers of the Gang of Four seize back power from Deng Xiaoping and reverse all his policies. The point was that Deng's line could never be firmly established so long as political power remained centralized rather than democratically based. Just as Chen

Erjin's booklet on "proletarian democratic revolution" brought the thinking of the *April Fifth Forum* group into a more radical phase, so "Tragedy" seemed to sharpen the focus of *Peking Spring*'s political writings. Thereafter the magazine concentrated on the problem of how to give the people more power in Chinese democracy. Its chief proposals included election instead of appointment of cadres, and greater leeway for free criticism of the party.

Enlightenment, April Fifth Forum, and *Peking Spring* were comprehensive magazines, publishing both literary works and political essays. Many other people-managed journals were strictly literary; they exploited literature's advantage of ambiguity to expose the horrors of the late years of Mao's rule. In a culturally managed society, it is hard to give clear definition to official standards of acceptability. When the line changes, the boundaries blur, to become clear again only as the authorities praise or ban specific works. In 1978–79 the test of acceptability was not how terrible a story of personal suffering was but that it held the communist system and the Great Helmsman blameless and attributed the horrors to the Gang of Four, local bureaucrats, or China's "feudal cultural tradition." But when a poem or piece of fiction concentrates on a victim's sufferings, it often remains unclear where the blame lies. A score of mimeographed literary magazines sprang up to operate in this dangerous territory. The most famous was *Today*, which proclaimed:

> History has finally given us an opportunity to sing aloud the song that has been buried in our hearts for ten years without encountering thundering punishment. . . . The difficult task of reflecting the spirit of the new era has fallen onto the shoulders of this generation. . . . What is past is already past, the future is still far distant. To our generation only today is today!

Today's editors were able to cut some of their stencils on a Chinese typewriter in an office to which one of their members had access, but like the staffs of the other people's journals they had to print and collate each issue themselves.

Campus literary magazines, which had just been restored in most universities, published similar kinds of material. Some were even sold at Democracy Wall despite the fact that they were supposed to be restricted to campus distribution. In August 1979, representatives of thirteen college literary magazines met and decided to publish an unofficial national literary magazine, *This Generation*. Since the campus literary clubs and their magazines were legal, they may have felt that a cooperative publication would be permitted. Printers in Wuhan accepted the job, but suddenly stopped work while the first issue was in press, apparently after receiving a warning from local party authorities. The sections already printed were distributed in November, but no second issue was ever published.

The boldest of the people's journals was Wei Jingsheng's *Explorations*. Like other people's magazines, it tried to stay within the law; it cited constitutional freedom of the press, published a liaison address, and sought to register and pay taxes. But it did not join the others in protesting its loyalty to the party or to Deng's reformist faction. Instead the January 1979 first issue stated, "We do not recognize the absolute correctness of any theory or any person." It contained the text of Wei Jingsheng's "Fifth Modernization" and a list of ten sarcastic questions about a January 5 Deng interview with American reporters—for example, "What would be the dangers to the interests of Chinese citizens if they were granted the same individual rights now enjoyed by U.S. citizens?"

Wei was employed as an electrician by the Peking municipal parks administration. According to one report, his father was deputy director of the cabinet-level State Capital Construction Commission. His mother was buried in Babaoshan, the elite cemetery of revolutionary martyrs. Wei had traveled widely in the 1960s and 1970s as a Red Guard and, later, an army man. In the northwest, he saw naked beggars and labor camps; in the south, mud villages emptied by famine. Like the Enlightenment group, he traced poverty to politics. Because he criticized Mao's dictatorship he quarreled with his superiors and was disapproved for party membership and suspended as a youth league member. At age twenty-eight, like many of his generation, Wei still lived with his father in a small apartment where one room had been set aside for him and a future wife. The father was dismayed at his son's unorthodox turn of mind, and told some of Wei's friends, "He is a counterrevolutionary. You better keep away from him." Wei calmly told his friends, "He made such a scene because he is a father and a decadent official"—a reference to the "feudal" faults of "patriarchalism" and "bureaucratism."

"The Fifth Modernization" appeared on Democracy Wall on December 5, 1978. "The hated old political system has not changed," it read. "When people ask for democracy they are only asking for something they rightfully own. . . . Are not the people justified in seizing power from those overlords?" Many readers were shocked and wrote disapproving comments. One recalled being attracted by such "refreshing" ideas, yet fearing the government's reaction and feeling unable to break with Marxism "after so many years of orthodox Marxist education." But a small group of readers went to the address given at the end of the poster and met the author. Although members of the group differed in their degree of skepticism about Marxism, they agreed on the need for unfettered theoretical investigation "to ascertain the real reason for the backwardness of Chinese society." They decided to found a magazine to carry out these "explorations." Among others, they included a college student (who was also a youth league member) and two factory workers. The first issue was mimeographed at the home of Wei Jingsheng's girlfriend, a woman of Tibetan origin whose parents, like Wei's, were senior party members. Most subsequent issues were printed in the room Wei's father had set aside for his married life. The number of copies ranged from 150 to 1,500 per issue, and the editors sold them on the street in Peking and, on one occasion, Tianjin.

The first three issues were dominated by Wei's writings, including "The Fifth Modernization" and two sequels and "Human Rights, Equality, and Democracy." They also carried material Wei garnered from foreign reporters who cultivated him, such as extracts from Amnesty International's 1978 report *Political Imprisonment in the People's Republic of China.* In the third issue Wei published a sensational exposé of Qincheng, the political prison for high-level cadres where his girlfriend's father had been incarcerated from 1960 to 1978.

Altogether, at least fifty-five people's periodicals were published in Peking, ranging from a single issue of some items to forty-three numbers of a journal called *Science, Democracy, and Law.* But the democracy movement was nationwide in scope. In Canton, a range of literary and comprehensive magazines was sold in the streets. The most famous was *People's Voice,* the organ of a part-time study group called the Scientific Socialism Study Society. *Voice* declared its loyalty to Marxism and Deng Xiaoping and discussed ways to combat bureaucracy and promote democracy. In Shanghai, lecturers from Peking appeared in late November 1978, and filled the huge blacktop People's Square until two or three in the morning with crowds estimated to be as large as 150,000. A French eyewitness reported a speech that opened with sarcasm:

> This evening I want to speak to you about our great socialist system and Comrade [Mao] Zedong. . . . [Mao] told us that our forces of production are backward but our relations of production and social system are the most advanced in the world—so advanced that even the capitalists envy us.

At this the crowd roared with laughter. The speaker continued with a play on words, based on the character *dong* in Mao's name, which means "east."

> Criticism of Comrade Mao is one of our most urgent tasks, for the party contains many small Mao-easts. It is also full of Mao-wests, Mao-souths, and Mao-norths.

According to one native, most Shanghai residents kept aloof from the square, fearing police action. Those who attended were mostly young men who enjoyed bantering with the speakers. When police appeared, the crowds mounted their bicycles and pedaled away, with the police copying as many license plate numbers as they could. But the police took no other steps and the discussions continued nightly for several weeks.

Besides those in Shanghai and Canton, there were Democracy Walls or people's periodicals in at least twenty-six other cities, and at least 127 titles were published outside Peking. The tally does not include campus periodicals, of which there were at least forty-five. There were doubtless still other cities and towns where Democracy Walls sprang up and people's periodicals were published that were never reported to the outside world. Nor will the total number of the participants in the movement ever be known. The publications' editorial boards ranged from one person to a score or more; each had its larger circle of contributors, anonymous advisers, and occasional helpers, as well as those who helped only by passing the periodicals from hand to hand.

Uniquely among democratic movements in socialist countries, the Chinese activists almost all saw themselves not as challenging the regime but as enlisting on the side of a faction within it. Unlike many people in the Soviet human rights movement, the democrats were not members of oppressed ethnic or religious minorities and they did not seek to emigrate. Unlike the Eastern European dissenters, they were not motivated by patriotic revulsion against foreign domination. Nor, with few exceptions, did they challenge socialism or Marxism. They angrily rejected the label of "dissidents" as implying antagonism to the state. Instead, they saw themselves in a traditional role—as remonstrators, not only loyal to the state but forming an integral part of it. Here lay the special source of their moral appeal to other Chinese, but also, because they had no grounds to resist the state's repression, the source of their movement's comparative fragility as well.

The tradition of remonstrance in China is ancient. Qu Yuan in the fourth century B.C. exposed to his king the errors of his policies and was in return angrily exiled to the primitive south. Yet he remained so loyal that when his predictions of disaster came true, he threw himself into the river in grief for his king and drowned. In the judgment of posterity, "he took loyalty as the highest good and valued the maintenance of integrity. He used bold words to preserve his state; he killed himself to achieve righteousness."

Although in later times the duty of remonstrance was concentrated in a special agency, the Censorate, honest advice to the sovereign remained the duty of every official. Over the centuries thousands of officials were flogged, demoted, banished, or exiled for having complained when the emperor neglected his ritual duties, tolerated corrupt officials, tampered with the line of succession, or disregarded the popular welfare. Tradition insists that the remonstrators were always unselfish. They never spoke to protect their personal rights; on the contrary, they put life and property at risk to awaken the ruler to his own interests and those of the state. When remonstrance failed, the act of self-sacrifice affirmed the moral character of the state and set an example for later generations of the minister's duty to guide the sovereign. "He who restrains his prince," wrote Mencius, "loves his prince."

Under Mao the duty of remonstrance remained, but its exercise became more dangerous than under even the most despotic of the emperors. According to Mao's "five fear-nots," a party member should speak the truth fearing neither removal from his post, expulsion from the party, imprisonment, divorce, nor "the guillotine." Mao chided his colleagues for treating him too timidly, inviting them to "criticize me day and night" in one speech and insisting elsewhere, "It is right to rebel." Yet he also regarded anyone who disagreed with him as a traitor, and millions were accordingly punished as "rightists," "revisionists," and "counterrevolutionaries" in the last twenty years of his rule.

To help restore people's willingness to speak up after Mao's death, the official press from 1977 on made heroes of those who had dared to remonstrate under Mao. For example, according to a 1980 newspaper story, in 1974 a factory worker in Changchun wrote fourteen anti–Jiang Qing, pro–Liu Shaoqi leaflets and sent them to fourteen offices in the city. He was arrested and during his interrogation tried to educate his jailers. He was executed by shooting in 1976, unrepentant, "head high, eyes blazing." In Shanxi a repairman in a broadcast station wrote twelve letters between 1974 and 1976 to Chairman Mao and other high officials, exposing bad behavior in the supposedly model agricultural brigade at Dazhai. "For the sake of pursuing truth, I have risked punishment and death to report this," he wrote. He was arrested, denounced in a mass meeting, tortured, and sentenced to eighteen years; his relatives were also punished. He refused to admit any crime and was cleared in 1979. In Jiangxi in 1966–67 a husband and wife, both medical-school teachers, sent the central authorities twenty-seven articles and letters expressing what were later deemed "correct opinions on a whole series of important issues" such as the errors of the Cultural Revolution, the faults of Lin Biao and Jiang Qing, and the injustices done to Liu Shaoqi and Deng Xiaoping. The husband was executed in 1970; the wife died the following year in a labor camp. "We do not fear plunging into boiling water, walking on fire, or having our bodies and bones broken," they were later quoted as saying, "so long as the great Chinese Communist Party can continue to exist and the great socialist fatherland can develop." The Jiangxi provincial party committee cleared their names in 1980. The most famous in this class of martyrs was Zhang Zhixin, "a good daughter of the party," who was tried in 1969 for expressing open criticism of the Cultural Revolution, Lin Biao, and Jiang Qing and defending the reputations of Liu Shaoqi and Peng Dehuai. (She had also criticized Mao, but the official press did not say so at the time of her rehabilitation because the party had not yet decided its own position on Mao.) She was sentenced to life imprisonment, but her unrepentant attitude in prison so unnerved the provincial party committee that they changed the sentence to death. Her throat was cut before execution so she could not shout her loyalty to the party. "At 10:12, the red flag flashed downward, the gun sounded, and Zhang Zhixin the woman communist fell. She had fallen, but her eyes were still wide open, staring angrily at the gray sky." There was even a "living Zhang Zhixin," a comrade named Guo Wei-bin who managed to survive eleven years in prison after speaking against Lin Biao and Jiang Qing at a meeting. In 1980 she served as a delegate to the National People's Congress and was warmly received by Zhang Zhixin's mother and Liu Shaoqi's widow. "Rather a broken jade," Guo said in prison, "than a tile intact."

All the officially published remonstrance cases had several features in common. First, the opinions for which the victims had been punished were judged correct at the time of rehabilitation; nobody was rehabilitated for using the rights of speech and correspondence to voice opinions still consid-ered incorrect. In particular, none of the rehabilitated persons was reported to have criticized Mao himself, only his lieutenants. Second, the victims had obeyed the party rule "Be open and aboveboard, don't intrigue and con-spire." Although in a few cases their letters or handbills were unsigned, none of them had made any attempt to protect himself or herself from arrest. Third, they took their punishment without resentment, although holding tenaciously to their "correct political stand." They underwent torture with composure and faced execution free of personal concerns, firm in the confi-dence that the cause of the party would win out and that the party itself would vindicate them. The moral of their stories was that the party was right in the end. Because they remonstrated rather than rebelled, the party's au-thority was strengthened. This was a model the democratic activists largely accepted. The difference between the twentieth-century remonstrators and their precursors from the fourth century B.C. on was one of social class. What used to be the responsibility only of the official elite was now a concern of every man and woman, and especially of the most politically conscious groups—students, workers, party members.

In many cities the democracy movement became intertwined with the activi-ties of petitioners seeking redress in the aftermath of the Cultural Revolu-tion. In Hangzhou, Xi'an, and Shanghai, local young people demonstrated to demand the right to return from their assigned posts in the countryside. The Shanghai demonstrations were the most serious. As China's largest city, Shanghai had produced over the years an estimated one million "sent-down youth"—middle-school graduates posted to distant corners of the nation for permanent service as farmers and frontiersmen. All of them looked to Deng Xiaoping's regime to liberate them from what they considered a kind of bondage. A National Work Conference on Educated Youth Sent Down to the Countryside met in Peking from October 31 to December 10, 1978. The policy it announced in mid-December was ambiguous—youth should be willing to stay happily in the countryside, but as many jobs as possible should be found for them in the cities. In January, thousands of sent-down youths returned to Shanghai on annual home leave for the lunar New Year. They joined hundreds of thousands of other youths (600,000, according to one estimate) already legally or illegally in Shanghai seeking permanent jobs. A series of irate demonstrations pressed the city government for assignments. On the night of February 5–6 the demonstrations culminated in a twelve-hour sit-in on the tracks of the Shanghai railway station that disrupted the travel of 80,000 passengers, according to the official press, and affected long-distance trains throughout the country for a week.

In Peking the petitioners' concerns were more diverse. Under the party's rehabilitation program, millions who had been arbitrarily demoted, transferred, fired, jailed, or had relatives executed during the previous thirty years were now to be politically rehabilitated, reemployed, given back their old houses, and reintegrated into society. Inevitably, many were not satisfied with the way their cases were handled locally. Tens of thousands came to the center of national power to seek redress. They posted their stories on Democracy Wall or told them to passersby at the front gate of Zhongnanhai:

Seeking to redress years of grievances, Comrade Liu, an air force political officer at Lanzhou, visited Lanzhou and Peking many times to air his grievances, and was placed in detention centers sixty-five times in Lanzhou and fifty-five times in Peking. . . .

Wang Dayuan of Datong Commune, Tianqingxian, Anhui province, and his whole family lost their residence registration as his father had been convicted on false charges. They had been petitioning for more than ten years, but were still unable to regain their residence registration. He and his sister were teenagers when their father was killed. Now his sister is twenty-nine years old and cannot find anyone to marry her because she does not have residence registration. . . .

Falsely accused of speculation and profiteering, Comrade Li Erli . . . was expelled from the party. His property was confiscated and he himself has become paralyzed owing to repeated struggles [interrogations]. His father, mother, and wife were hounded to death in four days. Li made several attempts to commit suicide. The case has dragged on for so long, over ten years, that his whole family is ruined and his children had to quit school. It is ascertained now that the charges were false. He got back his property, but nobody is adjudged responsible for the fiasco. . . .

A cadre who had accepted assignment to the countryside to lighten the burden on the official payroll during the famine of the early 1960s explained his case in a poem entitled "Where Is the Blue Sky of Shanxi?" (blue sky is a symbol of justice):

> *Eighteen years ago I went to help at the agricultural front,*
> *Responding to the call of the provincial party committee.*
> *I remembered the hard days of our revolution,*
> *And had the guts to take on the country's difficulties.*
>
> *Eighteen years ago I went to help at the agricultural front,*
> *With the guarantee of return after two years.*
> *But the provincial party committee went back on its word,*
> *And cut off my salary so I had no way to live. . . .*
>
> *These were eighteen years of tempests and storms.*
> *We sold our two children for three packs of corn. . . .*
> *My daughter died, my wife went mad.*
> *I lay deranged and half-paralyzed in my bed. . . .*
>
> *Eighteen years ago I went to help at the agricultural front,*
> *Sent on my way with the sound of gongs and drums.*
> *Eighteen years later I come back to appeal for justice,*
> *But they keep me locked outside the gate.*

The petitioners lived in desperate conditions in the city. They had often reached Peking on foot or by hobo rides on trains and trucks, dragging children and carrying their possessions in bundles. They clustered in the political center of town, some camping at the front gate of Zhongnanhai, perhaps hoping vainly to catch Chairman Hua or Vice Premier Deng going in or out. Others slept in the railway station or in doorways, cooking on fires kindled in the gutters or begging food from restaurants. Some peddled flowers, plastic tumbler holders, or handmade key rings in the streets. At least one woman put up a sign advertising her two children for sale. Several reportedly committed suicide. Later, many were housed in huts provided by the authorities, where several died from the cold. "Straight out of a Goya painting," French correspondent Georges Biannic called them, "sick, on crutches, dressed in rags and tatters, wretchedly poverty-stricken."

On January 8, 1979, the third anniversary of Zhou Enlai's death, the petitioners conducted a ceremony at Tiananmen Square. Contingents of factory workers and schoolchildren had arrived one by one to present wreaths at the Monument to the Revolutionary Martyrs. As reported by the people's journal *Reference News for the Masses:*

Their chests wearing white flowers [a sign of mourning], their eyes flowing with tears, wearing thin clothes and carrying small pieces of luggage on their backs, some carrying baskets in their hands containing items of everyday use, with solemn emotions they slowly entered the square. . . . After the column had paraded once around the square, the whole crowd gathered before the monument for a memorial ceremony. . . . When the crowd was in a very agitated state of emotion, a petitioner . . . made a speech: "Among those of us who have come to petition to Peking, already two have died of hunger. Now some have been driven away, some have been detained. We want human rights! We want democracy! . . . We want work, we want food, we want a place to live! We cannot drink the northwest wind." . . . At this time the audience numbered several tens of thousands. Some people in the back shouted, "Let's get rid of the remaining poison of the Gang of Four!" "We demand real resolution of our problems!" At the end they shouted slogans, sang "The Internationale," and left the square in an orderly manner in groups.

For the next several weeks a large group of petitioners sat at the front gate of Zhongnanhai. "We will not leave Peking until we have seen Chairman Hua to give him a letter containing our demands or until a good decision has been taken concerning us," one of them told a foreign reporter.

It was later revealed that the Central Committee and State Council had received over one million letters of appeal during 1979, an all-time high, and that during the busiest months of the petitioning movement, August and September, an average of seven hundred petitioners a day had come to the capital. Two hundred thousand cadres were eventually assigned to deal with these grievances, which the official press claimed were almost all redressed by the end of two years.

In the early part of 1979, however, the government was not prepared to handle the flood of cases, many of them impossibly intricate. In a wall poster, one petitioner complained that the government cadres' first step was "coaxing": the interviewer would write down the complaints, then draft a noncommittal letter of introduction to the authorities at home asking them to work out a solution. Since the original grievance was against these same authorities, the petitioner who was naive enough to go home with the letter was soon back in Peking with a new grievance arising from his treatment at home.

At first our petitions covered mostly a single issue. Then as our complaints multiplied, some petitions actually expanded to the size of a book, containing over 100,000 characters. . . . If we quit and went home, we would be judged counterrevolutionaries, and our relatives are still in prison. . . . Our only option is to remain in Peking.

But if they stayed they were subject to the second step, "suppression." The *Peking Daily* explained in an editorial:

> We must adopt a positive attitude in solving the problems raised in the masses' letters and visits. . . . But this certainly does not mean that any problem can be solved right away. . . . Some of the masses put forward excessive and even unreasonable demands. . . . When these demands cannot be met, they feel dissatisfied, pester people endlessly, and create an unreasonable uproar.

Persistent petitioners were sometimes detained in a prison called "Virtue Forest," whose existence was revealed in *Explorations*.

> Some fourteen people live in small, low-ceilinged, cold, wet, and dank rooms about eighteen meters wide. . . . Each person is given two steamed, half-steamed, or rotten dumplings, to be eaten with a bowl of dirty vegetable soup. Two people share a very dirty and louse-infested torn bedsheet. . . . They sleep on a bare and rough floor. . . .

According to this report, one of the police officers there told a group of detainees: "Because you made trouble, you have been asked to come here to be suppressed." (In Chinese Marxist terminology, "suppress" is a term for the function of the police vis-à-vis enemies of the state.) When one of the detainees protested, "Our papers have all publicized the constitution and the legal system," a policeman answered:

> We have five squadrons of a thousand policemen. We live by arresting people. Acting on orders of upper levels, we must carry out our duties. Papers are propaganda media that live on propaganda. They and we are like two cars running on separate tracks.

The petitioners had encountered the official limits of Deng's democracy.

2

OFFICIAL LIMITS

The central authorities at first seemed to encourage the democracy movement. Vice Premier Deng not only told an American reporter that "Democracy Wall is good"; he told a visiting Japanese socialist leader that "the masses' putting up big-character posters is a normal thing, and shows the stable situation in our country." This interview was published in the *People's Daily*, along with editorials with such titles as "Long Live the People" and statements like "Let the people say what they wish. . . . When people are free to speak, it means the party and government have strength and confidence." When the Third Plenum ended on December 22, 1978, its communiqué seemed full of plums for the poster-writers: Peng Dehuai was posthumously rehabilitated, Chen Yun was promoted, the Tiananmen incident was declared "fully revolutionary," and the party declared its intention to "shift the emphasis of the party's work to socialist modernization" and to "strengthen democracy in party life and in the political life of the state." On the first day of 1979, the pseudonymous poster-writing team Li Yizhe was released from prison, fulfilling one of the democracy movement's demands. In late January Deng Xiaoping departed for a trip to the United States surrounded by a halo of favorable press reports about American life.

But the local Peking authorities were discouraging from the first. "Democratic forums" met in Tiananmen Square for several nights after the epoch-making November 27 demonstration, but the forum of November 30 was disrupted by rowdies who were recognized as policemen in plainclothes and their friends and relations. Simultaneously a directive advised citizens not to participate in such demonstrations. No more were held. In January the municipality used the system of "transmission reports," in which cadres report orally to their subordinates information they have received at higher-level meetings, to tell people about "the spirit of a meeting of the Peking Municipal CCP Committee" at which a "responsible cadre" characterized the democracy movement as an "underground" movement that had close ties with foreigners, created disturbances, was utilized by enemies of the state, and was "impairing the state system." At the wall, plainclothes police recorded bicycle license numbers and private conversations, and later informed parents or factory security staff, who reprimanded their children or workers for having been there.

To the activists these events confirmed their theory of a struggle between the reformists, concentrated in the party center, and the conservatives, with strongholds in the Peking party committee and police. Seven people's journals held a meeting at Democracy Wall on January 29 and issued a statement that they would continue peacefully and openly to exercise their constitutional rights of speech, assembly, and publication. *April Fifth Forum* pointed out that the Municipal Committee's stand contradicted the national goals of democratic and legal reform and the Four Modernizations. *China Human Rights Paper* argued that "truthful, fair, and objective" identification of flaws in the generally good socialist system was aimed at "helping the party and government better to recognize and reform them" and should be welcomed rather than suppressed. Obviously the democrats were hoping that a sympathetic Deng would rap the knuckles of the zealots in the Peking party committee. *Explorations,* always the harshest, said that "some bigwigs in the Peking Municipal CCP Committee are afraid that the people might be able truly to enjoy democracy."

On January 18 the Peking police arrested Fu Yuehua, a leader of the petitioners' movement. The democratic publications protested that the police lacked a proper warrant, had failed to notify Fu's family within twenty-four hours, and had held her longer without an indictment than the law allowed. A delegation of people's journal staff called at the district police station that had arrested her to inquire about these points. The officer who received them was evasive. He said there were "internal procedures" that had been authorized from above; he was not obligated to explain them to persons who came posing as reporters without proper introductions from newsgathering units or journalists' identification cards. The journals published a transcript of this interview.

On February 8 Deng Xiaoping returned from the United States, and a little more than a week later Chinese troops invaded Vietnam in what the government called a "defensive counterattack" against border provocations. The invasion did not go well for the Chinese forces, who were withdrawn in the middle of March. This costly adventure brought the first check to Deng's freedom of action since his triumph at the Third Plenum in December; conservative party leaders who had been waiting to see how his reforms would go criticized him for moving too fast on several fronts. Deng's response was to defend the war and to attack the democrats in speeches on March 16 and 30. There were people misusing the pretext of democracy, he said, whipping up resentment over leftover problems from the Gang of Four era, forming secret or semisecret groups, and making connections with Taiwan agents and foreigners. He laid down "four basic principles" that no exercise of democracy could contradict. These were the socialist road, the proletarian dictatorship, Communist Party leadership, and Marxism-Leninism–Mao Zedong Thought.

Local governments throughout China quickly implemented Deng's message. On March 29 the Peking government issued a circular on public order in the capital. Citizens exercising their constitutional right to hold meetings and parades must obey the guidance of the police. No one should interfere with the work of public offices, instigate the masses to cause trouble, or obstruct traffic. Pictures, posters, slogans, or publications that contradicted the four basic principles were prohibited. And "it is not allowed to put up . . . posters on streets, public places, and buildings, except in places designated for such a purpose." The single spot so designated in Peking was Democracy Wall. Fire engines throwing water and teams of street-cleaners wielding scrub brushes removed posters from Tiananmen Square, Wangfujing, and elsewhere around the city. Other cities in China issued similar notices in March and April. *Peking Spring* reported how the former roomy and accessible Democracy Wall in Hangzhou, which had been spontaneously chosen for its convenient location, was closed in favor of a decrepit, narrow, badly lighted one in a secluded spot.

On March 25, Wei Jingsheng posted a bitter attack on Deng Xiaoping's March 16 speech. Entitled "Do We Want Democracy or New Dictatorship?" it accused Deng of "metamorphosing into a dictator." A few days later police arrested Wei and most of the rest of *Explorations'* staff and confiscated their mimeograph materials, books, notes, and funds. Police in Peking and other cities moved simultaneously to remove from among the democrats the minority of activists who were announced non-Marxists—besides Wei, people like Chen Lü and Ren Wanding of the China Human Rights League. Huang Xiang, who had returned home to Guiyang, was taken into custody there.

People's Daily greeted the third anniversary of the April Fifth incident with an editorial stating that that movement had been a struggle against the Gang of Four to uphold party rule. Its purposes had now been achieved. Those who pretended to inherit its mantle and who used its tactics to "present the state with unreasonable demands for their personal interests without considering the interests of the whole" were engaging not in democracy but in "ultrademocratization," a deviation characteristic of the Gang itself. In Tiananmen Square, wreaths in memory of Zhou Enlai were again placed at the foot of the Martyr's Monument, but a large sign reminded citizens that wall posters were prohibited.

These developments were no restriction of democracy, the official press argued. Democracy cannot be unlimited or absolute. "The kind of democracy we need is socialist democracy, or democracy enjoyed by the overwhelming majority of people," said the *Peking Daily*. "We don't want bourgeois democracy, which enables a handful of people to oppress the majority of people." The interests of the majority are defined by Deng's "four principles." So long as one upholds them (the "four upholds"), one is free to express any opinions. But the democracy movement, the paper said, harbored "counterrevolutionary elements," "black sheep" who used rumors and instigation to mislead well-meaning people, betray the nation to foreigners, and sabotage the Four Modernizations. "Socialist democracy," added the *Workers' Daily*, "is just a means, and it must serve the socialist economic base and socialist production. . . . In the present stage the criterion is whether or not it is conducive to shifting the emphasis of the party's work and speeding up the Four Modernizations."

The practical boundaries of democracy were defined by a number of actions in the next few years. A law-making process that had been interrupted in 1957 was resumed in July 1979, when the National People's Congress adopted seven laws, including a criminal code and a code of criminal procedure. The criminal law contained a section on counterrevolution, which it defined as acts undertaken "for the purpose of overthrowing the political power of the dictatorship of the proletariat and the socialist system and jeopardizing the People's Republic of China." In October 1979, the government brought Wei Jingsheng to trial on the dual charge of leaking secret information to foreign reporters and publishing counterrevolutionary statements. "Our constitution," the prosecutor told him, "stipulates that you have freedom of belief, and that you may believe or disbelieve Marxism-Leninism–Mao Zedong Thought, but it also states that you are definitely forbidden to oppose it—for opposition is a violation of the constitution." Wei was convicted on both charges and sentenced to fifteen years in prison. His appeal was expeditiously rejected. Fu Yuehua, the leader of the January 8 petitioners' demonstration, was also tried in October and sentenced to two years for violation of public order.

On November 29 the government closed a legal loophole by announcing that laws and decrees enacted since the founding of the PRC, despite their denunciation during the Cultural Revolution, remained in effect unless replaced by new laws. This reaffirmed the validity of, among other enactments, the 1952 regulations on registration of publications (the regulations that the people's journals had found too outdated to comply with); the 1951 Act on the Punishment of Counterrevolutionaries (which had been cited by the prosecution in the Wei Jingsheng trial); the 1957 Security Administration Punishment Act and State Council decision on reeducation through labor, which gave the police the right to impose without trial "administrative sanctions" ranging up to three years' detention in a labor camp for minor crimes, including political crimes; and the 1951 Regulations on Guarding State Secrets, which defined a long list of types of secrets, including "all national defense and military plans, . . . all state affairs which have not yet been decided upon or which have been decided upon but have not yet been made public, [and] all other state affairs which should be kept secret." These regulations, too, had been used by the prosecutor in the Wei trial to argue that information Wei gave foreign reporters constituted state secrets even though it was public knowledge among Chinese.

Now that posters were restricted to Democracy Wall, one democrat referred to it as "democracy in a shopping window," no more than "a display of samples." But late in 1979 the press reported that the National People's Congress Standing Committee regarded even this window as a problem. "People with ulterior motives" were using it, they said, again in collusion with foreigners, to "disrupt social order and security" with "adverse effect on the modernization drive." On December 6 the city administration announced that the wall would be closed, and sent teams of street cleaners to hose the posters off. But there were places where the ink had come through when the posters were fresh and soaked into the gray brick. The government soon constructed a line of large billboards in front of the wall.

From now on, posters could be hung only in Moon Altar Park, a place in a quiet neighborhood a couple of miles from the center of town, where old men played cards and toddlers used the slides and swings. Poster-writers were to register their names and workplaces at an office before hanging posters, to facilitate enforcement of article 145 of the new criminal law, which forbade the use of wall posters for slander or libel. In classic bureaucratic style, the office would be open from 8:30 A.M. to 5:30 P.M., except for two and a half hours off for lunch and two afternoons a week off for political study. Similar regulations were adopted elsewhere in the country. The *Peking Daily* ridiculed anyone who might see these developments as an assault on democracy:

> In our country, our people enjoy extensive democracy and have all kinds of channels and measures to exercise their rights to run the country and express their views. Political power at all levels in our country uses the system of people's congresses. There are blackboard newspapers and wall newspapers in factories, villages, offices, schools, shops, and all other units. . . . Party and government organs at all levels have set up organizations to handle the people's letters and visits. . . . However, some people have the audacity to say that there is no democracy in the whole of Peking or the entire country. . . . These words not only show ignorance, they are out-and-out slanders and distortions. . . . If we allow [people like Wei Jingsheng] to promote their so-called democracy, we will do harm to the just democratic rights of the masses of people.

At Moon Altar Park a few people hung posters of a personal nature, but without an audience these soon ceased to appear.

On January 16, 1980, Deng Xiaoping expressed his harshest evaluation yet of the democracy movement. Speaking at a central work conference called to review the country's progress since the Third Plenum, he said that "factors of instability" were hindering achievement of the Four Modernizations. These factors included not only criminal and counterrevolutionary elements but also, Deng said, "so-called democrats and dissidents who openly oppose the socialist system and the CCP leadership, such as Wei Jingsheng and his ilk." Although the democrats who were still active after the arrests of March and April 1979 considered themselves Marxists, Deng denied their socialist credentials by the standard of his own four basic principles. "They sometimes say that they too support Chairman Mao and the CCP," he said, "but they actually want to oppose CCP leadership and socialism." They were not to be treated as a loyal opposition, but as a potential "sabotage force" to be dealt with by the police. Nor should the police be stymied by the lack of a complete legal system. "The legal system must be gradually perfected in the course of its implementation; we cannot wait until it is perfected [to deal with criminal elements]," Deng said.

Deng demanded cancellation of the constitutional right to hang wall posters. To be sure, the "four great" freedoms of "speaking out freely, airing views fully, holding great debates, and writing big-character posters" had been formulated by Mao and were guaranteed in article 45 of the 1978 constitution, but it was now clear that these freedoms "have never played a positive role." "Therefore," Deng said to applause, "the party Central Committee is prepared to submit to the NPC Standing Committee and the NPC a motion to abolish the constitution's article concerning the 'four greats.'" In a nice illustration of the "leading role of the party over the state" that his speech had been aimed at affirming, Deng's suggestion was adopted at the next meeting of the National People's Congress in September. There was only one deliberately spoiled ballot to indicate any division of opinion, and even that was unusual enough to merit front-page comment in the *People's Daily*, which welcomed the anonymous delegate's courage as a sign of the new vigor of democracy in China.

Deng's January 1980 speech also contained the core of the party's doctrinal rebuttal of the democrats, offering themes that would be repeated in press campaigns over the next several years. "The core of the four basic principles," he stated, "is party leadership. . . . The party cannot be separated from the people, and the people cannot be separated from the party." A multiparty system, which some democrats had suggested, would sap the nation's unity. Under such a system "the strength of [a] country cannot be concentrated." Unless everyone accepts CCP leadership, "China will retrogress into divisions and confusions and will then be unable to accomplish modernization." Deng also rejected another argument frequently made by the democracy movement, its claim that free speech and political participation enable the people to correct the mistakes of the party. "Our party has . . . made serious mistakes," he said, "but these were always corrected by the party itself, not by any other force." "The whole party," he went on, "must obey the Central Committee. . . . No one is allowed to resist the leadership of the Central Committee by using the Central Committee's mistakes as a pretext."

The ideological counterattack included a campaign against the idea that America was a "democratic paradise." The people's periodicals reflected a widespread Chinese view of the United States as proving by its wealth and power the benefits democracy could bring. Deng himself had contributed to the image of America as a land of freedom and plenty during his visit by touring the Houston space center, ebulliently donning a cowboy hat, and thoroughly enjoying himself in ways that were reported home by the Voice of America and even beamed by satellite to Chinese television. Soon after his return a vast corrective literature began to roll off the party presses, most of it written by newspeople and scholars who began to visit the United States in considerable numbers after the normalization of diplomatic relations in January 1979.

So important was the propaganda campaign to take the bloom off America that articles on the United States seem to have outnumbered those on any other country for several years. Chinese writers exempted technology from their dark picture of the country, describing with admiration mechanized chicken farming, the Tennessee Valley Authority, Disneyland, and the defense consulting business. Otherwise, the visitors' gaze was directed to the "shadows" of America's "glittering skyscrapers"—to slums and arson, pornography and prostitution, derelicts and soup kitchens. To be sure, America had its super-rich: one billionaire, for example, with a villa so large that the servants lost their way in it, and another who kept twenty servants just to care for his dogs and cats. But the middle class wrestled with taxes, unemployment, and the burden of house and car payments so hopeless that families crumbled and the lonely individual turned to violence, suicide, or weird religious cults.

A Chinese-born American writer described the life of the average office worker living in New York City: up early in the morning, gulp a cup of coffee and two slices of toast, unlock three locks with three keys, spend an hour in urine-soaked subways, work all day with two ten-minute coffee breaks and an hour for lunch (the boss being too cheap to allow a proper Chinese-style siesta), ride home in a haze of marijuana, arrive to find the apartment burgled despite the three locks, and stay in all evening because it is too dangerous to go out. A college professor wrote to explain that his—to Chinese—astronomical salary of $33,000 did not go far because of mortgage payments, health and life insurance, and other expenses that the citizen of a socialist society need never dream of. Americans pamper dogs in unbelievable ways, wrote a correspondent, because in capitalist society a dog is a more faithful companion than a husband. In short, the message ran, instead of being a heaven of economic freedom and equality, America is a place where materialism and individualism lead to misery and injustice.

Racial discrimination—against blacks and especially against Chinese— was another major theme. To dissuade Chinese planning to settle in the United States, the *People's Daily* attempted to explode "six great illusions" harbored by Chinese emigrants: that jobs pay well, that it is easy to get work, that relatives will help you, that the work is easy, that it is easy to get permanent resident status, and finally, in general, that life is good.

As for the "colorful" drama of American politics, commentators presented the classical Leninist analysis that the competitive party system and the free press disguise the class dictatorship of the monopoly bourgeoisie. Without any real difference between the two parties, American politics are a "one-party system under the guise of a two-party system." Elections are an expensive show. Only the wealthy can put them on, and the techniques of campaigning have become so specialized that professional organizers manipulate the politicians, turning candidates into their creatures. The real conflicts take place behind the scenes among a few thousand men representing the "eastern," "western," and other financial cliques. There is universal suffrage, but it never challenges class rule. "How many top government figures in the West come from the common people?" asked a popular text. "Nearly all the American presidents from the past down to today were capitalists, big farmers, bankers, or politicians closely linked to monopoly finance. America's real rulers are the ten great financial cliques and the *Fortune* 500."

The ostensibly independent press of America, the analysis continued, hides oligarchical rule from the eyes of the people by pretending there is more at stake in election campaigns than there really is. The mass media actually belong to the same financial consortia that control the political game. They create a "lively atmosphere" in every campaign in order to sell newspapers, but suppress news of minor parties that might truly represent the masses' interests, and never allow fundamental criticism of the system. "If criticizing the government is the core of freedom of the press, then the U.S. press really enjoys tremendous freedom. . . . [But] press operations necessarily follow a given track and take the protection of the interests of certain persons or financial groups as their fundamental requisites."

Mao had spoken of "relaxing" and "restricting"—of a rule that should be alternately tight and loose in order to control the people without crushing their creativity. But the party's revulsion from the democracy movement after March 1979 was not a tactical tightening. It had always been a mistake, according to *People's Daily,* to confuse democracy with "anarchism" and "indiscipline." Democracy meant institutional changes in the "state system"—abolition of lifetime tenure for cadres, gradual introduction of directly elected people's congresses, an increased role for workers' congresses in government-owned factories, and reduction of direct interference by party committees in the technical business of offices and plants. It meant an end to "bureaucratism"—the arbitrary, inefficient, and self-serving use of power. And it meant the rehabilitation of millions arbitrarily punished in the last twenty years of Mao's rule—especially high cadres who had been purged for opposing him—and the introduction of laws that would prevent another such personal dictatorship. To the extent that the democrats shared these criticisms of the past and goals for the future, they were in accord with the party. But by their actions they offended against one principle from the past that the party could not yield: party control. This was so even though relatively few of them challenged the doctrine of party leadership in principle, simply because they spoke outside the party and in public.

Deng's temporary endorsement of the movement in late 1978 must have had something to do with the closely balanced struggle at the central work conference that preceded the Third Plenum. It was useful to have his rivals denounced in wall posters outside the Great Hall of the People where the conference took place, useful to hear shouts for the rehabilitation of his allies, and useful to be able to show that the "masses" wanted political reform and economic growth. When Deng acquiesced in the restriction of the movement in March 1979, it may also have been for factional reasons, because his policies of late 1978 had encountered difficulties and were under attack. But by February 1980, if not earlier, his political control was relatively firm. Now the democracy movement represented a threat to that control. Even more important, Deng was evidently surprised by the movement's persistence, and shocked by some of what the democrats had to say. For thirty years the party had made it so dangerous for people to speak out that it remained chronically misinformed about what was really on their minds. Deng had apparently hoped that the repudiation of the Cultural Revolution would not open questions of principle in anyone's mind about the way power was distributed between the party and the people.

Journals like *Peking Spring, April Fifth Forum,* and *Today* whose editors were close to the youth league or party kept publishing until they received a visit from an official of the youth league, city government, or police who told them to close down, usually giving as the reason the fact that they had failed to register under the 1952 regulations. Three *Peking Spring* editors reportedly made self-criticisms before the youth league Central Committee; they said they had realized their errors after hearing about Deng's January speech. *April Fifth Forum* sent registered letters to subscribers refunding the balance of subscriptions already paid and expressing its hope of being able to publish again sometime in the future. In Canton, *People's Voice* announced compliance with an order to close, but urged the National People's Congress to adopt a more practical publications registration law soon.

Sectors of the democracy movement that were not so close to the party managed to continue their activities for more than a year after Deng made his antagonism clear. In May 1980 the editors of eleven people's publications (some of them no longer being published) circulated a mimeographed open letter protesting the detention without trial of an activist named Liu Qing, who had been arrested in November 1979 for mimeographing and distributing the transcript of Wei Jingsheng's supposedly public trial. Soon after this protest, Liu was sentenced to three years of labor reeducation, an administrative punishment not requiring trial. An expanded group of seventeen organizations announced formation of a "National Committee to Save Liu Qing" and published another open letter, contending he was innocent of any crime. Several of the participants in this new committee were in turn arrested during a meeting in Canton on August 31. One of them, He Qiu, editor of *People's Road*, was held fifteen days on a charge of lacking proper household registration. Shortly after his release he was rearrested, this time for posting the first issue of a new mimeographed journal, *Responsibility*, which was published under the name of still another new organization, the "National People's Periodicals Association." He Qiu was released again after a few days. An activist in Shanghai, Fu Shenqi, managed to produce five issues of *Responsibility* through February 1981. In Peking and one other city, two small groups of democrats held what they grandly called "regional congresses of people's journals" in the late fall of 1980.

In fact, new mimeographed periodicals sprang up in cities around the country—perhaps in greater numbers than in the days of Democracy Wall. But now they were much more nearly "underground." Each was produced by a handful of people; they were thin and irregular, sometimes undated. The editors still printed their names and addresses on every issue to prove they were not conspirators. But they could no longer sell the publications on the streets. The issues passed from hand to hand among a tiny readership of the like-minded. Two of the best-known democrats, Wang Xizhe in Canton and Xu Wenli in Peking, resorted to mailing mimeographed "newsletters" that they claimed were personal correspondence protected under the constitution. On each issue they printed self-protective phrases like "intellectual exchange, for reference only."

The democracy movement had never had a large popular following. Already at Democracy Wall in the spring of 1979, Wei Jingsheng's acerbic response to Deng's March 16 speech drew scrawled comments such as "Pure shit!," "The whatever faction [the anti-Deng group] will warmly applaud you!," and "This is a purely reactionary poster." After his trial, Wei was portrayed in official propaganda as a chronic malingerer and troublemaker who

had sold military secrets to foreigners. The press labored to identify the remaining activists as thugs and traitors and to argue that anyone who resorted
to mimeographed newspapers, wall posters, and demonstrations wanted to
restore the chaos of the Cultural Revolution and the lawless ways of the
Gang of Four.

The democrats were able to make their views known to the public in several election districts where they competed for seats as people's deputies in
1980 (see Chapter 10). But harassment by police and postal authorities made
it increasingly difficult for them to circulate their writings to a wider audience. Most Chinese learned what they knew about the movement from denunciations in the official press or brief reports in the short-wave broadcasts
of the Voice of America or BBC. Chinese I later interviewed told me that
they agreed with some of what the democrats had to say, but thought they
were naïve to try to influence the government in the way that they did.
Others said that problems of democracy were of no concern to them, and
that they thought the democrats were behaving disruptively, "making a
mess." Intellectuals sympathetic to the democrats' values were afraid that
they were demanding too much too soon, and thought that the freedoms
being gradually recognized by the Deng regime had to be exercised with self-
restraint to avoid creating a counterreaction.

The party moved cautiously against the democrats in part because it recognized the value of the safety valve the movement provided during the deli-
cate process of negating the Cultural Revolution. The 1979 petitioners'
movement in Peking and demonstrations of sent-down youth in Shanghai
and elsewhere gave way in 1980 to factory strikes and university demonstrations, mostly distinct from the democracy movement and stimulated by the
government's own call for reforms. The Polish Solidarity movement was then
at its height, reminding the leaders that popular sentiments could take an
unpredictable course. The democracy movement was small and noncon-
spiratorial, mostly accepted socialism, and recognized the government's right
to restrict political activities according to law. Compared to terrorist and espionage organizations that the government claimed also existed, the movement was relatively harmless, and it helped provide information on the state
of mind of students and younger workers. Besides, the democrats had caught
the eye of journalists and diplomats in China and overseas Chinese in Hong
Kong and abroad. Hasty suppression could make domestic and international
martyrs of a group whose influence was otherwise relatively small.

A second reason why some cadres at the middle and lower levels were
"soft-handed," as Deng Xiaoping put it, was that until 1981 most officials
were not sure what the policy toward the democrats really was. In a society
that still seldom codifies its policies in the form of laws, the obstacle to bureaucratic compliance is not always the reluctance of lower-level officials to
obey, but sometimes, instead, their initial inability to discover what the lead-

ers really want amid the welter of abstract and contradictory editorials, speech transcripts, advisory notices, policy models, and other pronouncements emanating from the center. While gradually calling for restrictions on the democracy movement, the leaders also ceaselessly reaffirmed their commitment to democracy, legality, reform, and the cultural "Hundred Flowers." They implemented many of the democrats' suggestions and subjected their own party to criticisms of its past nearly as harsh in substance, if not in language, as most of the writings found in the unofficial journals. Just as the democrats themselves found signs of encouragement in all this, so lower-level officials saw reason to be cautious about going beyond the explicit instructions of the center. After all, their actions might later be denounced as excessive if the center's policies developed in liberal directions.

Finally, the democracy movement was able to remain active as long as it did in part because of the help of sympathizers within the party. "For instance," Deng Xiaoping complained in his January 1980 speech, "certain secret publications are printed so beautifully. Where did they get the paper? . . . Are there any party members in the plants which print these things?" (He may have been referring to the intercollegiate literary publication *This Generation*, which of course was not a secret publication.) Again in April 1980 a senior party ideologist, Hu Qiaomu, warned, "Comrade Xiaoping has said that we must not underestimate this group of people. They are organized. Their organizations are secret. They have programs and 'theories.' . . . These people are not entirely isolated in society; there is a fairly large number of people who harbor sympathy toward them or who even support them." As late as January 1981, just before the democrats were officially tagged illegal, party General Secretary Hu Yaobang reportedly stated that "illegal publications and organizations . . . are backed up by some people inside the party. These people think too highly of youths, believing that they are already able to manage state affairs."

Since many of the activists, in Peking especially, came from the small world of the government's company town, the charges of intraparty support are entirely plausible. In a vast peasant society, the college students and educated young factory workers of the capital represent a kind of elite. Apparently Hu Yaobang himself invited *Peking Spring* editor Wang Juntao and another activist to his home in Zhongnanhai to discuss the movement in its early days. The Academy of Social Sciences brought some of the democrats to a roundtable discussion and published some of their writings in its internal publications. The first party secretary of Guangdong met with editors of *Future*; the same may have happened in other provinces. In Peking, Canton, and probably elsewhere democratic activists were cultivated by cadres of the Communist Youth League as part of their normal work, the league cadres sometimes providing the inside information reflected in the journals' pages.

The league sponsored forums in both Peking and Canton in which democracy activists were prominent participants. Journalists working for official newspapers also sought them out, sometimes to gather information but sometimes also to share it. Ideas close to the democrats' found expression in the official press (see Chapter 5). Official literary magazines reprinted poetry from *Today* and short stories from *Peking Spring* and *Fertile Earth.*

Evidently the leaders saw promise in some of the activists. Avowed non-Marxists had been skimmed from the movement by the arrests of March and April 1979. During 1980 the party tested the loyalty of democrats who were youth league and party members by asking them to close their publications, a test most of them passed. Liu Qing was offered a post in the youth league apparatus, and says in his prison memoirs that "quite a few" others received similar hints; Wang Xizhe was offered a desirable job in the Pearl River Film Studio. Some of the young writers from *Today* and artists who had participated in an unofficial 1979 art exhibition called "Stars" were accepted into the official writers' and artists' associations and got plum editing and teaching jobs.

Perhaps the ablest of the democrats, in fact, were those who never went public, judging that the best route to influence ultimately lay inside the system. For each activist who worked publicly on a wall poster or magazine, gave a speech, or ran for office in the people's congress elections of 1980, there seem to have been several who advised them discreetly behind the scenes or pursued direct channels to the leaders. "I knew Wei Jingsheng," one such person told me, "and in late 1978 we debated whether to go public or make suggestions internally. He decided to put up wall posters. I sent my ideas privately to the leaders, and they accepted some." Such discreet activists, some of them members of elite families, have been among the members of the younger generation most assiduously courted by the leaders—recruited for jobs as personal political secretaries, invited to join policy study groups, asked to train as academicians and diplomats. Criticism articulated within the closed elite can be more sweeping than that expressed in public because the insider critic is licensed to speak and pledged to confidence. By bringing such chosen activists inside, the regime gained their cooperation. These democrats earned the opportunity to be heard, though at the price of dependence on their patrons and the patrons' political fortunes for any prospect of influence.

With a handful of exceptions, even the democrats who rejected the insider option nonetheless saw themselves as working in tandem with the reformers inside the regime to effect change. This was the key both to the democrats' optimism and to their inability to resist the government's decision to crush their movement when it finally came. *April Fifth Forum* editor Xu Wenli summed up the democrats' sense of mission:

Reform from below is impossible. For Chinese society and the Chinese people do not want disorder, nor have they created disorders. The historical experience of Chinese reform also makes it clear that reform from above cannot be carried through to the end. For the reform power of an upper stratum alone is not enough to overcome the bureaucratic resistance of the old system. Evidently the only practical road is a combination of reform from above and reform from below. China's business cannot be conducted by a minority any more. Government should be returned to the people and should be managed by the people of the whole country. Let us all work together, with one mind and one heart, to carry out reform and strengthen our nation.

Put this way, neither the issues nor the rhetoric had changed much from the 1890s. China had passed through a disaster, the Cultural Revolution, that revealed the weaknesses of the political system just as the defeat by Japan had done in 1895. Once again reformers saw the people as oppressed by a conservative bureaucracy that hindered modernization and kept the nation weak. Outsiders sensed a close battle between a conservative and a reformist faction in government, and those concerned about the fate of the nation felt obliged to support the reformists in government by mobilizing public opinion. Just as this was the spirit of Huang Xiang's venture to Peking in the fall of 1978, so it had been the mission of a group of young activists who had petitioned in Peking for reform eighty years earlier. They had been the first in China to promote the notion that political participation by the people was the key to modernization.

3

LIANG QICHAO AND THE CHINESE DEMOCRATIC TRADITION

In April 1895, eight thousand provincial degree-holders in their twenties and thirties who had assembled in Peking for the triennial national civil service examination learned that China had brought the Sino-Japanese War to an end by accepting a treaty on disastrous terms. Since these men were not yet officials, they had no right to concern themselves with national policy, but only with their studies. But because they believed China's survival as a nation was threatened, they enacted the protest that set China on the path to democracy. The conception of democracy they introduced proved lastingly influential. One of their number in particular, Liang Qichao, laid the foundation for the ideas of both the democracy activists and the party reformers of the late 1970s.

The leader of the protest in 1895 was Kang Youwei, a brilliant and eccentric thirty-seven-year-old examination candidate from the southern coastal province of Guangdong. He mobilized the candidates first from his own province and then from others to submit petitions to the Censorate, located on the site that later became Tiananmen Square. "Traffic was blocked in the streets as the scholars went back and forth in groups [to submit their petitions], and they surrounded the carriages of the high officials," Kang later wrote. "The provincial graduates from Taiwan [which had been ceded to the Japanese] wept as they volunteered their services to the state, and everybody sympathized with them." Over twelve hundred of the candidates signed a joint petition to demand rejection of the peace terms and fundamental government reforms. "The scholars, in high spirits, formed a line more than a third of a mile long outside the office of the Censorate. On May 2, we presented the petition to the Censorate. But the officials there refused to accept it, stating that the Imperial seal had already been affixed [to the treaty documents] and could not be canceled."

On rare occasions in earlier dynasties, examination candidates had demonstrated against corrupt officials or, less commonly, over matters of policy. But in three hundred years of the Qing dynasty no group of candidates had ever presumed to press the government on a matter of such high policy, much less to demand fundamental reforms. Kang and his followers soon broke with tradition even more radically by organizing study societies and newspapers, thus creating a permanent lobby for reform. They belonged to the first generation of Chinese to claim that government should be regularly supervised by the people, and the first to mobilize a public outside officialdom to try to exert influence on government.

Kang believed in democracy as the best political system, but he and his group argued for constitutional monarchy as the initial step. A constitution, Kang insisted, would not weaken the ruler but rather enhance his powers by mobilizing the energies of the people on behalf of the state.

> A constitution is enacted, which binds the rulers and all others alike. The ruler's person is inviolable; he can do no wrong, as administrative responsibilities are shouldered by the government. In this way the sovereign and the people are welded together into one body politic. How can the nation not be strong?

Kang argued that this was the "secret of the strength of Japan and the Western countries." In June 1898, the emperor launched the "Hundred Days of Reform" and embodied many of Kang's and others' reform proposals in decrees. But toward the end of September the conservatives at court carried out a countercoup. Six of the reformers, including Kang's younger brother, were put to death, and Kang fled to Japan. He lived until 1927, but intellectual leadership of the reform movement passed to a disciple, Liang Qichao.

Although occasionally a political organizer and in later life twice a cabinet minister, Liang Qichao is best known to history as a brilliant journalist and China's most influential modern political thinker. He stayed in exile with a price on his head until the Qing was overthrown in 1911, but he exerted immense influence by teaching and lecturing to Chinese students abroad and by managing and writing for a series of proreform magazines.

Liang was born in 1873 in a village in South China not far from Macao. As he recounted his childhood later, it was like a Confucian fairy tale. His uncles and cousins "cultivated the fields while engaged in studies, without becoming involved in the affairs of the outside world." As his grandfather's favorite, young Liang was tutored in the classics and "stories about the wise words and virtuous deeds of heroes and sages of the past." He went on to an academy in Canton, passed the provincial-level civil service examination at the age of sixteen, and received recognition as a precocious talent by the offer of marriage to the younger sister of the chief examiner. So far, his career was a classic example of the orderly rise of talent under the imperial system.

But in 1890 a friend introduced Liang to Kang Youwei, then a scholar of local repute. Without preliminaries, Kang assaulted Liang's examination-oriented literary learning as vacant and useless. "My interview with him," Liang later recalled,

> began at eight or nine in the morning, and lasted until eight or nine in the evening, when I begged leave. It was like a cold shower for me, or a blow right at the head with [the Zen master's] staff, suddenly depriving me of my defenses, leaving me dazzled without knowing what to do. I was both shocked and delighted, embittered and remorseful, frightened and uncertain. I stayed all night with [my friend], unable to sleep a wink. The next day I went to see the Master again, begging for his instruction on the right way to scholarship.

Liang devoted the next five years to studies under Kang. In 1895, student and teacher went together to Peking for the national-level examinations, which Kang passed. There they learned about the punitive peace terms with Japan and led the movement to petition the government for reform.

Liang was twenty-six when he fled the purge of 1898 aboard a boat bound for Japan. He stares out at us from photographs with the energy and assurance of a "man of resolve"—the Japanese-Chinese term that in his day denoted the type of young activist who had launched Japan on the road to modernization some thirty years before and whom the young Chinese radicals aspired to emulate. But while the Japanese Meiji revolutionaries appear in photographs in military costume with a sword by their side, or in a Westernized morning coat with full moustache and resolutely drawn brow, we usually see Liang pictured clean-shaven, in a scholar's gown, solemn and thin. The failure of the reforms deprived him of a position near the seat of power. "My daily work," he wrote despondently during his exile, "consists of enslaving myself with pen and paper, producing empty words that are of no help in [overcoming] current national difficulties."

Yet Liang largely succeeded in moving the massive political body of China on the fulcrum of his series of journals. The magazines were banned in China, but Liang's explorations of the relevance of Western thought for China and his exciting "new-style" prose were so popular that the journals were smuggled in and avidly circulated from hand to hand. "Even Napoleon at the height of his power could not have captivated a larger number of men in his armies than the numberless youths whom Liang held under the influence of his pen," one of Liang's translators contended. A man who later became a diplomat recalled that Liang's "sharp pen and overflowing emotion deeply moved me." He "stimulated my patriotic fervor," said a later government official; he was a "fountain of wisdom" (a college dean); his writings "completely capped the times" (a historian). A general wrote that he had decided to enter the military profession after reading Liang; a Buddhist leader resolved to "save the world through Buddha" after reading him; a literary critic writing in the 1950s claimed that "every Chinese intellectual in the last fifty years has been influenced by Liang Qichao." The philosopher Hu Shi wrote that Liang's essays were "capable of making us dance, of making us weep, of arousing us to a determined enthusiasm." For Chinese in the first years of this century, Liang's writings were the window on all that was modern and foreign and might be used to save China. He introduced new ways of thinking about literature, history, international relations, science, religion, language, the races of mankind, and the meaning of life. For political thinkers, his work defined the tradition within which later Chinese debates over democracy took place.

Liang's specific program wavered from revolution to reform and back to revolution again. After his flight to Japan, he agitated for revolution, anticipating by sixty-odd years the Cultural Revolution slogan "There can be no construction without destruction." In 1903, after a trip to America, he began to doubt that China was ready for a revolution and came to favor enlightened despotism. Nonetheless, when, in 1906, the Qing government announced preparations for constitutional government, he threw himself into the agitation to hasten the arrival of constitutional monarchy. But when the 1911 revolution overthrew the empire he became a committed republican. Some critics accused him of inconsistency. He agreed, writing of himself that he was a person who "had too few convictions [and] would often be carried away by events and abandon positions he had held."

Yet Liang's shifts were undergirded by a strong structure of principle. His work is suffused with ideas and vocabulary from Chinese Buddhism, Taoism, the I Ching, poetry, popular novels, and folk sayings. But his major training was Confucian. Chinese Confucianism in the 1870s and 1880s had already undergone the beginnings of a revolution, accepting for the first time within its dominant stream the notion that the nation is the political unit of concern and that the nation's survival is the prime problem for politics. Seeing wealth and power as the goals of the state, Confucian thinkers had already begun to view the active involvement of the people as one source of that power. The Qing school of "practical statecraft" focused on institutional change as a technique of rule. It remained for Liang Qichao to interpret the thought of the West in light of these ideas and values from his own tradition.

China in 1898 was only beginning to become acquainted with the ideas of the rest of the world. It was just in that year that the translator Lin Shu produced the first of his 180 renditions of Western literary works and Yan Fu issued the first of his political and philosophical translations, T. H. Huxley's *Evolution and Ethics*. The Chinese translation of *The Wealth of Nations* came out in 1900; of John Stuart Mill's *On Liberty*, in 1903; and of Montesquieu's *The Spirit of the Laws*, in 1909. On the boat to Japan after the 1898 coup, Liang started to learn Japanese. The Japanese had made a thorough study of Western political and legal theory before drafting their Constitution of 1889. They had translated into their literary language—which was very close to the classical Chinese in which Liang was versed—not only the works of such well-known theorists as Hobbes, Locke, Rousseau, Hume, and Bentham, but also those of persons less well remembered today, such as Benjamin Kidde, Johann Kaspar Bluntschli, and Gustav Bornhak. It was through Liang's essays that most politically aware Chinese were introduced to the ideas of these writers. Even the first Chinese mention of Marx was Liang's, although the reference was a passing and inaccurate one.

Liang's explorations of Western thought focused on a central conundrum: that the countries of the world that were powerful were also democratic—eighty years later precisely the perception of Huang Xiang, and still a riddle in Chinese eyes. Liang perceived a world of fierce competition among nations and races, in which the solidarity of the group offered the only means of survival. Yet he also considered popular participation a sign of civilization, an attribute of modernity, and an essential corollary to wealth and power. The question Liang brought to the works he read in Japanese translation was: How were the two values of statism and democracy to be reconciled? How were the interests of the individual connected to those of the nation? In a long tradition of discourse about the relations between public and private, Chinese philosophers had generally argued that harmony was essential to the strength of any social organism and that private interests must be suppressed to obtain that harmony. Yet Western philosophers seemed to reconcile the most boisterous individualism with the strongest states.

Liang had already begun to address this question before the Hundred Days in a series of essays called "A Comprehensive Discussion of Reform," published in 1896–98 in the journal he was then editing, *Chinese Progress*. Reflecting the consensus of contemporary reformist thinking, Liang portrayed democracy chiefly as a means of communication between government and people. The agents of communication he proposed for China were to be consultative bodies, which he referred to as "study societies" because they would maintain libraries, sponsor teaching and research, make translations, and publish technical journals. For one thing, he argued, such activities would overcome China's shortage of experts in the fields of commerce and technology. But new knowledge alone would not save China. "Although you may educate your people, this does not mean you can create a state." For a state is more than an agglomeration of individuals. It requires unity of will and effort: "ten thousand ears with one hearing, ten thousand powers with only one purpose in life." The experiences of Chinese antiquity, the Western countries, and Japan showed that study societies could create this unity.

In those instances, in order to have a state, they had societies. The prince held meetings. The officials held meetings. The gentry held meetings. The people held meetings. Every day things were discussed; every night they were mulled over. . . . What other way is there to unify ourselves?

In an 1897 memorial to the governor of Hunan, where he was teaching at a reform academy, Liang expanded on the potential role of study societies. He had privately urged the governor to be ready to declare the province's independence if the foreign powers took over the rest of China—by no means a farfetched vision at a time when Japan had seized Taiwan, Germany parts of Shandong, and the other powers seemed prepared to "carve China like a melon." Liang proposed that study societies should be set up in anticipation in each county and department and that the already established Southern Study Society serve as a sort of provincial-level legislature. (The society was so named because Hunan is in China's south.) For the moment, due to the backwardness of the people, participation would be limited to men with official degrees. Study societies would work with local officials in accordance with principles of division of power adopted from the West: the societies would have the right to discuss policies and enact rules, while administrative officials would carry out projects. At the provincial level, the governor would work closely with the Southern Study Society. When officials received telegrams or documents, unless they were top secret, they should be handed over to the society for discussion. All reform policies should be submitted to the society for discussion as to their advisability, appropriate methods of administration, funding, and personnel. This system would create intimate communication between officials and the gentry. The officials would learn from the study society members what the people needed; study society members would come to understand the need for certain projects and would voluntarily subscribe the necessary funds to support them. But what if there was a conflict between the governor and the study society over a policy decision? Who should have the right to decide? Liang provided no answer. Indeed, in none of his early writings did he even recognize the possibility of conflict between people and government.

How Liang then viewed the relations between people and government can be seen in another early essay, "China's Weakness Comes from Trying to Check Abuses." Here he argued the seemingly paradoxical position that the bureaucratic rules created to keep officialdom honest were the source of China's weakness. "In the West," he wrote, "each individual is said to have the personal right to do what is appropriate for him to do and to enjoy the benefits owing to him." But in China, governments have been obsessed with preventing corruption and have devoted their ingenuity to fashioning regulations to frustrate any nonroutine action by officials or subjects. By thus restricting its citizens' "rights" (*quan*), Liang argued, the state was at the same time restricting its own "powers" (*quan*), for

> a state consists of an accumulation of powers. A state with a full array of powers is strong; one with few powers is in difficulties; and one lacking them is lost. By a full array of powers I mean a situation where each individual member exercises his rights.

In contrast to the Western concept of rights as claims against the state, the broad Chinese concept of *quan*, meaning both rights and powers, enabled Liang to see rights as a kind of substance that could be accumulated so that the rights of individual citizens added up to the powers of the state.

But Liang's argument was more than just verbal. It rested on his conception of rights as consisting of that which it is appropriate for the citizen to do. He assumed that citizens going about their legitimate business would not clash with the general interest. Such an assumption was widely shared by contemporary thinkers, since their Confucian training posited a natural harmony of social roles. Liang also drew on the Confucian truism that the source of wealth and power lies in the activities of the people. Such activities, presumably, are entirely beneficial and in no way harmful. In fact, he argued, as subjects are admitted to the active role of citizen they shoulder particular "duties" much as a bureaucrat does when appointed to office. The duties of citizens are to love and be concerned about the nation. Hence political participation should unleash energies that will contribute to the collective welfare; it would not—as a Westerner might see it—enable individuals to pursue personal interests that might be competitive with that welfare.

Liang seemed to find his argument proven by negative example when he arrived in Japan in 1898 and saw the weakness of the Chinese merchant community there. In his analysis, his compatriots were at a competitive disadvantage with merchants of other nationalities because they lacked an organization—he called it a chamber of commerce—to gather commercial intelligence, prepare legal information, educate their children, improve social customs, and conduct public relief. And Chinese diplomacy was so weak that the Chinese alone of all nations were denied the right to reside and conduct business in the Japanese interior. In Japan, Liang began to see the issue for Chinese as not just the protection of their state but the very survival of their race. International competition, he said, no longer took the form of struggles among princes (he named Alexander, Genghis Khan, and Napoleon) who raised armies to pursue personal ambitions. Now entire populations were driven by the demands of the Darwinian struggle for survival to compete all over the face of the globe. The white race had already overwhelmed five of the six continents and also controlled large parts of Asia; it was gathering its forces for the assault on China. What did the Chinese have to counterpose against the white peril? At the moment, the Chinese abroad were in the forefront of the ethnic struggle. As a minority battling for their survival, the overseas Chinese should set aside "small conflicts" among themselves and unify for the "great conflict" against other races. Companies participating in the proposed chamber of commerce should cooperate entirely in the general interest without concern for their own profit or loss. The merchants should share commercial information, subscribe to community educational and legal funds, and give up gambling, prostitution, opium-smoking, and feuding because they damaged the reputation of the race.

But why should a group of businessmen set aside competition among themselves? Liang gave the analogy of the British East India Company, implying that the proposed Chinese chamber would be a joint-stock company in which people invested not capital but their racial fate. He also used the analogy of a swarm of bees to show that a community that united would be much more powerful than individuals in isolation. At the heart of his argument was the belief that all Chinese would be enslaved or wiped out if they did not cooperate to defend themselves. Under conditions of racial danger, each individual's interests were at one with those of the collectivity, for if the race died out so would each individual. The same reasoning applied to political reform at home. Just as Chinese communities overseas must organize to protect common interests, Liang argued, so the people of China must have a state that was no longer the private property of a dynastic family but an inclusive organization of the people. With the fate of each individual identified with that of the state, patriotism would flourish and the nation would survive.

Given that the individual's interests are served by the success of the group, how much freedom could the collectivity afford to grant the individual? Liang approached this question with the same optimistic view of human nature and its compatibility with the needs of the state that informed his view of citizens' rights. In a series of "study notes" and other essays on Western political philosophers written between 1901 and 1903, he summarized passages from Japanese translations of Hobbes, Rousseau, and Bentham, among others, and annotated them with analogies to Chinese philosophers, explications, and criticisms. These essays illuminate Liang's assumptions about human nature and politics by showing not only what he assimilated and disagreed with from the West, but what he misunderstood and overlooked.

In "Study Notes on Hobbes," Liang reviewed Hobbes's theory that to escape the war of all against all, people enter by contract into a state of commonwealth where the security of each is protected. For the most part, Liang said, he thought the argument logical. But why did Hobbes insist that the social contract establishes an absolute sovereign who has the power of life and death over citizens and against whom the citizens have no right to rebel? It would make more sense to reason that people seeking to assure their individual interests would set up institutions that guaranteed their liberty. Then everybody would be so satisfied that there would be no need to rebel.

Of course the answer to this question forms the heart of *Leviathan's* argument:

> If we could suppose the great multitude of men to consent in the observation of justice, and other laws of nature, without a common power to keep them all in awe; we might as well suppose all mankind to do the same; and then there neither would be, nor need to be any civil government, or commonwealth at all; because there would be peace without subjection.

In short, since human nature is envious, aggressive, and warlike, peace can be secured only by superior force. Not sharing this Hobbesian view of human nature, Liang failed to grasp a central part of Hobbes's argument.

The same blind spot appears in Liang's "Study Notes on Rousseau." Liang accepts the premise that to secure their freedoms, people join in a social contract which establishes the collective group as a sovereign animated by a general will. But he demurs when Rousseau asserts that the sovereign is "a moral and collective body" to which the individual is completely subordinate.

> Rousseau advocates the social contract on the basis of each individual's conscious freedom, but derives from the contract conditions which stress the state and ignore the individual. This cannot be what he really means.

Yet Liang was not arguing here for the right of the individual to do whatever he or she wishes regardless of the interests of the group. Instead, he was puzzled because he had overlooked Rousseau's argument that individuals may be animated by personal interests different from the general interest, leading to a contradiction that must be forcibly resolved in favor of the general interest. As Rousseau wrote,

> Each individual, as a man, may have a particular will contrary or dissimilar to the general will which he has as a citizen. . . . In order then that the social compact may not be an empty formula, it tacitly includes the undertaking, which alone can give force to the rest, that whoever refuses to obey the general will shall be compelled to do so by the whole body. This means nothing less than that he will be forced to be free.

Liang did not explain this problem of the particular will, just as in writing about Hobbes he had not made clear that Hobbes believed that people left to their own devices would oppress one another. Apparently for Liang, at this stage of his thought, the collectivity did not need to worry about granting freedom to the individual because the problem of antisocial motivations on the part of the individual did not exist.

In an essay on Bentham written the following year (1902), Liang acknowledged the conflict of public and private interests, but offered an easy solution for it. This essay, called "The Doctrine of Bentham, Master of Utilitarianism," summarized the pleasure-pain calculus and Bentham's argument that a social order should be judged by its ability to provide the greatest pleasure and the least pain for the greatest number of people. But, Liang asked, where does the standard of the greatest happiness of the greatest number come from? What could make people agree to the standard, when we know that "nine times out of ten the public interest and private interests are in conflict"? A Japanese Benthamite named Katō Hiroyuki had the solution to this problem, Liang reported, in his concept of "calculated concern for others." Calculated concern grows from the perception that one's own pleasures are largely dependent on the welfare of the group. In this light, all true weighers of their own interests will devote themselves to the collective welfare. Apparently, then, the private interests that appear to clash with public interests are only a kind of lower or illusory interest; at a higher level of reasoning, such conflicts disappear. The only residual problem Liang perceived was that uneducated people would not be able to reason so elegantly. Utilitarianism, therefore, could not yet be put into practice in China.

A crucial illustration of the higher compatibility of public and private interests arose from Liang's analyses of the past and future relationships of officialdom and the people. Writing again on "The Sources of China's Weakness," Liang argued that if the Chinese people were slavish, ignorant, selfish, dishonest, cowardly, and passive, it was because officialdom had kept them that way in order to prevent popular uprisings that would challenge officials' control of property they had seized from the people. All government policies described in the twenty-four dynastic histories had one of three purposes—to make the people stupid, to weaken them, or to disunify them; and all used one of four methods—tempting, taming, enslaving, and surveilling. The alienation of the people from the government was thus due to oppression by officialdom rather than to innate rebelliousness. In an essay on the virtues of a constitution, Liang argued that a constitution that provided for popular participation in government would actually strengthen the state. Although the constitution would set limits to the monarch's powers, in exchange the monarchy would be eternally guaranteed against domestic disorder. For under an autocratic regime, he submitted, there are three potential sources of disorder—struggles over the succession, power-grabbing officials, and popular suffering. Under a constitutional regime, the succession is fixed, the powers of officials are fixed, and the people can always complain about policies they do not like. "Thus a constitutional form of government can never suffer from disorder."

Liang enlarged on the benign nature of freedom in "The Dialectical Unity of Five Pairs of Virtues." He paired freedom with discipline, defining freedom as acting autonomously as long as one does not invade others' freedom, and discipline as the virtue of respecting others' freedoms. Thus freedom is marked by obedience to law and to the public interest. In a letter to his dismayed mentor, Kang Youwei, whose own thinking was becoming more conservative, Liang conceded that freedom could be abused by an undisciplined people, as occurred in France after 1789. But he felt there was little danger of this happening in China, for the French were overactive by nature while the Chinese were passive to a fault. In any case, he argued, what he favored was freedom properly understood, something that might better be called personal self-government since it entailed governing oneself, letting others govern themselves, and everyone joining in obedience to the law.

Liang's faith in the harmony of individual and state reached its high point—as did his influence with the young, radical reading public in China—in the early years of a new fortnightly journal, *The New Citizen*, which he founded in Tokyo in 1902. The magazine was smuggled into China, where it created a sensation and achieved a circulation of fourteen thousand copies per issue—unmatched even by his own previous journals—and a readership of perhaps two hundred thousand, since each copy was passed from hand to hand. In a serial essay, likewise called "The New Citizen," Liang wrote in a visionary mood about the kind of personality the Chinese citizen of the future must have so that China might be cohesive, progressive, and strong. Accepting the racial and national-character stereotypes common at the time, Liang reminded his readers that in the worldwide struggle among the races, the white race was currently dominant. Among the whites the Teutons were most successful, and among the Teutons the Anglo-Saxons (i.e., the British). The British now controlled over one-fourth of the world's surface and population. English a century ago had been spoken by 12.7 percent of those using European languages and was now spoken by 27.7 percent. (Liang must have gotten these odd figures from some of the Japanese materials he read so voraciously.)

To analyze the source of Britain's strength, Liang quoted an anecdote he had read in a book by Rudolf von Jhering, a German political theorist teaching in Austria. An Englishman was overcharged a few shillings in a continental hotel. Instead of dropping the matter, he stayed on several weeks to contest the charge, at a cost many times the money at stake. An Austrian (or, Liang adds, a Chinese) might think the Englishman a fool, but it is this spirit of "rights consciousness" that makes a nation great. Combativeness over a few shillings is by no means equivalent to the petty pursuit of profit, Liang insisted. The two are really opposites: rights must be defended at any price, while the profit-minded person will ignore humiliation if it is too costly to seek redress. A nation whose citizens allow themselves to be cheated of a shilling here and a shilling there cultivates "an ideology of appeasement and a greed for peace." Such a nation will at first accept the foreign annexation of small bits of barren land (as China did in the nineteenth century) and later acquiesce in the loss of large parcels of land or even in total colonization. The attitude of "yieldingness" taught by China's ancient philosophers had created a nation that was a "boneless, bloodless, breathless monstrosity" in a world of competition. It had created a people whose sense of rights was inferior to that of all other peoples except "the black barbarians of India, Africa, and Southeast Asia." Only when the Chinese cultivated the attitude that no one was willing to give up the smallest right would the nation stand up to its oppressors. For

> the rights of the portions add up to the rights of the whole. The accumulation of private rights-consciousness of individuals makes the rights-consciousness of the nation. . . . People who can put up with eunuchs and petty officials extorting their small change will also put up with foreign countries slicing off a province. . . . The door through which extortionate government enters [that is, popular acquiescence] is the door through which foreign invaders enter.

So too with freedom, the subject of another installment of "The New Citizen." According to Liang, two kinds of freedom were particularly urgent for China. The first was political participation, which could be understood as "freedom that the citizenry as a whole has achieved vis-à-vis the government." The second was national freedom, or "nation-building," which exists "when the people of a nation get together with those of the same race and establish their own state, and do not allow other races or states to exercise any sovereignty over them, to interfere in the slightest way in their internal affairs, or to seize an inch of their territory." Although it might seem that the freedom of citizens against the state would detract from that of the state against other states, in reality the two freedoms were linked. The individual could have no freedom if the group to which he belonged was conquered, so the freedom of participation required the independence of the state. On the other hand, since true freedom is not licentiousness but voluntary obedience to the internal discipline of the group, it could reasonably be argued that "the freedoms of individuals, added up, make for the freedom of the group."

"Self-rule" was a final heading under which Liang explored the relations between individual and group. Rule, Liang pointed out, is the opposite of disorder. It was a well-known Confucian precept that any person, household, or state in a condition of disorder is likely to be taken over and ruled by others, while a group that keeps its own house in order will prevail. Although one side of human nature is undisciplined and uncooperative, there is also an "inner conscience" that teaches people to discipline themselves. In Western countries, Liang said, everyone from king and prime minister down to peddlers and butchers goes to work at eight in the morning, has lunch from twelve to one, and goes home at four or five in the afternoon. The nation works as one and rests as one. Although perhaps not a very realistic portrait of London or Berlin, this idea posed a sharp contrast to the tumult Liang's readers could observe in any Chinese city. These Western nations are so efficient that they are like armies or even machines, Liang concluded; the secret of their success is the voluntary hard work and rigorous scheduling of self-governing citizens.

In the essays written between 1896 and 1903, Liang repeatedly performs an act of philosophical legerdemain that is bound to baffle Western readers. Into the hat go individual rights, freedoms, and autonomy, and out of the hat come group rights, freedoms, and autonomy. Even after following this trick several times, one cannot easily analyze how it is done. The answer lies in Liang's refusal to admit that individual interests might conflict in any fundamental way with those of the group.

By assuming that harmony is natural in the political order, Liang was freed from having to answer for China the central problem that the thinkers he studied tried to answer for the West—how to reconcile the conflict between individual and collective interests. Hobbes and Rousseau argued that individuals have particular interests contrary to the general interest but can be forced to serve the latter because they also partake in it; Liang saw no need for compulsion. Darwin argued that the members of a species compete with one another but that this leads to the evolution of the species because the fittest survive; Liang treated the struggle for survival as something that occurs among groups, with the individual benefiting from the survival of the group. (Yet he ignored the implications of this reading of social Darwinism for the internal politics of multiethnic China, in which the majority Hans struggled for political power and territory with the minority Manchus and more than fifty other ethnic groups. Liang found it more convenient to refer to them all—quite inaccurately, and with the Japanese thrown in for good measure—as "the yellow race.") Liang did not argue, like Adam Smith, that individuals pursue selfish ends but that an invisible hand turns these efforts into a general increase in welfare; he did not argue, like the American authors of The Federalist, that government can be insulated from factional pressures by a series of institutional chambers and baffles. At this stage of his thought he posited no reconciliatory process—institutional, natural, or logical— whereby private interests could be transformed into public interests. He simply did not see private interests antagonistic to public interests as a serious problem for politics.

This faith in the innate potential harmony of human beings in the social order was a tenet of the Confucianism in which Liang was trained. During centuries when Western philosophers labored over the question of how humanity's selfish nature could be reconciled with life in society, Confucian thinkers instead discussed ways of educating people to follow their instincts for social cooperation. When Western thinkers were trying to design political systems as vessels to contain irrepressible conflict, Chinese philosophers aimed to design systems where no such conflict would be engendered.

Confucian reformers traditionally fell into two types, depending on their estimation of how good or how corrupt society was at the time that they wrote. Optimistic reformers argued that a mere change of institutional arrangements could tap the energies of officials and people to produce an immediate transformation of society. For example, when a group of early Qing decentralizers urged the emperor to disperse power more widely among officials, they assured him that the decentralized power would automatically be used for the common good. Liang carried the same idea into the modern age when he demanded power for the people, claiming that democratic institutions would bring quick results in national dynamism and modernization. Until 1903 he was able to be a radical democrat because he was a Confucian optimist.

Confucian pessimists, on the other hand, perceived society as corrupt, and argued for long-term indoctrination and education by moral example to teach people to see their higher interests in those of the collective. Liang became such a pessimist after a tour of America in 1903. The shift did not change his faith in natural social harmony. But it altered his prescription for the type of political reform needed to bring this harmony into play. This change in Liang's thought showed how the premise of natural social harmony could be compatible not only with radical democracy but, on a darker reading of China's backwardness, with authoritarianism as well.

Liang went to America to recruit supporters and raise money for his and Kang Youwei's political organization, the Protect-the-Emperor Society. He serialized his diary of the trip in The New Citizen and published it in 1904 as Abridged Diary of a Trip to the New Continent. Now barely remembered, this tour was actually one of the most influential Chinese-American encounters of the century. Liang traveled by ship from Yokohama to Vancouver and by train across Canada. He arrived in New York on May 12, 1903. Chinatown took the day off and several hundred Chinese met him at the station. There were welcoming speeches at an auditorium. Liang marveled at the huge size of the city (population three and a half million) and how busy and elegant it was. In the best hotel, he reported, a luxury suite decorated in the style of a palace of Louis XIV cost $150 a night. Even the famous statesman Li Hongzhang, who visited on an official tour in 1896, had been able to afford only a second-class room. Up on Morningside Heights Liang visited Grant's Tomb, where his famous predecessor Li had planted a memorial ginkgo tree (it still stands).

Giant economic trusts were a revelation. Liang visited J. P. Morgan, "the king of trusts, Napoleon of the business world." He had heard that no matter what, Morgan never went out to see anyone; presidents and prime ministers had to call on him, and he always disposed of an issue, no matter how complicated, in one to five minutes. Liang actually had no business to conduct, but was curious to see "the most powerful man in America." Morgan gave him three minutes.

From New York Liang made side trips to Boston and Philadelphia, visiting Plymouth Rock, Harvard Yard, and the Liberty Bell. He was amused by the way, when a woman walked into a room, the men all stood up and took off their hats. President Theodore Roosevelt received him at the White House and praised the work of the Chinese Empire Reform Association, a U.S. organization of Chinese adherents of Liang's and Kang's ideas. Liang went on to Baltimore, Pittsburgh, and Cincinnati. In New Orleans he deplored lynch law but unhesitatingly accepted its premise that blacks had an inordinate lust for white women. He visited the Chicago stockyards and recorded the boast that they "used everything but the grunt." He crossed Montana on the Great Northern Railroad and ended his five-month tour in Seattle, Portland, San Francisco, and Los Angeles, before embarking again from Vancouver for Yokohama.

American democracy was a disappointment. He was struck first by the tremendous number of immigrants in New York and noted that they resisted assimilation and voted as blocs. (A bit confused on the details, he reported that the licentious immigrants voted with the Mormon bloc in order to promote polygamy.) Politicians were afraid to offend the large blocs, so anti-immigrant sentiment was taken out on the Chinese, a small, defenseless group who were not allowed the same immigration privileges as other races. The spoils system, of course, was another weakness. Not only was it corrupt, but the constant change of officials at all levels made it impossible to carry out a coherent national policy. Liang deplored the constant electioneering—the presidency every four years, the House every two, many state and local offices annually. Every election offered an opportunity for more corruption. After his meeting with Roosevelt, Liang wrote that few American presidents had been men of talent. The parties' smoke-filled rooms produced compromise candidates distinguished only for their lack of enemies. As a puppet of the party bosses, the president tried to avoid offending anyone for four or eight years so he could find a good job after leaving office. In view of these and other defects, Liang wrote, "My trip to America has made me feel that the republican form of government is not as good as constitutional monarchy, which has fewer flaws and functions more efficiently."

More painful still was Liang's disappointment in those of his compatriots whom he met in the New World. American Chinese should be much more advanced than those at home, he said, since their economic and educational standards were higher and they enjoyed the benefits of freedom. Instead they seemed to have imported all the flaws of the national character, which Liang pointed out as pitilessly as only a countryman can. The Chinese overtired themselves working excessively long hours; they employed too many personnel in a single business; they snored and talked when attending a lecture; they spat and threw garbage in the streets. They walked too slowly, bowed too low to others, and talked too loud. By far their worst characteristic was that given the opportunity to organize in a free country, the Chinese had proven politically incompetent. "There is no society in the world more chaotic than that of San Francisco Chinese," wrote Liang. Their community organizations were either run autocratically or degenerated into factional battles over every issue. "Can a people like this carry out a consultative system?" And their elections were conducted strictly on grounds of hometown or clan loyalty, often leading to gang warfare in the streets. "Can a people like this carry out an electoral system?"

If the Chinese abroad were not ready for democracy, how could the Chinese at home be? As Liang prepared to leave he wrote the following summary of his observations:

Freedom, constitutionalism, republicanism: these are but the general terms which describe majority rule. But China's majority, the great, the vast majority of Chinese, are as I have described them here. Were we now to resort to rule by this majority, it would be the same as committing national suicide. Freedom, constitutionalism, republicanism—this would be like wearing summer garb in winter, or furs in summer: beautiful, to be sure, but unsuitable. No more am I dizzy with vain imaginings; no longer will I tell a tale of pretty dreams. In a word, the Chinese people must for now accept authoritarian rule; they cannot enjoy freedom. . . . Those born in the thundering tempests of today, forged and molded by iron and fire—they will be my citizens, twenty or thirty, nay, fifty years hence. Then we will give them Rousseau to read, and speak to them of Washington.

Liang's disgust at the Chinese and despair of democracy induced a painful rethinking of his position after his return to Japan. He became quite depressed. A friend in China who received a copy of a photograph wrote to Liang that he did not look himself. He expressed his confusion in an essay called "The Theory of the Great Political Scientist Bluntschli," published in *The New Citizen* a few months after his return. Johann Kaspar Bluntschli, a Swiss teaching in Germany, had written a book positing an organic theory of the state that was popular in both Europe and Japan. As Liang summarized the argument, Bluntschli refuted the idea of a social contract as the basis of the polity because it placed too much emphasis on the individual. Bluntschli showed that the state is an organic entity, far more than just an aggregation of individuals. Instead of deriving its existence from the citizens, the state is actually the source from which individuals derive their status as citizens and all their legal rights. For a people to enjoy the status of citizens they must form a strong state.

For certain disciplined and experienced peoples, the republican form of state could be made to work. But in China, Liang now felt, the pressing problem was the lack of social order and of a national-interest outlook on the part of the people. Even the educated youth, upon whose shoulders the task of building a nation rested, were beset by factionalism.

> Groups of activists have been unable to organize a solidly based association; or if one does get formed, it disbands almost as soon as it gathers. Someone's recent remark is most apt: "They can neither organize an association of more than three people nor maintain a party for over a year." Can people like this create a state that will survive in this world of fierce competition?

Where the public ethos is corrupt, Liang went on to summarize Bluntschli, a strong form of state such as constitutional monarchy is necessary. Citing Gustav Bornhak, a German professor, Liang predicted that a Chinese republic would quickly degenerate into mob rule with corrupt elections and incompetent politicians like those he had observed in America.

"For years I have been intoxicated with the idea of a republic," Liang wrote near the end of his essay. "Now reading Bluntschli's and Bornhak's theories is like having cold water poured down my back. My beliefs have lost their grounding overnight. I am in confusion, not knowing what road to take. Of the qualifications the two doctors regard as necessary for citizens of a republic, my countrymen lack even one." For a political leader who had cultivated a tone of certainty such a reversal was painful, but, Liang informed his readers, "All my life I have challenged received opinion, so I am not afraid now to challenge my former self."

Not until 1905 did Liang find his new solution to China's state-building problems. He explained it in "On Enlightened Despotism." China must have an autocracy that would rule in the public interest and gradually raise the level of popular education and civic consciousness until the conditions were ripe for a transition to constitutional monarchy. To compete successfully, a race must work together and compromise its internal conflicts. Such compromise cannot occur by itself; a system of authority is necessary. "With domination, society will survive; without it, disappear. From the viewpoint of society, it is not too much to say 'Domination is sacred.' "

No one should consider domination illegitimate. For the strong, such a system legitimates their privileges; for the weak, it secures their access to whatever goods they enjoy, which would otherwise not be protected. But even more important is the common interest all members of a state have in national survival. A state that succeeds in regulating internal competition in order to make itself more effective in external competition is ruling in the common interest of its members. In fact, "even if a governmental system deprives the people of much or all of their freedom, it is a good system so long as it is founded on a spirit of meeting the requirements of national defense."

Liang had come a long way from his earlier view that "a state whose people have rights is a state with rights." Yet in certain important respects the two views were similar. Liang was still insisting on an identity of interests between the individual and the collective. Now he was prepared to see that particular interests exist which could undermine the collective; he referred to them as the corrupt lust for fulfillment of personal desire, or as "internal competition" resulting from the existence of "small groups." But he maintained that there was still a higher level at which individual and collective interests unite. In both his pre- and post-American writings this higher level was defined by the survival of the race, identified in turn with the vigor of the state. Before 1903, Liang believed that the higher interest would be perceived automatically. Afterward, he believed that ill-educated, undisciplined people would overlook it, and that the common interest would therefore have to be temporarily enforced by an authority that would guide or tutor the people toward a higher civic consciousness. But both before and after 1903, he gave particular interests no legitimate force. This was where he crucially differed from Western liberal philosophers. He consistently regarded particular interests not as permanent, inevitable, and useful, but as temporary, misguided, and damaging. Under the constitutional monarchy that he advocated before 1903, particular interests would be sacrificed willingly; under enlightened despotism, they would be suppressed by authority. In neither case would private interests have to be accorded a legitimate role of their own, because in Liang's view it was only the collective level of interests that had any final reality.

Just as Liang's advocacy of democracy had adapted the optimistic strain of Confucian reformism to the modern world of mass participation, so his turn to enlightened despotism drew on the tradition of pessimistic reformism to justify subordinating the individual to the needs of the modern state under conditions of backwardness. The natural harmony of the political order could not be realized immediately if the people were backward. They must be trained as citizens first; until then, freedom would lead only to disorder. Liang thus laid down the rationale that would be used to justify authoritarianism, and the acceptance of authoritarianism, throughout China's democratic era.

Mao Zedong would later dismiss Liang Qichao's generation of reformers as "bourgeois democrats," advocates of a "bankrupt" ideology. (This was one of many verdicts revised after Mao's death; Chinese historians now consider Liang progressive for his time.) The communist regime did not reprint Liang's works until after Mao's death. Liang's essays ceased to be read in schools as exemplars of modern prose style. The democratic activists, among the most inquiring minds of their generation, were fond of referring in their writings to Montesquieu, Bacon, Descartes, La Rochefoucauld, and an assortment of other thinkers whom they must have read in old copies of old translations, but they rarely referred to Liang.

If the democrats' thinking on key points was nonetheless close to Liang's, it may ironically have been Mao who was the chief conduit of influence— not by citing Liang directly, which he did rarely, but by persistently framing the issue of the relationship between citizens and state in the way Liang had pioneered. Mao, after all, had come from Liang's world. He was born in 1893, only twenty years after Liang. After helping his father in the fields the teenaged Mao would secretly read Liang's current magazine, *The New Citizen,* in his room. When he went away to school, he later said, "I read and re-read [the writings of Kang Youwei and Liang Qichao] until I knew them by heart. I worshipped Kang and Liang." A biographer who inspected a copy of *The New Citizen* that Mao read found the following Liang-like marginalia in his hand:

> When the constitution of a constitutional state is drawn up for the people, the monarch will enjoy their support. To the contrary, when the laws and decrees of an autocratic state are formulated by the monarch, he will not convince the people.

The two men even came close to working together. In 1921 Liang heard about Mao's activities as an adult educator in Hunan and wrote to a friend suggesting that Mao join him in a project called the Study Together Society in Tianjin. Liang did not know how far Mao's path was already diverging from his: the founding meeting of the Chinese Communist Party had been held only a few months earlier, with Mao in attendance. By the time Liang died in 1929, Mao was a guerrilla leader in the Jinggang Mountains, well on his way to implementing his strategy of peasant-based revolution.

Liang had consciously rejected the Marxist philosophy that Mao adopted. China needed economic growth, Liang said, not class warfare: to promote a labor movement at this early stage in China's development would be like teaching elementary school students about the problems of married life. Mao, going to the other extreme, was conspicuous even among Marxists not only in seeing class conflict everywhere but in keeping it alive as a force in China's political life after the revolution, when his party colleagues would have preferred to let the issue fade away. Mao insisted that every Chinese carry a designated "class background"—landlord, poor peasant, worker, "revolutionary cadre," "bad element," and so on. These labels were inherited, and they intimately affected one's educational prospects, career choice, marriage chances, and opportunities to join the party. (The class label system has been deemphasized since Mao's death.) Students of "good" and "bad" class backgrounds were set against one another in the competition for careers; Red Guard groups made up of the two kinds of students fought armed battles during the Cultural Revolution. Not only did the "old exploiting classes" remain to be struggled against in the new society, according to Mao, but a new exploiting class, the "newly emerging bourgeoisie," was generated both within and outside the party by inequalities that would continue to exist until the realization of full communism. Even after communism arrived, society would be riven by "contradictions" between leaders and led, between party and people, between state and individual, between backward and advanced elements, and among different nationalities.

Yet the assumption of a natural harmony of social interests survived the transition from Confucianism to Marxism. In some personal reading notes written in the early 1960s, Mao put this as clearly as could be wished:

Public interests are in apposition to private interests. Private interests are in apposition to public interests. Public and private interests are the unity of opposites. There can be no public interests without private interests. Likewise, there can be no private interests without public interests. . . . Public interests come first and private interests come later. The individual is an element of the collective. When collective interests are increased, personal interests will subsequently be improved.

The premised identity of personal and collective interests governed the meaning of the various democratic procedures that Mao invented or adapted from Lenin. Thus "democratic centralism" meant discussion of an issue within the party (or among the people) followed by unified implementation of whatever decision was reached at the top. "The mass line" involved gathering information from the masses before making a decision, then persuading the masses to accept the decision. "Unity-criticism-unity" was frank discussion of issues among comrades proceeding from and followed by an awareness of shared goals. In no case were these procedures designed to encourage pursuit of personal or local interests or to achieve compromises among such interests. In principle, their purpose was to discover under party leadership the objectively correct general line of the historical moment and to guarantee its wholehearted implementation by everyone, even those personally disadvantaged by it. The correct line would be the one that led to national strength and prosperity and the survival of socialism. Like Liang's ultimate goal of the survival of the race, these Maoist public goals subsumed any conceivable private interest, for what Chinese (except a class enemy, by definition not a member of the people) could enjoy personal happiness if the nation were subjugated or if the system of class exploitation were restored? Likewise the higher interest justified rule by a single party, since there were no legitimate rival interests that should be represented by other parties.

Moreover—again an echo of Liang—these public goals could be achieved only by collective effort. Disunity, selfishness, privatism—what Liang called the "internal competition" of "small groups"—in Mao's view were damaging to economic growth and likely to help restore class exploitation. Political participation, for Mao as for Liang, had an instrumental goal—to open the channels of communication between above and below and thus to promote unity of will in the pursuit of common ends. However, democracy could achieve its full flowering only when party-sponsored education had produced sufficiently widespread civic consciousness among the people. Thus the leader had a tutelary role to perform for the people, serving meanwhile as the trustee of the higher interests the people would sometimes fail to perceive. Mao, like Liang, believed that it was necessary to balance democratic processes with powerful rulership in order to prevent people from acting ill-advisedly on their ultimately illusory private interests.

Fifty years after Liang's death and two years after Mao's, the Enlightenment Society of Huang Xiang was only paraphrasing them both when it said that "in order for China to become strong . . . it must have a stable democratic government . . . which can mobilize the enthusiasm and wisdom of every member of society." This view of the promise of democracy was shared by the democratic activists and the party leaders alike. In the words of the party journal *Red Flag*, "Democratization of the country is a necessary guarantee of the modernization of our country." Or in the more excited phrases of the people's journal *Four Modernizations Forum*, "The emancipation of the mind has commenced; facing us is our golden world filled with cars, television sets, and refrigerators!"

But equally agreed-upon in the late 1970s was that the promise of modernization through democratization glimpsed in the 1890s was as yet unrealized. At the time of Mao's death the institutions of Chinese democracy—study groups, mass movements, revolutionary committees, the "mass line"—were hollow. The country was backward and the people withdrawn. What had gone wrong, and what was the cure? The disputes that broke out in 1978, both in public and within the party, concerned not what democracy could do for China but the nature of the obstacles to its realization and the ways of overcoming them.

4

DEMOCRACY AND
BUREAUCRATISM

Chinese thinkers from Liang Qichao on identified two major obstacles to the realization of democracy: the people's backward culture, and interference by bureaucrats in the natural solidarity between ruler and people. How politicians proposed to bring the people's energies to bear to cure China's weakness depended upon which of these two problems they considered to be primary. Liang, for example, believed during his optimistic early phase that the root cause of the people's retreat from active cooperation with the ruler was the existence of a cadre of oppressive, corrupt officials. The passivity and selfishness of the masses, he argued, had been instilled in them by generations of "people-robbers" (plundering officials) who took the people's property, made it their own, and then encouraged the people to remain passive and ignorant so that they would not challenge the theft. But after 1903, disillusionment with the quality of his countrymen's political culture caused him to decide that only the tutelage of an enlightened dictatorship could prepare the people for democracy.

It is significant that neither Liang nor other modern thinkers until the democracy movement showed much interest in a third possible theory about the obstacles to cooperation between ruler and people—that the ruler himself might plunder the people and so suppress their enthusiasm for the state. A critique along these lines had been presented in the seventeenth century by Huang Zongxi, a scholar who resisted the conquest of China by the Manchus and then tried to analyze why the preceding Ming dynasty had failed. Huang argued that the Ming rulers had treated the empire as "an enormous estate to be handed down to [their] descendants, for their perpetual pleasure and well-being."

In ancient times the people were considered the proprietors and the prince was the visitor. All of his life the prince spent working for the sake of the people. Now the prince is proprietor and the people are visitors. Because of the prince people can find peace and happiness nowhere. In order to achieve his ends, people must be harmed and killed and their families broken up—all for the aggrandizement of one man's fortune. . . . In ancient times men loved their prince, thought of him as a father, likened him to God; and truly this was no more than just. Now men hate their prince, think of him as a mortal foe, call him an "outcast"; and this is perfectly natural.

Huang's book was a rarity, a critique of despotism erected on Confucian premises. The late Ming rulers, in Huang's view, lost power because they abandoned the principle of unity between the prince's interests and the people's. A proper sage-king would rule with the interests of the people in mind. By ceasing to be the people's enemy, he would secure greater power for himself and more stability for his house than would a tyrant.

Two hundred years later, Liang Qichao adopted only part of Huang's argument. Huang's book had been banned by the Qing rulers, but Liang and his colleagues reprinted it for secret circulation during their agitation for reform. Its influence showed in Liang's advocacy of study societies to strengthen the relationship between ruler and ruled, and in his analysis that the imperial institution weakened itself by treating the state as its private property, rather than as the common property of the nation. Yet Liang, while acknowledging the potential disparity of interests between ruler and people that Huang had identified, chose not to explore more deeply the antidespotic possibilities Huang had located in the Confucian tradition. This was in part because Liang was arguing during much of his career for constitutional monarchy, against the creation of a republic. But the main source of Liang's reticence about the dangers of despotism was his perception of China's weakness in the Darwinian struggle among nations, his fear that the Chinese race might literally be extinguished. The urgent message of all his writing was national solidarity for survival. Rather than checking the power of the ruler, Liang wanted to enhance it. This was why he concentrated on the bureaucrats and the people's culture as the main obstacles to the strong democratic state. His choice of targets would dominate Chinese political thought until after Mao's death.

In a famous 1900 essay, "Young China," Liang framed what would become the classic Chinese indictment of doddering bureaucrats.

They cannot get into office or get promoted without chanting examination-style prose for decades, copying documents for decades, serving in subordinate posts for decades, . . . without decades of passing name cards, flattering superiors, kowtowing and cultivating connections. Out of a hundred who finally make it to a responsible post either at court or in the provinces, ninety-six or ninety-seven have lost the use of some of their senses. If they aren't blind they are deaf. If their hands aren't palsied, their feet are lame or they are half paralyzed. For this one body to eat and drink, walk and see, hear and speak, it requires three or four other people to stand by his side and hold him up so he can get through the day.

How could you expect people like this to act decisively in a national crisis? Liang asked. All they want to do is make it to the end of their lives without trouble. If it is necessary to "give the foreigners a province or two or sell a few million of our people into slavery" to keep the peace, such officials are happy to do so. It was in the context of this analysis that Liang argued for the constitutional grant of political rights to citizens so that they could not only regain the initiative, but also help the emperor to check the corruption of the bureaucrats. Indeed, he argued, the people could supervise officialdom more effectively than the limited corps of censors: "Since their interests are closely involved they will not tolerate any coverup. The eyes and ears of public opinion can never be deceived by evasive reports."

After 1949 the problem of bureaucratism assumed an even more central position in Chinese political thought. Mao's government, like other communist regimes, had had to build an incomparably larger apparatus than the country had ever had before in order to carry out its program of social change and economic planning. The late Qing regime had required only about 27,000 civil and military officials in the capital and the provinces—assisted by several million clerks and runners—to govern a population of some 450 million. This in turn was just a few thousand men larger than the government apparatus at the start of the Ming six centuries earlier, despite the fact that China's population had increased by a factor of six. Yet by the time of Mao's death the administration had grown to encompass approximately 28 million state bureaucrats; an equal or greater number of commune and cooperative-factory officials not formally listed as employees of the state; and an armed force of 4.2 million officers and troops. In addition, there were 35 million Chinese Communist Party members who formed a part of the ruling stratum although they did not all draw their salaries from the state payroll. Allowing for the overlapping positions of some party members as state and local cadres, the total size of the governing apparatus must have numbered well over 75 million. This still did not include 100 million–odd nonadministrative workers on the state payroll in government-owned factories, farms, and service trades.

Not only was the bureaucracy huge under Mao, it almost choked itself on its own complexity. The preliberation Communist Party and army kept their organizations relatively simple in order to work under conditions of insurrectionary war. After 1949 the party decreed administrative "regularization" along the lines of Soviet experience. Government personnel were organized into systems of ranks and grades—thirty ranks for administrators, twenty-six for law-court staff, seventeen for technical cadres, and so on. Job assignments and salaries were made to depend on rank; promotion depended on seniority. Housing, clothes, and transport depended on status, as did access to special shops, publications, movies, and to some extent educational and job opportunities for one's children. Party cells were established in virtually every office, factory, school, village, and residential neighborhood from the bottom of society to the top, charged with enforcing party policy and reporting difficulties to the levels above. Paperwork grew heavy. Regular and specially commissioned reports crammed with statistics (not infrequently fabricated, according to later revelations) moved up the parallel party and state hierarchies. "Orders," "directives," "notices," "circulars," "regulations," and "bulletins," each binding to a specified degree, flowed down. Officials had to attend constant meetings to discuss, decide, specify, and explain policies. Telephones and phone lines, in limited supply, were devoted mainly to official communications, including "telephone meetings" (conference calls).

Daily life was rationalized for better central control. Births, deaths, and changes of residence were registered with the police, who also issued the ration coupons needed to buy grain, cloth, cooking oil, and other necessities at fixed prices. Each person was registered as either a "peasant" or a "worker" and had to stay on the land or in the city accordingly. Everyone also carried a more specific, inherited class label that was taken into account in various administrative decisions. Each citizen belonged to a "basic-level unit"—a production team, factory workshop, residents' committee, schoolroom, office, or army company—that answered to "higher levels." Movement from one unit to another was nearly impossible, except in the cases of a young person going to school or the army, a woman marrying into her husband's village, or an official enjoying a promotion. A middle-school graduate went to the job assigned by a committee in the school, which filled slots allocated to it by government plan. If the assignment was to the countryside, as was often the case for city youth in the 1960s, there was almost no way to resist it. College-bound students—fewer than 1 percent of their generation even after the reopening and expansion of the colleges in the late 1970s—were accepted by a single department of a single university. Job posting after college graduation was again the responsibility of an assignment committee, working in response to a central government plan. Beginning in the 1970s the government decided how many births would be permitted each year, and assigned the right to participate in each year's quota to prospective mothers through the residents' committees, factories, and communes.

Even the frequent campaigns designed to prod the bureaucracy were bureaucratic. There were seasonal campaigns to wipe out insect pests, improve sanitation, or help with the harvest, and special political campaigns to oppose corruption or "rectify" erroneous thinking and "styles of work." Each campaign was run by an ad hoc hierarchy, which usually coincided with the hierarchy of party branches, committees, and cells. The campaign committee in each unit received documents from higher levels, convened meetings, and guided the campaign through the phases of study, exposure of targets, criticism and self-criticism, and application of sanctions. During the Cultural Revolution, in which virtually the entire bureaucracy was the target, the Red Guard and "revolutionary rebel" groups carefully organized themselves by school or factory affiliation and then into county- or citywide alliances, following the lines of existing administrative divisions. They elected leaders and steering groups, held meetings, issued documents, and competed bitterly over their fealty to the directives of the Central Cultural Revolution Group in Peking.

Control of the bureaucracy inevitably became a prime concern of Mao and his colleagues. They adopted both the techniques of the dynasties and those of the socialist world. From the past they took the methods of ideological indoctrination, private channels of communication, censors, spies, patronage, and exemplary punishments. From the Soviet Union they adopted a range of inspection and discipline mechanisms. A local official might be visited by an investigative reporter for a party newspaper or by a "work team" sent by higher levels to "squat on a point" and interview people in the unit. The party discipline inspection commission might call on the official to answer charges of infractions of party rules and policies. Mao or another leader might pop up unannounced on an inspection tour to compare the local unit's performance with that of some "key point" or model unit. According to later revelations, a number of the highest officials ran their own secret police networks. Competing factions in the central government also had their loyalists scattered throughout the bureaucracy, making reports.

The party also ran numerous "rectification campaigns" in which officials criticized one another's ideology and "work style" in accordance with documents provided by the center. In each campaign a few who failed to "pass the gate" were purged, while the records of the criticism sessions were preserved in the others' dossiers. The campaigns attacked such bureaucratic "deviations" as "formalism" (literal-minded enforcement of procedure without substantive accomplishment), "sectarianism" (haughtiness toward nonparty people), "factionalism" (cliquish power-seeking), "mountain-topism" (resisting cooperation with other units), "commandism" (issuing too many orders), and "tailism" (giving insufficient leadership to the masses).

Communist states normally keep their methods of bureaucratic supervision and control within the apparatus. But in the mid-1950s Mao began to conclude that inner-party methods were not enough. Officials had become inured to investigations and campaigns. No matter what orders came from above or how enthusiastic the masses below were for rapid progress, he said, the bureaucrats "tottered along like a woman with bound feet, . . . complaining all the time, 'You're going too fast, much too fast.' "

Mao's war on bureaucracy began to carry him beyond the thought of either Lenin or Liang. On the one hand, he began to tamper with the most basic premise of Leninism, that the vanguard party is a more reliable representative of the people's interests than the people themselves. At the same time, perhaps without noting the precedent, he began to revive the forgotten theme of Huang Zongxi's seventeenth-century argument, that the selfish interests of the rulers might turn them into exploiters and oppressors of the people.

In part Mao merely reasserted Liang Qichao's familiar position that the nation would benefit if the people were involved in supervising the bureaucracy. Speaking to the party Central Committee in 1956, for example, he said that the party should welcome popular strikes and demonstrations against local officials.

> If you alienate yourself from the masses and fail to solve their problems, the peasants will wield their carrying-poles, the workers will demonstrate in the streets and the students will create disturbances. Whenever such things happen, they must in the first place be taken as good things, and that is how I look at the matter.

Here Mao was within the bounds of Leninism, pitting party and people together against the bureaucrats. But his suggestion a few moments later that local party officials might develop into an "aristocratic stratum divorced from the masses" contained the germs of a less orthodox position. It implied that the party might become (or might harbor within itself) an independent social interest, so ceasing to represent exclusively the interests of the masses.

Mao's thought developed further in this direction when he encountered resistance within the party to one after another of his new policies. In 1957, over the objections of many of his senior colleagues, he launched the first campaign of "open-door rectification" to subject party bureaucrats to the criticisms of the public. This "Hundred Flowers" movement led to unexpectedly harsh attacks and was suppressed by designating hundreds of thousands of critics as "rightists." The following year, Mao summoned the peasants to organize huge communes combining agriculture, industry, commerce, education, and military affairs under a unified, pared-down, and nearly self-sufficient administration. Without the drag of bureaucracy, he claimed, China would "surpass England within fifteen years." But the Great Leap Forward led to economic disaster, and Mao retired to the "second line of power." In 1963 he ordered the establishment of "poor and lower-middle peasant associations" to provide continuous supervision for rural cadres in a movement

called the Socialist Education Campaign. This time his purposes were sub-
verted by contravening directives from other leaders.

The more his initiatives failed, the darker became Mao's analysis of
bureaucratism. He began to see bureaucracy as not just an unwieldy tool of
government, and its problem as not just the moral backsliding of a fraction of
its members. He came to view it, instead, as a separate social group with special interests opposed to those of society as a whole. In the Chinese polemics
of the early 1960s against the Soviet Union, which Mao directed, the Chinese side put forward the concepts of "revisionism" and "capitalist restoration," defined as the takeover of power in a socialist society by a new
privileged stratum of cadres and intellectuals whose power is based on their
managerial control of the means of production. In launching the Cultural
Revolution Mao applied this idea to China, introducing the concept of "capitalist-roaders in the party"—leaders who were so satisfied with their privileges gained in the revolution that they did not want to carry social change
any further. The masses were supposed to "drag" these people out for criticism and punishment regardless of their rank. In the early 1970s party
theorists working with Mao put forward a theory of "newly engendered
bourgeois elements" who emerge from among the party members, state
cadres, and better-off workers and peasants and seek to overthrow socialism
and restore capitalism.

Such theories left unclear whether the entire party had become an alien
social force. When Mao used terms like "capitalist-roaders" or "new bourgeois elements," he hinted that only a minority of leaders within the party
were corrupt. But when he spoke of a "bureaucratic stratum" or a "bourgeois
headquarters in the party," he implied that the concentration of power and
privilege inevitably produced an antipopular special interest at the top of society. In one 1965 directive he went so far as to write:

> The class of the bureaucrats is a class in sharp opposition to the working
> class and the poor and lower-middle peasants. These people have already
> become or are in the process of becoming capitalist elements sucking the
> blood of the workers.

If the bureaucrats were really a "class," then in Marxian terms they must
have their own political interests and their own party. If this party was the
CCP, then Mao was calling in effect for a new people's revolution against his
own regime.

But Mao never fully developed this Djilas-like "new class" theory. In
fact, he strenuously denied kinship either with Djilas or with Trotsky—
whose theory of the Soviet Union as a "degenerate workers' state" also resembled his views in some ways. Mao veered away from the idea of a bureaucratic class, insisting that his theories did not contradict the idea of the

"leadership of the party." In a directive discouraging the formation during the Cultural Revolution of a "Shanghai commune" that did not include a role for the party, Mao said, "There must be a party somehow! There must be a nucleus, no matter what we call it." Each formal directive of the Cultural Revolution recognized this principle of party leadership.

Only because of his unique position as the infallible spokesman of Marxism in China could Mao embrace the paradox of calling on the masses to overthrow the party leaders while insisting on the principle of party supremacy. Much as he wished to deny it, his attack on bureaucracy ended by undermining the rationale for party dictatorship. If, as Mao said, "the masses are more progressive than we are," then who could speak for them? If party leaders other than he were not good guides to the higher interests of the people, who was? If Mao Thought itself was the answer, who could interpret it after Mao was gone? As a confused Red Guard leader asked when Mao summoned her to Zhongnanhai to demand that she demobilize her armed supporters, "Chairman, I have a question. If ten or one hundred years from now . . . one faction claims that they represent Mao Zedong Thought and another faction also claims that they represent Mao Zedong Thought . . . what should we do?"

By abandoning the Leninist precept of the infallible party center, Mao had opened the door to diverse challenges, if not yet explicitly to the concept of party rule itself, then to the authority of anyone other than himself who ruled in the party's name. A widely circulated Red Guard document in 1968 called for "overthrow of the rule of the new bureaucratic bourgeoisie, complete smashing of the old state machinery, realization of social revolution, carrying out the redistribution of property and power, and the establishment of a new society—the 'People's Commune of China.' " The Li Yizhe poster of 1974—whose authors' rehabilitation was to become one of the democrats' demands in 1978—demanded "revolutionary supervision by the masses of people over the leadership at various levels in the Party and the state." Within the party leadership itself in the early 1970s, the faction that was in the minority argued for the continuation of "two-line struggle" to resist what they called the "new bourgeois elements and upstarts who have totally betrayed the proletariat and the laboring people [and who] emerge from among Party members, workers, well-to-do peasants and personnel in state organs." Once Mao died, his legacy would enable challengers to invoke either "the people" or Mao Thought itself to deny the authority of whoever happened to be running the party at the time.

Meanwhile, the twenty-year campaign against bureaucracy had only exacerbated the weaknesses of the Chinese apparatus. At first, government offices in Peking and the provinces were half-emptied, but the "cadre schools" where purged officials went still belonged to the ministries, and the "students" remained on government salaries. When the Cultural Revolution ended, they went back to work. There they found their desks occupied by newly promoted acolytes of Maoism who had risen "like helicopters" through political activism. With both groups in service the bureaucracy was larger than ever, and its operations were impeded by new grudges and jealousies. Its responsibilities for control of the economy and social life were as broad as before, but now all rules and regulations had been "smashed" by the Cultural Revolution, so bureaucratic decisions were harder to make and more arbitrary than ever. In the eyes of the post-Mao leaders, bureaucratism was as bad as it had ever been. Premier Zhao Ziyang complained of "the intolerably low efficiency resulting from overlapping and overstaffed administrations with their multi-tiered departments, crammed full of superfluous personnel and deputy and nominal chiefs who engage in endless haggling and shifts of responsibility." *People's Daily* revealed that a city trying to take over some land to build housing had to get approvals from thirty-nine separate organizations. A county official complained that he received 120 pounds of documents a year and had time to read only their titles. An essayist described the "twelve stations" of an official document within a single office from reception through circulation and drafting of a reply to sealing, registering, and sending out a decision. Bureaucrats became for a time the chief butt of satiric cartoons in the official press (see pages 76–79). Summing up the leaders' exasperation, Deng Xiaoping complained:

> Bureaucratism is expressed in sitting high above the people, using power in an indiscriminate way, becoming divorced from reality and the masses, being fond of keeping up appearances, a liking for uttering empty words, mental ossification, sticking to old ways and conventions, swollen bureaucracy, delaying the handling of matters, paying no attention to efficiency, failing to take responsibility, failing to keep one's word, endless circulation of official documents, and mutual passing of the buck. All this results in a stuffy official atmosphere, reprimanding others on the slightest provocation, retaliating against people, suppressing democracy, cheating those above and hoodwinking those below, acting in an imperious and despotic way, engaging in bribery and corruption, and so on. Both in domestic affairs and international dealings, all this has reached an intolerable stage.

Once again the leaders resolved to use democracy as the corrective, although it was to be democracy of a different type from that of Mao's Cultural Revolution. On August 18, 1980, Deng Xiaoping gave the charter speech of the political component of his reforms to his colleagues in the party Politburo. He identified five major political obstacles to modernization— "bureaucratism, overcentralization of power, the patriarchal way of doing things, lifelong tenure of leading posts, and various kinds of privileges." To

1. "Imperturbable" (a neo-Confucian virtue). He grasps slips of paper labeled "mass opinions." According to an accompanying poem, not shown here, he pretends to welcome suggestions but always finds an excuse to ignore them.

三思而后行

（原载《贵阳晚报》）

2. "Think Thrice Before Acting" (a quotation from Confucius's *Analects*). The bureaucrat's head is an abacus, implying that he is always calculating, always cautious. 3. "Account of a meeting." The officials gather; they all agree to wait for instructions from higher levels; the meeting is adjourned.

4. With the masses' opinions stuffed into a wastebasket behind him, a bureaucrat sews "small shoes" (a slang term for hard assignments, delayed promotions, and unpleasant working conditions) in response to critics.   5. "Kung-fu." The cadre breaks a stone bearing "the masses' opinions" with his head; sleeps on a bed of nails consisting of the masses' opinions; smashes a brick inscribed "the masses' opinions."

6. "The Lazy Barber." "Problems" await shearing but the barber, labeled "bureaucratism," snoozes in his chair.

7. "The Thinker." Although the work before him concerns important policy matters, the official's head is filled with thoughts of a new house, a car, a TV set, a vacuum cleaner, imported liquor, and study abroad for his children.

8. "Playing Chess." Seated in important government positions, bureaucrats exchange choice jobs for their sons and daughters.

圆桌会议　　　　　　　　　韦君琳 作

9. "Roundtable Discussion." Faced with "problems," each official tries—
and fails—to elicit a real opinion from his neighbor.

1. RMRB 1980.9.21.3.
2. RMRB 1980.12.17.3.
3. RMRB 1980.8.28.8.
4. RMRB 1979.8.25.3.
5. RMRB 1980.11.12.3.

6. RMRB 16 August 1979, JPRS 74430: 12.
7. RMRB 1980.9.20.8.
8. RMRB 20 August 1979, JPRS 74430: 14.
9. *Anhui Huabao* No. 3 (1979), JPRS 74430: 13.

combat them, he called for creation of "a democracy which is at a higher level and more substantial than that of capitalist countries." In the Chinese "stem-and-branch" chronological system, there are sixty names for years, used in succession. Just as the Hundred Days of Reform was referred to as the Wuxu Reform after the name of the year 1898, so the leaders called their new political program the Gengshen Reforms because 1980 was the Gengshen year.

Behind political reform lay the fact that the Deng group wanted to change the organization of the economy—to open the country to foreign trade and investment, to decentralize management of the land by giving responsibility to individual farmers who worked on contract for the production teams, and to reduce the number of mandatory targets that the state plan imposed on managers of state-run factories. These economic changes in turn required, they felt, a political cure for the passivity inherited from the Cultural Revolution. According to one of Deng's advisers, Liao Gailong, democracy would allow social conflicts to be expressed and resolved peacefully in the common interest, give the leaders the benefit of everyone's advice in making decisions, enable the people to understand and accept government policies, and help the leaders find able younger people to bring into the leadership. It would, in short, overcome "the bureaucratism and autocracy which suppress the people's creativity and enthusiasm."

The Gengshen Reforms included changes both within the bureaucracy and in the relations between it and the people. Changes internal to the bureaucracy included sharper separation between party cadres and unit managers; emphasis on collective decision-making within party committees; more rapid promotion of younger cadres; and, starting in 1982, a program of streamlining to cut the number of state bureaus and personnel. Changes in the bureaucracy's relations with the public centered on restoring means of popular supervision of the bureaucracy. "There must be," Deng said in his speech, "a system of mass supervision so that the masses and ordinary Party members can supervise the cadres, especially the leading cadres. The people have the right to expose, accuse, impeach, replace and recall according to law all those who seek personal perquisites and privileges and refuse to change their ways despite criticism and education."

Deng's group had already taken steps to encourage the masses to expose and accuse cadres when they announced in 1977 that the miscarriages of justice of the Cultural Revolution would be repaired. This stimulated the flood of appeals that led to the Peking petitioners' demonstrations of early 1979. In 1978 the leaders announced further that all offices must restore the tradition of "letters and visits work," which had fallen into abeyance after the Great Leap Forward. Under this policy, major government and police agencies, party units, and newspapers opened reception centers. Any citizen with a grievance could line up during office hours, take a number, and state his or her case. Alternatively, a citizen could detail complaints in a letter. Cadres serving as the equivalent of social workers were to give each case their full attention, investigate the facts if necessary by telephone or mail, and try to find some way to resolve the problems brought before them. "They must read carefully all the letters and patiently listen to what the visitors have to say," instructed *Red Flag*. "They must not show any annoyance if the visitors do not deliver their complaints in a coherent manner. As to those visitors who cannot control their temper, they must patiently console them and must not grumble at their bad attitude." Citizens not satisfied with the answer they got at their own level of the hierarchy had the right to appeal all the way to the State Council or the Central Committee in Peking, enjoying the protection of the state and party constitutions and the criminal code of 1979 against any retaliation by the cadres they were complaining against.

In an administered society where officials routinely control a citizen's educational opportunities, job prospects, income, marriage choice, and place of residence, grievances are common. Party discipline inspection commissions alone—only one of several kinds of offices to which citizens could appeal—handled 7.7 million letters and 2.6 million visits from 1979 to 1982. The appeal system helped heal the wounds of the Cultural Revolution and so removed obstacles to the cooperation of citizens and government. It also helped higher-level officials identify local cadres who were not carrying out the government's announced policies. The party press praised officials who gave letters and visits work its proper prominence, especially provincial governors who "personally listened," "personally checked," or "personally went" to handle a number of cases themselves. It criticized localities where, in the words of the *People's Daily*, "letters and visitors . . . travel up and down from central authorities to provincial, prefectural, and county levels or go around various central and provincial departments . . . [and] the rate for closing cases is low." On the other hand, satisfaction was by no means guaranteed. Since the country was short of housing and desirable jobs, not all appeals could be satisfied immediately even if they were justified. "Even if you are right you cannot create a disturbance," headlined the *People's Daily*. Petitioners who were disorderly or who kept coming back after their cases were closed were sometimes detained or sent for labor reeducation as "habitual troublemakers."

A second reform in the political role of the public was the revitalization of the system of unit-level elections. Before the Cultural Revolution the party had established procedures for the election of cadres in rural communes, urban residential areas, state-owned factories, and local chapters of the national trade union. It is not known how widely these regulations were carried out, but they were disrupted during the Cultural Revolution. In his 1980 speech, Deng called for the reestablishment of elected workers' and staff congresses in state-owned enterprises. The National People's Congress adopted the necessary regulations in 1981, mandating that the congresses be elected at two-year intervals and meet once every six months to supervise the decisions of factory management. By the end of 1981, workers' congresses were in place in about 101,000 enterprises. In some factories, not only congresses but also managerial cadres were elected by the workers. To revive elections in urban neighborhoods and in the countryside, the government republished regulations dating from 1954 and 1962 respectively, providing for elections of urban residents' committees, rural team, brigade, and commune management groups, and urban and rural people's mediation committees. The national trade union organization adopted a system of elected congresses and committees in its 1983 constitution.

Third, the Gengshen Reforms also involved an attempt to revitalize the press, the party's main organ for informing the people of its policies and arousing their enthusiasm for it, and also one of the leaders' key sources of information on the state of the popular mind. As one of Deng Xiaoping's advisers explained,

> In order for the media to play the role of quickly and effectively propagating the policies and decrees of the party and the government, opportunely inform the people of all important events aside from a minority of secrets concerning national defense and diplomacy, and opportunely reflect the people's criticisms of and suggestions to the party and state organs, we should permit, require, and encourage the media, the journalists, and commentators independently to assume the responsibility of reporting or publishing news, letters from the masses, and comments. I think that such broad freedom of the press, freedom of speech, and freedom of publication carried out under the leadership of the party's line, principles, and policies, is of prime importance in democratizing the party and the state.

The press reforms and their effectiveness form the subject of Chapter 9.

Finally, the reformers took steps to reinvigorate the people's congress system. People's congresses, called soviets in the USSR, embody popular sovereignty in all socialist systems. Constitutionally they exercise supreme state authority, appointing and supervising the work of officers of the administrative and judicial branches of government, although actually they usually have relatively little power. Soviets were first established in communist-ruled parts of China in 1931. The 1953 election law and 1954 constitution established a four-level hierarchy of congresses: communes and towns, counties, provinces, and the National People's Congress. Only the lowest-level congresses were directly elected, with delegates to those above being elected by deputies at the congresses below. Six elections were held under this system from 1953 to 1966 and three national-level people's congresses were chosen, meeting an average of once a year for two or three weeks at a time. The work of the congresses was interrupted by the Cultural Revolution. The national congresses resumed meeting in 1975 but convened only twice before 1980, acting merely to pass new constitutions and hear speeches by the central leaders. Local-level congresses met for the first time in early 1979, but their members were not really elected—they were appointed by the party and confirmed by a show of hands. According to one of Deng's advisers, speaking shortly after Deng's 1980 speech, "It is probably correct for people to call our NPC a 'rubber stamp.'"

The September 1980 session of the NPC began to correct this image. Delegates at that session cross-examined government ministers more vigorously than ever before (or since), leading to the dismissal of one, and tabled some 2,300 "motions" (suggestions for government work). From then on, the national congress met regularly. Laws and policy decisions continued to originate with the central party leaders, but deputies used the opportunities of regular meetings and generous press coverage to raise numerous suggestions for government work in specialized areas of concern. Besides holding regular sessions, both the national and the local people's congresses were empowered under the 1982 constitution to establish more powerful standing committees, which began to meet frequently to pass regulations and review government actions. The national congress also established a series of specialized committees in such areas as foreign, economic, and minority nationalities affairs. Finally, the reformers moved closer to the long-standing ideal of direct popular election of people's congresses by passing a law providing for the direct election of deputies not only to the local-level, but also to the next higher—county-level—congresses. These elections provided the final opportunity for the democracy movement to try to participate as a partner in the reforms, with results that will be described in Chapter 10.

Deng's version of Chinese democracy as reflected in the Gengshen Reforms represented both an extension of and a reaction against Mao's conception of democracy. It accepted the classic assumption that the state must draw on the energies of the people to become strong. And it accepted Mao's diagnosis of bureaucratism as the immediate obstacle to realization of this promise as well as his prescription of more democracy as the cure for the disease. Democracy, said the party journal *Red Flag*, "is the basic way to insure that the staff of state organs maintain their spirit of serving the people, to prevent them from seeking privileges and degenerating, and to eliminate various drawbacks in our state organs, in particular the trend toward bureaucracy." But the party leadership drew a clear line between this supervisory function and Mao's radical conception of a violent people's movement to smash a bureaucratic stratum or class. There was no "bourgeoisie within the party," the leaders said; there never had been and never could be. The people could make constructive suggestions and expose particular corrupt officials, but they had no legitimate need to rise up against or oppose the leadership itself. As Shanghai Radio put it, democracy was like playing basketball: "The contest should be held in a space confined by four lines." These lines were Deng's "four upholds": socialism, dictatorship of the proletariat, Marxism-Leninism–Mao Zedong Thought, and party leadership. The last, Deng had said, was the most important.

These were views that most of the democrats accepted. They seldom questioned that the purpose of democracy was development. As Li Jiahua of the Enlightenment group put it, democracy "is the recipe for curing the Chinese nation of its age-old sickness." Without it, "people . . . cannot contribute their ability and wisdom to society." Nor did the democrats challenge the conventional vision of what the democratic condition was like. In a democracy, Li said, people "will share the same views . . . and have identical ideals. In lofty and harmonious unity they will produce, live, think, invent, pioneer, and explore together." His colleague Lu Mang stated, "in a democratic atmosphere . . . the nation will no longer be plagued by interference and undercurrents of resistance. Unity of the people is the spiritual condition for a nation to be stable and develop." Nor, finally, did most democrats disagree with the authorities that the chief obstacle to democratic harmony and rapid development was the estrangement of the people from the power-holders due to bureaucratism. Antibureaucratism, indeed, was the dominant theme of the unofficial press. The bureaucratic love of privilege, for example, was seen in Wang Dongxing's alleged action of building himself an expensive house in Zhongnanhai. The fact that government offices were not open to the public made China's officials more inaccessible than those in the capitalist West. The petitioners' movement was a gallery of bureaucrats' victims, and the way officials treated the petitioners showed their callousness toward the people.

The people's magazines devoted a great deal of space to analyzing the causes of bureaucratism. Excessive concentration of power was one: Since the party secretary was at the same time almost always the factory manager, school principal, or commune director, there was too much power in one pair of hands. Secretaries could not meet all the demands on them and still keep in touch with their subordinates' opinions and needs, nor was there anyone to interfere in their overlordship of their small private kingdoms. A second cause was lifetime tenure in office: Except for extraordinary events like the Cultural Revolution, bureaucrats stayed in office for decades. Most of those purged in the Cultural Revolution had been returned to office since 1969. They became autocratic and took privileges for granted. They rewarded flatterers and punished the outspoken, who, under China's assigned-job system, had no chance to move elsewhere. A third cause of bureaucratism, according to the democrats, was the system of appointment from above: It meant that ambitious officials had to please only their superiors, not the people they ruled. Fourth, the democrats argued that people who had entered the bureaucracy after liberation were often motivated by a desire for power and comfort rather than for public service. They were careerists, poor models of the simple living and hard work the party demanded from the people. Consistent with these diagnoses of the sources of bureaucratism, the majority of the democrats accepted the Gengshen reformers' program as the appropriate cure.

In seeking the ultimate roots of bureaucratism, the party reformers and most of the democrats rejected Mao's theory of a corrupt ruling stratum or class. They returned instead to the theory of cultural backwardness that Liang Qichao had used to explain his 1905 conversion to the theory of enlightened dictatorship. The source of bureaucratism, the party press explained, was China's "feudal cultural tradition." Even though the socialist economic system had been established for thirty years, "the concepts, habits, and traditions of feudalism, formed and developed over the past several thousand years, are deep-rooted." It was feudal culture that manifested itself in cadres' autocratic behavior, in the cult of the individual, in the acquisition of bureaucratic special privilege, in patronage and favoritism, and in officials' habit of setting their individual authority above the law. Reprinting an article of Liu Shaoqi's from the 1940s, *Red Flag* made the point that "bureaucracy exists within our party because the influence of the nonproletariat within the party is very strong"—that is, because of the party's peasant base—"and it is more so because of the inadequate standards of education of China's proletariat and laboring masses." The democrats agreed, pointing out the persistence of old-fashioned ideas about the perquisites of office. An official was expected to reward sycophants, provide for his children, accept small gifts from people he helped. He would feel humiliated if he did not wear better clothing than ordinary people, including leather shoes and a good watch, and, if his rank was high enough, he would expect to ride in a chauffeured car and live in a large apartment.

In the post-Mao world, a theory of "feudal culture" or something like it was necessary for the party leaders to explain why curing bureaucratism required reaffirming party dictatorship. Mao had raised the possibility that the very concentration of power in the rulers was the source of their corruption; "feudal culture" placed the blame back on the people. "The bureaucratic phenomenon found today is not inherent in the socialist social system," explained the *China Youth News*. "On the contrary, it is a force alien to socialist public ownership and is the opposite of people's democratic dictatorship." Mao's theory suggested that the people should have the power to supervise the rulers (except for Mao himself); "feudal culture" meant that the people needed to undergo cultural transformation under the tutelage of the leaders. In the next few years, the government conducted a series of campaigns to improve the quality of the people's culture: campaigns on patriotism, on "socialist spiritual civilization," on "communist morality."

In an attack on the democracy activists a few months before the April 1981 wave of arrests that effectively ended the movement, *People's Daily* argued that "eliminating the pernicious influence of feudalism from the people's minds" would take time. In the meantime, only "stability and unity" could promote democracy. It charged that people who wrote wall posters, held demonstrations, boycotted school, "established ties and issued declarations" were reviving the political methods of the Cultural Revolution, which would only hinder China's progress. The party was once again the reliable vanguard, and democracy meant participation under its dictatorship, to discourage bureaucratism and promote the common social interest.

5

THE CHALLENGE TO PARTY DICTATORSHIP

In May 1979, *Peking Spring* published a futuristic short story entitled "A Tragedy That Might Happen in the Year 2000." It was part of a small body of democracy movement writings that questioned the principle of party dictatorship, and thereby so threatened the leaders that they ultimately decided to suppress the movement.

In that target year of the Four Modernizations, the story ran, Democracy Wall still exists, but in the shadow of an elevated expressway, and when handbills are dropped it is from a thirty-story office building near the Peking Railway Station. China's population has grown to 1.5 billion in the twenty good years of Deng Xiaoping's rule. But Deng has died in 1998. In the ensuing power struggle, many of the leaders associated with him die mysteriously, some in car and airplane crashes. The Central Committee's investigation blames the deaths on the surviving Deng followers, and show trials of these followers are conducted. As the year 2000 begins, the new leaders launch a purge to "liquidate the counterrevolutionary conspiracy group's [i.e., the Deng group's] social foundation at the grass-roots level." "Leftist" policies are reintroduced, including the old cult of Mao's personality, a wage freeze, strengthening of the police, heightened ideological vigilance, and a break in economic and cultural ties with the West. Deng's "erroneous line of the previous twenty years" is criticized, and ceremonies are held to rehabilitate leftists who died in disgrace during Deng's rule.

At this point in the story a poster appears on Democracy Wall. It is a copy of one which, the story goes, was first posted in 1978, pleading with Deng Xiaoping's then-new regime to provide itself with a democratic base: otherwise, Deng's "reform measures can be as easily abandoned as they are imposed. At a certain time they may be repudiated in the same fashion as they are ordered." Deng had failed to take this advice in 1978, and now in 2000 the predicted tragedy has occurred. The poster's author is arrested, tried, and sentenced to life in a labor camp, where the authorities soon do away with him in an arranged accident. His wife immolates herself before Democracy Wall. Shortly afterward, the wall is bulldozed. The pessimism of the ending is slightly relieved when "a certain Politburo member" drives up in his deluxe sedan to place garlands at the wall's site. Troops surround the Great Hall of the People and a mysterious central work conference begins— perhaps signaling another turn of the political wheel and a restoration of the Deng line.

The pseudonymous author of this story, Su Ming, puts his main message into the text of the wall poster, which takes up about half of the story's length. Although Deng's policies are good, the poster states, overcentralization of power exposes the nation to the vagaries of the struggle for power at the top. Even Marx and Lenin did not solve this problem of excessive centralization. The answer lies in democracy—not "Western democracy" but a new type, which might be called the "power of supervision." This power

> is not like the type that has been propagandized until now, where the people bring their opinions before the official masters begging them to take a look, and the masters turn a few pages and with a word or two dismiss what may be the fruit of a person's efforts of several years or several decades.

It should instead be a real independent power of the people to be the masters of the state. This requires protection of three kinds of rights.

First is the right to vote, to exercise a genuine choice among rival candidates for a post. Under the present system where officials are appointed from above and have lifetime tenure, the poster continues, the vote is a formality accompanied by a great deal of propaganda about why the people should be happy with the candidates the authorities have presented. Second are the personal rights of citizens. These are listed in the constitution, but people are punished for exercising them, making democracy "too much of a luxury for the pragmatic Chinese people." Third is the "right of propaganda." Only if the people can publicly express what they really think can bad rulers be exposed, as happened in the United States in the Watergate case. "There can be healthy democracy only when it is protected by publicity." Protection should be extended to Democracy Wall, people's publications, strikes, and processions. The government itself should publish a forum-type journal in which the people "can air their views freely."

"Tragedy in the Year 2000" demonstrated the irrepressibility of the issues that Mao had raised during the Cultural Revolution and that the Deng regime desperately wanted to avoid. To be sure, the regime itself was soon to call for an end to lifetime tenure and for electoral competition among rival candidates for some low-level official posts. It was already on record in favor of protection of citizens' constitutional rights and of the opportunity to express criticisms in letters and articles in the official press, if not an actual "right of propaganda." To identify democracy with "supervision" was uncontroversial, and to speak of a potential leadership coup and accompanying reversals of policy was only to recognize historical facts of life—and that after paying generous homage to Deng Xiaoping's modernization policies.

But in the hands of Su Ming these unobjectionable elements were shaped to make an unwelcome point—that the party is fallible as a guide to the people's interests. For its highly centralized power can be seized by bad persons and used to impose erroneous policies against the people's will, just as Mao claimed had happened in the years before the Cultural Revolution. Following out Mao's logic, Su Ming therefore suggested that government could not be kept on a true course by the party but only by the people themselves, who know their own interests more reliably than the party does. If the party wants to represent the people it must allow itself to be controlled by them—not claim to know their best interests through theory. Just adopting a more democratic "work style" will not help, as another writer in *Peking Spring* explained:

> After all, both Duke Zhao and Prince Wei [rulers who were good at listening to advice] were feudal rulers. Their so-called democracy was only a tactic of domination and this tactic can be easily replaced if necessary.

The sensitive issue of the party's trustworthiness was raised from another angle by Chen Erjin, in a book-length essay "On the Proletarian Democratic Revolution," mimeographed in June 1979 as issue No. 10 of *April Fifth Forum*. Chen built his argument on the concept of "revisionism" that Mao had used in polemics against the Soviet Union. As he restated the theory, revisionism is a system of class exploitation by a "bureaucratic monopoly privileged class." This system exists in the Soviet Union and was staved off in China by the Cultural Revolution. But Mao had warned that it could reappear at any time so long as China continued to be ruled by privileged bureaucrats. In one of his "supreme directives" late in life Mao asked, "What will you do if revisionism appears in the Central Committee? It may well do so." Chen Erjin's monograph presented an answer: the Cultural Revolution of the 1960s must be followed by a "proletarian democratic revolution" of the 1980s that would challenge the party's monopoly of power and the cronyism, conservatism, slavish mentality, and bureaucratism that grew from that monopoly.

Chen did not say how this revolution would be carried out. Naïvely, he seemed to want the party leaders to implement it from above. But he gave some details about the system he thought should result. Its "Marxist constitution" would draw the best elements from the experience of socialism, the

Paris Commune, and European and American political institutions. It would provide for an elected president, limited to two four-year terms. Law-making powers would reside in an elected legislature. Judges, too, would be elected for life. In factories, villages, and the armed forces, power would be held by elected committees. Most importantly, to force the Chinese Communist Party to obey the constitution, there would be a rival party, also Marxist but competing with the CCP for votes. Chen argued that the two-party system was effective in consolidating capitalist rule in America. Like Su Ming, he gave the example of the Watergate incident to show how one party prevented the other from abusing power and so maintained the stability required by the ruling class. In the same way, the two-party system would protect the socialist system in China by forcing the ruling party to abide by the people's interests. "The proletariat," Chen concluded, "cannot allow any single party or group to place its own sectarian or small-group interest above that of the people as a whole."

The multiparty idea was also suggested by Fu Shenqi, the activist who, besides working as a repairman in the Shanghai Generator Factory, was editor of the democrats' national journal, *Responsibility.* Fu contributed an essay called "Democracy and Socialism" to one of the other democrats' mimeographed correspondence bulletins. He argued that although competing political parties represent competing class interests in capitalist society, this is not the case in the stage of socialism. With the disappearance of classes, parties can serve as spokesmen for diverse policy viewpoints and strategies, all of which serve the common interest of the working class. "Independent, autonomous political parties," he said, "are of decisive significance for democracy. Where there are not two or more such independent parties, democracy cannot fully develop. In such places the legislature always becomes a cover for one-party dictatorship and the press becomes an echo of the single party." Similarly, the journal *Sea Spray* argued, "When the social structure consists of only one party which monopolizes all authority, neither violation of law nor the corrupt use of office for public gain can be subject to supervision by any well-matched authority." The anonymous author recommended a "multiparty socialist republic" to give teeth to the people's "power of supervision."

Many of the democrats' proposals showed the effects of Mao's having put forth the Paris Commune as a model of "proletarian democratic dictatorship" during the Cultural Revolution. Marx's *The Civil War in France* had told how the communards "smashed the old state machinery" and ruled through an elected council closely controlled by the working people. Taking Marx's account as his text, Lenin in turn put forward the theory in *State and Revolution* that under socialism, the state as a separate apparatus "begins to wither away." And Mao had built on this canon in launching the Cultural Revolution, calling for "a system of general elections, like that of the Paris

Commune, for electing members to the cultural revolutionary groups and committees." The democracy activists often referred to this model to justify their call for election of local-level cadres. But several went further, drawing conclusions inimical to the authority of the party.

In January 1979, *Peking Spring* published an article by Lü Min called "Gradually Abolish the Bureaucratic System and Establish the Democratic System Modeled on the Paris Commune." Lü said that China's problems could not be solved merely by "toppling [particular] bureaucrats" like Lin Biao and the Gang of Four. It was necessary, he said, to "destroy the old state machinery" as an institution. As a first step, the system of appointing cadres from above should be replaced by a system of election of factory managers along the lines of Yugoslav factory democracy. And, Lü continued in another article, "since class struggle is withering now, the party should also gradually wither." Party rule should be replaced by that of factory councils at the lower levels and of the National People's Congress at the top. The people's congress, of course, was constitutionally the supreme organ of state power. But while the official reformers wanted only to strengthen the congress's symbolic and advisory rule, Lü Min wanted it to exercise real power in place of the party.

Lü Min's articles exemplified the ironic tendency of some democrats to identify the "old state machinery" that the Parisian militants supposedly smashed with China's Communist Party. The distinction between state and party was hard to keep in mind in the China of 1979, where the top officials in every office of the state apparatus were party members who, meeting as a party committee, made all important personnel and policy decisions. With a twist that may have been clever rhetoric or just a misunderstanding, some democrats turned Marx's celebration of smashing the old regime's bureaucracy into a call for discarding the Chinese new regime's Marxist party.

Wang Xizhe, writing in the *People's Voice* of Canton in July 1979, called up the Paris Commune image to similar effect. Wang was perhaps the leading theoretician of the democracy movement, having been the major author of the famous Li Yizhe poster of 1974. In an article called "Strive for Proletarian Class Dictatorship," Wang followed Chen Erjin in echoing Mao's theory of revisionism. He warned that "the Communist Party's dictatorship may gradually divorce itself from society's control and become a sort of oppressive force above society. . . . The dictatorship of the advanced stratum of the proletariat may become a dictatorship of 'communist bureaucrats.'" To prevent this China should install the Paris Commune's institutions of election and recall of cadres, and low salaries for officials. "Gradually" party dictatorship would give way to "proletarian dictatorship exercised by organizations of the proletariat as a whole." What this vague formula signified was here left unclear, but Wang elaborated in an essay given privately to friends in Hong Kong and published there after his arrest.

"When the people discover that the Communist Party has turned from a party devoted to the interests of the majority of the people into one serving the selfish interests of, or controlled by, a privileged class," he wrote, "the people should have the right to replace this 'Communist Party' that is no longer a true communist party. If we are true supporters of Marx's theory on the dictatorship of the proletariat, which is the basic principle of the Paris Commune, then we should dare to pose this theoretical question."

In some democrats' minds, Mao's long vendetta against the bureaucrats and the other party leaders had even raised questions about the reliability of Mao himself as a guide to the people's interests. If so many other leaders could turn into revisionists, wasn't Mao also subject to error? If the Marxist party with its arsenal of theories and its collective leadership was not infallible, who could be sure its chairman was? While Mao lived and briefly after his death, the cult of personality stifled public expression of this question. Criticisms of Mao's policies were directed only at Lin Biao, the Gang of Four, or other scapegoats. Even the Li Yizhe poster criticized Mao's policies indirectly, under the rubric of the "Lin Biao System." Zhang Zhixin, the party member mentioned in Chapter 1 who dared to criticize Mao by name while he was still alive, was executed for doing so. In 1978–79, avoidance of Mao's name was still the course preferred by most of the democracy activists. A few asked the party to rehabilitate Mao's enemies. Some said the time had come for a historical judgment of Mao himself. One or two were more explicit. A handbill distributed in Canton argued that the political movements sponsored by Mao since the early 1950s had all been aimed at "strengthening his dictatorial despotic emperorship, realizing his one-man rule, and making millions of heads roll." A writer in *China Human Rights Paper* recalled that during the Cultural Revolution the slogan "do unto others as you would have others do unto you" was declared counterrevolutionary humanism; accordingly, Mao "did to everyone else what he didn't want done to himself, and did it with the instruments of the state." Mao, charged Wang Xizhe, "was not really an enemy of the bureaucratic system. . . . It was not the bureaucratic system that he hated, but the existence in the party of an opposition force that prevented him from disposing of the people's fates as he wished."

The heart of the matter was penetrated by Huang Xiang, the Enlightenment group poet. In his poem about an idol thrusting itself among the people, without mentioning Mao, Huang wrote:

> *Why can idols control the will of millions,*
> *Why can they manipulate the life and death of the populace?*
> *Why do we have to show respect and worship the idol,*
> *Let superstition imprison our living will, emotion, and thoughts?*

Certainly Mao was the main idol Huang symbolized, but the image reached beyond the errors of a single man. Other writers on Mao committed lèse majesté; Huang addressed the generic problem of tyranny.

Tyranny, of course, was the problem Chinese democratic thinkers since the time of Liang Qichao had avoided. To be sure, both Liang and Mao recognized that a leader might make a mistake, and they provided for a citizen's duty of remonstrance to set him right; Mao had even reopened the theme broached in the seventeenth century by Huang Zongxi—the possibility of fundamental conflict between the interests of the regime and those of the people. But Liang had avoided the question of tyranny because his theory required a ruler to guide the backward people to democracy, and Mao had refrained from extending his analysis of tyranny to himself, preferring to see himself "alone with the masses," as he put it once, against the revisionist bureaucrats. But what if power corrupted not just the bureaucrats but the ruler himself? Or, even more seriously—the assumption, of course, of much of Western democratic thought—what if the very function of rulership implies not an identity of interests with the people but a permanent if partial conflict of interest with them? Then a theory of democracy that stresses cooperation between ruler and people to supervise the bureaucracy is sadly beside the point. The real issue is whether the people can limit the leader's reach and assert their own ultimate control. As one of Huang Xiang's colleagues explained,

> Idols and fetishes hold that their very existence represents a living code, the supreme "bible" in human society and finally the "ultimate truth." . . . In all spheres under their tyranny, people dare not voice what is really true. . . . All [China's] shortcomings can be summed up as the result of the evils of autocracy and fetishes.

Once the question of Mao was seen to involve the general problem of absolute rulership rather than personal flaws, it became a particular case of the larger question raised by "Tragedy in the Year 2000," by Chen Erjin's theory of proletarian democratic revolution, by Fu Shenqi's theory of the role of parties under socialism, and by Lü Min's and Wang Xizhe's interpretation of the significance of the Paris Commune—the question of party dictatorship versus people's power. These more daring among the democrats were saying that China's problems had been caused neither by the moral corruption of individual bureaucrats nor by the people's feudal culture (although these might play a role), but by the systemic overconcentration of power; that the absolute power of one or a handful of rulers, unchecked by popular influence, creates arbitrariness, injustice, and unpredictability, makes bureaucrats watchful, anxious, and cautious, and turns politics into a competition for friends at court and for the emperor's ear. If the party said that too many "feudal" customs survived, Huang Xiang's group pointed out that the biggest feudal survival of all was "Qin Shi Huang's totalitarianism," that is, overconcentrated and absolute power. The more radical democrats therefore argued that only the people can represent their own interests; that they can do so not by writing letters to newspapers, paying visits to government offices, participating in discussion meetings, reading official propaganda, and electing low-level officials from controlled lists of candidates—not by playing a restricted role in a system of power dominated by those who claim to represent them—but by exercising real power, specifically through an independent press and competitive elections. They breached a philosophical taboo of at least a century's standing: they proclaimed China's problem to be neither bureaucratism nor political culture, but dictatorship.

Although the wall posters and mimeographed articles of the more radical democrats put the challenge to party dictatorship most openly, a more alarming spectacle in the eyes of the leaders was the spread of similar ideas within the party itself. There was no doctrinal reason why the arguments the democrats were making could not be made by Marxists—which, of course, most of the democrats claimed to be. To be sure, the notion that socialist democracy could be pluralist had been a minority view in international Marxism since the time of Lenin. The orthodox theory was the one codified by Stalin in his commentary on the Soviet constitution of 1936:

> The party is part of the class, its vanguard section. Several parties and consequently freedom of parties can only exist in a society where antagonistic classes exist whose interests are hostile and irreconcilable. . . . But in the USSR there are no longer such classes as capitalists, landlords, kulaks, etc. . . . Consequently there are no grounds for the existence of several parties, and therefore for the existence of freedom of such parties in the USSR. There are grounds for only one party, the Communist Party, in the USSR.

Yet there was also a long Marxist tradition identifying socialism with free and competitive political institutions. Marx himself had said that socialism would be democratic, although he wrote little about the institutional conditions this would require aside from his essay on the Paris Commune, which left many crucial points vague. Until the Russian Revolution, most Marxists took it for granted that socialism would protect and enhance the democratic institutions and political freedoms inherited from bourgeois society, just as the socialist economy would build on, not discard, the achievements of bourgeois industrialization. When the Bolsheviks took power and suppressed not only rival parties, but also freedom of speech and intraparty factions, there were protests from such eminent Marxists as Karl Kautsky, Rosa Luxemburg, and Y. O. Martov, who condemned these actions as a betrayal of Marxism's democratic goals. Wrote Luxemburg, in her 1918 essay *The Russian Revolution*,

> [W]ith the repression of political life in the land as a whole, life in the soviets must also become more and more crippled. Without general elections, without unrestricted freedom of the press and assembly, without a free struggle of opinion, life dies out in every public institution, becomes a mere semblance of life, in which only the bureaucracy remains as the active element.

Trotsky, too, during his time in power the most enthusiastic architect of Soviet dictatorship, wrote in *The Revolution Betrayed* after Stalin had driven him into exile that a true Marxist regime would "restore freedom of Soviet parties" and "give the youth free opportunity to think independently, learn, criticize, and grow." After Stalin's death, multipartyism and an independent press became key proposals, although never realized, of Marxist reformers in Hungary, Czechoslovakia, and Poland, and were even suggested in the Soviet Union by the dissident Marxist Roy Medvedev.

It is not clear how much the democrats knew about the history of pluralist ideas in Marxism, since they referred relatively seldom to Marxist writers other than Marx, Lenin, Stalin, and Mao. But Chinese academics and party theoretical workers did have access to many non-Leninist works in translation, including Leszek Kolakowski's masterwork *Main Currents of Marxism*, which summarizes the ideas of all the main Marxist critics of party dictatorship. Such Marxist-pluralist ideas found echoes in a number of writings that appeared in the official Chinese press from 1978 to 1981. Often disguised as philosophical or historical disquisitions, the articles were far more cloaked in ambiguity than those of the democrats. The authors protected themselves with disclaimers and "yes-but" statements and by stating the controversial parts of their arguments with obscure brevity. Although they identified problems in socialist society directly or by implication, they never specified solutions, so one could never be sure that they were advocating the same programs that the democrats were. Yet certain writings stood out against the background of hundreds of perfectly conforming essays.

The presence of code words like "Paris Commune," "bureaucratic class," "idols," or the "withering of the state" could alert readers to the presence of beliefs that at least to some degree resembled those more clearly expressed in the uncensored mimeographs of the democrats. An article in the February 1979 issue of *Philosophical Research*, for example, referred to the emergence of a "privileged class" from among the bureaucracy as a danger still existing after the fall of the "Gang of Four," and recommended Paris Commune–type measures to enable the state to begin to wither away. "The possibility of government assuming dictatorship over the people is already present," the authors warned—something of an understatement to foreign ears, but a daring observation in light of the party's claim that the exercise of dictatorship against the people had ended with the purge of the Gang. In another scholarly journal, *Historical Research*, two specialists writing about the seventeenth century stated that bureaucratism at that time had not been an independent problem but had its roots in autocracy: "the existence of the ruler's absolute authority and the feudal 'master-slave' relationship inevitably made it necessary for big and small subjects and workers to do things only in accordance with 'His Majesty's will.' " It had been hopeless for the dynastic reformers to try to improve the bureaucracy's functioning so long as the autocratic system remained in place, the authors concluded— making a point of relevance to the present as well. The historical journal also published an admiring account of Thomas Jefferson's theories for limiting and controlling governmental power to prevent the rise of tyranny. A social science journal published an article contradicting the official slogan that "democracy is a means to serve the socialist economic base." Its author wrote that "Lenin did not take democracy simply as a means, but as the basic content of the socialist political system, and as rights which every citizen really enjoys." *Cinema Literature* published a filmscript called *Bitter Love* by Bai Hua, a professional writer employed by the People's Liberation Army. Echoing Huang Xiang's poem about "idols and fetishes," Bai Hua wrote in obvious reference to Mao of an idol "blackened by the smoke of burning joss sticks and candles of faithful believers." Bai Hua's case became an international cause célèbre in 1980 after the official army newspaper denounced him for "anarchism, ultraindividualism, and bourgeois liberalism."

Not only academics and literary figures but the party's own ideological specialists sometimes gave hints of wanting to transfer real power to the people. In a party journal published in Guangxi Province, an author pointed out that the power to purge cadres was still held by the party "leading organs" and not by the people; as long as this continued to be the case, he said, nothing could prevent "conspirators" from seizing power in the way that Lin Biao and the Gang of Four had done. An article in the *People's Daily* criticized the phrase "democracy under centralized guidance" which had appeared in the 1945 and 1956 party constitutions and which may have been under consideration for inclusion in the new party constitution being prepared for adoption in 1982. Democracy means rule by the majority, the author argued; this majority cannot in turn be subjected to guidance by one or a few leaders, or else it would create "the theoretical basis to practice autocracy and deny democracy." Someone important enough to sign as a "contributing commentator" wrote in the *People's Daily* that although democracy is a means, it has "its own laws" that cannot be tampered with at will. Real, not sham, power must be exercised by the people if democracy is to exist.

In the heady days of 1979 and 1980 when the limits of Deng Xiaoping's Gengshen Reforms were not yet clear, some within the party evidently advocated shifting a significant amount of real power to the people. In the optimistic tradition of Chinese reform, it must have seemed to many that this could be done without challenging the principle of party leadership; the people and the party would work together in the common interest. But party secretariat member Hu Qiaomu later claimed that there was also a substantial number of party members who went beyond such ideas of cooperation to advocate what he called "bourgeois liberalization." This he characterized as ideas that "oppose the four basic principles, oppose party leadership." Ideas of bourgeois liberalization, he said in 1981, had had "great impact" and "are found inside and outside the party and the army to a greater or lesser extent. . . . A handful of people," he added, "would even fan the flames and say: . . . 'Unless we practice a two-party system, allow absolute freedom of speech, of publication, of assembly and of association, and start another revolution, how can China be modernized?' "

Hu was claiming in effect that a significant number of established intellectuals and party theoreticians shared the radical democrats' thesis that there is no effective democracy without a free press and competitive elections. Given the veiled nature of the party's internal intellectual life, it is impossible to confirm this charge unambiguously from published evidence, yet the public record suggests it was true. There were a series of remarkable academic and ideological debates in the Chinese press between 1977 and 1983. Whether the topic was agrarian socialism, humanism, the Paris Commune, or the nature of bureaucratism in Chinese society, the real themes were China's political problems and their sources. The same was true of discussions of existentialism, Freudianism, and "philosophy of life." Economists debated "the objective of production under socialism"—whether it is to serve human welfare and happiness or to strengthen the state. The idea of class reconciliation and tolerance for individuality was explored in literary controversies over the content of human nature and whether decent individuals could be found among the bourgeoisie. As a whole, these discussions showed strong support among the intelligentsia for some sort of democratizing reform. The policy implications of such writings, however, were always left self-protectively vague. An article written with the intent of supporting the Deng reform program might contain a careless phrase or formula that wrongly implied that the author wanted to go beyond it. Alternatively, an author who wished to signal that the Gengshen Reforms did not go far enough might protect himself by limiting specific policy recommendations to those the party had already approved.

The intellectual controversy of the period that most strongly suggested the attractiveness of some form of pluralism within party and intellectual circles was the debate over the theoretical issue of alienation. Alienation is one of the fundamental terms in Marx's writings. It refers to the theory that under capitalism both the worker's labor and the products of that labor become commodities which, because they are bought and sold, enslave the worker to the capitalist. More broadly, alienation refers to humankind's creation of any power that oppresses it—religion, injustice, political power. Communism, Marx promised, would bring an end to alienation in all its forms.

According to one count, over six hundred articles discussing the linked topics of alienation and humanism appeared between 1978 and 1983. A key author in this literature was the deputy editor of the party newspaper *People's Daily*, a theoretician in his fifties named Wang Ruoshui. In June 1980, Wang gave a talk at the *Daily*'s journalism study class, portions of which were later published. "Is there still alienation under socialism?" he asked.

> Socialism should wipe out alienation, but has it actually already wiped it out? Is there no more alienation? I think we should acknowledge that practice proves that there still is alienation. Not only is there ideological alienation, but there is political alienation and even economic alienation.

It was controversial enough to assert that alienation was an important topic in Marxism, since the orthodox Chinese view had long been that the concept belonged only to the immature writings of the early Marx. Others, however, had already broached alienation as an academic topic. What was more remarkable was for Wang to assert that alienation exists under socialism, and that it affects at least three major spheres of socialist life. (In an article in a Shanghai newspaper also apparently drawn from his *People's Daily* speech, Wang extended the idea to a fourth sphere, literature and art.) For Marx had limited his discussion of the subject to capitalist society and said that it grew from the class exploitation that the revolution was supposed to end.

When Wang came to discussing the political implications of his theoretical position he stayed within the bounds of the established reforms. In discussing ideological alienation he criticized the cult of Mao, saying the party should recognize that "the source of wisdom is the popular masses." With respect to political alienation, he suggested that the "main danger" to socialism comes from socialism's public servants, the bureaucracy, and recommended the Paris Commune system of election of and low salaries for officials, as well as "developing democracy, strengthening the legal system, establishing rules for party life, and getting rid of the lifelong employment system." In citing examples of economic alienation, he mentioned overinvestment in heavy industry, pollution, and irrational construction policies, but did not say what should be done to prevent such things from happening in the future. As for alienation in literature and art, he said that literature should not "paint a false picture of peace and prosperity" as it had done in the past, but should protect the people by protesting against bureaucratism and other evils whenever they occur.

None of these proposals individually departed from the program of the party reformers. Yet seen as a whole, and especially when grounded in the theory of alienation, they appeared different in an important way. The public rationale of the Gengshen Reforms was not to challenge the preeminence or infallibility of the party but to restore its "democratic work style" of close co-operation with the people. Alienation, on the contrary, implied some sort of structural antagonism between the powerholders and the people. It suggested that party dictatorship was a force created by the people but no longer at one with them, a power which had become separate and antagonistic. Speaking to a visiting delegation of American scholars of Marxism-Leninism, Wang even referred approvingly to Kautsky's criticism of Lenin:

> Kautsky raised the question: Was it going to be the dictatorship of the class, of the party, or of leaders? Lenin thought it was an absurd question, since he believed that the leaders carried out the wishes of the party which in turn carried out the wishes of the class. Now practice has told us that leaders don't always represent the party, the class, or the people.

If the leaders did not automatically represent the interests of the people, then logically they could perform good service only if effectively subordinated to popular supervision. "Self-criticism is a good medicine," Wang wrote elsewhere, "but [the party] requires the people to see that it takes it." Left to the imagination, as usual, was what institutional means the people needed to be able to force the party to take its medicine.

It is possible that Wang was merely laboring to provide a better Marxist rationale for the Gengshen Reforms than they had yet been given. Since bureaucratism, the target of the reforms, belongs to the "superstructure," a Marxist party needed to explain the socioeconomic roots of the problem. For these purposes the theory of "remnant feudal culture" was, in strict Marxian terms, too "idealistic," because it ascribed to disembodied ideas the power to influence society even after their economic base was removed. Alienation, as a classic Marxian concept, might serve to explain why socialist society was imperfect and needed to be improved.

But when alienation theory came under attack, its critics took a darker view of its implications. In October 1983, Politburo member and principal of the Central Party School Wang Zhen launched a campaign against "spiritual pollution" in a speech to a Peking conference of ideological specialists. Two wrong views, he said, were held in party circles and must be criticized. The first was the idea that China was not yet socialist, that Chinese socialism was still only agrarian socialism. (This view had been expressed outside the party

by Wang Xizhe and others. Its chief implication was that China was peas-
ant-dominated, backward, and "feudal" and hence more authoritarian in politics than a proletarian regime ought to be.) The second idea, which became
the main target of the ensuing campaign, was the concept of "socialist alienation."

In the campaign, many charged that the theory of alienation in socialist
society was intended to destroy the party's authority. As Nanking's *New
China Daily* asked, if the party doesn't represent the masses, then who does?
One prominent philosopher said that the alienation theory means, "in politics, it is best not to have concentration of power; in economics, it is best to
have absolute freedom . . . ; and in ideology it is best to have no restrictions."
To attribute the problems in socialist society to alienation, he continued, is
to negate the superiority of socialism to capitalist society. The party's senior
ideologist, Hu Qiaomu, accused proponents of the alienation concept of
being the utopian socialists of today, meaning that they negated the need for
authority during the building of socialism. Deng Liqun, the head of the CCP
Propaganda Department, even accused the alienation writers of opposing the
four basic principles, including party leadership. After some months of such
criticisms, early in 1984 Wang Ruoshui lost his post with the *People's Daily.*

We can hardly accept the charges of Wang's critics as a dispassionate account of what he and other alienation writers were trying to say. In fact he
always carefully affirmed the principle of Communist Party leadership, although avoiding the Leninist term "party dictatorship." It is hard to see how
he could have retained his editor's post as long as he did without the support
of Deng or another high leader. On the other hand, it is hard to see how the
Gengshen Reforms, limited as they were, could ever have satisfied the requirements for reform implied by his theoretical position.

While Wang Ruoshui's purposes and those of others like him remain obscure to outsiders, at a minimum the alienation and related debates revealed
that some party and academic figures accepted a diagnosis of China's political problems fundamentally similar to that of the radical democrats. The debates showed that some intellectuals' thinking about the Cultural Revolution
had led them to the conclusion that the cult of the individual, the irration-
ality of economic policy, and the lack of personal security were not accidents
of Mao's personality, or of factional infighting that brought evil people to the
top, but had something to do with the structure of Chinese political institutions. By accepting that overconcentrated power is inherently subject to
abuse, this view implied the existence within the academic and party establishment of at least a potential disenchantment with party dictatorship.

Yet agreement on the diagnosis did not in all cases mean acceptance of
the radical democrats' prescription for the cure. Many intellectuals and party
members wished only for a more democratic style of decision-making within
the party, for a humane socialism in which the party trusted the people more,

listened more sympathetically to their cries, and gave up its dogmatism without compromising its ultimate authority. Indeed, to many intellectuals both the democrats' use of wall posters, demonstrations, and handbills and their freedom-seeking political program seemed to threaten a reprise of the Cultural Revolution rather than offer a way to prevent its recurrence. Most intellectuals within and outside the democracy movement continued to assume that true democracy should lead to unity and harmony. They shared the alarm expressed by Hu Qiaomu, who said in 1980 that if party leadership was abridged and "we are not uniform [in our thinking], then our steps will be confused. Some would be going east, some west, some south, and some north, and our rank and file would not be able to march forward. Then we would not be able to unify our forces into a consistent body and speed toward our common destination; we would become split into fragments and could accomplish nothing."

Hu was voicing the old fear of disorder that had prompted Liang Qichao to declare that "Domination is sacred" after observing the street wars of San Francisco Chinese clans and the splintering of Chinese student organizations. It was that same fear of disorder that led Mao, at the height of the Cultural Revolution, to call out the army to suppress the Red Guards and restore the rule of the party. The Mao who said "the masses are more progressive than we are" had spawned the democratic challenge, but the party leaders echoed something deeper in Mao and in the Chinese tradition when they suppressed the democracy movement in the name of unity and order.

Deng Xiaoping recalled this deeper tradition in the series of inner-party speeches he delivered during 1980. "China has always been called a plate of loose sand," he reminded the central work conference of January 1980, quoting a metaphor used by Sun Yat-sen. "But our party became the ruling party and the core force uniting the whole country, bringing to an end the countless splits and little kingdoms.... China is led by the CCP and China's cause of socialist modernization is carried out under the leadership of the CCP. This principle cannot be shaken. If it is, China will regress into divisions and confusion, and will then be unable to accomplish modernization." In August 1980 Deng warned further, "In a big country like China, without a political party whose members possess a high degree of political consciousness, sense of discipline and spirit of self-sacrifice . . . it would be inconceivable that the ideology and strength of hundreds of millions of people could be united to build socialism." He underscored the point in December: "China would be certain to fall to pieces and be incapable of achieving anything without the leadership of the Communist Party." In short, after seven decades of a republic the Chinese people in Deng's view were still incapable of exercising power on their own. If they tried to do so they would splinter and drag the nation to collapse. They needed authoritative leaders who could tell them where their interests lay.

In hundreds of articles taking their cues from Deng, the official press began in 1980 to rebut the democrats' arguments point by point, at the same time negating many of the points raised by Mao. China, it said, echoing though not naming Stalin, has no need for more than one political party since there is only one social interest to be represented—the people's. As the representative of the people, the party has no separate interest of its own, so the people need not fear that it will do anything but serve them. Of course, in serving them the party cannot show "blind faith in the spontaneity of the masses"; it must "never forget the differences between the vanguard and the masses" and the vanguard's responsibility to lead. The regime could never spawn a "bureaucratic class" under socialism because under socialism the state serves the people. The people do not need to exercise direct power to prevent the party from making mistakes or from being taken over by conspirators. Although mistakes have been made in the past, "all . . . have been corrected by the party itself" without outside help. Using freedom of speech to try to hold the party to the correct course is not only unnecessary but counterrevolutionary, since speaking up might "undermine the stable and unified political situation." People who think that party dictatorship is undemocratic are indulging in "anti-Marxist petit-bourgeois thinking," a kind of "anarchist thought with the individual as the center." What really distinguishes socialist democracy from bourgeois democracy is that it is more "disciplined and orderly." As for the Paris Commune, although it was a glorious episode it cannot be taken as "the model of proletarian dictatorship"; it was "imperfect, incomplete." Besides, the meaning of the Paris Commune lies in the smashing of the old state machinery, and "we did it thirty-one years ago." It is true that eventually our own state must wither away, but that will not be for a very long time. To talk about it too far in advance will "spoil the prospect of historical development."

In June 1981 the Central Committee adopted a resolution on the knotty problem of Mao himself. If the leaders were tempted simply to cashier the Great Helmsman posthumously in view of what he had done to most of them as individuals, they knew that to do so would reopen the question of authority in a way not favorable to their own hold on power. Because they believed that chaos was a more present danger than tyranny, the party leaders held that the principle of authority was more important than the mistakes made in its name. As Deng told the central work conference of December 1980, "If people are swayed by emotion and go to excesses in talking about [Mao's] mistakes, that can only damage . . . the prestige of the party and the socialist system and can only sap [our] unity." And as the party's resolution put it, "In no case should one use the party's mistakes as a pretext for weakening, breaking away from or even sabotaging its leadership." So the party acknowledged Mao's mistakes as its own, even though its leaders were among his victims, in order to renew the claim to the authority he had used to commit those mistakes. It willingly conceded that Mao had been fallible, but did so not in order to admit that dictatorial power had proved dangerous but instead in order to discredit each of the Maoist precepts that might help to support the democrats' arguments.

The resolution, "On Questions of Party History," listed as "erroneous 'left' theses" Mao's concepts of the bourgeoisie inside the party, mass revolution from below against revisionism, and "continuing the revolution under the dictatorship of the proletariat." The Central Committee created a new orthodox canon of Mao's thought, which included such law-and-order concepts as party-building and the "people's democratic dictatorship." "It is entirely wrong," the resolution concluded, "to try to negate the scientific value of Mao Zedong Thought and to deny its guiding role in our revolution and construction just because Comrade Mao Zedong made mistakes in his later years. Socialism and socialism alone can save China. . . . Any view denying this basic fact is wrong." In the end, the party's analysis of the historical lessons of Mao's mistakes neatly reversed that of the democrats. Theirs challenged the idea of dictatorship; the party's sought to save it.

While classifying Mao's errors as lying to the "left," the party charged the democrats, because of the Western tone of some of their ideas, with deviating to the "right." So shortly after the adoption of the Mao resolution the leaders launched an ideological campaign against "bourgeois liberalization" that was directed against the democrats' kind of thinking. "The essence of bourgeois liberalization is opposition to party leadership," Deng Xiaoping stated in a meeting with top propaganda officials in July 1981. At an August "forum on problems on the ideological front" Hu Qiaomu called for refutation of the ideas of a two-party system and absolute freedoms of speech, publication, assembly, and association. "Any person who is identified with this trend," Hu warned, "is a representative of bourgeois ideology if he insists on publicizing a programmatic proposition which goes against socialism and party leadership, and refuses to correct his mistakes; it makes no difference whether he is a party member." The bourgeois liberalization campaign continued off and on until the focus shifted in late 1983 to "spiritual pollution," another tag for contamination by Western ideas.

That the party labored to suppress the democrats' ideas at least three years beyond the time when it had suppressed the democrats themselves is a tribute to the importance of ideology in legitimizing communist power. In a system of Leninist dictatorship the legality of the state is derived entirely from the party's claim to represent the interests of the people, and not from any actual award of popular support, except perhaps during the original seizure of power. Any challenge to the party's claim to infallible progressiveness thus threatens the state's existence. The defenders of party dictatorship won the battle against the democrats with a combination of classic Leninist arguments, an appeal to the fear of disorder, and decisive political power. Yet the experience of the Cultural Revolution had made the points the democrats raised so pressing to Chinese that it is doubtful whether they can be permanently suppressed.

The controversy over democracy was also significant for the area of consensus it reaffirmed. A line of thinking important in the Western democratic tradition was all but absent from the debate. This was the argument that the individual's interests are separate from the group's, that certain of them are so basic as to have the status of "rights," and that democracy is first of all a system that protects these rights. Wei Jingsheng's was the only extended statement of a position close to this liberal Western mainstream. But the argument Wei offered for a rights-based view of democracy was too isolated from the central tradition of Chinese democratic thought to get much support.

"Autocratic rulers of all ages," Wei wrote, "have invariably taught the people that since men are social beings, social interests should predominate; that since social interests are common to all people, centralized management or administration is necessary; that since rule by a minority, or even by a single person, is most centralized, autocracy is the most ideal form." This was a telling summary of China's democratic tradition as understood both by the authorities and by most of the democrats. But Wei contended, "Society is composed of different individuals, and in his natural condition, each individual exists independently of the others. People's social nature is formed of the common characteristics and common interests of many different individuals. . . . People's individuality is a component of human nature which is prior to their sociality." In short, the individual is prior to society and has interests independent of it.

To defend this theory, Wei resorted to the term "human rights" (*renquan*), which had rarely appeared in a century of Chinese democratic writing. "From the moment he is born," Wei wrote, "a human being has the right to live and the right to strive for a better life. These are what people call heaven-given [natural] human rights. For they are not bestowed by any external thing. Just like the right of any object to exist, they are bestowed by the fact of existence itself. This is like the case of a stone: since it occupies a bit of space by virtue of its existence, it has its right of existence relative to the things around it. No external thing has to give it this right. It has it most naturally." Wei argued that a strong state—the aim of the government's Four Modernizations—was not the highest goal. "We want to be masters of our own destiny. . . . Freedom and happiness are our sole objectives in accomplishing modernization. Without this fifth modernization, all the others are merely another new promise."

Socialism, Wei believed, is "essentially inclined toward democracy" because it aims to give everyone a share in society's wealth. But because it has arisen in backward countries with feudal traditions, it has abandoned its democratic potential in favor of "blind faith in a small group regarded as saviors and leaders." To be authentic, democracy must entail not only the right to share in society's material and cultural products but the right to defend one's access to these benefits by action in the political arena. Otherwise, people enjoy their share in society's wealth on the sufferance of their rulers, who in fact, Wei believed, always monopolize advantages for themselves while trying to delude the people with the promise of a better future—what he called "trying to satisfy people's hunger by showing them a picture of a cake, and their thirst by showing a picture of a plum." The rights of speech, assembly, association, the press, and so forth should not be considered favors granted by the state or privileges tied to duties of political loyalty, nor can they be restricted to actions that will serve the state's or the collective's interest. They are necessary powers for the individual, and their aim is to allow the individual "to satisfy his personal desires in life and to fight for survival." Democracy, then, is a system in which "all men have an equal political right to fight for the rights of [material and cultural] existence."

In making his case for rights, Wei suffered from the lack of a strong Chinese tradition of natural-rights thinking. Why should people accept his argument that they had a natural right to defend their personal interests when the whole weight of Chinese intellectual tradition warned them that this meant chaos and national weakness? Wei could draw the analogy between a stone's mass and human rights, but the analogy is fallacious: a stone has no rights. Rights cannot be derived from inert existence but only from specifically human qualities. Moreover, Wei failed to confront realistically the consequences of the kind of rights he defined. He was no more willing than other Chinese democratic writers since Liang Qichao to accept the fact that democracy entails conflict and disorder. Like the other democrats, he insisted that democracy would be a state of harmony and development. But he did not solve the riddle that Liang had faced, of how the struggle of individuals in defense of their personal interests could produce harmony.

Besides his analogy of the stone, Wei supported his idea of rights with the classic Confucian argument that government has a duty to satisfy its subjects' needs. Everyone knows, he said, that people want to be happy and free; otherwise life would not be worth living. The people will not settle for less and it is government's duty to satisfy them. But if rights derive from government's responsibility to give its people as good a life as it can, then as conditions change rights also change. As Wei put it, "Human rights are limited and relative rather than unlimited and absolute. This limitation constantly grows and changes with the development of the history of mankind and with man's quest to tame and control his surroundings. This explains why the main points of the concept of human rights constantly change and are constantly being improved." Intending to claim more and better rights as society advanced, Wei thus admitted a relativism that bordered on the official view of rights as limited by the nation's "stage of development" and contingent on the general welfare as defined by the party.

The idea of the political primacy of rights had few supporters in the democracy movement besides Wei. The term "human rights" appeared in the titles of two people's periodicals, *China Human Rights* and *China Human Rights Paper*. But, judging from copies available in the West, neither journal had a clear conception of rights or presented an extended argument for their primacy in politics. Two articles in other publications expressed such a view, but neither appears to be part of a substantial body of writing by the same author. In fact, most of the democrats rejected Wei's theories. After his trial and conviction *April Fifth Forum* published several articles criticizing the trial on procedural grounds, but also admitted that Wei's views "are opposed to Marxism and violate our constitution." Individual rights are not absolute, the journal argued (something Wei had actually conceded). They are limited by the interests of society. Democracy is not an end in itself but is "a means . . . to concentrate various forces to serve the Four Modernizations." Xu Wenli of *April Fifth Forum* told a visiting reporter from Hong Kong that the China Human Rights League and its few allies were "naïve youngsters" who have "mistaken citizens' rights for human rights." "They are not a force to reckon with," he stated. And Xu's views were probably among the most sympathetic to Wei at Democracy Wall and in the movement as a whole. Wei was admired by many in China for his courage but by few for what he said.

Chinese legal thought had given political rights a major role since the start of the century. The purpose of rights, however, had never been to protect the individual against the government, but to enable citizens to work better to strengthen the state. To defend himself against the charge of counterrevolution at his trial, Wei argued that he had only tried to educate people so as to encourage gradual reform of the political system. But that defense would have been valid only in a system that already accepted the concept of rights he was arguing for. Under Chinese law, the prosecutor reminded him, his posters and mimeographed essays in their editions of a few hundred copies constituted political action—action to "overthrow the political power of the people's democratic dictatorship." Ours is a class society, the prosecutor told the court. "In a class society, the law and the state are the same. The law itself represents the embodiment of the current ruling class system." The prosecutor's terminology was Marxist, but his view of political rights as limited by the needs of the state was founded in eight decades of the Chinese constitutional tradition.

6

POLITICAL RIGHTS IN THE CHINESE CONSTITUTIONAL TRADITION

Political rights have always occupied a prominent place in the modern Chinese political order. They have been featured in each of eleven major central government constitutions and constitutional drafts under four different types of regimes. By political rights I mean rights to take actions to influence the choice of government personnel or policy, including the right to vote, serve in office, petition, and appeal; some of the rights often called civil rights, such as those to speak, publish, assemble, and associate; and any other rights that bear on the citizen's opportunities for political action. In any modern nation, the constitutional and legal provisions for these rights define how citizens can legitimately attempt to influence government. Some Chinese constitutions were not in effect for very long, and none was fully obeyed by the regime that promulgated it. Yet all embodied the negotiated consensus of dominant groups in society about what they considered the proper power relations between citizen and state. As constitutions defined them and laws and political practice spelled them out, political rights in China were consistently regarded as a grant given by the state to the citizens, to enable them to contribute their energies to the needs of the nation.

The table on pages 108–109 summarizes the content of political rights in China's major constitutions and drafts. The first text, Principles of the Constitution, was an outline promulgated by the Qing government in 1908 as a step towards transforming itself into a constitutional monarchy. Since the monarch was intended to be both sovereign and all-powerful, the Principles devoted fourteen of twenty-three articles to listing the future powers of the monarch and only nine to subjects' rights and duties. The rights included the freedoms of speech, writing, publication, assembly, and association "within the scope of the law," as well as rights to serve in office if qualified and to submit petitions for judgment. An outline electoral law added that subjects with proper legal qualifications would have the right to vote. These rights

Political Rights in Chinese Constitutions

Right or Freedom	Principles	Provisional Constitution	Temple Draft	1923	1931 (Tutelage)
Speech	X	X	X	X	X
Writing	X	X	X	X	implicit
Publishing	X	X	X	X	X
Assembly/Association	X	X	X	X	X
Teaching/Study	O	O	O	O	O
Petition/Appeal/Suit	X	X	X	X	X
Compensation	O	O	O	O	O
Secrecy of correspondence	O	X	X	X	X
Equality before law	O	X	X	X	X
Popular sovereignty	O	X	implicit	X	X
Voting	implicit	X	X	X	locally
Running for office	implicit	X	X	X	O
Serving in office/ Sitting for exam	X	X	X	X	X
Election/Recall/ Initiative/Referendum	O	O	O	O	locally
Residual freedoms/ rights	O	O	O	X	O
Supervision of production	O	O	O	O	O
Participation in armed revolution	O	O	O	O	O
National minority self-determination	O	O	O	O	O
National minority autonomy	O	O	O	O	O
Political asylum	O	O	O	O	O
Rights for foreign nationals	O	O	O	O	O
Procession/ Demonstration	O	O	O	O	O
Freedom of culture: scientific research, literary and artistic creation, other cultural activities	see Writing	see Writing	see Writing	see Writing	see Writing
Supervision of state organs	O	O	O	O	O
"Four greats"	O	O	O	O	O
Striking	O	O	O	O	O

Notes

   X = conferred by constitution, although perhaps not in exactly these words.
   O = not conferred.

1946	Jiangxi Program	1954	1975	1978	1982
X	X	X	X	X	X
X	O	see freedom of culture	O	see freedom of culture	see freedom of culture
X	X	X	X	X	X
X	X	X	X	X	X
X	O	O	O	O	O
X	O	X	X	X	X
X	O	X	O	O	X
X	O	X	"freedom of"	"freedom of"	X
X	working classes	X	O	O	X
X	working classes	X	X	X	X
X	working classes	X	"democratic consultation"	X	X
X	working classes	X	X	X	X
X	O	O	O	O	O
X	election + recall	election + recall	election + recall	election + recall	election + recall
X	O	O	O	O	O
O	X	in capitalist enterprises	O	implicit	X
O	working classes	O	O	O	O
O	X	O	O	O	O
O	X	X	X	X	X
O	X	X	X	X	X
O	working classes	O	O	O	O
O	O	X	X	X	X
see Writing	O	X	O	X	X
O	O	X	O	X	X
O	O	O	X	X	O
O	O	O	X	X	O

were supposed to enable citizens who met property qualifications to participate in electing a parliament that would advise the emperor and strengthen
the ties between the ruler and the people in the way that reformers like Liang
Qichao had envisioned.

Before the constitutional transition was completed the dynasty fell. Except for some short-lived imperial restorations, subsequent Chinese regimes
were republics. The early republican governments until 1928 were based on
the principle of popular sovereignty exercised through Parliament. The par-
liaments were constitutionally supreme—that is, their enactments were not
subject to judicial review—but in fact nearly powerless in the face of warlord
domination. The Provisional Constitution of 1912, the so-called Temple of
Heaven Draft of 1913, and the Constitution of 1923 all restricted the right to
vote on the basis of property and education. The republican constitutions
added a number of rights to those envisioned in the late Qing Principles, including secrecy of correspondence. Like it, they provided that such rights
could be restricted by law.

The Guomindang, or Nationalist Party, which came to power in
1927–28, continued to recognize the principle of popular sovereignty but
modified it with the theory of "tutelage," under which the party was to supervise the gradual introduction of full democratic institutions. Under the
Tutelage Constitution of 1931 the party appointed and controlled the government. In 1946 the Guomindang ended tutelage by promulgating a permanent constitution, which remains in effect in Taiwan today. The 1946
constitution gave the citizens some new rights, including that of teaching
and study, the right to compensation for damage suffered as a consequence
of illegal acts of officials, and a category of residual rights—rights and freedoms not otherwise listed but in the public interest. As in earlier constitutions, the two Guomindang texts made the exercise of rights dependent upon
limits established by law and gave the power to interpret the constitutionality
of laws to the party (in the Tutelage Constitution) or the government itself
(in the 1946 text).

The communist constitutional tradition began with the Constitutional
Program, an outline charter adopted in the party's Jiangxi base area in 1931.
It continued through several base-area constitutions before 1949 and the four
national constitutions of 1954, 1975, 1978, and 1982. The communist texts
added some new political rights, varying from document to document, such
as the rights to procession and demonstration, political asylum, supervision
of state organs, and the right to strike. The rights were not granted to all citizens, but to "the people"—that is, that majority of citizens belonging to the
progressive classes. As in earlier constitutions, rights were to be defined and
restricted by law. Laws in turn were passed by the hierarchy of soviets or
people's congresses that embodied popular sovereignty. The soviets also had
the power to review the constitutionality of any law.

These eleven texts represent the thinking of four very different re-gimes—the last imperial dynasty, the liberal early republic, the authoritarian Guomindang, and the socialist People's Republic. One constitution was mo-narchical, the rest republican. The early republican constitutions envisioned competitive politics; those written under Guomindang and Communist aus-pices allowed a single party to dominate. The relation between the president and the cabinet, the executive and the legislature, the center and the prov-inces, changed from one era to the next. As the regime moved from monar-chical to republican, from multiparty to single-party, and from Guomindang to Communist, different guiding ideologies were placed in the constitutions and different institutions established.

All constitutions granted a common core of political rights consisting of speech, publication, assembly, and association. The rights of petition/ap-peal, voting, and popular sovereignty were virtually universal. But the right to serve in office and/or sit for the official examination was limited to precom-munist constitutions; the right of election/recall/initiative/referendum was predominantly a feature of Guomindang constitutions; and rights of proces-sion and demonstration, national minority autonomy, political asylum, su-pervision of production, supervision of state organs, the "four greats" and the right to strike were limited to communist constitutions, although not found in all of them. The concept of residual rights was found in three constitu-tions, all precommunist; the right to compensation also in three constitu-tions, one of them precommunist. Several rights were provided in only one constitution each: teaching and study, participation in armed revolution, na-tional minority self-determination, and rights for foreign nationals.

Despite differences, the series of constitutions established a tradition of continuity with respect to the basic nature of rights.

First, in none of the constitutions were rights considered to be derived from human personhood; they were derived from citizenship in the state or, in the communist period, from membership in the progressive classes known collectively as "the people."

Second, the very variability of rights from constitution to constitution was an important point of continuity. Chinese constitution writers felt able to add and withdraw rights fairly casually because they held that rights are granted by the state and can be changed by the state.

Third, some rights in each Chinese constitution were programmatic—that is, they were presented as goals to be realized. This feature was funda-mental to the Qing Principles, the Guomindang's Tutelage Constitution, and the communist constitutions, all of which were explicitly written as polit-ical programs. And in all constitutions the feature was implicit in the fact that rights were mentioned that in fact could not be enjoyed.

Fourth, every Chinese constitution implicitly or explicitly gave the gov-ernment the power to limit rights by acts of legislation. The protection that rights offered lay in the fact that they could not be restricted except by law, not in their forming a limit to law.

Fifth, and consequent to the fourth point, none of the constitutions established an effective procedure for independent review of a law's constitutionality. The organ that made the law—emperor, parliament, ruling party, or people's congress—was considered to have sovereign power to do so, and could not be checked by any other branch of government.

Sixth, while all but the Qing constitution recognized popular sovereignty in principle, none provided for its effective exercise by the people. In no constitution was the executive directly elected. The national legislature was always elected either indirectly or by a limited electorate and had very limited authority in government affairs. The influence of the citizens over state policy was so buffered and checked as to be negligible in practice.

The meaning of these six points can be sharpened by comparing them to analogous aspects of the American tradition. The purpose of such a comparison is not to tag the Chinese constitutional tradition as deviant. In fact, it is the American Constitution that is more unusual by world standards. But just because the two are so different, an American comparison, rather than one with the Soviet or Japanese tradition, highlights most clearly what was characteristic and consistent in Chinese constitutions over the course of eight decades. Although American thinking about rights has been diverse and the content of rights in the American Constitution has changed over the course of two centuries, a central tradition is not hard to find. First, although rights are codified by the state, they are not considered to originate in a grant by the state but to be inherent in the dignity or personhood of the individual—to be, as some say, "natural." Second, since rights are seen as discovered rather than enacted, changes in their content are considered to arise from a changing understanding of what is necessary to secure the dignity of the person, not from the changing needs or goals of the state. Once rights are recognized, they are unlikely to be withdrawn. Third, rights are claimed and exercised in the present. They are not goals for the future and cannot legitimately be withheld because conditions are not ripe. Fourth, rights limit legislation rather than vice versa. The exercise of rights is constrained by considerations of other persons' rights and of the public good, but to be enacted into law limits on rights must meet stringent political and legal standards. Public opinion and watchdog groups make it hard for laws limiting rights to be enacted. When enacted and challenged in the courts, such laws have to be shown to serve clear and compelling public interests or they are likely to be thrown out. Fifth, an organ independent of the legislature and the executive is empowered to enforce the superiority of the Constitution to other law by testing laws against the standard of the Constitution. Finally, in the American system citizens have effective mechanisms to influence the selection of state personnel and policies. Because of this, political rights have been used by citizens to make demands on government. The freedoms of the press, demonstration, and association and the enforcing power of the vote have helped to protect rights from encroachment and to expand them.

In short, the American constitutional tradition sees government, however necessary, as partly an adversary of the individual. The power of the state is constitutionally limited in order to protect individual interests against invasion. The individual has recourse to appeal, on behalf of frankly selfish interests, not only against bureaucrats who act in disregard of state policy but against state law and policy itself. By contrast, Chinese constitutions assumed a harmony of interests between state and citizen. They did not encourage or even recognize the possibility of conflict between the two. For them the purpose of citizen participation was to mobilize popular energies to serve the state. Although means were provided for the citizen to appeal against the acts of individual bureaucrats, no avenue was open in any Chinese constitution for the citizen to defend private interests against laws and policies of the state that might damage them.

The Chinese ideology of rights is an amalgam of elements from the Chinese tradition and from the West, including Marxism. Although the idea that China should have a constitution and that the constitution should specify rights came from abroad, the substance of both constitutions and rights came to be understood in Chinese terms. First, the constitutional tradition was shaped by a theory of the unlimited scope of state power that interpreted foreign theories of law in the light of ideas from the Chinese tradition. Second, rights were interpreted in terms of long-standing Chinese views on the relation between individual and collective interests, on political obligation and moral heroism, that interacted with Western individualistic and Marxian currents of thought. Third, the Chinese understanding of political democracy integrated Western theories with traditional schools of thought on the relations between people and state. Finally, the Chinese discussion of political rights drew on the modern idea of social utility, understood in the light of China's condition of backwardness.

Chinese thinking about the functions of law was shaped by two ancient schools, Legalism and Confucianism. Both accepted the ruler's right to make law. The Legalists viewed this right as absolute, as unconstrained by any higher moral order. They held that the ruler could and should create any laws necessary to strengthen his state, and that harsh laws worked better than soft ones. The Confucians argued, by contrast, that to be effective law must comply with the moral order inherent in society. The laws and the ruler must be fair and just and must encourage the virtues of filial devotion, loyalty, and social compassion. This Confucian view was parallel in a broad sense to the

Western concept of natural law, in that it posited a moral order independent of the laws of the state.

For the Confucians, however, this was a moral order created by humans, not nature. More important, their moral order differed in content from that which underlay modern Western theories of natural law such as those of Hobbes, Locke, and Rousseau. Confucians did not see the moral order as limiting the powers of the ruler. Instead, they saw it as calling for the fulfillment of the ruler's and the people's innate promptings as social beings. For the ruler, complying with the moral order meant extending his charismatic virtue to the full. As Wm. Theodore de Bary puts it, "moral restraints . . . are intended not to make [the Prince] less of a king but to help him be a king." In particular, the Confucian moral order contained no belief in the rights of the individual as a limit on any kind of authority—including that of the clan, the family, parents, or husbands. So while the Chinese tradition like any other had its own sense of what was naturally right, neither Legalism nor Confucianism saw moral laws or individual rights as limiting the power of the state.

At the time that Chinese thinkers began to look abroad for guidance in modernizing the legal system, they found the idea of natural rights wrapped in what was to them a particularly mystifying guise, social contract theory. When Liang Qichao introduced Chinese readers to Hobbes and Rousseau, he treated the notion that humans had ever existed outside of society in a state of nature as a curiosity. He expressed shock at the primitive morality of Hobbes's vision of the war of each against all. Liang was far more comfortable with the ideas of Johan Kaspar Bluntschli, the Swiss political scientist whose works he had discovered through Japanese translations. Bluntschli's argument that the state is not merely an aggregation of individuals but an organic entity proved to Liang that individuals' status as citizens and therefore their rights derive from the state, not the other way around.

Moreover, at the time Liang wrote, natural-rights ideas were in retreat in the West. European and American legal theorists were increasingly influenced by the doctrine of legal positivism developed by the English theorist John Austin (1790–1859). According to Austin, the so-called laws of God, nature, or morality are just expressions of philosophers' preferences, dressed up with the claim to be law. Properly speaking, laws are whatever commands are enacted by a political sovereign and backed up with the threat of punishment. This theory could be taken in diverse directions. It was associated in Britain with the liberal reform philosophy of utilitarianism and in America with the school of "legal realism" that directed attention to the factors influencing the actual behavior of courts. But in Germany, Italy, and the Soviet Union, legal positivism combined with doctrines of the absolute state to help provide the ideological foundations for fascism and Stalinism.

In China, too, beginning in the late nineteenth century, the theory of legal positivism was put to the service of creating a strong state. With increasing urgency after 1895, Chinese were searching abroad for methods of strengthening their government. The study of foreign legal theory was part of their quest. Before the Principles of the Constitution were drafted the imperial court sent two groups of commissioners overseas to study constitutional models. The tours resulted in lengthy compilations built around the theme of how constitutions augmented the power of the state in Europe and Japan. The Principles were submitted to the Empress Dowager accompanied by the following summary of their spirit:

> First, the sacred majesty of the sovereign may not be offended against. Second, the sovereign has absolute power, which he exercises in constitutional forms. Third, the [subjects], according to the laws, have privileges to which they are entitled and duties which they owe.

As the century wore on, returned students dominated the university law schools, comparative government faculties, and legal drafting commissions of successive governments. Because of linguistic and geographic convenience, the Japanese influence was particularly strong. There was also considerable German influence, both directly and through Japan. Both countries' jurisprudence was based on the doctrine of legal positivism. One scholar during the Guomindang period summarized the then-accepted view of law and rights as follows:

> It must be realized at the outset that constitutional rights should not be based on the theory of natural rights. It is beyond controversy that any enforceable right is the creation of the law. Only when the law recognizes a certain right is such a right legally protected. It naturally follows that the law may make the right and also may unmake it. Constitutional right as a form of legal right is no exception.

With the arrival of communism came the Marxist theory of law as the will of the ruling class expressed in fixed form. As explained by *Red Flag*, "In a class society, only after obtaining political power can the ruling class, by means of the form of law, transform the will of its own class into the will of the state, and rely on the coercive force of the state to safeguard its own class interests." So far as the theory of rights was concerned, this did not involve a major shift. Like the Guomindang, the communists rejected the concept of fixed and universal "human rights." Again in the words of *Red Flag*,

> Human rights are not "heaven-given," they are given and regulated by the state and by law; they are not universal, but have a clear class nature; they are not abstract but concrete; they are not absolute but limited by

law and morality; they are not eternally fixed and unchanging but change their nature and proper scope in accordance with changes in the functions and position of people in the midst of shifting conditions of material production.

Thus the communist state recognized only "civil" (or "citizens' ") rights, created by the state and granted to its citizens. As explained in a Chinese radio talk, "The content of civil rights may not be completely identical [even] among countries with the same political systems, because the civil rights are specifically stipulated by each country's own constitution."

In short, Chinese predispositions and the foreign models Chinese selected combined to forge a philosophy of law as the state's will and rights as the state's creation. This philosophy, in turn, helps explain several of the characteristics of the Chinese constitutional tradition. First, if rights are created by the state, it is reasonable for rights provisions to be programmatic. The constitution need not list preexisting limits on state powers, but can announce what rights the state hopes to provide in due course, without embarrassment that these rights are not yet available. Second, it is reasonable for the state to grant rights only to those who are friendly or loyal to it or who are its "members," and to deprive of rights those who are hostile to its purposes. As the *Worker's Daily* put it with respect to freedom of speech, this "is not an innate right which can be exploited even after the proletariat succeeds in seizing power. . . . In order to protect socialist public ownership and consolidate its political rule, the proletariat must give political rights and freedoms, including freedom of speech, to the masses instead of to the antagonistic classes or their remnants."

Third, since the state creates rights it is reasonable that it have full powers to restrict them, so long as it does so in the same way that it grants them—by legislative enactment. As the chief drafter of the 1946 constitution, John C. H. Wu, put it:

> Rights are entrusted by society to the individual; society is the source of rights. The individual apart from society has no rights to speak of. Since society bestows rights, at times of necessity it can also remove rights; at least it can limit their scope.

Or, as explained in the journal *Democracy and Legal System,* "The state has the right to intervene in all civil activities which run counter to state planning and state laws and decrees." Fourth, since the state acts legitimately when it restricts rights by law, no law can be invalid because it restricts rights, and no procedure is needed to determine whether particular laws do violate rights. For example, when the democracy activists tried to defend their right to mimeograph and distribute periodicals on the basis of the constitutional guarantee of freedom of speech and publication, there was no institution with which to lodge their appeal except the same police precincts that were closing them down.

Most modern legal theories, including Marxism, make a distinction between the decisions of the ruler or the ruling party and the laws of the state. The word "state" is reserved for the sovereign authority and the word "law" for the general rules that it commands its subjects to obey. To say that rights may be restricted by law therefore means that they can be restricted only in keeping with general rules enacted through the formal procedures of specific legislative organs, not on the basis of the policies of the ruling party or the case-by-case preferences of officials. But Chinese political leaders have sometimes stretched the idea of law as the will of the state beyond the boundaries of what their own legal theory strictly permits. For one thing, until recently the Communist Party has held that it can legitimately restrict rights through its own decisions or policies rather than only through state law. In this interpretation, party policies have the same effect as law. "We work according to party policies and the interests of the people," a legal official told a foreign journalist in 1974. "There is in the country now no published code but we have individual regulations concerning penalties against counterrevolutionaries. If the case is not covered by one of the special regulations we deal with it according to the policy of the party." Under this system tens of thousands of persons were punished for violating party regulations or policies they did not know existed, or for acts that were judged culpable by local party leaders. Verdicts and sentences were decided in batches by party officials in camera.

Speaking in 1984, Peng Zhen, chairman of the Standing Committee of the National People's Congress, stated, "We must gradually make the transition from relying on policy in managing affairs, to establishing and strengthening the legal system and relying not only on policy but also on law to manage affairs." Under Deng Xiaoping, legal reforms have returned the responsibility of decision in criminal cases to the courts, where verdicts and sentences are supposed to be based on enacted laws. In interpreting and applying the law, however, judges are still required to be guided by party policy. According to one commentator, "The party's policies for the life of the state are accepted by state organs as the policies of the state . . . [and] do, in fact, play the role of law." A 1981 college law text states:

> Legislation must take party policy as its basis, and administration of the law must take party policy as its guide. When legal provisions are lacking, we should manage affairs in accordance with party policy. When legal provisions exist they should be accurately applied, also under the guidance of party policy. . . . Policy occupies the leading position, . . . law serves to bring policy to fruition.

A second stretching of the notion that law is the state's will has occurred on several occasions when the authorities suspended rights—either for limited numbers of persons or for the whole population—without following legal procedures for doing so. One such instance was the Nationalist government's imposition of martial law in Taiwan in 1949, which did not follow the procedures required by the 1946 constitution. Under the state of siege still in effect today, the scope of political offenses has been broadened, their penalties have been increased, and military courts have taken jurisdiction over them. During the Cultural Revolution on the mainland, people were persecuted by ad hoc authorities through nonlegal procedures for acts that were deemed political crimes on no legal basis. The head of state, Liu Shaoqi, was deposed without action of the National People's Congress and imprisoned without a criminal charge or a trial. All this was officially defended at the time as "revolutionary legality" required for class struggle. As recently as 1980, the newly enacted criminal and criminal procedure laws were disregarded in the "trial of the Gang of Four and Lin Biao counterrevolutionary cliques." In this instance the irregularities were explained on the ground of the extraordinary nature of the case.

Propelled to some extent by the lobbying of Chinese lawyers, the idea of the supremacy of law in the affairs of the state is being reemphasized and may eventually become an entrenched part of the evolving Chinese concept of rights. If this happens the limits of rights will be more clearly defined, but that does not necessarily mean that they will be significantly widened. For example, three laws currently restrict the scope of one of the most important political rights, freedom of speech (or expression). First, the constitution establishes an obligation for each citizen to uphold the four "basic principles" of party leadership, socialism, dictatorship of the proletariat, and Marxism-Leninism–Mao Zedong Thought. Second, the state-secrets regulations of 1951 prohibit the revelation of matters that are classified as secrets of state or that "ought not to be revealed." Finally, the 1979 criminal code contains a number of articles restricting acts of speech, such as instigating others to crime, lodging false charges, making libelous statements, or making false identifications or appraisals.

The most important speech-related provision of the criminal code is Article 102, which prohibits counterrevolutionary incitement or propaganda. If an act of speech is held to constitute counterrevolutionary incitement, it becomes a crime drawing a penalty of imprisonment for no less than five years. The code defines counterrevolutionary offenses as "acts undertaken with the purpose of overthrowing the political power of the dictatorship of the proletariat and the socialist system and which harm the Chinese People's Republic." In principle, then, counterrevolutionary crimes require an intention, an act, and a harmful consequence. But in the cases of Wei Jingsheng and other democracy activists, the mere posting or mimeographing of critical essays or the dropping of leaflets was punished as counterrevolutionary incitement even though there was no explicit call for the overthrow of the regime, no inciting act beyond dissemination of written material, and no measurable damage done to the state.

Summarizing the law's provisions, *Red Flag* pointed out, "A person is free to express any opinion (including erroneous ones) and will be protected by law so long as he stands on the side of the people and safeguards the constitution and the law. . . . [But] no one is allowed to air antiparty and antisocialist views." Conversation, academic discourse, and correspondence can all be punished if their content is objectionable. As one newspaper explained, "Speech takes place; it enters the realm of reality and there is the possibility that it may attach itself to certain kinds of conduct." The only act of speech unambiguously designated as exempt from prosecution is writing in a diary, so long as no steps are taken to disseminate the ideas in question. Yet even diary entries have been used as evidence of counterrevolutionary intent, making serious crimes out of acts that would otherwise have been punished less severely or not at all.

In the current state of Chinese law, other political rights are equally weakly protected. The rights of assembly and association and of procession and demonstration are restricted by constitutional and criminal provisions against damaging public order, interfering with traffic, disrupting work, harming social morals, and damaging state property. Officials have treated almost all demonstrations and unauthorized public meetings as if they were in violation of these restrictions, and have sometimes called them counterrevolutionary besides. The right to petition and appeal has been narrowed in the same way. Appeals that are importunate, persistent, or "unreasonable" are punishable as counterrevolutionary incitement or violations of public order, or by work-unit officials or the police as ideological deviations. The right to publication is governed by the outdated publications regulations that set conditions private publications cannot meet and by the state secrets regulations, which classify state secrets broadly enough to include any state matter not already officially published.

In practice, the difficult constitutional and philosophical issues of the permissible boundaries of the exercise of all these rights have often been left for resolution to the police rather than to the courts. Under the 1957 regulations on rehabilitation through labor the police may sentence to renewable terms of three years' service in a labor camp "counterrevolutionaries and antisocialist reactionaries who, because their crimes are minor, are not pursued for criminal responsibility"—i.e., who are not given court trials. Most political dissidents have been dealt with in this way, including most of the democracy movement activists arrested in 1979–81.

* * *

The strong state did not collide in China with the kind of individualism that might have offered a bulwark against extensive use of its legal power to restrict rights, as has been the case, for example, in England, where parliamentary supremacy is checked by the forces of common law and public opinion. In China, political philosophy did assign a great role to individuals. But since Chinese thinkers perceived the relation between society and the individual very differently than most modern Western thinkers, they valued an individualism of a different kind. In contrast to the dominant Western attitude, Confucianism saw private interests not as individual but as belonging to a group—a family, lineage, or community. People are born into society and cannot prosper alone; the individual depends on the harmony and strength of the group. Selfish behavior—which of course existed—was viewed as reflecting a failure to understand that one's welfare was tied to a larger entity and as a futile attempt to isolate oneself. The individual should cultivate himself but should do it not for himself but in order to contribute to the welfare of family and community. To behave selfishly was the mark of the moral "small man," who had neither the power nor the right to influence events.

Confucianism recognized the power of the "great man" (*junzi*) to change the world. Such a person was an individualist in that he followed his own moral beliefs. But he was never motivated by selfish ends: a transcendence of personal interests was the very source of his power of moral suasion. Confucian heroes like Qu Yuan, the remonstrator described in Chapter 1, followed their personal visions of the truth, not in order to aggrandize themselves but to affirm morality and serve society. Their individualism led to personal sacrifice rather than gain.

It was against this background that modern Chinese thinkers confronted Western ideas of the role of the individual in politics. In 1896, Liang Qichao argued that unlike China, Western countries were strong because their citizens had rights. He explained this by defining rights not as individual claims against society but as the power to do within and for society "that which it is appropriate to do, and to enjoy the benefits that are owing to one." If Liang in his early phase did not envision that rights granted to the individual might be used in ways contrary to the interests of the state, he also did not worry that a strengthened state might threaten the interests of individuals:

> The individual cannot survive alone in the world. Society thus arises, and the individual manages his existence in collaboration with his fellows. . . . One who is good at pursuing his own interests will first see to the interests of his collectivity, and then his own interests will be advanced along with it.

Indeed, the identity of individual and collective interests was even more compelling now than in earlier times, in Liang's view, because now the survival of the Chinese race was at stake. With the famous translator Yan Fu, Liang taught a generation about the new science of Darwinism that showed how, according to them, individuals might perish but their interests were served if their race survived.

The early decades of this century were years of liberation for Chinese intellectuals. Iconoclasm flourished. Confucian social bonds and duties were challenged by young rebels. No school of thought, including the most individualistic, lacked its handful of believers. Yet it is hard to find even among the Chinese anarchists, Ibsenites, and Nietzscheans a consistent defender of self-interested individualism. The impulse to defend liberation as serving society was too strong. For example, the anarchist Liu Shipei wrote that "we stand for . . . uniting all the people of the world into one great mass to plan the complete happiness of mankind." The liberal Hu Shi introduced Ibsen's slogan "Save yourself" with the defense that "such egoism is in fact the most valuable kind of altruism. . . . If society and the nation do not possess [men of] independent character, they are like wine without yeast, bread without leaven, the human body without nerves. Such a society has absolutely no hope of improvement or progress." Chen Duxiu's famous 1915 essay "Call to Youth" cited Nietzsche in calling on Chinese youth to shake off the "slavish" Confucian morality and become "completely independent and free personalities" because, said Chen, "I would much rather see the past culture of our nation disappear than see our race die out now because of its unfitness for living in the modern world." Guo Moruo, a Chinese disciple of Nietzsche, Goethe, Carlyle, and Whitman who wrote a poem with the line "My ego is about to burst," also wrote soon afterwards that "the minority who are farsighted should sacrifice their own individuality, sacrifice their own freedom to save the masses, to reclaim the individuality and freedom of the great mass of the people." As heirs to the literati tradition of social service, and as citizens of a threatened nation, modern Chinese intellectuals were unable to justify the liberation of the individual on the frankly selfish grounds so often employed in the modern West.

With the arrival of Marxism, the ethic of selflessness was preserved in tandem with the Marxian emphasis on material interests. Marx saw the proletariat as compelled by self-interest to liberate humankind. The workers are driven to revolution by hardship and exploitation. They end by creating a society so productive that each individual has access to all the goods he or she needs and to the leisure to develop fully as a person. Thus the individual material interest of each member of the proletariat is an important goal of socialism, in Marx's view. Chinese Marxism accepts the legitimacy of individual interest, but only in a limited sense; it argues that this interest is subordinate to the higher interests of party, class, and nation. Individual and collective interests may sometimes seem to come into conflict, but this conflict is reconcilable. As Mao wrote, "The individual is an element of the collective. When collective interests are increased, personal interests will subsequently be improved." The party leads the people to see that, in the words of a Chinese philosopher, "the benefits of the social collective are more important than individual benefits, long-term benefits are more important than short-term benefits, and complete benefits are more important than partial benefits." "When people struggle for socialism," stated *Red Flag*, "they not only are bringing benefits to other people and future generations but are objectively striving for their own immediate and long-term interests."

In this view, not all individual interests are recognized as legitimate: "The legitimate individual interests that we say should be protected by the party and the nation are those individual interests of the worker that are at one with national and collective benefits." In case of conflict, members of a socialist society should be selfless, even to the point of self-sacrifice:

> The spirit of selflessness is a reflection of the essential disposition of the proletariat. Our party . . . demands that both party members and the masses take the selfless spirit as the moral norm of their own words and deeds and make a rupture with bourgeois individualism. Under the nurturing of the party, the vast ranks of the party members and the masses all take selflessness as a glory and selfishness as a shame.

"When individual interests and party interests are found to be inconsistent with each other," writes another commentator, "we should be able unhesitatingly and without any reluctance to obey party interests and sacrifice individual interests."

The ethic of proletarian selflessness still leaves room for the heroic individual, but, as under Confucianism, such a person's goals must be selfless. The former defense minister Peng Dehuai, for example, is now considered a hero because he spoke up against Mao's Great Leap policies in 1959 and then accepted the punishment of living out the rest of his life in obscurity. But, like such other martyrs to the public good as Zhang Zhixin, who was executed after criticizing "ultra-leftists" around Mao, Peng had to be found to have made his criticism solely in the public interest, and that criticism had to be judged correct in retrospect; otherwise he could not have been posthumously rehabilitated and praised for his action.

The factual proposition that the individual's interests are inseparable from those of society, and the ethical injunction to place the interests of society first, have buttressed the Chinese constitutional tradition at several points. First, they gave added justification and latitude to the state's power to restrict individual rights. They suggested that the state might properly restrict rights not just for reasons of extreme urgency but in whatever ways served the interests of society, for in so doing, the state would actually be serving the higher interests of the individuals who were being restricted. As the journal *Legal Research* explained:

> Even some members of the ruling class itself must suffer the restraint of law if they clash with the basic interests of their class. . . . Freedom under socialism is freedom which does not contravene the basic interests of the broad masses of the people; it is freedom which respects the social order and which respects necessary discipline.

Individuals in turn should recognize such restrictions as serving their higher interests and should embrace them willingly.

Second, the ethic of selflessness demands moral self-restraint in the exercise of individual rights that sometimes goes beyond the restrictions imposed by law. As the *Enlightenment Daily* explained in 1981, there is a distinction between "legal individual interest" and "legitimate individual interest." "Not all individual interests in accord with socialist laws are necessarily morally legitimate," the newspaper argued. "Whether they are legitimate or not depends upon their relation to the collective interests of the society at a given time." Thus the fact that a person has a certain right under the constitution does not make it morally correct to exercise that right to the fullest. Appealing and letter-writing, for example, are protected under both the party and state constitutions, and officials are forbidden to retaliate against those who complain through proper channels. But frankly self-interested appeals remain of doubtful legitimacy. Appeals that are importunate or demand compensation that the state cannot afford to provide have been ruled "unreasonable" even if the citizen involved has the law on his or her side. In the realm of speech, "We often emphasize 'not saying anything that is not good for unity,'" according to the *Workers' Daily*, "and if anyone publishes this kind of opinion, although he will not be punished by law, he will be criticized and denounced by the opinion of society. Every citizen who has socialist awareness . . . should conscientiously use socialist morality to restrict his own speech."

Third, the state and the ruling party have undertaken to see that the ethic of selflessness is widely understood. In the words of one newspaper,

> [Socialist] freedoms can exist and develop only when, under the leadership of the party, we educate and guide the vast ranks of the masses of people by making use of the communist world view and view of life, when we overcome the individualism, departmentalism and bourgeois view of democracy and freedom that still exist in the thinking of some people, when we establish communist morals and customs.

The Tutelage Constitution spoke of education in the Three People's Principles, and the 1946 constitution of the responsibility of educators to inculcate patriotism and civic morality. In the 1982 constitution moral training in selflessness was included as a task of the state:

> Article 24. . . . The state advocates the civic virtues of love for the motherland, for the people, for labor, for science and for socialism; it educates the people in patriotism, collectivism, internationalism and communism and in dialectical and historical materialism; it combats capitalist, feudalist and other decadent ideas.

Finally, the concept of higher interests helps clarify why Chinese constitutions since the founding of the republic have recognized popular sovereignty in principle but have not contained provisions to enable citizens actually to influence government personnel or policy. In both Guomindang and Chinese communist theory the ruling party is the representative of the nation or the vanguard of the progressive classes. It has no interests of its own and rules solely in the interests of the nation and the people. It follows that rule by the party's leaders is rule in the people's interests and by definition democratic. A commentary on the 1982 constitution explained:

> In socialist countries, as the people are the masters of the country and the government is the people's government, the subject and object of management are consistent with each other. In other words, the masses of the people are simultaneously conductors and objects of state management. This determines that in the socialist state administrative management bears the nature of a democracy.

In this conception, democracy is a matter of the interests rule serves rather than of procedures for selecting rulers; procedural guarantees of democracy are relatively unimportant. Mao once remarked, "I don't trust elections. . . . I was elected from Peking [to the NPC], but many people have never even seen me! If they haven't seen me, how can they vote for me? They've just heard my name." Mao's point was that he represented the people not because he was elected by them but because he stood for their interests. Chinese analysts argue that the procedural freedom of bourgeois democratic systems is illusory: it allows individual workers and farmers to speak, vote, and lobby without restraint, but in the end serves the interests of the bourgeoisie. Because socialist democracy is based on public ownership of the means of production, it serves the people's true interests by definition. "It may not appear as colorful in form as bourgeois democracy, but it is the most extensive and substantial democracy in mankind's history."

As applied to freedom of speech, for example, this means that the people have such freedom by virtue of the fact that the Communist Party controls the press.

> Is it not freedom of speech when several hundred newspapers and nearly a thousand magazines unfold contentions and debates on numerous major problems of theory and practice, such as the criterion of truth, the purpose of production, autonomy for enterprises, distribution according to labor, democracy and the legal system, the educational system, literary and art creation, the meaning of life, and so forth? Is it not freedom of speech when the masses of cadres and people, through letters and visits and through newspapers, magazines, television broadcasts and other media, are criticizing the shortcomings and mistakes of party and government organizations at all levels and their workers and putting forward suggestions on work in various fields? . . . Why is it that some people turn a blind eye to all this or write this off as not being a manifestation of freedom of speech? The problem lies in their having a totally different understanding of what is, after all, freedom of speech. Some people think that so-called freedom of speech means "speaking without any fear," speaking without any restraint, saying reactionary things without being criticized, and saying counterrevolutionary things without being punished by law. True, there is no such "freedom of speech" in our country, nor can it be allowed to exist.

✻   ✻   ✻

Despite their lack of esteem for assertive individualism, the writers of Chinese constitutions included rights prominently in every constitution. As we have seen, their purpose was not to protect the individual against the state, but to enable the individual to function more effectively to strengthen the state. This idea of rights as means to a healthy political order was new in China, but it drew on traditional concepts to make sense. Classical Confucianism stressed the charisma of the emperor and his officials as the chief means of taming unruly nature and a disorderly populace. Any weakening of imperial authority had been seen as an invitation to tax evasion, banditry, natural disaster, and rebellion. But late Qing reformers like Liang Qichao observed that Western kings and presidents not only survived the individualism of their citizens, but seemed to channel these energies to the uses of the state. To explain how this was possible, Liang and his colleagues drew on an early Confucian dictum, "The people are the basis of the state."

This line appeared in the *Book of Documents* and had been elaborated by Confucius' disciple Mencius. When Mencius was advising kings, China consisted of several weak, thinly populated states whose feuding rulers were each trying to unify the country and become emperor. Population was the key resource for making war, but the ruler had to be skillful in husbanding this resource. When King Hui of Liang complained to Mencius that even though he gave out relief grain in bad years, people did not come to his country from neighboring kingdoms, Mencius answered that relief was not enough. The ruler must consistently subordinate war-making to the needs of agriculture, fishery, forestry, silk-raising, animal husbandry, and moral training. Then "persons of seventy will wear silk and eat meat and the common people will suffer from neither hunger nor cold. For the ruler of such a state not to become emperor is unheard of." Rulers who squeezed their people to raise and support large armies thus defeated their own purposes, for the people would look on the invader as a savior. "When . . . the inhabitants meet the invading army with flagons of drink and baskets of food," Mencius warned King Xuan of Qi, "there can be only one reason: they see in the invasion a chance of escape from flood and fire."

Mencius therefore advised rulers to choose ministers who would serve the people's interests and to punish those the people disliked. In a well-ruled kingdom, he said, when the king has someone put to death, it is said that "the people killed him." Even a ruler was dispensable if he was not a good one. A certain King Wu who had come to power by killing his predecessor, Zhou, was defended by Mencius against the charge of regicide on the grounds that Zhou had not been a true king but a mere "robber and ruffian": "I have heard of the cutting off of the fellow Zhou, not of the putting to death of the sovereign [Zhou]." Given that he accepted the institution of kingship, Mencius's advice to kings seemed paradoxical: "It is the people who should be valued, the gods second and the ruler last." But this did not mean that the prosperity of the people was an end in itself. The point was that princes would fall if they displeased the gods and gods would be abandoned if they failed to produce good harvests, but the people could not be changed. The king who would become the son of heaven had to win the people first.

Mencius' idea of the people as a resource had been elaborated by later thinkers, who in turn provided the basis for the late-nineteenth-century reformers' interpretation. Among the most influential figures in this line of transmission were the Qing thinkers loosely referred to as the "statecraft school," ranging from Gu Yanwu in the early part of the Qing dynasty to Feng Guifen and others in the mid-nineteenth century. They suggested reforms in the overcentralized bureaucratic system to enable local landowners and literati to play a more active, independent role in government. They claimed that local rule would lead to greater prosperity and security and thus help strengthen the dynasty. It was against the background of such ideas that the late Qing reformers forged their interpretation of modern democracy.

As suggested in Chapter 3, the reformers argued that Western democracies were strong because they enabled the ruler fully to use the people's energy and wisdom. In the new, Darwinian world of competition among nations and races, China could no longer afford to use the people as merely a passive base for the ruler, but must mobilize them as an active source of strength. If the ruler binds and represses the people in the exercise of their natural faculties, they are prevented from contributing their full strength to the state. Kang Youwei summed up these points in a memorial to the emperor in 1898:

> The reason countries East and West are strong is invariably because they have established constitutions and opened parliaments. In parliament the ruler and the people consult together on the affairs of state. . . . The ruler and the millions of citizens are joined together in one body. How can the country not be strong?

This argument became the basis for the Qing court's promulgation of the Principles of the Constitution.

The interpretation of the strength of Western democracies in the conceptual language of this tradition—called *minben,* "people-as-the-basis"—entailed a radical extension of its original idea. The people's only claim in the Mencian conception of government was for welfare, and even this was not a right they could demand but a responsibility the ruler was urged to shoulder for both moral and prudential reasons. The people were seen as a resource, most productive when least abused. People-as-the-basis had never meant people's rights (*minquan*) or people's rule (*minzhu,* "democracy"). But interpreting the classics to meet new needs was itself a long-standing tradition of Chinese thought. By analyzing Western democracies through the prism of *minben* ideas, nineteenth-century thinkers explained to themselves how individual rights could be a means to state power. The modern *minben* thinkers, like their Confucian predecessors, addressed their counsel to the rulers rather than the people. They treated political rights as something the ruler should grant rather than recognize. They stressed the advantages of political democracy for the state rather than for citizens. They valued political rights for what they enabled citizens to contribute to the state rather than for what they enabled them to protect for themselves.

What the citizen could contribute was valued by modern Chinese thinkers to an almost mystical degree. Liang Qichao's image of a constitutional state was "ten thousand eyes with one sight, ten thousand ears with one hearing, ten thousand powers with only one purpose of life. . . . When mind touches mind, when power is linked to power, cog to cog, strand around strand, and ten thousand roads meet in one center, this will be a state." Sun Yat-sen wrote, "Building a new state is like building a new steamship. . . . [I]f we install high-powered machinery, the vessel will have a high rate of speed, will be able to carry heavy freight, and will bring in large profits." Mao said,

"The masses' tide of enthusiasm is like atomic energy." Hua Guofeng declared to the National People's Congress in 1979 that "Without a high degree of political democracy, without the pooling of the wisdom and efforts of the masses on the basis of such democracy, . . . there can be . . . no four modernizations." In short, democracy was seen as a highly efficacious means of tapping the vast energies latent in the masses to propel the country out of backwardness and into a position of world power fitting for a nation with rich natural resources and an enormous population. The enthusiasm for democracy of most twentieth-century Chinese political thinkers and leaders has been no less real or eager than that of most American thinkers and leaders. Only their vision of its purposes has been different.

This conception of the benefits of democracy provides a further explanation for many characteristics of the Chinese constitutional tradition. If the purpose of granting rights is to elicit the individual's contribution to the nation, then it makes sense that the exercise of rights should be limited, both by law and by the citizen's morals, to actions that are constructive. Since it is the state that grants rights and that channels the energies that democracy releases, it is the state that can best determine where the boundaries of constructive action lie. The use of rights for self-seeking purposes cannot be part of their legitimate purpose, and may even be damaging if it undermines the ability of the state to channel citizens' energies in a unified direction.

Moreover, the *minben* tradition helps explain the preoccupation of Chinese constitution writers with providing rights of supervising, correcting, and appealing against the bureaucracy while overlooking judicial review or other channels for appeal against the state as such. The notion of people-as-basis reinforced the idea of a harmony of interests between people and ruler (or the ruling party) in a legitimate state. While, however, the relation between the citizen and a legitimate ruler could not be fundamentally antagonistic or adversarial, that between the citizen and particular bureaucrats could be. Solidarity between ruler and people was not threatened and was even enhanced by admitting that blundering or corrupt bureaucrats might come between them. Since democracy universally involved rights to complain, remonstrate, appeal, and petition, it made more sense in the Chinese tradition to direct these activities against particular bureaucrats than against the ruler or ruling party itself.

Finally, the *minben* tradition tends to reinforce the standard Marxist-Leninist view that political rights are no more important, and possibly less important, than socioeconomic welfare rights. In the Mencian tradition welfare is the state's chief obligation to the people, and even it is subordinate to higher goals—in Mencius' time uniting the empire, in modern times assuring the survival of the nation and the building of socialism. Every Chinese constitution since 1931 contains an extensive list of welfare rights—rights to work, vocational training, rest, social insurance and assistance, public health facilities, retirement, education, and so on. In the Chinese constitutional tradition these are not second-order goals of government to be striven for on the premise that political rights are guaranteed, as the American tradition suggests. They are among the highest goals of the state, among the ends to which political rights are a means. Political rights must be justified, at least in part, by their utility in achieving these higher goals.

The claim that rights have such utility has been the chief argument for their expansion put forward by late Qing reformers, anti-Guomindang civil libertarians, and PRC reformers and democracy activists. As with so many other Western ideas, the first writer to introduce utilitarianism to a Chinese audience seems to have been Liang Qichao, in his 1902 article "The Doctrine of Bentham, Master of Utilitarianism." The point of utilitarianism, Liang contended, was not to encourage selfish hedonism but to help individuals see how their "pleasure and profit" (utility) are tied up with the welfare of the collective. For the basic principle of the utilitarian philosophy is "the greatest happiness of the greatest number." This principle shows that "the interests of the collectivity have no separate existence apart from the interests of the constituent individuals; hence, Bentham makes the argument that public and private interest are one and the same." In this way Liang detached Bentham's utilitarianism from its native purpose as a standard by which to judge legislation's benefit to individuals and imposed a collectivist purpose more in keeping with Chinese preoccupations.

Liang's interpretation was hardly idiosyncratic. The Chinese translation of Mill's *On Liberty* that Yan Fu brought out the following year contained the same shift of emphasis. Where Mill speaks of the development of individuality as an end in itself, Yan says that the development of strong personalities will strengthen the state. When Mill says that the individual should be allowed to do what he likes unless the interests of others are affected, Yan's translation implies that too much government interference will stifle civic virtue. Benjamin Schwartz summarizes, "If liberty of the individual is often treated in Mill as an end in itself, in Yan Fu it becomes a means to the advancement of 'the people's virtue and intellect,' and beyond this to the purposes of the state."

Under the Guomindang a utilitarian argument for rights was presented by Luo Longji (1896–1965), a Western-trained professor who was probably modern China's best-known rights theorist (and ultimately a prominent victim of the Anti-Rightist campaign of 1957). In his 1929 essay "On Human Rights," Luo defined human rights as "whatever conditions are necessary to be human, [i.e.,] (1) to support life; (2) to develop individuality and cultivate personality; (3) to attain the goal of the greatest happiness of the greatest number of the group." Freedom of speech, for example, he defended as enabling people to contribute more fully to the welfare of society. Luo said that as human society advanced, more and more rights became necessary. The original European and American conception had been rather narrow, but "now—in 1929—in China" the people were demanding thirty-five rights. These included not only such classic items as popular sovereignty, free speech, and equality before the law but many specific demands pointedly relevant to liberalizing the Guomindang regime: for example, that military officers should not hold concurrent civilian government positions, that government bureaucrats should either be elected or be chosen by competitive public examination, that the tax burden should be progressive, and that government finances should be public.

In authoritarian settings Liang Qichao or Luo Longji could use the concept of social utility to argue for a growing list of rights to meet new needs of the time. It would have been more difficult to make the same case on natural-rights grounds to a Chinese audience concerned about national survival, insofar as natural rights imply a restriction on government rather than an aid to it. But the weakness of social-utility arguments lay in the fact that the authorities could so easily meet the liberals on the same ground, taking over their assumptions and using them to argue that rights must be narrowed rather than expanded for the public good. Indeed, in the crisis-ridden decades after 1895 not only the authorities but increasing numbers of intellectuals were inclined to see the greatest good of the greatest number as identical with anything that would strengthen the disastrously weak state. Liang himself, as we have seen, converted to an authoritarian position for this reason in 1905. Sun Yat-sen explained in lectures in 1924:

> Europeans rebelled and fought for liberty because they had too little liberty. But we, because we have too much liberty without any unity and resisting power, because we have become a sheet of loose sand and so have been invaded by foreign imperialism . . . , must break down individual liberty and become pressed together into an unyielding body like the firm rock which is formed by the addition of cement to sand.

Under the pressure of Japanese invasion and political disorder in the 1930s, the superior utility of dictatorship seemed obvious even to former liberals. The political scientist Qian Duansheng wrote in 1934:

> [S]ince dictatorship is really able to advance the welfare of the majority (which is almost all the people), then one cannot, because of the suppression of the freedoms of the minority, insist on maintaining a democracy which is not the equal of dictatorship in planning benefits.

One of the few Chinese intellectuals to retain his faith in democracy in the 1930s, Hu Shi, was reduced to arguing for what he called "kindergarten democracy"—the exercise of a few simple democratic rights by the people, which would actually strengthen the state, he said, by encouraging more public affection for government.

With Marxism came a narrower definition of whose interests were to be the standard of utility: those of the proletariat and its allies. But the principle remained the same: "All political rights, including freedom of speech, must serve the ruling class and protect the economic foundation of the society." As *Red Flag* pointed out, "Democracy, like centralism, dictatorship and other political forms, is a means subordinate to the economic base. The socialist economic base determines that we must uphold the socialist democratic system, and if this democratic system does not suit the economic base, it must be reformed and improved step by step." When the party adopted economic development as its goal the Xinhua news agency asserted, "In the final analysis, the result of democracy should be measured by whether it benefits or harms our modernization program." When the Politburo determined that the right of free speech should be limited by the "four basic principles," Shanghai radio declared, "In discussing democracy we must take the people's interests as the boundary line and should not break the bounds to follow the path of evil." In attacking the democracy movement Hu Qiaomu warned, "Our society is not a park [like Hyde Park], where everyone can voice his opinion and when everyone is finished no harm has been done, no flowers or trees have been injured, and everyone leaves the park and goes home." Ideas were to be judged by their consequences. The power of deciding what degree of political freedom would serve the socialist system naturally lay with the authorities.

Throughout the century, what most decisively turned the idea of social utility into a support for authoritarianism was the widespread perception that China was backward. Whether social utility could best be served by liberal or authoritarian institutions depended for most Chinese thinkers on their evaluation of the state of the people's culture. Under the conditions of this century, few of China's rulers have believed for long that the Chinese people were ready for democracy. Chiang Kai-shek defended tutelary rule on the basis of China's backwardness. In 1980 Deng Xiaoping echoed Sun Yat-sen in calling China a "sheet of loose sand" that needed authority to stay together. The party leaders referred to cultural "remnants of feudalism" to explain the slow development of Chinese democracy:

> We have been building socialism in a country where feudal society prevailed for more than 2,000 years and where semifeudal and semicolonial society existed for more than 100 years. . . . The feudal system of political domination and exploitation can be overthrown by violent means, but feudalistic ideology, traditions, and habits cannot be solved in this manner. Their solution is more complicated and difficult and will take a long time.

The problem of feudal remnants, the party claimed, did not alter the superiority of proletarian democracy over bourgeois democracy, but it meant that proletarian democracy could only be realized gradually:

> Proletarian democracy is history's highest form of democracy, but this does not mean that it can be put into practice immediately after the victory of the revolution. . . . After thirty years of national construction our productive power is still low and our culture is still comparatively backward. So we still can only manage the state through the proletariat's advanced stratum [the party]. This shows the incompleteness of proletarian democracy.

If the backwardness argument was used by rulers to justify the restriction of rights, for a majority of reformers and liberals it mandated a softening of political demands in favor of long-term cultural, educational, and social change—a virtual flight from politics to the safer, traditionally sanctioned realm of social education. Just as the disillusioned Liang Qichao wrote in 1903 that his countrymen did not possess a single one of the qualifications necessary for citizens of a republic and would have to undergo a slow process of education in democratic virtues, so later in the century rural reconstructionists like Y. C. James Yen and Liang Shuming devoted themselves to solving the problems of peasant literacy and livelihood in order to prepare the masses to exercise democracy. In one way or another, this was the mission most twentieth-century Chinese intellectuals set for themselves—to change culture before trying to change politics. Given the backwardness of the people, it was necessary to accept the government's authority, and to work from within the system for slow change, lest disorder ensue. The democracy activists belonged to this tradition of non-adversarial reformism. They made it their policy not to conspire and not to rebel, but instead, by means of posters and publications, to try to change public opinion and remake popular culture. For them as for their predecessors, establishing democracy remained a matter of exerting moral pressure on the rulers while trying to educate the people—both being functions of propaganda.

7

THE RISE OF
PROPAGANDA

"Constitutional government," wrote Liang Qichao in 1910 during the abortive preparations for enactment of a Qing constitution, "is in essence government by public opinion. All the discussions and actions of [legislative organs at various levels] are, without exception, the reflection of public opinion." Seeing constitutionalism as a way of tapping the energies of the people to strengthen the state, Liang naturally believed that the people must be awakened to politics in order to play their new role. But he warned that the mere expression of people's ideas would not make for a public opinion valuable to the state.

> What will be of value is a healthy public opinion, . . . an amalgam of the views of the majority that is at once unified and continuous. If it isn't the amalgam of the views of the majority, it can't be called public opinion; and if it isn't unified and continuous, it can't be called healthy.

Public opinion, then, should not be an arena of conflict among partial views, but a stable consensus regarding the nature of the common good.

Such a constructive public mind would have the virtues of knowledgeability, sincerity, honesty, public-spiritedness, and temperateness, Liang stated; and virtues like these would not emerge by themselves. "If public opinion is to possess these five virtues, those of us who create public opinion must first strive to exercise them ourselves and must then urge them on our countrymen. Although public opinion arises from many sources, the most powerful among the organs that produce it are newspapers." Newspapers, Liang urged in conclusion, must shape the public mind by performing "eight duties": remonstration, guidance, encouragement, repetition, taking the large view, concentrating on main themes, propagating knowledge, and penetrating society. These were the tasks that others later in the century would sum up in the term "propaganda."

Politicians and intellectuals who turned to propaganda as the way to promote political change drew upon a long tradition. "From Heaven the people receive their potentially good nature," wrote one of the early Confucians, "and from the king the education which completes it." Based on their faith in the natural harmony of people in society, both imperial rulers and village gentry had long used indoctrination as one of their chief methods of social control. The examination system encouraged the elite to spend years mastering the Confucian classics. Village schools and clan temples reinforced the code of social obligation by their teachings and rituals. To strengthen the moral training of the common people, the Kangxi emperor in 1670 promulgated a *Sacred Edict* of sixteen maxims and ordered local officials to lecture on them twice a month. All forms of popular culture, including storytellers' manuals, reading primers, popular almanacs, songs, and village operas, were infused with moral lessons.

Traditional methods of moral indoctrination sought to train but not to mobilize the people; to maintain but not to remake society. In the democratic era the demands made on propaganda would increase. Leaders would use it not only to bring out people's inherent social natures but to make them perceive and act on the overriding common interests they shared with the state. Intellectuals would use it to transform a culture considered too backward for the needs of the times. The media would become increasingly specialized and complicated, and would demand more and more of the citizen's attention. They would serve as a central force in the creation of Chinese democracy in the early decades of the century, and as a central institution in its daily functioning in the years after 1949. For Chinese citizens, participating in a democracy came to mean living in an environment dominated by propaganda.

Western missionaries started the transition from traditional indoctrination to modern propaganda in the early nineteenth century, when they experimented with the use of periodicals as instruments of proselytization. Traditional Chinese periodicals were few in type and number, and served narrow functions. A number of privately published Peking gazettes copied central government memorials and edicts for the information of officials throughout the empire. Similar local gazettes emanated from provincial capitals. In the cities, popular newssheets came out irregularly whenever there was a fire, earthquake, riot, or sensational trial to report. Local guilds published price circulars. But the missionaries, who were banned from traveling in China's interior until the treaty signed at the end of the Opium War began to force open China's doors, decided to try to use magazines in place of sermons to win converts. A Protestant named William Milne pioneered with *A General Monthly Record*, published from 1815 to 1828 in Malaya for distribution inside China.

The strategy behind this undertaking was the classic one for propaganda in any culture. "To promote Christianity," Milne wrote, "was to be [the magazine's] primary object; other things, though they were to be treated in subordination to this, were not to be overlooked. Knowledge and science are the hand-maids of religion, and may become the auxiliaries of virtue." The religious message was thus embedded in more general content, which would at once win readers and show that Christianity was part of a civilization that had much to offer.

None of the early missionary periodicals was widely read in China. Milne's *Monthly Record* had a circulation of only two thousand, including Chinese in Southeast Asia. But the idea of proselytizing through publications sowed seeds in the minds of some important Chinese. One of the leaders of the mid-nineteenth-century Taiping revolutionary movement, Hong Rengan, had worked under the missionary James Legge in Hong Kong at the time when Legge was publishing a Chinese magazine. In 1859, Hong proposed that the revolutionaries establish newspapers to circulate in the areas they had taken over:

> Newspapers will be useful in educating people to obey the laws, to distinguish between good and bad, to develop a moral sense, and to be loyal to sovereign and parents. When education is carried out the law is clear; when the law is clear the people know their duty to the sovereign—so much so that people will supervise one another, talent and virtue will flourish, and popular morals will constantly improve.

This was probably the first proposal by a Chinese to use modern instruments of propaganda to perform the traditional function of moral indoctrination.

Some years later the government itself began to use periodicals to promote adherence to its policies. Traditionally, private entrepreneurs had been allowed to publish collections of official documents so long as the materials were printed without deletions or editorial comment. As late as 1851 the court rejected a proposal that it sponsor an official gazette on the grounds that bureaucrats with a need to know would receive their orders by official post. But in 1896, in the aftermath of the defeat by Japan, the agency in charge of foreign affairs was allowed to print two journals carrying selected memorials and edicts as well as translations of foreign documents calculated to promote reformist ideas among officials. After the failure of the 1898 reforms the two journals were closed; but when reformism revived after the Boxer debacle, new ones emerged. A gazette founded in 1901 stated in its inaugural issue:

> There is certainly no small number of private papers which are broad and penetrating in their knowledge and views and suitable for awakening the

unenlightened; but among them there are also those with erroneous, un-balanced theories which may mislead ignorant people and cause them to lose their sense of right and wrong. Only by relying on an official newspaper can we find a way to communicate between above and below and only in this way can we make everyone realize that new policies and the study of new things cannot be delayed if we are to set our nation on a firm foundation.

Soon there were many provincial and central government gazettes. In 1906, when the decision was made to move toward constitutional government, an official publication called *Political Gazette* was established "to cause gentry and people clearly and fully to understand government affairs, so as to serve as a basis for the preparation for constitutionalism."

Although the gazettes' sponsors defended them as merely a new way to discharge the traditional function of educating the people in their duty of obedience, they had actually gone beyond this conception. The Qing reformers believed that government must move the people, meaning mostly the literati, beyond passive compliance to active cooperation with its pursuit of wealth and power. To do this it must provide more information about the substance of policy and the reasons for it. A stream of supporting documentation, much of it bearing the prestige of translation from foreign languages, aimed to create a constituency for reform programs in the bureaucracy and among the gentry. The growing idea of government as public business was expressed in the last year of the dynasty by the decision to have new laws and regulations take effect as of the date of publication in the *Cabinet Gazette*, as the chief government gazette was now called.

Until 1895 the main line of development of the nongovernmental press was commercial rather than political. Foreigners congregating in the treaty ports demonstrated the commercial possibilities of the press with a series of English-language papers published on Chinese soil, starting with *The Canton Review*, a biweekly launched in 1827. The first daily paper in the Chinese language was the *Chinese and Foreign News*, published in Hong Kong beginning in 1860. The Chinese-language papers of the late nineteenth century concentrated on news of trade, for their potential readers were mainly Chinese businessmen. The Shanghai *New Paper* stated in its inaugural issue in 1861:

In a place like Shanghai people from all over are mixed together. They have problems doing business, such as the inability to understand one another's dialects and the failure to hear about news. By glancing at this *New Paper*, you can learn that a certain cargo is to be sold on a certain day, and you can personally go to inspect the cargo and negotiate the price. You will thus avoid the endless delay and procrastination of agents and can avoid making a bad purchase on speculation.

The press evolved new techniques to serve the interests of the business audience. The *New Paper* began using headlines in lieu of what had previously been unchanging section titles. The *Shanghai Report* introduced poems and literary essays, although it did not pay the authors. It offered a lower price per copy for bulk orders and encouraged people outside Shanghai to subscribe by post. The Shanghai *News* featured exclusive Chinese translations of Reuters dispatches, published the same day they were printed in the English-language parent newspaper. Other papers that printed the dispatches were unable to use them until the next day. Editors developed a new, plain writing style and tried to improve layout and punctuation so that readers could scan more easily. As the audience grew in the twentieth century, profitable papers were established to serve special audiences. The Shanghai *Times* carved out a readership of young people by stressing sports news, gossip, and attractive layouts and printing; the Shanghai *Upright* made a name by covering the news in brief tabloid form. But papers like *Shanghai Report*, which continued to serve the broad business audience, remained the most successful.

The business-oriented papers avoided political advocacy or controversy. They had no wish to offend readers of varying persuasions or to invite government harassment such as denial of post office and telegraph privileges. "When you open one of these papers," Liang Qichao complained in 1901,

the page is clogged with words like "Bureaucratic Bustle in Shanghai," "Official's Spouse Coming South," . . . "Robbery Plan Fails," . . . "Willing to Die for Love." All the articles are alike. . . . As for the editorials, if it isn't "An Examination of How Western Learning Originated in China," then it's "China Should Urgently Plan for Wealth and Power." They plagiarize from one another over and over. When you read them you are only afraid of falling asleep.

But the commercial audience required increasing amounts of political news as China's crisis deepened. In 1882, the *Shanghai Report* used the newly built Tianjin-Shanghai telegraph to publish the first wire dispatch in Chinese journalism. In 1884 it raised circulation with on-the-scene coverage of the French naval attack on Ningbo. Major papers competed to carry bulletins from around the country, each headlined with heavy type and emphasized with circular punctuation marks running down the side of the column next to each word. Less important events were covered by mail dispatches and press excerpts from other cities.

The circulation of the commercial papers shot up to new highs in the late 1890s—that of the Shanghai *News*, for example, from 5,000 in 1895 to 12,000, largest in the nation, in 1899. China's defeat in the war with Japan and the signing of the Treaty of Shimonoseki—which granted Japan a two-hundred-million-tael indemnity, the right to open new treaty ports and establish factories and businesses in China, and control over Formosa and the Liaodong Peninsula—had persuaded many Chinese that their nation was in literal danger of extinction and stimulated their appetite for news and political discussion. The experience of a young man named Bao Tianxiao, who later became a journalist himself, was typical:

> Our country and Japan were warring over Korea, and the Shanghai newspapers carried news about it day after day. Previously young Chinese readers paid no attention to current events, but now we were shaken. I often went out and got a Shanghai newspaper to read, and, however incompletely, began to understand current events and to discuss them, and I accounted myself as pro-reform. . . . [After the loss of the war and the establishment of a Japanese concession in Bao's hometown,] most educated people, who had never before discussed national affairs, wanted to discuss them: why are others stronger than we are, and why are we weaker?

This was the question still being asked by Huang Xiang and other Democracy Wall activists eighty years later, the obsessive theme of Chinese politics throughout the century.

The defeat suffered at Japan's hands not only brought the issue of national weakness to the attention of a wider public, it started the process of political mobilization that would enlarge this public, with the mobilizers hoping that popular participation in politics would be the key to ending China's weakness. The war gave rise to a kind of newspaper new in China— the political journal, devoted largely to essays of political dispute and advocacy. The first was Liang Qichao's *Chinese and Foreign News*, published for a few months in Peking in 1895. Avoiding editorial polemic, it limited itself to retailing proreform memorials and edicts and translating foreign materials supportive of reform thinking. Unlike contemporary commercial papers, it looked like a gazette—six inches high and three inches wide, bound in Chinese-book form in yellow covers. In fact, the magazine was printed in the shop of one of the gazette companies and distributed free to some three thousand of its subscribers.

The reform press soon became an alternative channel of expression for younger literati who could not gain access to the emperor through the "road for speech." When, in 1897, Kang Youwei could not find a sponsor to forward a reform petition for him to the court, he had the document published in a Shanghai newspaper. As the reformers evolved from a literati faction in capital politics to a pressure group, they sought to promote change by creating something new in China—public opinion.

The new political press soon surpassed the commercial press in numbers, circulation, and liveliness. One historian of journalism identified 216 newspapers and 122 magazines that were pubished in the few years after 1894. Many of them were short-lived, so that in 1901, for example, Liang Qichao counted only 80 newspapers and 44 magazines being published—still a considerable increase over the dozen or so journals of the early 1890s. While many journals had circulations of only a few hundred, the more popular ones broke records. Liang's own *News of the Times,* published in Shanghai, achieved an unprecedented circulation of 12,000 in 1896. A decade later his *New Citizen,* published in Tokyo but read largely in China, reached a claimed circulation of 14,000.

In the optimistic period before the failure of the 1898 reforms, Liang and his colleagues tried to minimize the differences in function between their publications and the gazettes approved by the government. "Newspapers are beneficial to the state," Liang argued in 1896, because they increase solidarity between "above and below" and enable both people and government to be better informed about commerce, technology, foreign affairs, and other topics important to strengthening the state. But in his first essay written in Japan, "Preface and Regulations of the *China Discussion,*" Liang set down the aims of a new journal that would propagandize for reform from outside the country, now that the government had proscribed reformist publications at home. Service to the regime in power was no longer an aim of Liang's journalism, which from now on would appeal directly to the people to demand change, although still in the ultimate interest of the state.

By 1901, when *China Discussion* had published its hundredth issue, Liang had developed the idea that magazines and newspapers could be the leading force in the development of national culture. They exercise the freedoms of thought, speech, and publication, he argued, which drive civilization's progress; promote policies later adopted by governments; provide knowledge of new world ideas and trends; and cleanse citizens' minds of old ideas while introducing new ones. Politically, he claimed some time later, the press should be the supervisor rather than the handmaiden of government:

Government is entrusted by the people, is the people's servant. And newspapers represent the people in expressing public sentiment and speaking for the public. So a newspaper regards the government the way a father or elder brother regards a son or younger brother—teaching him when he does not understand and reprimanding him when he gets something wrong.

These statements suggest how far Chinese journalism had traveled, from a limited idea of the media as a source of business information and an instrument of indoctrination for obedience, to a modern idea of the press as a central institution in the functioning of a democratic polity.

In the first decade of the century, however, the Chinese press was far from being able to perform the functions Liang Qichao envisaged for it. One of the chief obstacles was the Chinese language itself. At the end of the Qing the predominant language of public documents and the press was the austere "Tongcheng style," named after the birthplace of the people who had promoted it in the eighteenth century. The Tongcheng masters themselves had been reacting against the ornate obscurities of the previously esteemed parallel prose called "Six Dynasties style." They said that writing should be clear and clean, with emphasis on substance rather than show. Like many of his generation, Liang had studied the Tongcheng anthology of prose models as a boy, and his early writings showed their influence. But after his flight to Japan he began to go beyond them toward a style that was more accessible, more rousing, and more modern. His "new-style prose" was a response to the needs of propaganda journalism for a style that could reach a larger audience. It became one of Liang's major contributions to modern Chinese culture.

The change in prose style began to be visible in Liang's earliest writings in Japan. Classical references, common in his essays before the 1898 reforms, were reduced to a minimum. In their place Liang began to employ foreign terms and allusions that would have been at once exotic and impressive to his audience—references to Mazzini, Napoleon, the trans-Siberian railway, brandy. The objective, reasoning tone characteristic of his pre-1898 policy briefs gave way to a tone of exhortation. Stately cadences were replaced by exciting rhythms. His essays offered a pressured flow of ideas and images connected less by logic than by feeling. As described by Chen Duxiu, an intellectual of the republican period, Liang's style created the impression of "flashing light and fleeting shadow."

Liang's prose in Japan showed changes in vocabulary, syntax, organization, and even punctuation—all aimed at making his writing more effective as propaganda. He was one of the first Chinese writers to make extensive use of Japanese terms—that is, Chinese-character compounds that either were coined by the Japanese or, though existing in ancient Chinese, were given their modern meanings in Japan. Liang employed these compounds not only for such relatively specialized terms as "culture," "history," "law," and "sovereignty" but also for everyday concepts like "hope" and "method." He could have chosen terms that were more familiar in Chinese prose for all these ideas, but he preferred the Japanese variants because their allusions, if any, to ancient Chinese were less well known to his readers, so that they could be used exclusively in their modern senses. Liang also began to free himself from classical grammar. In classical Chinese nearly every clause is grammatically self-sufficient, in the sense that it is possible to translate it by a separate English sentence (so translated, a passage would sound choppy and repetitive in English, though it is terse and balanced in Chinese). After arriving in Japan, Liang began to employ longer, more complex sentences reflecting the syntax of the foreign books he was reading in Japanese translation. He could express logical relationships more explicitly this way and so give fuller exposition to the foreign ideas he was introducing. At the same time, moving away from classical grammar brought his style closer to spoken Chinese, which is wordier and more flexible than the terse documentary style. Liang's foreign-influenced grammar was thus, ironically, more easily understood by ordinary Chinese who had limited training in the classics. Around 1900, Liang started to use punctuation marks, paragraphing, and topic sentences—all foreign devices—to help his readers find their way. About a year later he brought in quotation marks, perhaps because he was quoting more frequently from foreigners and wanted to set off their statements. Soon he began to reproduce foreign names, book titles, and even whole phrases in roman type, and to use tables and charts both to present quantitative data and to organize parts of his argument. Increasingly he presented his argument in a series of numbered points.

All these features later became standard in modern Chinese writing. In many writers the effect was unfortunate—a kind of Europeanized formalism almost as hard for the average person to decipher as the prose of the Six Dynasties style. The critic Qu Qiubai complained in 1932 about the "new classical style" that the May Fourth movement had given rise to: "It completely ignores the habits of spoken Chinese and adopts bits of grammar from classical Chinese, from European languages, from Japanese, and turns it all into a kind of so-called vernacular which you can't even read; even if you can, you can't make any sense of it." Later, Mao would complain about "party eight-legged essays" that combined Marxist jargon and Germanic syntax in a high-flown bureaucratese that the masses could not follow. But no such flaws affected the new writing as practiced by Liang himself. As he wrote truthfully of his own prose, "His style had a clear structure and the flow of his pen was often passionate, with a rare magical kind of power for the reader." The diplomat Huang Zunxian said, "It alarms and moves people, each word like a thousand precious coins. In a style no one can match you say what everyone thinks, so that even men of stone or iron must be moved. Since ancient times, the power of the word has never been so great." And Hu Shi testified, "In a traditional society undergoing great disruption, Liang's free new style had an immense appeal."

The loosening of style by Liang and others pointed toward vernacularization—the abandonment of all classical syntax to write in the grammar and vocabulary of the spoken language. Fiction had been written in the vernacular for centuries, but a high level of literacy was needed to understand these books, which were intended to entertain the elite rather than to instruct the masses. Now a number of Liang's contemporaries proposed writing textbooks, technical manuals, and newspapers in a level of vernacular simple enough for barely educated common people to understand. In a suggestion typical of the sort being made at the time, Liang even proposed writing simple texts with a very small number of characters, each one standing not for a word as it usually would, but for a sound—a sort of quasi-alphabetic use of Chinese ideographs. None of Liang's contemporaries went so far as to suggest that serious writing should be in the vernacular, a suggestion which was made twenty years later by Hu Shi and came then to be widely accepted. But Liang and his colleagues started a movement against excessive archaism even in writing for the highly literate portion of the public. Criticizing Yan Fu's translations, Liang wrote, "In his style he is too much concerned with profundity and elegance. . . . The object of translation is to spread civilized ideas among the people, not to make a useless reputation."

Besides his pioneering use of the periodical press and his adaptation of language to the needs of political journalism, Liang was the first to see the modern propaganda potential of the traditional media. In an early essay, "A Comprehensive Discussion of Reform," he advocated reforming the primers used in elementary education. Instead of teaching Chinese characters through rote memorization of the classics, he said, teachers should use new-style vocabularies, grammars, dictionaries, and storybooks written in the vernacular and imbued with modern knowledge and values. Instead of punishing students for humming, as Chinese schoolmasters traditionally did, they should take advantage of students' love of music to teach songs about history, astronomy, geography, and physics. Songs promoting patriotism could "renovate the people, mobilize talent, and guarantee the strength of the state."

Believing that an assertive, rights-conscious culture was the key to national survival, Liang paid special attention to reforming those media that he thought had the deepest influence on people's values—music, drama, poetry, and fiction. In *The New Citizen*, Liang ran a regular column on music, poetry, and Chinese opera called "Talks on Poetry from the Ice-Drinker's Studio." In Prussia and France, he said there, the national anthems stirred patriotism. Chinese must write some patriotic poems and set them to martial music. Again, he noted that traditional operas had had a deep influence on public mores, but the ideas they conveyed were backward. China needed "music reform," and this was already beginning with the admission of a Chinese student to a Tokyo music school. In his own Datong School in Yokohama, Liang had the students perform a new patriotic drama which, he said, "opens new territory for popular opera." Its first verse ran, "Tell the people that the countries of the world are in a struggle for survival." Liang himself wrote three unfinished operas, the first in Chinese to deal with contemporary themes. One was about the unification of Italy, intended as a model for Chinese patriotism. In poetry, Liang championed the so-called new poetry, recommending especially the work of his friend the ex-diplomat Huang Zunxian as "nourishment for the youth of our poetry revolutionary army." He praised Huang for employing modern references and idiomatic expressions in his verse, and for addressing contemporary political themes and praising militant nationalism.

Elsewhere Liang explored the political uses of fiction. In 1896 he said that simple works of fiction could be used instead of classical texts to teach reading and at the same time instill patriotic values. In 1897 he wrote, "The Japanese reforms [the Meiji Restoration] depended on the power of popular songs and fiction—for nothing is better than these for pleasantly training children and painlessly guiding the uneducated." In 1898, after his arrival in Japan, where political fiction was in vogue, Liang extended his analysis. Classics, orthodox histories, religious and legal writings influence only the literate minority, he argued, while fiction reaches everybody, if not in the written form then through tea-shop and marketplace storytellers. Fiction can change culture. The great European revolutions, he contended, all started with changes in public opinion triggered by fiction, and fiction continues to stimulate the progress of the advanced countries. He concluded that the reform movement should translate foreign political novels in order to impart their dynamic values to the Chinese.

In 1902, Liang presented his most profound analysis of fiction's impact as a tool of cultural renovation. In a famous essay, "On the Relationship Between Fiction and Democracy," he claimed that fiction has a unique power to "smoke," "soak," "prick," and "pull" the masses of humankind, and hence to determine whether a national culture is decadent or vigorous and whether democracy is possible or not. He charged that traditional Chinese fiction had taught people to be superstitious, mercenary, cowardly, untrustworthy, calculating, lustful, weak, and lawless. "Only by renovating a nation's fiction can you renovate its people," he said. Liang founded the pioneer New Fiction magazine and began work on his own political novel, The Future of New China, which he never finished.

Unlike later-developing countries, China in its first decades of political mobilization had no radios, TV sets, or newsreels to bring politics into the small towns and villages; politicians did not come into the countryside to electioneer, and the government did not put roads, electricity, and bus services into the villages as a way of building popular support. The quickening of late Qing political life was achieved to an extraordinary degree by the single medium whose development Liang Qichao had led, the political journal. In the years after 1895, to hold such a journal in one's hands was an intensely exciting experience for many Chinese who had never before considered national government a legitimate matter of concern, had never had the means to learn about it, and had never been summoned to form opinions about it. Bao Tianxiao recalled that the publication in 1896 of Liang's *News of the Times* "was like the explosion of a large bomb, which woke many people from their dreams. . . . It wasn't just that Liang's writing was good; it was also that what he said seemed to be just what we had stored in our hearts and wished to express ourselves." The writer Cao Juren recalls:

> *The New Citizen* was published in Tokyo, but its distribution was so wide that it reached into poverty-stricken villages and remote places. . . . It took a month to reach our family village, 400 *li* from Hangzhou, by post, yet my late father's thought and writing style were influenced by Liang Qichao; *The New Citizen* leaped over the "three gorges" [of the Yangtze River] and penetrated as far as Chungking and Chengdu, changing the perceptions of the gentry.

And the diplomat Huang Zunxian wrote to Liang:

> In the last half-year [during 1902] all forty or fifty newspapers in China have taken up the arguments you promote. Your phrases are plagiarized everywhere: in the terminology of new translations, the language of common gossip, the memorials of officials, the examination topics set by civil service examiners.

At the turn of the century the press was concentrated in Peking and the major treaty ports. Shanghai alone had the modern rotary machines essential for rapid production of a large number of copies of a newspaper, as well as access to the imported paper they required. On Chinese soil the police could close any journal and arrest its publisher, but their authority did not reach into the foreign concessions. Added protection could be gained by registering a paper in the name of a foreign citizen paid for the purpose. The big cities also commanded the transport and communication facilities needed to receive news and send out papers. Their cosmopolitan cultures attracted writers and readers. Besides the treaty ports, the biggest Chinese publications center of the late Qing was Tokyo, with its more than ten thousand students and exiled politicians publishing a score or more of journals.

The urban-centered press received wide circulation throughout the country, thanks partly to new roads and railroads, the growing and increasingly efficient foreign-managed Chinese post office, and a spreading network of bookstores, and partly to traditional letter-carrying firms and river paddleboats. Each of Liang Qichao's late-Qing magazines, even those that the government tried to prohibit from circulation, listed the names of scores of sales agencies in cities and county capitals throughout China. When Bao Tianxiao started his own magazine in Suzhou around the turn of the century, he induced general stores in local towns and markets to stock it by offering a 30 percent discount for bulk orders. A customs commissioner from one of the towns near Shanghai reported in 1891, "What in 1881 was the exception is now the rule in all good families in Chinkiang as well as in the interior—that is, for every intelligent adult to take a glance at the Chinese daily paper brought here from Shanghai." In a county seat in south China in 1902, recalled the politician and educator Zou Lu,

> a bookstore was established at a Confucian temple near our house. It not only had material of the reformers and modern Europe and America, but also bits and pieces of the rarely seen writings of the revolutionaries. I frequently went there to read. . . .

Hu Shi recalled students going home for vacation from school in Shanghai smuggling the banned *People's Journal* into the interior sewn into their pillows. Cities had long been cultural centers, but now a smaller number of them became foci of influence over a growing nationwide audience.

No one knows the size of the late-Qing periodicals audience, but there are several ways to arrive at an estimate, and they all point to roughly the same conclusion. First, fluctuating and unreliable tallies exist for numbers of periodicals published and for claimed per-periodical circulations. There were about 100 substantial periodicals being published at any given time in the last decade of the Qing, and on the average each published about 3000 copies per issue, for a national circulation of 300,000.

Post office statistics offer further help. In 1908, for example, the Imperial Post Office received nearly 36 million items of "newspapers and printed matter" for delivery. To translate this into a national circulation figure we must first separate the periodicals from other printed matter, then estimate how many copies were circulated outside post office channels, and finally divide the total number of copies by the average number of times each journal was published per year. The result will vary according to the estimates involved in the calculation. It will also vary year by year, since postal business changed rapidly as post offices were opened or closed, newspapers started or stopped, business shifted from native letter-carrying firms to the government post office, and political disturbances and economic cycles stimulated or depressed activity. But the 1908 figure can be used as an illustration. Newspapers constituted about 69 percent of printed matter, if we use the ratio characteristic of the 1920s when postal statistics first separated newspapers from other printed matter. Applying this to 1908's 36-million-plus printed-matter items we get about 25 million periodicals delivered through the mails. Anecdotal evidence suggests that no more than half of all newspapers went by post, the bulk being delivered or sold locally by delivery boys and vendors.

Then the total number of copies circulated in 1908 must have been something over 49 million. If we assume that daily publications contributed two-fifths of this annual flow and weekly, ten-day, and monthly publications one-fifth each, the weighted average periodicity was 166 issues per year. Divided into the estimated annual flow, that represents approximately 295,000 copies. This is not far from the 300,000 estimated on the basis of periodical circulation data.

But each copy had many readers. Newspapers and magazines were passed from person to thrifty person—or sold for a steadily diminishing price "until, too ragged to be longer legible, they are carefully burnt." The American journalist Agnes Smedley tells the story of the young Zhu De, later a top communist general, then a college student in Sichuan, finding a copy of the antigovernment *People's Journal* "which someone had slipped under his pillow in the dormitory. The paper had passed through so many hands that much of the print was obliterated. . . . Zhu read and reread the little sheet, then slipped it in the bed of another student." In 1904, when Bao Tianxiao was serving as a school principal in north China, the Shanghai *News* was received in the prefectural yamen, then after several days passed on to the school. An American reported even more extensive multiple readership, although this was in the 1920s and in the highly developed Yangtze Valley region:

> The daily paper first goes to the city people, and after they have read it, the paper is given the various country boat lines for distribution in country towns from which it is passed on to the villages. On occasions there are gatherings at which a good reader reads, in a very dignified manner, to an audience. A further method used for spreading news is that of posting the paper on a wall or board where passersby may read it.

One specialist estimates the per-copy readership of some late Qing periodicals at 10 to 20 persons.

If readership averaged 15 persons per copy, then the circulation figure of 300,000 suggests an audience on the order of 4.5 million. But some people may have read many periodicals, and others may have seen only an occasional copy. If we assume for the sake of discussion that the average periodical reader regularly read two periodicals, then we would have to divide our audience figure in half, to reach an estimated audience of 2.25 million. In fact, there must have been people who were able to read several periodicals regularly and others in remote towns and villages who could obtain a few copies a year. In any case the rough estimate for the total audience remains in the neighborhood of 2 to 4 million.

The plausibility of this figure can be checked against demographic information. China's population is estimated at 394 million in 1893 (excluding

Taiwan and Manchuria), of which the urban population was 6 percent, or 23.5 million. Roughly 63 percent were age sixteen or over, and slightly over one-half were men, so the urban adult male population was about 7.4 million. Evelyn Rawski has recently shown that literacy in late imperial China was more widespread than scholars used to think, especially among urban males. If one-quarter of them were occasional periodical readers, then the urban audience would have numbered about 1.85 million. A great many literates also lived in the countryside as landlords, teachers, students, and businessmen. If they formed an audience of roughly equal size to the urban one, the total readership would have numbered about 3.7 million, the same range suggested by other data.

Another benchmark can be derived from the size of the gentry, the landlord-official-literati class defined by ranks achieved in the government examination system. In his study *The Chinese Gentry*, the scholar Zhang Zhongli determined that there were about 1.4 million members of this class in the late nineteenth century, together with another 2 million or so "junior students" who had passed a preliminary examination. Not all of these 3.4 million highly literate men were necessarily interested in reading the new periodical press, but those who were not were probably replaced as readers by literate tradesmen, women, students who had not yet taken the preliminary examinations, and former students who had given up trying to pass them.

Even though the assumptions used to interpret each of these four kinds of evidence—circulation information, postal statistics, literate urban population, and gentry size—are speculative, the fact that each line of argument leads to the same rough audience size of 2 to 4 million tends to lend plausibility to the common result. It would be difficult, at least, to contend that the audience was less than one million or more than ten million. It was, then, about one percent of China's population in the last decade of the Qing. In about a decade, the new periodical press had created the largest, most far-flung audience in Chinese history. But the audience still consisted of a highly literate minority.

In succeeding decades the audience expanded rapidly. Elementary-school enrollments went from 1 or 2 million in the late Qing to 5 or 6 million in the early 1920s to 10 or more million in the 1930s. Middle-school enrollments increased in the same period from a few tens of thousands to half a million or more. Even if only one-third of the students who entered primary school each year went on to complete a substantial portion of the seven-year course, by 1940 the schools would have added roughly 13 million medium-literates to the population. And a middle-school education was no longer necessary to read all periodicals. There were now many papers for the working class. The Shanghai *Upright*, a popular tabloid of the 1930s, had three supplements aimed at different classes: the "Forest of Words" for "cultural circles," the "Fruit and Flower Mountain" for "upper and middle classes, the professions and commercial circles," and the "Little Teahouse" for "the ordinary working class." In Shanghai there were also a hundred or more "mosquito" tabloids that were sold for a few pennies on street corners, featuring gossip of politics and the entertainment world. Thirty-two of 58 working-class families studied by Olga Lang in Peiping in the 1930s included men who read newspapers. There were women readers in two families.

By the mid-1930s there were 910 newspapers published in China and perhaps as many as 900 magazines. Thirty years earlier the largest claimed circulation had been 20,000; now the big Shanghai papers claimed sales of 150,000 or more. Postal statistics confirm the curve of growth: mailed newspapers doubled every few years to a high of 235 million in 1936. We cannot conclude that the audience grew at exactly the same rate, since conditions such as the percentage of papers circulated by post, periodicity, and multiple readership may have changed. But the reading audience for newspapers alone in the 1930s has been estimated at 20 to 30 million.

Of the thousands of journals founded from 1895 to the 1940s, most were born to serve causes. Periodicals eschewing politics in favor of commerce, belles lettres, or humor were rare. "The individual is no longer an individual," wrote Lin Yutang in the 1930s,

> but an ardent servant of party and clique propaganda who takes orders telling him what to think and what to say. A shortness of temper—a bitterness of opinion—a lack of toleration and incapacity for taking the round view—cheap and self-deceiving patriotism—impatience to save the country with the desire to prevent everyone except oneself and one's own party from saving China. Writers today are more interested in bombastic nonsense than in self-knowledge, gentle understanding and sweetness and light.

After the late Qing no component of entertainment or belief—music, art, fiction, drama, language, religion, history, or clothing—would again be produced innocent of political intent.

Liang Qichao and his contemporaries had ushered China into the modern world of managed culture. The writer's contribution would now be measured not by fealty to the truth but by results. In Liang's words,

> Once a journalist has fixed on a goal, he should press it with the most extreme arguments possible. Even if he is somewhat biased or excessive, it is not a flaw. Why? . . . If we concede to one another and speak accommodating, ambiguous words, then all over the country people's nerves will be calm and democracy will stagnate. For it is human nature to be

comfortable with the familiar and afraid of something new. We must make the startling familiar; only then can people's knowledge advance.

At first, Liang continued, people are startled by something new. So one shows them something else that is twice as startling. This shifts their sense of shock from the first thing to the second, and makes the first one quite familiar.

> Leading them on in this way in an infinite progression, as the level of what it takes to shock them increases stage by stage, so does their tolerance. When you get to the point that the strangest, most unheard of, and unusual theories in the world have no shock value, then the knowledge-level has reached its ultimate. . . . Today, among the intellectuals in our country, there is probably only one in a thousand who is not shocked by the idea of revolution; one in a hundred who is shocked by the idea of revolution but not by that of popular rights; and virtually none who is shocked at the ideas of reform and Western learning. This shows the effect of journalists in leading the people. If you want to lead people to the idea of reform, you must shock them with people's rights; if you want to lead them to people's rights you have to shock them with the idea of revolution. . . . And if any theory can be brought forth more shocking still than that of revolution, then even the theory of revolution will lose its power to shock.

When Liang defended freedom of the press, therefore, it was not for its contribution to uncovering objective truth but for its usefulness in stimulating controversy and seizing public attention. The voice of the press in his view was properly polemical, even at the cost of extremism and polarization. "One must intend to use one's words to change the world," he wrote. "Otherwise, why utter them?"

The competing ethic of political detachment and impartiality had some advocates during the century, but it never gathered the force to dominate Chinese literature or journalism. The large commercial papers nurtured a handful of professional reporters who described the complexities of Peking politics during the 1920s and the war scenes of the 1930s and 1940s. Professionalization was encouraged by the establishment of journalism courses or departments at Peking, St. Johns, and Yenching universities in the years around 1920. But reporting remained a profession generally held in low esteem. It was considered less a branch of literary endeavor than a modern reincarnation of the lineage of copyists who sat at yamen doors gathering materials for the old gazettes. According to popular superstition, publishing news about strangers brought bad luck: if it harmed their reputations or caused their deaths by suicide, these offenses would be deducted from the reporter's accumulated merits in the afterlife.

Journalism was ill paid. The hours were long and there were no vacations. To make ends meet, reporters often accepted retainers from political factions or served as stringers for as many as eight or ten newspapers at once. Reporters on local beats supplemented their incomes with hush money earned for not reporting embarrassing court cases. The small staffs of even major newspapers had to cope with difficulties that made it hard to maintain standards of accuracy. Bao Tianxiao recalled that sometimes space would be set aside for a telegraph report that did not arrive. One editor got so good at fabricating reports to fill the space, Bao claimed, that it was hard to tell his stories from the true ones carried the same day in the other papers.

Nor did the profession of journalism receive support from the law. In the late Qing, papers were covered by general provisions against "weird writings or talk" and spreading secrets. When a law specifically regulating printed matter was enacted in 1906, it provided for registration of printers and submission of two copies of all publications to the police. Slander was defined so loosely that accurate reporting was not protected. The press was just as subject to government regulation at the government's option as any other form of enterprise, and derived no special protection from its role as the citizen's chief source of information; to the contrary, it was subject to especially intensive oversight as part of government's traditional duty to protect the people's minds from baneful influences.

Printing was cheap, so every small party and faction could afford its own organ. Most politicians had their captive newspapers and magazines and so did the foreign powers. The Japanese alone gave financial support to fifteen newspapers in China in the late 1920s, of which three were in English, six in Japanese, and six in Chinese—the latter including one of the major Peking papers and the leading paper in Canton. Most of these subventions were unknown to the public. Publicists even developed something called "newspaper setups"—ordinary-looking four-page newspapers with the contents mostly lifted from the major Shanghai papers. Three sections were left blank—the title, the editorial column, and "major news." For a small price a warlord's agent could fill these with praise for his boss's latest maneuvers and have a few hundred copies run off to show favorable "public opinion."

In the twentieth century, writing in the service of a political goal was considered by most Chinese a higher calling than dispassionate reporting detached from the national struggle for survival. The sense of national crisis had lent urgency to political disputes, and mobilizational politics meant they had to be further exaggerated for the edification of distant publics. The mandarin style of political discourse—genteel and prudential, rooted in allusion to shared values—was gone. There was nothing to restrain a press that saw itself as a political instrument serving its masters at any cost.

The authorities' response to agitation was censorship. For thousands of years the publishing industry had been quite free of government interference. If it had no legal protection, neither was it governed by laws of registration or censorship. Except for occasional literary inquisitions, officials had no time to concern themselves with what was being printed in thousands of small shops using cheaply-cut wood blocks. But now that the press had become a political medium, the stakes were higher. The Qing published the first law specifically governing publications in 1906. A revised version in 1914 included a provision against "any writing, drawing, or picture" that "aims to change the form of government" or "is harmful to the public peace." Prepublication censorship was introduced by the Guomindang under its doctrine of tutelage. Nothing could be published that was "designed to undermine the Nationalist Party or violate the Three People's Principles." Although the application of the laws was spotty, over several decades scores of writers were arrested and journals closed. Outside the law, journalists were assassinated and newspaper offices burned. By the 1930s, according to Lin Yutang, the major newspapers dared to print only what was "official, correct, friendly, time-tested, and untouched"—i.e., government press releases.

Serious writers of the thirties opposed to the government honed the skills of satire, irony, and Aesopian discourse. The public learned to believe nothing and to decipher everything. People hungry for facts had to turn to the rumor-filled mosquito press. But they read its stories much as they read contemporary "butterfly" fiction, for escape and sensation. Tragically, many Chinese experienced their own political history as if it were a tale of duplicity and revenge like the ancient legend of the Three Kingdoms or a bandit adventure like *All Men Are Brothers*. The public had a lively voyeuristic interest in politics but grew detached and cynical—the paradoxical result of the press's efforts over several decades to mobilize it.

Toward the end of the 1940s the public's cynicism abated, at least toward the leftist section of the press, in the atmosphere of hope generated by impending communist victory in the civil war. But from 1949 on, the problems of the media took a new turn. Now the press came under firm central control and obtained a command audience which soon grew far larger than any it had enjoyed in the past. But central control of the media and its message eventually produced their own problems of effectiveness. When the press had been fragmented the competition of voices warned the citizen to be wary; after it came under party control the unity of its voice would come to have the same effect.

8

THE MEDIA IN THE
SERVICE OF THE STATE

The establishment of the People's Republic brought a fresh opportunity to realize the potential of propaganda. In 1950, all book publishing was brought under the government's General Bureau of Publications, while book selling was centralized in the Xinhua chain. Magazines and newspapers were reorganized, with some journals being closed and the rest brought under party control by the mid-1950s. The work of distributing periodicals through subscriptions and kiosks was assigned exclusively to the post office. Except for the Red Guard tabloids of the Cultural Revolution, there were no more private publications until the democracy movement's mimeographed periodicals of the late 1970s.

For the first time, a Chinese regime had the political will and institutional means to try to control the entire realm of public culture. Together with fuller control came the assignment to the media of new missions, and expansion of the media network to reach virtually every Chinese with propaganda in several forms. Especially in the later years of Mao's rule, when other political institutions were weak, the press acted as the most important institutional connector between citizens and the state.

Under the system established in the 1950s and still in effect today, the final power to control the realm of culture in its broadest sense rests with the Propaganda Department of the Central Committee. Located within the party's central secretariat, the Propaganda Department in the late 1970s and early 1980s was one of only four Central Committee departments (the others overseeing organization, united front work, and international liaison). It supervised not only the mass media, but also literature, art, music, education, publishing, scientific research, public health, sports, and more. From 1976 to 1977, the department was headed by Deng Xiaoping's close associate Hu Yaobang, who continued to supervise its work when he was transferred to head the Organization Department in 1977. In 1980 Hu became the party's general secretary.

The top leaders routinely participate in the management of only a few official publications of the Central Committee, such as *People's Daily, Red Flag,* and *Enlightenment Daily.* Mao, for example, published many of his important writings as unsigned *People's Daily* editorials, while Zhou Enlai is admiringly said to have "read every word and corrected thousands of manuscripts" for the newspaper. Journals that do not speak for the center report to other institutions. *Liberation Army Daily,* for example, is the organ of the PLA general political department; *China Youth Daily* is run by the youth league; and *Southern Daily* is the organ of the Canton provincial government. Scholarly and specialist journals belong to universities or professional societies and literary journals are run by branches of the writers' association. Performing arts, scientific and educational work, and other aspects of culture are managed by such government organs as the ministries of culture, education, radio-television, and public health.

Whatever organ they report to, however, all publications, along with other media and cultural enterprises, are answerable to the Propaganda Department through several effective channels of control. Each publication, radio or TV station, film production studio, or performance troupe includes a contingent of party members—amounting to as much as 50 percent of the professional staff in many units—and is led by a party committee. Nonparty reporters and editors, like those who are party members, are obliged by State Council regulation to "support Communist Party leadership, warmly love socialism, strive to study Marxism-Leninism–Mao Zedong Thought, and implement the party's line, principles, and policies." Each local-level media organization accepts the close supervision of the party secretary of the city or province as to what to cover and how, and sends important articles to the secretary's office to be checked before publication. Newspapers depend for major news on the centrally controlled New China News Agency, which does most of the national and international reporting for the entire press, and reprint important theoretical and policy articles from the *People's Daily.* They get many of their local stories from "spare-time correspondents" who are party members or activists in the grass-roots units being reported on, and who submit their work to their own party secretaries before sending it in. As a matter of courtesy, newspapers customarily clear articles that they produce themselves with the party secretary at the next level above the unit they are writing about.

What is true of the news media is also true of scholarly and literary journals. They are led by their own party committees and supervised by the propaganda officials of the committees above. They rely chiefly on contributors who are professors at government universities and research institutes or salaried members of state-run cultural organizations like the Chinese Writers' Association, the Chinese Dramatists' Association, and the Chinese Artists' Association, organizations whose members are bound by a 1982 pact to "love the motherland, be loyal to the people, uphold the four basic principles, [and] wholeheartedly serve the people and socialism." Like journalists, many scholars and writers are party members. Party members or not, all are frequently made aware of the leaders' priorities for academic and literary work. For example, at a forum for playwrights held in February 1980, Hu Yaobang spoke for several hours on how literature should treat such currently problematic topics as the party, society, the intellectuals, the army, and Chairman Mao; suggested four subjects that literary workers could safely write about (modernization, the history of the communist revolution, the history of the precommunist phases of the revolution, and stories and legends of the working people of the past); and offered the party's help in designing such works and providing historical material. Hu's speech was widely circulated as a guideline for literary and art workers in all fields, not just playwrights. Such briefings on academic and literary topics by the leaders occur often.

The media's functions today would all sound familiar to Liang Qichao. The first is to propagate the party's policies to the people. A speech by Mao to the editorial staff of a north China communist paper in 1948 is considered the classic statement of this duty:

> The role and power of newspapers consists in their ability to bring the party program, the party line, the party's general and specific policies, its tasks and methods of work before the masses in the quickest and most extensive way.

Although the party has its own elaborate organization reaching into virtually every work and residential unit in Chinese society, the press remains the leaders' fastest and most efficient direct voice to the people. In 1945, Mao told a group of journalists that the party center had to rely upon the press for 90 percent or more of the work of leading local party units: "It is generally through newspapers and news agencies that we propagate the party's policies so that they become known to the broad masses." After 1949, despite the establishment of other means of communication with the local authorities, the press still played a key role in the transmission of policy. Wrote Mao in a 1958 note to some local officials: "When it comes to the work of the whole province and all the people, a newspaper has the greatest effectiveness in organizing, stimulating, criticizing, and motivating."

The press's second mission is to provide intelligence to the leaders on the public's feelings and behavior and the performance of lower-level cadres. This function was explained by Liu Shaoqi, then general secretary of the party and the person in overall charge of press work, to a group of north China journalists in a speech in 1948:

> The party doesn't fear anything—except for one thing. We never feared American imperialism or the atomic bomb. . . . We only fear becoming divorced from the masses. . . . The center relies on you as an instrument to keep in touch with the masses. . . .

Truthfulness is important to this intelligence mission. "Don't add soy sauce, don't add hot sauce, don't wear colored glasses," Liu once told reporters. "If the masses are against us they are against us, if they welcome us they welcome us, if they misunderstand us they misunderstand us; don't be afraid to report these things truthfully." In 1956 he reminded a group of correspondents that the central leaders relied on their investigations to find out when policies were incorrect, were being incorrectly implemented, or had run into unforeseen problems that required adjustments. "For example, a reporter stationed at the Anshan Iron and Steel Factory for a long time naturally has a clear view of things there, so he should publish his views in the form of a critique of the factory's achievements, good points, and bad points." (This choice of example incidentally implied that even the model Anshan works patronized by Mao had flaws that could constructively be written about.) Reporters, said Liu, must avoid two kinds of bias: on the one hand, refusing to cooperate with the local party people and acting too independently; but on the other, "believing everything the party committee says and putting out exaggerations." Reporters had to preserve a measure of independence in order to serve as a check on the reporting filed by bureaucrats on themselves.

But uncovering shortcomings and errors in the party's work was not an end in itself; "to report everything is objectivism," said Liu, "it is automatic recording." Critical reports should be selected for "immediate benefit to the party in its current struggle." They must reflect a Marxist standpoint: "If you write things that oppose Marxism, of course they must be restricted." And if it seemed likely that publication would benefit the enemy more than the party, Liu instructed, "don't report it publicly; you can write something for the *Internal Reference News*"—a domestic intelligence newsletter for top officials.

The press's third task is to help the leaders and people supervise the bureaucracy through a process called "criticism and self-criticism." Criticism in this context means exposure of official wrongdoing; self-criticism refers to the malefactor's statement of repentance. The process can occur in closed party meetings or in the public forum of the press, where it takes the form of publishing letters to the editor or investigative reports. The importance of conducting a portion of the party's criticism and self-criticism in public view was explained in a 1950 Central Committee resolution:

> With the end of the war on the mainland today and with our party in control of the whole country, shortcomings and mistakes in our work could easily hurt the interests of the people. . . . If we cannot make public and timely criticism and self-criticism throughout the party and amidst the broad masses of the people, we will be poisoned by severe bureaucratism. . . . To carry out criticism and self-criticism in newspapers and magazines is an essential method for consolidating the party-mass relationship, safeguarding the democratization of party and state, and speeding social progress.

To assure the press's ability to perform this function, reporters have quasi-official, although unwritten, investigatory rights. They can enter units, interview workers, and see files; if local-unit cadres refuse access, the reporters can go to the party secretary at the next higher level for a directive that the unit be opened to investigation. This work might bring the journalists into conflict with local party officials, Liu Shaoqi once acknowledged. "You criticize him, he is unhappy; you puff him and pat him and he is delighted." But he urged the reporters to stiffen their backs and show some fighting spirit for the party's larger goals. "On behalf of the people you can go through some wind and frost, some storm and waves, take a bit of tempering, get a little experience. How can you get tempered if you don't take a few knocks?" Whether the results of such investigations are published in the open press or in classified bulletins depends upon the judgment of editors and party secretaries as to which form of publication in the particular case will be most helpful to the party's prestige among the masses. But open publication constitutes the essence of criticism and self-criticism, for it serves to separate the party from acts of arrogance and corruption committed in its name and so assures the public that the leaders care for their welfare.

Closely allied with criticism and self-criticism is "mass work," or the receipt and processing of letters to the editor and a smaller number of personal visitors. Although some are letters of praise, most contain the masses' grievances, complaints, and exposures of wrongdoing. By writing to newspapers instead of appealing through the bureaucratic hierarchy, citizens hope to get effective action and avoid retribution. All major newspapers and some magazines maintain "mass work sections" that are often the largest section of the editorial department, some with staffs of forty to eighty employees. These sections do in China what social work agencies and congressional offices together do in America—help thousands of individual citizens solve their problems with government. All letters are supposed to be either answered or passed on to relevant party or government offices for action. In the 1950s, the

People's Daily even maintained a card file on the letters and systematically queried the government organs on each case until the paper was satisfied that the problem had been resolved. Important but sensitive letters are published in internal periodicals. Others appear in the letters columns of the open press, sometimes without comment but often with an authoritative ruling on the question involved, provided either by the paper itself or by a government office to which the editors have applied for a decision. Some letters serve as tips that start investigations by the newspapers' reporters. Finally, the newspapers use the letters to compile content analyses of trends in the masses' concerns for the information of the leaders.

Until recently, the high point of the Chinese media had been reached in the mid-1930s, when nearly 2,000 periodicals had a reading audience of probably well over 30 million. The Japanese invasion and the civil war disrupted circulation, and according to one estimate, aggregate newspaper sales in 1946 amounted to no more than 2 million. In 1953, after the reorganization of the media and several years of economic recovery, the number of newspapers and magazines stood at 560, still not up to the mid-1930s level. Circulation amounted to about 18 million. By 1965 the number of newspapers and magazines had risen to 1,133; aggregate circulation reached a new high of about 54 million. But during the Cultural Revolution most periodicals were closed. Total circulation slipped to about 15 million in 1967. The media network rebounded from 1970 on, but a 1973 catalogue of the Peking post office still listed only 3 newspapers and 61 magazines available for subscription to residents there. Citizens in other cities had a choice of some of the same and some different titles.

The media have expanded more rapidly since Mao's death than at any other time in Chinese history. Periodicals attacked during the Cultural Revolution were rehabilitated, their records cleared as ceremoniously as if they were human beings. And hundreds of new journals were launched to serve specialized interests. By 1980 there were some 155 social science journals published by institutions of higher learning, about 200 literary magazines, and about 900 science and technology magazines. Special-interest periodicals included a soccer magazine, an abacus magazine, a nature magazine published by a consortium of museums, a popular journal on family planning, a quarterly on fashion, and an academic journal called *UFO Exploration.* The pace of expansion moved a newspaper correspondent to complain that organizations were launching magazines without coordination. "Readers feel that under the present conditions of difficulty in the national economy, in paper supply, in post office warehouse space, and in railway transport there should be some consolidation among periodicals whose content is redundant."

The paper shortage had always been one of the chief constraints on the growth of publishing. Now the government made a decision to allocate increased supplies to the most popular journals. *China Youth News*, a weekly, was able to set a record for the highest circulation in Chinese history in 1980 when its weekly print run was expanded to 11,110,000. The second most popular publication appears to be *Reference News*, a compendium of foreign wire-service and newspaper reports in translation, with a circulation of about 9 million. Third is *Popular Cinema*, which always has a picture of a movie star on its cover and sells about 8 million copies. Fourth is *People's Daily*, with a circulation reported to be in the range of 5–6 million. The *Daily's* editors reportedly told a Japanese delegation in 1980 that they intended to increase its circulation to 50 million by the end of the century.

The Chinese post office runs magazine stands in towns and cities, and has recently begun to allow private individuals to peddle periodicals on commission. But most readers obtain their periodicals through subscription. Postal carriers deliver almost six times as many periodicals as they do other items of mail. Newspaper subscriptions are ordinarily available for one or a number of months up to a maximum of a year, magazine subscriptions for a season (three months) or several seasons up to a year. Although short-term subscriptions require more paperwork, they are convenient for people who do not have much cash. As of 1981, the post office delivered to 99.8 percent of China's rural townships. But this did not necessarily mean house-to-house service. One letter to the *People's Daily* told how a commune mobilized 148 elementary-school students, one from each production team, to take home from school newspapers that the commune's one postman could not hope to deliver himself.

Until recently each post office had a limited quota of each periodical to sell as a result of the paper shortage. One rural postmaster complained that although he had more than fifty schools in his district he was allocated only sixteen copies of the *China Youth News* and similarly small numbers of other popular youth publications. Some journals have been in such short supply that the aspiring subscriber had to travel to a major city to apply. Even *Popular Cinema* and *People's Literature* had to be ordered at a county seat, and the customer who went there to place an order was likely to be told that the quota was filled. At the same time the system left post offices with surplus supplies of unpopular magazines. A soldier complained in a letter to the editor that when he sent a friend to buy copies of *Popular Cinema* and *Cinema Pictorial* the salesman insisted on a package deal—the two movie magazines plus three thick, boring literary periodicals costing over one yuan each. Only with the improvement of paper supplies since about 1980 has the post office been able to end quotas on most periodicals.

Despite its expansion in recent years, the press is not yet able to serve its public primarily through individual subscriptions. The total per-issue circulation is still far less than half the comparable number in the United States, about 165 million versus some 403 million in 1980, for a population five times the size. The Chinese published 2,800 periodicals in 1983 compared to over 13,000 in the United States, and the record circulation of a little over 11 million for *China Youth News* is less than two-thirds of the 18-million circulation of the most popular American magazine, *Reader's Digest.* The paper shortage is not the only reason for these limits. Another is the consideration of cost to the consumers. In 1979, for example, *People's Daily* cost 1.50 yuan (about a dollar) a month, the weekly *China Youth News* .09 yuan (about 6 cents) a month and *Popular Cinema* .90 yuan (about 60 cents) a season. These prices were low, but not negligible in a country where the average peasant spent only some 3.70 yuan (roughly $2.40) a year on recreation and services. Household subscriptions have been rare until recently, especially in the countryside. One rural postmaster reported in 1979 that only 21 of more than 1,800 newspaper subscriptions in his district were private. The cost of a magazine bulks large enough in most people's pockets so that rental stalls continue to flourish in the cities.

In 1979–82 I did a series of interviews with Chinese émigrés designed to learn how effectively the media reach Chinese citizens and how they influence citizens' knowledge of and attitudes towards politics. My research assistants and I spoke with sixty-nine Chinese émigrés who came from communes, factories, schools, mines, and other kinds of units in eighteen different provinces (for details, see the Appendix). The experiences the émigrés described dated mostly from the mid- and late 1970s.

One finding of the interviews was to confirm the important role of communal media facilities in reaching the public. A technician attached to a large state-owned coal mine, for example, explained that its reading room subscribed to over thirty newspapers, including those of all the provinces because it had workers from many different areas. The reading room also contained sixty or seventy magazines. In addition, each administrative department of the mine subscribed to five or six newspapers and about twenty magazines for use in the office. A medical equipment factory established a trade-union-managed workers' club with numerous newspapers and magazines, books, a stage for performances and political meetings, ping-pong tables, Chinese billiards, and two black-and-white TV sets. In a large petrochemical plant the party committee ran a reading room for the workers containing all national and provincial newspapers and some thirty to forty magazines. Each workshop subscribed to *Reference News, People's Daily,* and several other papers, and had a TV set. The factory maintained a separate collection of technical materials and a room where party members could consult internal documents. It also published its own four-page weekly tabloid on production achievements.

The Chinese press has recently reported the establishment of elaborately equipped "cultural stations" in rural villages; one posed-looking picture in

People's Daily shows seven solemn peasants seated around a table full of magazines while six browse at book-filled shelves. But the facilities in the rural units described by my respondents were far more limited, and varied from spot to spot. A young woman who spent time on a remote state farm on Hainan Island said that her team's administrative office subscribed only to *People's Daily*, *Red Flag* magazine, and the daily papers of Guangdong Province and of Hainan; *Reference News* was available to party and youth league members. A man who served on an army-managed farm said that the company commander's office contained four or five newspapers for common use. A farmer told me that *People's Daily* and one local paper arrived at his production team in batches and were stored in the team accountant's office, but because they came so late hardly anyone bothered to read them.

Unit facilities are usually provided even to people in out-of-the-way places. One national and one local paper were brought to the work site for members of a traveling road construction brigade. A construction worker told me that each workers' study group was issued free subscriptions to *People's Daily*, *Red Flag*, and the provincial paper. A worker on a harbor barge said he had access to a reading room at headquarters on his two days a week on shore, and that the company even maintained a newspaper display board on the barge, although the newspaper was often out of date. A young woman who tended sheep in Inner Mongolia said that the cluster of yurts where she lived subscribed to as many as twenty newspapers because the sent-down youth there came from a wide range of places. The papers were kept in the yurt that served as a brigade office. The Chinese press recently reported that Peking Municipal Prison has a library with over 17,000 books, and that each detachment of prisoners has its own reading room.

Although maintaining some kind of unit reading facility is considered one of the obligations of leaders, units do sometimes fall through the cracks. An electrician told me he was one of four technicians living at a small mine remote from the headquarters of the commune that owned it. The commune had a reading room, but the four men at the mine received only the county newspaper. A farmworker said that her production brigade had a copy of *People's Daily* posted and a second available in the brigade school, but the closest reading room was in the commune headquarters miles away. Another rural resident said there were no newspapers at all at the team or brigade headquarters in her area, and even the commune had only a display board with one national and one provincial paper.

There are no comprehensive statistics on the distribution of unit reading facilities, but clearly they are widespread. The government claimed in 1980 that over 90 percent of rural communes and production brigades subscribed to one or more publications, although many basic-level production teams did not. An American study of sixty-three south China villages based on émigré interviews found that over half the production teams studied subscribed to two or more newspapers as of the early 1970s. Of my sixty-nine respondents, thirty-one said their units had formal reading rooms; thirty-two said newspapers were available in unit administrative offices, either instead of or in addition to those in reading rooms; and ten described other collective reading facilities, such as workers' clubs, newspaper racks in a schoolteachers' lounge, and distribution of free copies of *Red Flag* to unit members—even, in one instance, to patients in a hospital. Only one respondent's unit had no public reading facility. In addition, forty-nine respondents said their units maintained either a wall newspaper or a blackboard newspaper, generally to report political and production achievements.

Although the network of communal reading facilities puts newspapers and magazines within the reach of virtually the entire population, this does not assure that everyone reads. My respondents' reading habits were not typical. Forty-eight of them reported that they or their families had at least one periodical subscription at home. Forty-seven said that they did some reading at their units at least once a week, several claiming to spend two to three hours a day, and one four hours. Nine told me that they borrowed reading material from the unit facilities to take home. But all of my respondents were literate and all but one had at least some secondary education. In the population as a whole, 23.5 percent of those aged 12 and over are illiterate or semiliterate, according to the published results of the 1982 census. Literacy is defined as knowing fifteen hundred characters—enough to read simple newspapers, but not with ease.

Many nonreaders continue to be produced by the school system. According to the education ministry, 93 percent of school-age children start primary school, but only 65 percent finish the five-year course and only about half of these are able to pass the graduation examination—a pattern referred to as the "9-6-3 system." The dropouts are concentrated in the countryside, where many families cannot afford the modest tuition fees and the loss of a child's labor. A Central Committee rural investigation reportedly found that nonreaders ranged from 50 to 70 percent of the population in the villages studied. Frequent readers averaged no more than one-tenth of the population—mostly sent-down youths, teachers, students, local enterprise employees, and cadres and technicians rather than peasants. In the countryside newspapers are often used to paper walls, cover windows, and wrap food. A former resident of a commune in east China told me:

> The leaders set up a reading room but the peasants started to store potatoes and tools there. When a political movement started the leaders cleared out the room again. The postman brought the papers in batches and dumped them on the floor. The peasants started to fight over who

could take them to use. The team leader threatened to cut off all the subscriptions, but the brigade chief said the team had to subscribe whether it wanted to or not.

To encourage reading the government has not only increased the press runs of the heavily illustrated *Popular Cinema* and the simply written, practical *China Youth News* but has revived county-level newspapers and peasant editions of provincial papers. Comic books comprised one-fifth of the total number of books published in 1980. Educated young people are encouraged to establish reading groups where they read the daily press aloud to the peasants. In 1980 a magazine was launched specifically to carry stories meant to be read aloud, many of them adapted from the oral storytellers' tradition that is centuries old.

Since the press message continues to be chiefly political, the major forum for group reading is the political study group. In principle the members of all units in China are divided into these groups, which meet one to six times a week for an hour or so to assimilate party policy. Although the intensity of such meetings dropped off after Mao's death, fifty-seven of my respondents said that study meetings were held at least once a week in their units, including units in the city and the countryside and covering periods both before and after Mao's death. In many cases the printed media were intimately involved in the meetings. A factory manager told me that a youth league cadre read the newspaper to a group of about a hundred workers, and then they split up by workshop to discuss the contents. A laborer said he read the press most intensively when there was a political movement in progress. "If you don't read every issue of *Red Flag* during a movement," he said, "you can get into trouble." A young man assigned to a state farm said, *"People's Daily* would be read aloud at the front of the study meeting, and some of us would gather around in back to read *Reference News."*

Because of reading rooms and study groups, Chinese periodicals continue to have nearly as large a multiple readership as they did in the late Qing. An American scholar, Paul Hiniker, has estimated that as of about 1962, there were 11.5 readers of each copy of a Chinese magazine and 9 readers of each copy of a Chinese newspaper. (The corresponding figure for American magazines is 4.64.) These projections were based on interviews with 413 Chinese émigrés in Hong Kong and Macao and, because of various assumptions used, may be biased in an upward direction. Yet no audience survey of comparable scope done in China has been released, and no better one has been done abroad. Hiniker's figures suggest that by the early 1960s some 500 million people, virtually the entire adult population of China, were exposed to the print media either directly or through discussions in study sessions.

To supplement the print media the government has encouraged the growth of electronic communications. Radio came to China in 1922, but its early spread was slow. By 1937 there were only 93 broadcasting stations, of which almost half were in Shanghai, which had an estimated 100,000 receiving sets. There were about 300 movie theaters with an aggregate seating capacity of 300,000, likewise concentrated in Shanghai and a few other large cities. The coming of the war set back the radio and movie industries as it did the publishing world. Although electronics production grew rapidly after 1949, over 95 percent of the output was at first devoted to military and industrial uses. The mass distribution of consumer electronics equipment had to wait until the mid-1970s.

The first nonprint medium to approach universal distribution was the cheapest—wired loudspeakers. The program began in the early 1950s, using corvée labor to link each county seat with its surrounding villages. Locally produced iron or steel wire was strung on wooden poles and powered by small hydroelectric generators. Inexpensive speakers, often locally manufactured, were placed in factory workshops, on street corners, in brigade headquarters and farm fields, and in peasants' homes. The program gained momentum after 1969. According to one estimate, by 1974 there were 141 million speakers in use, widely available in cities and reaching into 90 percent of the production brigades and teams and 65 percent of rural households. In the early 1980s, broadcasting had a larger audience than newspapers, most of it reached by speaker. Among my sixty-nine respondents, sixty-two reported that there were loudspeakers either in their work units, in their residential neighborhoods, or both. Exceptions included a small coal mine, a harbor barge, a large central government office, and two rural units that had no electricity. But a worker on another nonelectrified farm told me that loudspeakers were run six hours a day there using electricity generated by a tractor.

Some units simply relay broadcasts that emanate from city or county stations. But increasing numbers of local units also have their own programming facilities run by full- or part-time staff. Even in the countryside one can see elaborate banks of receivers, recorders, microphones, and amplifiers run by the units that used to be called brigades and teams. A leading popular-science magazine, *Radio*, carries instructions for assembling and repairing such equipment. Local personnel tune in, record, and rebroadcast news, opera, sports, and drama from central and provincial radio, and also produce their own programs of local propaganda, calisthenics, weather reports, and emergency bulletins. Thrice-daily broadcasts were the most common pattern revealed in my interviews, but there were other schedules as well. In some factories broadcasts go on all day even though they are hard to hear over the noise of the machines. In others, broadcasts are made only during rest periods. At a middle school, I was told, the speaker was used between classes; in another school, before school and at lunch; in a hospital, during the midday and evening meals. Only ten of my respondents said that the loudspeakers in their units or neighborhoods were used rarely—perhaps as amplifiers at large meetings or to call people to meetings or the telephone.

Private radios have lagged behind loudspeakers as a form of mass communication partly because of the cost of individual sets. Until the 1960s, most were made with expensive vacuum tubes. With transistorization, in China as elsewhere, the price went down, and radios became a mass consumer item. But a transistor radio still costs around 40 yuan (about $25), or five to ten times more than a good-quality household loudspeaker. Another hindrance to the spread of radios has been the difficulty of broadcasting throughout the vast hinterland. By 1982 China had 118 broadcasting stations and 506 transmission and relay stations. Although many broadcasts are in shortwave, 35 percent of the population still did not have adequate reception by 1984.

Nonetheless, beginning about 1970 the government began to promote wider use of personal radios. Output had averaged only some 800,000 sets a year until then. Thereafter production expanded rapidly, reaching a high of 40 million sets in 1981. Until recently, private radio ownership was mainly a phenomenon of the cities. According to a Chinese government survey, less than a fifth of rural families had radios in 1978. In the last few years, as the agricultural reforms have channeled more spending money to the peasants, radios have been among the consumer items they have chosen to buy. By 1982, according to the same survey, radios were owned by half of all peasant households.

The Chinese film industry produces a little over a hundred feature movies a year, together with cartoons, newsreels, documentaries, and educational films. Tickets are cheap, and frequently free when distributed by a factory or office. Most viewing takes place in work-unit auditoriums or under the stars. Many factories and communes maintain their own projectors. In addition, projection teams travel around the countryside. Nationwide, projection facilities in 1982 were said to number 140,000. Of my sixty-nine respondents, twenty-eight said that their units either handed out tickets or showed films. Forty-one went to the movies at least once a month (in two cases, as often as twelve times a month), and another twenty-three less frequently. Official sources have given contradictory figures on the national film audience, ranging from over 10 billion to nearly 30 billion, suggesting that every Chinese goes to the movies ten to thirty times a year on the average.

The medium of the future in China is television. A senior propaganda official explained in the *People's Daily* in 1981:

Television is the most mass-oriented propaganda instrument, capable of being seen and heard at the same moment by thousands and millions of people. . . . To see movies you need a theater or a projection team, . . . and a theater can only hold an audience of limited size. It can't show the same program to tens of millions at once as on television. . . . At present, there is no propaganda medium that can beat television.

China's first television transmission was made in 1958 in Peking, and over the next decade or so stations were established in most provincial capitals. As recently as the mid-1970s there were only a few hundred thousand sets in use. Then major investment in TV factories and transmission facilities created a mass video audience overnight. Annual production of sets grew from about half a million in 1978 to nearly 7 million in 1983. According to one report, the government aims to have 200 million sets in use by the end of the century. There are now forty-seven broadcasting stations, each transmitting on several channels, mostly in the evening from about 5:30 to 11:00. The central station in Peking provides one set of programs, mixing news, sports, entertainment, and documentaries, via landlines and microwave relay stations. Each of the provincial capitals normally originates one or two channels of its own. The program guide *Television Weekly* has become one of China's most popular magazines, and several people I interviewed said that the TV listings were the main feature they looked for in the daily paper. But poor reception remains a problem in many areas, and the government has announced plans to launch a broadcasting satellite to improve nationwide coverage for both radio and TV.

As programming has increased, TV sets have become so desirable that in some places they have had to be rationed by allowing units to award purchase coupons to their most deserving members. Prices have gone down as production has increased. In 1980 a black-and-white set cost from 370 to nearly 900 yuan, up to twice the annual income of most urban workers. Color models, produced in significant numbers since 1982, cost 2,000 yuan or more (one yuan being equal to roughly 60 cents U.S.). Since the quality of domestic sets remains poor, Chinese traveling abroad often bring home foreign models and pay a substantial duty. There has been a black market in foreign sets, especially in the areas of south China most often visited by overseas Chinese, who have the right to bring sets as gifts for their relatives. The highest concentration of private TV ownership is in the urbanized parts of Peking, where one family in three has a set. More commonly, televisions are owned by the unit. Of my sixty-nine respondents, thirty-five reported that their units had TVs, usually black-and-white sets acquired in the late 1970s. The units without sets were predominantly rural communes, state farms, and village schools. Some collectively owned sets, even if they have small screens, may be watched by a hundred or more viewers at a time. The Chinese government claims a regular audience of about 30 million—an average of three or

four watchers a set at the time the figure was issued—but for special programs like the 1984 Olympics, the audience is said to reach 200 million or
more—an average of twenty or more viewers per set.

The curve of growth of the Chinese media public has been sharp—from
roughly 1 percent of the population in the first decade of this century to
near-universality now that radio and television have become widespread. The
media have expanded most rapidly in the last fifteen years. In this sense,
China's mass audience is a recent creation despite its century-long gestation.
With huge investment and innovative social design, the party has created a
network that reaches people even in remote and backward places. How the
people respond to the media, however, is a more complicated question—and
more crucial to the media's ability to perform their functions for the Chinese
state.

A portion of my interview questionnaire was devoted to exploring the
impact of the media network on people's knowledge of politics. Using two
separate tests, I found that as of the early 1970s the media delivered information with remarkable effectiveness. First, I named thirteen news items I
had selected from the period 1969–74 and tested respondents' knowledge of
each (for details, see the Appendix). The results are displayed in the table on
page 167. The proportion of persons familiar with each item ranged from a
low of 38 percent to a high of 100 percent with an average for all items of 77
percent. Almost half of the respondents were able to identify eleven or more
items. This range of responses shows that respondents were willing to admit
they did not know some items, thus lending credibility to their claims to
know the items they said they knew. More importantly, to be counted as
knowing an item the respondent had to give information beyond what was
contained in the question itself, as explained in the Appendix.

By discussing how the respondents learned about each item, I found that
different levels of recognition depended mainly on the government's decisions about how to publicize each piece of news. The government could
double or triple the rate of mastery by featuring, emphasizing, or repeating
information, and it could influence the way an item would be received by its
method of treatment. The Lin Biao incident is an example. According to official reports, Lin, Mao's chosen successor, had made an abortive attempt to
assassinate Mao, then tried to flee to the Soviet Union, and died when his
plane ran out of fuel and crashed. Fifty-five respondents recalled hearing the
news in dramatic "relay briefings"—oral reports by their cadres, who in turn
had been called away some days earlier for secret briefings at higher levels. By
keeping the news secret until it could be presented in the controlled briefing
format, the government was to some extent able to shape reactions to this
shocking news. Although there was some gossiping in the aftermath of the
briefings, public doubts centered on minor aspects of the story such as

Percentage of Respondents Demonstrating Familiarity with News Items

Item	Percentage Familiar
1 In 1969, it was reported that two Americans landed on the moon.	70
2 In 1970, it was reported that China had launched its first manmade satellite.	94
3 In 1970, it was reported that "Japanese militarism, which has revived under the wing of U.S. imperialism, is attempting to realize its old dream of a 'Greater East Asian Co-Prosperity Sphere.' "	51
4 In 1971, it was reported that "Rich harvests have been gathered nine years running. A new upsurge is emerging in industrial production. Prices are stable."	92
5 In 1971, there was a report as follows: "Defying the U.S. government's ban and intimidation, several hundred thousand American workers, black people, students, teachers, women, ex-servicemen, soldiers, and people of religious circles took to the streets, demonstrating once again their will and strength in the face of U.S. reactionaries."	38
6 Let me ask you about the Lin Biao incident.	100
7 Now let me ask about the Nixon visit to China.	100
8 I would like to ask you about Premier Zhou Enlai's illness.	97
9 Do you remember hearing about a person named Zhang Tiesheng?	97
10 Do you recall hearing about a place called Xiaojinzhuang?	78
11 During 1973, there was a report that the commanders of all eleven of China's military regions were shifted.	68
12 In the fall of 1973, there was a report as follows: "On 6 October, Israel flagrantly launched a large-scale military attack on Egypt, Syria, and the Palestine guerrillas."	68
13 During 1973 and 1974, there was a report that China signed contracts with foreign companies to buy thirteen large chemical fertilizer plants.	52
Average	77

Note:
Six questionnaires were not used because the respondents had left China before all the events happened.

whether Lin's plane had really run out of gas or had been shot down. The more incredible charge that he had plotted to assassinate Chairman Mao was accepted by almost everyone I talked to.

In the case of Zhou Enlai's illness, the government followed the opposite strategy. Without mentioning the illness, from the spring of 1975 on the government allowed citizens to see newsreels and photographs of the increasingly feeble premier receiving foreign visitors in the hospital. Citizens began to speculate among themselves that Zhou was ill, so that news of the death of this extremely important leader in January 1976 created less anxiety than it might have otherwise. When China's first satellite was launched, citizens were forewarned to stand by their radios for what turned out to be a broadcast from space of the Maoist anthem, "The East Is Red." The Nixon visit was announced in relay reports and covered on the front pages of the newspapers. Repetition explains the high scores for the news items on rich harvests and on the young man named Zhang Tiesheng, who handed in a blank college entrance examination as a protest against the idea of basing college admissions on exam grades. News on both items was repeated over and over, so that respondents could give details of the stories but could not recall where they heard them first. By contrast, the less-well-known items were those that had been less intensively reported, some never reported at all in the open press (items 1, 11, and 13). Yet even these less-emphasized items were identified by substantial percentages of the people I interviewed.

As a further test of media effectiveness, I asked respondents whether they could give the names of a number of officials whom they might have heard of through the press: the members of the Politburo, the foreign minister, and the chairman of the Standing Committee of the National People's Congress as of the time they left China. Depending upon the date of departure, this allowed respondents to list twenty to thirty officials. The results confirmed the media's impact. Thirteen persons reeled off 10 or more names. One respondent named 17. The average number of officials correctly named was 6.5. Most of the respondents named 5 or more officials, and only three persons could name none.

These data illustrate how effectively the Chinese media were able to convey political information to at least one collection of diverse individuals living in city and countryside, in eighteen different provinces, and working in state farms, communes, mines, factories, schools, and offices. The respondents' command of political items resembled Americans' grasp of advertising slogans more closely than it resembled the average American level of political information. In one survey, for example, 79 percent of Americans questioned could identify the product associated with the slogan "Plop plop fizz fizz," but in another study in 1970 only 49 percent of the American public knew which political party held the majority of seats in Congress. Such comparisons, however, must be interpreted with caution, for, as I explain in the Appendix, my respondents were not a statistically representative group of Chinese.

Other contrasts with the dynamics of public opinion in most countries can be more firmly established. The first concerns the interaction of political information and media use with political interest and participation. In most countries, individuals' command of political information and their attention to the media vary directly with their level of political interest and activity. My respondents indeed made significant use of the media: 89 percent of them spent at least half an hour a day reading newspapers or listening to broadcasts over radio or the loudspeaker. But their high scores in media use and political information were achieved despite the fact that a substantial majority—63 percent of those who were asked—said they had little or no interest in politics. Moreover, their rates of political participation were low. None had been a Communist Party member; fifteen had belonged to the Communist Youth League; one to a minority "democratic party"; and one to a professional association (for other affiliations, see the Appendix). When asked how often they engaged in a series of nine political acts, only twenty-nine said that they often or regularly spoke up at unit meetings, and usually only because everyone was required to speak. Seventeen said they often discussed personal problems with the unit leaders, and thirty-five said they often discussed politics with other members of the unit. But virtually none had ever written a letter to the editor, sent a complaint or appeal to higher officials, or used the suggestion box that exists in virtually every unit.

In a second unusual association, I found that the media were able to reach my respondents despite their relatively low levels of trust in the responsiveness of the political system—what political scientists call the sense of political efficacy. To measure this attitude, I asked four hypothetical questions about the individual's perceived ability to influence official decisions directly concerning his or her life (see the Appendix for details). Only 39 percent said that they would try to do something if their local residential unit was considering a decision that they felt was "very unjust or harmful." Even those who said they would do something often stipulated that they would speak out only if the issue was exceptionally serious, and most added that they would not expect to succeed in altering the decision. When asked about bringing a personal question such as a problem of housing or job assignment to a local government office, only 31 percent said they would expect fair and equal treatment. The other 69 percent said that government offices are so overwhelmed with housing and job problems that they could do little to help in any case. They would probably respond with excuses and delays, unless the individual concerned had personal connections with someone in the office.

Stronger feelings of efficacy were expressed in connection with the work unit. Forty-four percent of the respondents said that they had had some influence on the way "decisions were made on your job," in most cases concerning technical details of the work or a change in job assignment during an illness. Forty-seven percent of those who answered the question said they would have spoken up about a decision affecting their work that they disagreed with strongly, although several said they would have spoken only if they had good personal relations with the leaders and that their objections in any case probably would have carried little weight. These data, like others reported above, can neither be generalized to the population as a whole nor compared to figures from other countries that were gathered through sample surveys. Since as far as we know no such surveys were done in China in the 1970s, we will never know how representative my respondents' attitudes were. But judging from recent private testimony and official revelations they were not unusual in either their experiences or their reactions to them. The attitude of political alienation and passivity—"a thousand horses stand mute"—was officially admitted to be widespread as late as the early 1980s. As described in Chapters 4 and 9, a major goal of the Gengshen Reforms was to reverse this attitude, so that citizens would begin to participate more frequently and with more confidence in getting a hearing.

But the interviews showed that even before the reforms, in the early 1970s media use and political information were often high despite many individuals' low levels of political interest, political participation, and sense of efficacy. Further questioning suggested an explanation for this pattern in what might be called a motive of defensive curiosity. Seventy-two percent of those asked stated that government had a great effect on their lives. They cited policies on wages, schools, youth-to-the-countryside, economic development, and emigration, among others, as having virtually determined their life chances. "You may not want to pay attention to politics," several of them told me, quoting a common saw, "but politics will pay attention to you." The questionnaire included an item originally intended to probe the sense of civic obligation: "Some people say that even if a person is not very interested in politics, he or she still has an obligation to pay attention or get involved. What do you think?" A surprising 61 percent expressed agreement with this statement, but when I probed into their answers it became clear that they had understood the question in a way I had not anticipated. "It's dangerous not to be informed," one said. "You could put a foot wrong and get into bad trouble." They recognized an obligation to keep informed not in order to get involved, but in order to keep from getting too involved.

Aided by the institutional framework of work and residential units, study sessions, and political campaigns, the Chinese media not only have reached citizens but have often compelled their attention to information that the government felt was vital for them to know. People have usually spent more time with newspapers, magazines, loudspeakers, radio, and TV than with any other government-related institution outside their units. For most people, the media have been the authoritative and direct voice of the state, the arm of government they were likely to encounter most often, and their chief source of knowledge about politics and policy. But by the 1970s, the technological and political power of the media had outrun their ability to engage their audience. The media were reaching the people but were failing in their mission of moving them to belief and action.

9

WINNING BACK
THE PUBLIC

By the early 1970s, the Chinese citizen's relationship to the media had come
to resemble the "war of spiritual enslavement waged by high-pitched loudspeakers" described a few years later at Democracy Wall by the poet Huang
Xiang. The insistency, repetitiveness, and monotony of Chinese propaganda—the very fruits of central control—had fostered reactions opposite to
those the propagandists intended: instead of being persuaded and mobilized,
people increasingly withdrew from belief. The challenge the post-Mao reformers faced in attempting to win back the public was revealed in my interviews with 69 Chinese émigrés.

I had selected the thirteen news items on my questionnaire (see page
167) simply as a cross-section of well-known and lesser-known news about international and national affairs that had been treated in a variety of ways by
the Chinese press. They were not untypical of the material that appeared in
the Chinese media at the time. Yet in fact not a single one of these items had
been reported promptly, completely, and objectively. Three were simply
false: in 1970, there was no revival of Japanese militarism; in 1971, the economy had been sluggish rather than thriving for nine years and there was
slight inflation; and in 1973 the Arabs attacked Israel rather than the other
way around. Three sounded like, and were later alleged to be, fabrications:
the story of Lin Biao's coup attempt and flight; the tale of the model revolutionary youth Zhang Tiesheng; and the doings of the model cultural village
Xiaojinzhuang. Two items were reported tendentiously: the launching of
China's first man-made satellite was made a festival of patriotism; the report
of American antiwar demonstrations was slanted to show the imminent collapse of the American government. Nixon's impending visit was signaled by
terse announcements of Kissinger's presence; then when Nixon arrived, his
visit was treated as a tribute mission. Zhou Enlai's illness was revealed only
by printing photographs of the premier receiving foreign visitors in the hos-

pital. Three of the items were not reported at all in the open press: the American moon landing, the 1973 transfers of military commanders, and the purchase of foreign fertilizer plants. My respondents had learned about them, if at all, through relay reports, internal publications, foreign broadcasts, rumors, or delayed references in the public media.

My respondents' reactions to propaganda placed them in three groups, which I tagged the accepters, the skeptics, and the decipherers (for the classification technique, see the Appendix). The accepters adopted an attitude of detached receptivity to most of what the media said, viewing it as the information the party wanted them to have, without holding any strong conviction that it was the truth. A state farm worker told me that when he heard about China's rich harvests nine years running, he "felt it was a good thing." The Lin Biao incident struck him simply as "a serious matter." He was envious of Zhang Tiesheng, of blank-examination fame, because it seemed that people with good class backgrounds were always doing the right thing. A middle-school student who knew ten of the thirteen items had no opinion about any of them. "I didn't think much about it," she said. Another student read the press simply to see what "the reporter comrades" wrote. She never wondered why they wrote what they did.

Some of these individuals were actively contemptuous of the media's veracity when asked about it. One student observed that the *People's Daily* reported only good news, not bad; that all the papers "blew a big wind of propaganda." Yet these individuals did not bother to analyze the slant of news items or to speculate about the truths behind them. It was precisely their perception that the press was unreliable that had stilled their curiosity. As one said, "We did not pay much attention to radio and newspapers because we did not believe what they said." But for them "not believing" did not lead to active questioning.

There were two reasons for this response. First, this group of respondents was composed primarily of people who lived in units with poor media facilities. (See the Appendix for the evidence for this and related conclusions.) Information in China is filtered through a series of concentric rings of communication. The inner layers consist of many kinds of classified, "internal" publications, including foreign and domestic news bulletins for high officials, specialized scientific and scholarly periodicals, classified works of translation, and even restricted movies "for reference viewing." Under the post office subscription system, journals published for audiences in particular localities cannot be obtained outside those areas except through special procedures. Many specialized publications can be bought only with a certificate or letter from one's unit attesting to need. And most journals—local periodicals, specialized journals, and house organs—are not even listed in the post office catalogues and so are effectively hidden from potential readers outside the target audience. The importation of Chinese-language publications from abroad is in most cases forbidden, and during the early 1970s anyone caught listening to foreign radio broadcasts was punished. Most of the transmissions were jammed anyway. Thus the government's success in penetrating the population with its media was matched in many units by success in preventing the intrusion of competing information, not just from foreign sources but from domestic media aimed at other audiences. And this discouraged people who could not get around the information monopoly from asking questions about news reports even if they did not feel they were true.

The other characteristic of the accepters was that they had no special reason to make additional efforts to learn more. They were mostly young, of unexceptional class background, and more of them than of the respondent pool as a whole were female. They had suffered less in political campaigns than other respondents on the average, and had less reason to feel vulnerable. Politics did not absorb them. They needed to know only enough to get by in study sessions. Theirs was not the credence of the true believer, but the assent of the apathetic.

The second group of respondents was the skeptics. Like the accepters, the skeptics came from information-poor units with access mainly to official media. The difference was that they decided to reject what the accepters chose to accept. In this sense, they were less apathetic, since they cared more about identifying the truth. But unlike the third group, the decipherers, the skeptics were so alienated from the official media that they refused to try to quarry meaning from them, preferring to withhold judgment or to speculate rather than to read between the lines. "Everything is chosen to show that communism is good," one student told me. "I could never be sure whether newspaper stories were true or false." Said a farm worker commenting on the Lin Biao affair: "I didn't think Lin was bad or Mao was good; I only knew you can't have two tigers on one mountain."

Skepticism was sometimes simply a reaction to the pressure to accept official opinions. The very insistency of the party line signaled that alternative views were possible, and some readers felt they must be quite substantial to draw such strong rebuttal, even if one did not know quite what they were. In other cases, skepticism was triggered by reports that were at variance with the reader's own experiences. A worker on a state farm said about the claim of good harvests, "We didn't know whether to laugh or cry. If things are so good, why is life getting harder and harder? You could only buy a tenth of a piece of soap a month, there was no toothpaste, and we did not have meat for half a year. Once I found seven stones in one mouthful of rice. Our daily lives contradicted everything the newspapers said." A student said that the official line on the miseries of life in Hong Kong was belied by the tourists he met from there. And a peasant told me that his own village was a famous model brigade—not because of its accomplishments but because of the support of higher-level officials. "I've become totally cynical myself," he said. "I don't know what socialism is any more; I only know how to talk about it."

After rejecting much of what they read, the skeptics often did not know what to believe. For example, all but two of my respondents accepted the *People's Daily* report that Israel had attacked the Arabs in 1973. Most Chinese lacked the background in Middle Eastern affairs needed to detect any problem with the story. But several speculated that perhaps Israel had some good reason for its attack, and others concluded that Israel had dared to attack because of its superior technological achievements.

The last group of respondents was the decipherers. They usually lived in units with relatively rich media resources and paid close attention to the public press. But in contrast to the accepters and skeptics, the decipherers refused to accept the limits on information that the public media attempted to impose. They tried to decode the open press, but first obtained all the information they could from a hidden information network consisting of rumor, foreign radio, and the regime's internal media.

Rumor was the most readily available of these supplementary sources. Forty of my respondents reported getting information about Zhou Enlai's illness from "side-street news," as rumor is called. In this case the government had encouraged rumors by publishing pictures of the ailing Zhou without any description of his condition. Facts about his condition leaked from medical circles in Peking through relatives to people in all parts of the country. The rumors in different parts of the country were consistent with one another and, from what we know in retrospect, accurate—that he had been treated for cancer beginning in 1972.

In the late Mao years talking about overtly political subjects could be risky. Attitudes expressed in private might be brought up for criticism in study meetings. Many respondents said that was why they never discussed politics with other members of their units (see Appendix, Table 7). But if the temptation was too great to resist in the case of Zhou's illness, the same was true with the Lin Biao incident. Before the incident was announced through relay reports, two respondents learned from friends with contacts in aviation circles that all planes had been grounded, and they surmised that a crisis had occurred. Later, many Chinese shared with friends their doubts about the official story that Lin had crashed when his plane ran out of gas. They asked how the head of the Chinese military could have taken off in a plane without a full tank. Rumor supplied a story to fill the gap—that the plane had been shot down. One version had Zhou Enlai asking Mao, "Shall we shoot him down now?" and Mao replying, "Wait until he crosses the border. Until then he is still the vice-chairman." Another subject of rumor was the 1973 transfer of military commanders. Nineteen respondents learned about it from side-street news. Several heard the same story about why Mao decided on the transfers. He asked Deng Xiaoping what China would be like in ten years, and Deng answered in two words: "Great disorder." Mao asked, "What should I do?" and Deng answered again in two words: "Transfer commanders."

As this example shows, rumors shaded into stories and even jokes, all helping people draw more vivid, if largely imaginary, pictures of the handful of mysterious men, and one woman, who ruled them. The popular imagination placed the leaders in roles familiar from thousands of years of storytelling and opera—the worried emperor (Mao), the sagacious counselor (Zhou), the buffoonlike villain (Lin Biao), the evil empress (Jiang Qing). Zhou Enlai was the modern Zhuge Liang, a strategist whose invention was equal to every occasion. In one story people told, Zhou and Khrushchev meet in the halls of an international communist congress after each has attacked the other's country in his speech. They shake hands. Then Khrushchev pulls out a handkerchief, wipes his hand, and puts the handkerchief back. Zhou pulls out his handkerchief, wipes his hand, and throws his handkerchief away. In another version Khrushchev remarks, "It's interesting, isn't it? I'm of worker origin while your family were landlords." "Yes," replies Zhou, "and we each betrayed our class."

A third tale pits Zhou against Kissinger, who asks, "Why do you Chinese always walk around with your heads hanging, staring at the ground? We Americans stick our chests out proudly and look ahead." Zhou answers, "America is going downhill. If you leaned forward it would hasten your fall. We are moving up the mountain, so naturally our heads are bent forward." People liked to tell how Zhou was informed that Nixon and Kissinger had pilfered a famous flying horse statue on their visit to the Forbidden City. Zhou invited the Americans to a special magic show, in the course of which the magician made a replica statue "disappear," only to be "retrieved" from the President's pocket.

Tales of the early 1970s depicted Mao as befuddled and Deng Xiaoping as bitingly laconic. Mao asks Deng, "How much money do we have in all of China?" Deng replies, "Eighteen yuan and eighty-eight cents"—the sum value of the units of currency in everyday use. Another story has Wang Hongwen, Mao's last heir apparent and a man popularly considered none too bright, coming to Deng for help because Mao has assigned him to tally the total number of public latrines. "That's easy," Deng says. "Tell the Chairman two: the men's and the ladies'." Respondents also told stories about Mao's wife, Jiang Qing—how she had given interviews to an American scholar, how Mao was furious, and how Zhou Enlai had been deputed to prevent the book's publication by buying its copyright. (In fact the book was published in 1977 as *Comrade Chiang Ch'ing*, by Roxane Witke.) A widely told tale concerned how Mao's chief palace guard, Wang Dongxing, recruited the young women who were always seen around the elderly chairman in photographs and newsreels—how the girls were kidnapped from their families, forced to divorce their husbands, and impressed into serving the chairman's sexual whims.

Some stories about the leaders crystallized into hand-copied stories and novels that were circulated furtively from reader to reader. One was about Mao's mistress, a woman called "Little Zhang." Another concerned Zhou Enlai's resourceful defeat of a Soviet agent. Other stories were Cultural Revolution adventures and love tales—the most famous being *The Second Handshake*, which concerned the long-lasting love of two patriotic scientists, and was cleared after Mao's death for official publication. Twenty-six of my respondents had seen one or more of these hand-copied manuscripts. It was said that one novel, *A Maiden's Heart*, was so sexually explicit that any number of sent-down male youths had been driven to suicide by the frustration caused by reading it.

The second major source of unauthorized information was foreign radio. Almost all Chinese radios are produced with shortwave receiving capability because the hilly terrain forces the government to make many of its own broadcasts in shortwave. As a result, almost any Chinese with a radio is equipped to listen—depending on location—to the Voice of America, BBC, Radio Moscow, or stations emanating from Austrialia, Japan, Mongolia, Hong Kong, Macao, Taiwan, or the Philippines. Forty-two of my respondents told me that they listened to foreign broadcasts at least occasionally—usually in secret, late at night, and with earphones, in some cases keeping this activity hidden even from their families. Taiwan and Russian radio were not popular because they were considered no more reliable than the Chinese media. Chinese listeners preferred VOA and BBC, which broadcast in both English and Chinese, not only for their reports on the outside world but for the news they gave about China. They reported the Lin Biao incident and Zhou Enlai's death, for example, before the Chinese press. After Mao's death the government withdrew the ban on these stations, and in recent years many people have been tuning in for English lessons as well as for information.

Finally, enterprising Chinese could sometimes get access to Chinese internal media or foreign media that they were not eligible to see. Nine respondents told me they had been able to see a few copies of foreign magazines. (Nine others had seen foreign magazines in the course of their work and another two had seen selections in Chinese translation.) A young man got tickets to internal movies (films, mostly foreign, not cleared for public viewing) from a relative. Only one of my respondents had been cleared for the high-level publication *Reference Materials*, but fifteen others had glanced at copies in offices or when visiting friends whose parents were high cadres. None, however, had seen any of the other, still more sensitive, internal bulletins. An unemployed young man who lived in a big city made a project of obtaining internal books, especially translations from Western languages. Sometimes he borrowed them from friends and sometimes got fraudulent letters of authorization that enabled him to visit the special bookstores located upstairs from the bookstores open to the public. Classified works available at the time included Shirer's *Rise and Fall of the Third Reich*, *Khrushchev Remembers*, Nixon's *Six Crises*, and *Jonathan Livingston Seagull*. After Mao's death works of this sort became available on the open shelves, but the classification system as such has continued in effect. Despite its lapses, the system appears to have been fairly effective. Forty-one percent of my respondents saw internal media that they should not have seen, but in most cases it was no more than an occasional glimpse of a translated work or *Reference Materials*. Forty-two percent had never seen any internal movies, books, periodicals, or documents at all as far as I could judge, except for the widely available *Reference News*.

Reference News, a lightly edited four-page selection of foreign news reports in translation, was in fact the most popular printed source among my respondents. Forty-six percent of them said that they studied it most closely of all the official media, many poring over it for an hour or more a day—more time than some of them devoted to all other journals combined. Their chief reason was that it was more truthful and detailed than the rest of the press. This made it interesting even to those who were not especially concerned with the foreign news that it specializes in. Many paid special attention to articles on China, which they believed *Reference News*'s editors selected not only as indicators of foreign opinion but also as indicators of trends of thought in the Chinese leadership itself.

Reference News was only formally an internal publication. The term "reference" in China implies raw facts not subjected to ideological processing and not necessarily expressing the correct political attitude. In contrast to the strictly controlled content of the public media, almost anything can be circulated for reference because nobody has put himself behind it, and because people who might be wrongly affected are supposed to be protected from confusion by the fact that the item is classified. Despite this rationale, in 1957 Mao picked out *Reference News* from among all the internal media and directed that its circulation be increased from 2,000 to 400,000 in order, he said, "to put poisonous weeds and what is non-Marxist and anti-Marxist before our comrades, before the masses and the democratic personages [non-communist dignitaries], so that they can be tempered." Its present circulation of about 9 million is higher than that of the *People's Daily*. Anyone with cadre standing, including technicians and teachers, is able to subscribe, as are industrial employees and university students. Most work units get copies, even in the countryside. Only persons with bad class backgrounds or political labels are forbidden to look. As a consequence, as one of my respondents pointed out, ordinary Chinese are better informed about the outside world than would be expected by anyone who supposes that Chinese know only what appears in the open press.

Armed with clues from rumor, foreign radio, and such internal media as they could obtain, the decipherers among my respondents turned finally to the open press, adopting interpretive techniques similar to those used by Pekingologists in the West. They looked for a missing stock phrase, a reordering of leaders in a photograph, a change in the emphasis of coverage. A warehouse worker told me, "Beginning in late August 1971, I noticed there were no photographs or reports about Lin Biao, so I figured something was wrong. In early September the city-level cadres received a relay report and some rumors started to come down the line. Then I noticed that more generals were missing from the papers. Finally in early October the story was transmitted to the masses." Asked about the Nixon trip, the same worker said, "In 1971 I noticed in *Reference News* that Nixon had referred to China as the 'People's Republic of China,' and I thought U.S.-China relations might improve. In late 1971 anti-American propaganda started to ease up. The emphasis was placed on Soviet social imperialism rather than American imperialism. Small reports began to appear on American life—not favorable, but relatively objective—and on the bitter life in the Soviet Union and Eastern Europe. I felt a thaw in relations was coming." Other respondents interpreted reports of Zhou Enlai's sixteen-hour workdays as early denials that he was sick; the story of examination candidate Zhang Tiesheng as an attack by radical forces on the restoration of college entrance exams favored by Deng Xiaoping; and reports on Japanese militarism not as news of an event but as a warning to Japan not to rearm. Several claimed to have sensed in advance the brewing power struggle that broke into the open after Mao died. A factory worker said he and other workers were watching Zhou Enlai's funeral on television when they noticed that Jiang Qing refused to take off her cap. They all felt that this showed Jiang's opposition to Zhou and his successor, Deng. A middle-school teacher said that in April 1976 the New China News Agency distributed a report that included a quotation from Zhou. He and his colleagues noticed that the *People's Daily* printed the quotation while the Shanghai newspapers deleted it. "We all knew that this meant that the Shanghai political forces opposed Zhou's followers," he said.

Those who tried to decipher the press were tacitly accepting its usefulness as a source of information. In this sense they were less alienated from the regime's propaganda than the skeptics or even the accepters, for they felt that the press contained something meaningful and spent hours trying to figure out what it was. In fact, it was the decipherers among my respondents who were most likely to defend the guarded quality of the press, contending that what Americans might think of as "the whole truth" was not suitable for publication in official media whose every line carries the imprimatur of the party. They would have been disturbed if the media were a cacophony of competing voices and undigested facts; they were used to treating the official line as a fixed point in their analyses of events. When asked whether the government should always tell the truth to its own people, 37 percent of the respondents who answered the question said that it should sometimes lie. This did not mean, however, that the decipherers approved of the way the official press was performing its role. Most seemed to feel that the press was not skillful enough in providing substantial information in the context of a plausible ideology. Too often the facts it gave were unbelievable or the interpretation failed to encompass facts that readers knew.

Forced to find their own ways of thinking about fragmentary information, the decipherers, like the skeptics, often reached conclusions opposite from those intended for them. One felt that if Japanese militarism had revived, Japan must have become quite prosperous; maybe China should follow its model. Several believed that the anti–Vietnam war demonstrations reported in *People's Daily* showed how much freedom the American people enjoyed. China's launching of a satellite prompted one worker to reflect on the vigor of American rather than Chinese science, because China's chief space scientist was American-trained. A sent-down youth told me that the more reports she read of urban middle-school graduates enthusiastically accepting assignments to the countryside, the more strongly she sensed that new graduates were resisting the policy.

Thirty-nine percent of my respondents turned out to be accepters, 39 percent skeptics, and the remaining 22 percent decipherers. Completely missing among them was a category of audience members whom I would have called believers had I found any—those who viewed what the media said not merely as the authoritative government line, but as a true representation of the facts. It is likely that the distribution of types among the Chinese population in the early 1970s was different from that among my interview group. There must have been some believers; the proportion of accepters was probably higher, especially among the hundreds of millions of poorly educated country people and workers in small factories who had limited access to the media and little desire to know much more than they were told; and there must have been correspondingly fewer skeptics and decipherers. Yet my interviews do suggest the nature of the "crisis of confidence" acknowledged by the Deng regime when it came to power.

The Chinese media could not perform their missions for the state unless they not only informed but also persuaded the people, not only reported good news but also provided accurate intelligence to the leaders, not only promulgated policy but also helped uncover bureaucrats who failed to implement it. The press portion of the Gengshen Reforms was aimed at restoring the ability of China's media network to perform the functions for which it was designed.

The first step was to declare a clean break with the past. The press denounced its former style of journalism as "Gang of Four–style eight-legged essays." *People's Daily* apologized for its past performance, claiming that Gang member Yao Wenyuan had ruled it with peremptory phone calls and arbitrary orders. He had scotched a prominent display of photographs in memory of Zhou Enlai, demanded publication of articles by his hand-picked writing group, and ordered journalists to "trump up" paeans to models now revealed as frauds, such as Zhang Tiesheng and Xiaojinzhuang. The Gang had supposedly used the press to quote Mao's words out of context, fabricate quotations, tamper with photographs, and, according to a character in a stage drama, "employ a bunch of hacks who specialize in churning out crap explaining why black [reactionary things] should be red [progressive]." Yao Wenyuan was even reviled as "China's Goebbels."

In order to win back the public's interest, the media began to publish a wider range of material. The number of books and journals increased; subscription quotas were lifted on the most popular items; material that would have been published in internal publications appeared in the open press and on bookstore shelves; evening papers, with lighter content than the major dailies, began to appear in the cities. So many pretty girls appeared on magazine covers that conservative readers wrote in to protest. The newspapers carried more information on regions of special curiosity to Chinese like America, Taiwan, and Eastern Europe. They printed divergent opinion on historiographical and philosophical issues, and even some policy questions, before the party leaders decided on the correct line. TV viewers saw "The Man from Atlantis" and other imported programs; movie theaters screened not only North Korean and Rumanian epics but American cowboy movies and science fiction dramas like *Futureworld*. Artists once again depicted traditional landscapes and bird-and-flower themes. There was a revival of light music and Western-style symphonies.

As in the missionary periodicals of the nineteenth century, diversity established a context of liveliness and believability for the political message, while often helping to convey subtle themes of its own. "Man from Atlantis," for example, helped popularize science, as did the revived genre of science fiction. Traditional landscape painting signified love of country. Translated works were mainly those of wholesome and progressive foreign authors, or those that threw an unflattering light on bourgeois society. Sentimental music depicted people with socialist and patriotic feelings, while "yellow" (pornographic) love music from Hong Kong and Taiwan remained officially banned, although popular on smuggled cassettes. Broadening the boundaries of propaganda did not mean abandoning its purpose. *News Front*, the magazine of the Chinese Journalists' Association, summarized the strategy as "placing [communist] education in the midst of material full of knowledge and interest," so as to "influence people without their noticing it."

Third, the press tried to restore its tradition of factual reliability. Accu-

racy had often been subordinated to other goals in Chinese journalism. Although the missions of supervising the bureaucracy and providing intelligence to the leaders required factual accuracy, the task of propagating policy
could be hampered by publishing too many negative examples and reports
about problems. Reporters as an independent corps of investigators were
supposed to discover the truth, but as minions of the party they were obliged
to accept the guidance of central and local leaders about what to publish.
Only when they had strong editorial support have Chinese reporters given
the public, or even the leaders, all the unpalatable facts; otherwise they have
concentrated on what is known as "good people and good events." "You report good news and never bad," Liu Shaoqi had complained to a group of
People's Daily editors as he tried to check the "wind of exaggeration" that
blew during the Great Leap Forward:

> How much of what your newspaper prints is true? Every day you print
> leading stories in big type, one day saying how great production is over
> here, the next day saying how wonderful communist mess halls are over
> there. How much of this is really true? . . . I never read [these stories].
> When the paper comes I just look at the international news and features.

Liu then ordered the press to report both bad news and good; to report selected foreign criticism of China; and to report on certain issues "as problems, not necessarily waiting to report on them until a conclusion has been
reached." He instructed the New China News Agency in its reporting for
foreign audiences to be "objective, truthful, fair, and complete, at the same
time as it has a political standpoint. Only in this way can we establish our
credibility in the world." These instructions had been denounced during the
Cultural Revolution as a bourgeois doctrine of "class-free objective reporting." But they were restored to a place of honor in the new campaign to raise
standards of accuracy in the press.

For thirty-five years it had been rare for the Chinese press to correct itself.
Now the reporters' professional magazine, *News Front*, took the lead in exposing falsehoods that appeared in the media. It revealed that a 142-year-old
man reported in *People's Daily* as "full of vigor and able to walk with steady
steps" was only 82. A report on the enthusiastic reception given to Chinese
artisans at Bloomingdale's department store in New York was said to have
been made up by a reporter who had never been there. A water-control
project that was reported to be in service turned out to be incomplete; a reporter learning by phone of rain and snow in one part of a drought-stricken
area had assumed wrongly that the drought had been lifted all over.

Analyzing the sources of falsehoods, *News Front* determined that reporters too often relied on unchecked facts given them by party sources. Even
statistics taken from intraparty reports were not necessarily true, it warned.

Stories fed to the press by local party officials were often inaccurate as well. In "extremely few isolated cases," said the magazine, journalists were motivated by active bias against or in favor of some individual being reported on. Some reporters, added *People's Daily* in its contribution to the campaign, publish lies in order to advance their careers: "As soon as they hear that a 'new guideline' has been issued by higher levels, they rush to cite examples and to find facts to verify it." Such practices of the past could no longer be allowed. To improve professional standards journalism departments in Chinese schools gave new emphasis to techniques of investigation and fact-checking. Foreign professors were invited to lecture on the arts of asking questions at press conferences and interviewing the man in the street.

Accuracy, however, still had to serve propaganda's purposes. *News Front* reminded reporters that stories on model units and individuals—which remained a mainstay of the daily press—"are not a form of naturalistic recording of all that we hear, not the mechanical reprinting of a copy or photograph. They require selection, refinement, generalization, and elevation. But these processes should never depart from the reality of the model itself." *News Front* criticized stories about events that were contrary to the party or state constitutions or to law. A *People's Daily* article that bragged about a criminal being caught, indicted, tried, sentenced, and rejected on appeal within eight days, for example, ignored the fact that the procedures it described legally required a longer time to complete. Such reporting, even if true, the journal said, was not helpful to the task of publicizing legal knowledge among the masses. Accuracy was useful to the extent that it served the purposes of propaganda and not as an end in itself. As a writer in *People's Daily* observed, "The reason propaganda can play a great role and can sometimes exert tremendous authority is not mainly because of the quality of the propaganda work itself but because of the objective facts." False reports are like "rat droppings in soup"—they ruin the effect.

The most ambitious press reform measure was the attempt to revive the press's role as an independent investigative force, a kind of modern censorate that could supervise the bureaucracy and voice the concerns of the masses directly to the leaders—the work of "criticism and self-criticism." As a first step, *People's Daily* and other major papers reestablished their "mass work" departments, closed during the Cultural Revolution. In the early 1980s *People's Daily* handled tens of thousands of letters a month; the mass work department of Peking's *Enlightenment Daily* about two hundred letters a day. Despite the revival of "letters and visits work," newspapers were still the only organizations in China's complex bureaucratic system that had at once the authority and the incentive thoroughly to investigate people's complaints against cadres at the middle and lower levels. County and provincial officials who could also handle such problems had insufficient time and little inclination to get involved with the complex, sometimes insoluble, complaints of ordinary people. For journalists, on the other hand, this was the work they were trained to do and in which they took pride. Moreover, letters and investigations have always been among the press's most popular copy. So when letters to the editor brought interesting complaints about local officials, papers sent their local correspondents or even special teams to investigate. The reporters were sometimes harassed, slandered, or even beaten in the pursuit of their investigative duties; after a spate of such incidents *News Front* published an editorial entitled, "The Proper Rights of Correspondents Are Not to Be Infringed Upon."

Often the subject matter of an investigation was minor, but pursuing it showed the party's concern for the application of policy to individual cases. A photographer complained that a cadre of a state-owned photography shop seized her camera when she tried to sell portraits to tourists at West Lake in Hangzhou. A worker said that cadres of the Shanghai Number 2 electrical machinery plant used the factory's welfare fund to hold banquets. A party official was living too luxuriously; collectively owned agricultural land was sold off illegally for housing; an accountant who refused to falsify production figures was harassed by his boss. A citizen wrote to say that a bus driver and ticket-taker on a route in Shanghai allowed a rider to carry a piece of wood which was longer than regulations permit. No case was insignificant if it had some human interest and typified in some way the application of current policy.

Editors at *Enlightenment Daily* told me in an interview how readers' letters tipped them off to beatings of schoolteachers in Sichuan, corruption in a cigarette factory in Shanxi, and harassment of a private film-projection team in Hunan. In all cases local cadres tried to deny wrongdoing. But the paper kept publishing details to bring pressure to bear until the targets admitted their guilt and made restitution—a course of events that did no harm to the paper's circulation. When an investigation upholds a complaint, it is customary for the offending cadre to submit for publication a letter of contrition. One vindicated letter-writer even wrote to complain about a new practice of "paying special visits to make apologies." After *People's Daily* upheld his complaint about a dirty railway station, a delegation of station personnel came to apologize personally, so incurring considerable expense not only for their own unit but for his, since he had to entertain them.

The second source of material for criticism and self-criticism was original investigative reporting by news staff. *People's Daily*'s new editor, Hu Jiwei, appointed in 1977 under the aegis of Deng Xiaoping, explained his creed on investigative work in a speech carried in *News Front*. Criticism, he said, should be constructive and should be guided by party organs, but it must also be strict and fearless in order to "place the party's work under the supervision of the masses." He rebutted the claim of some that bad publicity about high-ranking cadres would harm the party's image. One must not be afraid of being taken advantage of by enemies, he said, so long as the healthy process of criticism and self-criticism benefits the people more. He warned that his newspaper would go after "tigers" as well as "flies," and would break with the tradition of never giving the names of higher-level officials criticized until they had been purged.

Hu was as good as his word. Although the bulk of investigative stories in *People's Daily* in 1979 and 1980 concerned abuse of power, waste, corruption, privilege-seeking, nepotism, and resistance to change by lower-level officials, the paper also published a series of exposés of important officials, serving in each case the interests of Deng's faction either in consolidating its power or in enforcing compliance with its policies. In 1980 the newspaper carried a series of articles exposing political oppression and economic mismanagement in the former model agricultural brigade of Dazhai even though its leader, Chen Yonggui, had not yet been dropped from his vice-premiership. After a foreign newspaper revealed the sinking of an offshore oil rig, the Bohai Number 2, in a storm, the *Daily* exposed an eight-month coverup of the case and blamed the oil minister, who had to resign. The paper aggressively pursued another story about the minister of commerce eating free meals in a public restaurant. He too left office.

Resistance to exposure reporting in conservative sectors of the elite came together with uneasiness about Deng's reforms generally—including concern about the continued activities of the democracy movement in 1980—to spark a controversy over the limits of reform in the work of the press. How far should the press go, as an independent investigative arm of the party, in prosecuting cases against those who outrank the press people themselves? When might news of leaders' errors tar the image of the party? When did the zeal of reporters for their role as the people's tribunes turn into competition with the party leaders for the right to represent the highest interests of the masses? The conservatives' thinking on these questions was given by Guangdong First Party Secretary Ren Zhongyi in 1980 during a visit to the offices of the *Southern Daily* in Canton. "Exposures of our dark side should not be too frequent," he told the staff, "nor should they be too highly colored. Otherwise, we might give people the wrong impression, weaken the party's prestige among the masses, and affect stability and unity in ways that are not beneficial to socialist construction."

People's Daily published a series of statements in defense of aggressive exposure writing by the press. Some comrades, one article charged, prefer to expose errors in internal circulars that are read by no one below the level of county officials. But this often produces little effect, whereas exposure in the open press brings quick results. "Under the very eyes of the public, it is difficult for those practicing bureaucratism to say nothing, make excuses, pass the buck, or get off scot-free." The paper claimed that each of its investigative articles had elicited hundreds of spontaneous letters of support from the public. Of course, criticism should be conducted prudently, in consultation with the party committees involved and through exposure of a limited number of cases, the paper conceded, but it remained the best method for keeping the masses on the party's side. *News Front* reprinted Liu Shaoqi's old directives in favor of exposure reporting, and in its last issue of 1980 carried what was to be the first of two lectures by Hu Jiwei further defending criticism and self-criticism against those "many comrades whose understanding of its importance is still insufficient." Hu's second lecture was never published. Instead, the January 1981 issue of *News Front* contained a table of contents so hastily rearranged that part of it was pasted over the original printed text.

The magazine had fallen into line with a compromise policy just enunciated by the party center in its Document No. 7 of 1981. This document, "Decision on the Present Propaganda Policy for Magazines, Newspapers, and Broadcasting," laid down the governing principles for the role of the press, and by extension writers and other cultural workers, under the Deng regime. The document ruled, first of all, that exposure reporting had gone too far. From now on, fewer criticism articles should be published, fewer names should be mentioned, and criticism should be aimed mainly at trends rather than individuals. If a person was to be criticized by name, the document imposed stringent procedures. The newspaper must verify the facts with the person concerned and the leaders of his or her unit and must negotiate the nature of the criticism with the target's superior party and government organs. In the later words of Ren Zhongyi, critical reports must meet four criteria: they must be accurate, they must follow through and inform the masses of the disposition of a case, they must "pay attention to social effects, helping raise the party's prestige and strengthen the masses' confidence," and "they should not create problems for the leaders: problems that for the time being cannot be solved should not be publicized; you can bring them to the leaders' attention through other channels."

To reinforce the message, some of Mao's statements on journalism were brought from the archives and republished. "We must defeat the tendency of propaganda personnel to push for independence," he was quoted as having said in 1942. "Newspapers must unconditionally propagandize the party center's line and policy," he had said in 1948. "Criticism [in newspapers] must be accurate, it must be beneficial to the people, it can't be all over the lot," he directed in 1954. "Whether or not to name names should be carefully studied. Management . . . is the key. If the party committee doesn't manage it, criticism cannot be launched and cannot be well conducted."

The new policy did not mean an end to criticism and self-criticism. As explained by an editor of the *People's Daily*, "By relying solely on reports of the good side, it is hard to move some people; it is also hard to find anything new to say. By exposing a few negative examples, news reports more easily make an impression." The proper proportion of praise to blame, this editor indicated, was about 80/20. So letters to the editor continued to expose the peccadilloes of local bureaucrats, sparking press campaigns about careless handling of goods in transit or mistreatment of intellectuals returning from overseas. The press did its share in the campaign against economic crimes. The Central Committee brought the pressure of the newspapers to bear on slow-moving local officials—for example, exposing laxity in rehabilitating teachers at Hunan University and criticizing continuing "leftist" influence in Guangxi Province. But the targets were more carefully circumscribed to avoid painting too dark a picture of socialist society in the aggregate. In 1982 Hu Jiwei lost his editorial control of the *People's Daily* when he was appointed to a newly created post as director, and a year later he was forced into early retirement.

A similar cycle of reform and retreat occurred from 1977 to 1981 in other sectors of the propaganda front—for example, in literature. Chinese writers beginning in 1977 were allowed to experiment with what came to be called "wound" or "exposure" literature. At first these stories portrayed the horrors of the Cultural Revolution, but then they began still more daringly to describe the pessimistic attitudes of contemporary youth and the continuing corruption of some cadres. (Several collections of this literature have been published in English, including *Mao's Harvest*, edited by Helen F. Siu and Zelda Stern, and *Stubborn Weeds*, edited by Perry Link.) The exposure writers carefully observed certain conventions: Although their stories, set in the late Mao period, portray the depths of winter, spring is always sure to come. Their heroes work tirelessly for the nation regardless of illness, hunger, age, or other infirmities. It is never the party that is oppressing them, but the "remnant poisons of feudal ideology" or what some of these fictional characters anachronistically recognize as the "Gang of Four," although this term did not enter public usage until after Mao's death. Nothing can shake these heroes' faith in the ultimate correctness of the party, so they endure ten or fifteen years of oppression quite cheerfully, rightly confident that they will be vindicated in the end. The "leftist" villains of these pieces are not presented as committed ideologues, which would be giving them too much credit, but as opportunists moving vaguely with the current ideological winds.

By depicting the "dark side" of recent history, the exposure writers and the editors who published their works hoped to exorcise some of the problems of Chinese society and prevent their recurrence. At the Fourth National Congress of Writers and Artists in November 1979, leading writers begged for latitude to serve the revolution through the presentation of the complex realities that party literature had traditionally avoided. But for some party leaders the writers, like the newspaper journalists, were coming too close to claiming to speak for the people against even the party. After long debate, the party leaders ruled against them. In the same Document No. 7 that had limited investigative reporting, the party center reaffirmed that the role of writers was to "inspire the whole party, the whole army, and the people . . . to work concertedly and vigorously to accomplish the great cause of the Four Modernizations." To do this, they must "fervently praise the socialist-minded new people and pioneers of modernization" and "write less" on themes of exposure, because "too many works on these themes will produce negative results."

The document thus reiterated, for literature as for journalism, the classic doctrine of both Soviet and Chinese communism that literature, like other propaganda, must be judged by its social effects. Mao had given this doctrine its definitive Chinese formulation in a speech at the Yanan Forum on Literature and Art in 1942:

> The purpose of our meeting today is precisely to ensure that literature and art fit well into the whole revolutionary machine as a component part, that they operate as powerful weapons for uniting and educating the people and for attacking and destroying the enemy, and that they help the people fight the enemy with one heart and one mind.

The Yanan Forum doctrine was now reaffirmed. Articles published in the aftermath of Document No. 7 argued that writers could not discharge their duty just by "depicting reality" without regard to effects. One "must have the sense of responsibility of a politician" in gauging the impact of one's works. Nor could a writer's duty to the people justify publishing damaging works. "There are now some writers," observed the veteran literary bureaucrat Zhou Yang, "especially young writers, who like to talk about the so-called conscience. This is a very difficult notion to understand. They do not like to discuss loyalty to the revolutionary cause, which can actually be examined and tested." In a textbook example—it may have been intended as such—of how the concern with social effects must override the criterion of mere truthfulness, the party press unanimously criticized a 1982 novel, Yu Luojin's *Fairytales in Spring*, although no one could challenge its veracity as a thinly disguised account of its author's actual experiences, because it painted too negative a view of socialist society.

The struggles over exposure writing in journalism and literature ended by restating the fundamental doctrine of propaganda that Liang Qichao had enunciated at the beginning of the century—that truth is instrumental to action goals. After all, asked an article in *People's Daily*, "What is truthfulness? It is a pity that this problem has not yet been solved very well theoretically. Some articles hold that it is truthful to write about events in real life. This view is too simplistic." "Literature must contain facts," stated *Red Flag*, "but facts are not necessarily a form of literature." Chinese writers must seek what is known as "the truthfulness of typification" rather than the untruth of objectivism. Perceiving the outer appearance of a thing is only the first step in correct understanding, explained another *Red Flag* article. The propagandist must grasp the inner essence which, properly understood, is always conducive to the party's goals.

> When we are doing propaganda work, we should always guide the people to understand the matter correctly so that they will take their effective action in the interests of the people's cause. We should on no account adopt the so-called purely objective attitude of propagating everything we have seen.

*   *   *

Even in the early 1970s my respondents, including the skeptics and decipherers, had been deeply influenced by propaganda. They absorbed a great deal of information about government policies from the press and did most of their political thinking in terms of its jargon. No matter how alienated they thought they were, they accepted many of the values and goals defined by the government. And after they had sifted through the facts presented by the press their picture of the world was still made up largely of the material that remained. In this sense even those who were least persuaded were still captives of their information environment. Few of my respondents had access to enough outside information, and none had enough time and intellectual energy, to construct the kind of independent view of the world that the handful of democracy activists had. The fact that the democrats were so few, and that even their thinking was constrained by official categories, attests to the ability of the propaganda network to reach people, to inculcate ideas through repetition, and to exclude contrary ideas and information.

My interviews suggested that the new diversity and accuracy of the media after Mao's death were further increasing the media's impact, as intended. My classification of respondents as accepters, skeptics, or decipherers was based primarily on their responses to the thirteen news items from the early 1970s. But respondents who left China after the press reforms began in 1977 said they had started to read more, go to more movies, and watch more television as the contents of the media became more interesting. They trusted more of what the press said—not only as the authoritative government line, but as a basically accurate account of the facts and a plausible interpretation of their significance. They were beginning to move into the fourth category of audience members that might be called believers. If the press continues to present a relatively complex and accurate view of the world, the proportion of believers in the population can be expected to grow.

The Chinese citizen, however, continues to be aware that the media are centrally coordinated instruments of persuasion. No effort is made to keep this fact secret. In fact the Central Committee Propaganda Department often publishes its directives on the front pages of the major papers. For example, the themes to be emphasized by the press during the spring festival of 1982 were laid out on page one of *Enlightenment Daily*:

> All localities . . . must energetically propagandize the series of achievements on various fronts since the party's Third Plenum [when Deng took over], the ten policies for economic construction, and the bright prospects for the future. All fronts, professions, and enterprises should select advanced personnel for praise. You should propagandize their good ideology, good work styles, and good experiences in order to encourage people to fight their way forward, to strive to make new contributions for the state.

Citizens reading the directive could count on hearing the slogans that it carried repeated throughout the festival period.

Even when propaganda guidelines are not published they are easily discerned by noting their influence in the press. Leaders' speeches or Central Committee documents provide themes and slogans that are echoed by editorials and news articles. Examples include the promotion of the four basic principles after Deng introduced them in March 1979, the denunciations of the "four great freedoms" prior to their abolition by the National People's Congress in 1979, the 1979–80 campaign on properly understanding the U.S., and the 1981–82 movement against bourgeois liberalization. In each of these cases the coordinated use of arguments and phrases in all the media revealed the existence of a guiding directive, although the texts of the directives are not all available to us.

The reader is further reminded of the propagandistic aims of the media by the eulogistic tone of much that appears in the form of news. For example, the *People's Daily* reported that the slogan "Five Stresses and Four Beauties," which promotes various forms of civic virtue, "quickly found favor among the broad masses of people and became a principle governing social life soon after it was formulated." In Peking, the press reported, more than a hundred thousand young people formed "Learn from Lei Feng Groups" to assist elderly people (Lei Feng was a model soldier). Peasants throughout the country were said to have formed voluntary "village pacts" to promote socialist ethics, maintain order, discard old customs, and improve sanitation. A young party member killed helping pedestrians resist a mugger was found to have left a diary full of correct sentiments about self-sacrifice. While the old model village of Xiaojinzhuang was no longer mentioned, attention was given to new model villages such as the Wangxi brigade in Shanxi, a "spiritual civilization village" full of "cooperation and unity, respect for the elderly and love for children, love for the collective, obedience to discipline and law, pleasure in helping others, and household diligence and thrift." On the production front, an agricultural brigade was reported to have gone from rags to riches in a year thanks to reform of its collective sideline production. The new model county of Fengyang became a showcase of peasant consumerism under the impact of the responsibility system in agriculture. Even the old model brigade of Dazhai, whose supposed achievements under Mao had been exposed as a fraud, was now reported to be setting new production records because it had changed to the new system.

Such stories may have been founded on elements of truth, but no one intended them to be read as the whole truth. They belonged to the old category of edifying reports on "good people and good things" intended to encourage people to follow the directions mandated by policy. Between the Chinese media and their audience the understanding remains that reported facts have an official meaning. (An exception is the growing category of strictly informational articles and advertisements on technical and economic subjects in specialized publications.) The Chinese citizen's belief in the press remains, accordingly, guarded. A reader survey conducted by Chinese researchers in 1982 in Peking revealed that only 24.2 percent of those polled regarded the newspapers as "believable"; another 55 percent considered the papers "basically believable," while the remaining 20.8 percent found them often or always untruthful. Readers in a Tianjin survey contemptuously accused the papers of "swaying and swinging," "blowing up whirlwinds," "riding the waves," and "bending like grass on a wall." A critique published in *News Front* in 1984 reported that many readers disbelieved on principle 20 to 50 percent of what they read in the press, and the critique's author blamed this on the fact that "the propaganda flavor is still too thick."

According to my interviews, however, it was not its propagandistic tone as such that was most damaging to the press's relationship with its audience—most members of the public accepted the media's role of speaking for the party line. The deepest problem was the changeability of the line itself over the course of several decades. The Lin Biao incident, in particular, broke citizens' confidence in the reliability of the line. During the Cultural Revolution many had accepted the charge, incredible though it was, that the long-honored head of state Liu Shaoqi was a capitalist agent. But when Mao's second chosen successor turned out to be a hidden traitor too, people began to doubt Mao's infallibility and to realize that no policy, no matter how vociferously expressed, was safe from reversal. Later, although many Chinese welcomed the purge of the "Gang of Four," they were cynical about the way all of China's problems were blamed on the Four. The new leader, Hua Guofeng, claimed to have inherited Mao's mantle but was himself criticized and demoted a few years later for rigid adherence to Mao's ideas. Although media credibility has improved, it remains hostage to political stability. A decade of careful work in winning back the audience will be undone if the press is required again to denounce leaders it has earlier praised. And so long as the Chinese public knows this can happen, its trust in the media will remain tinged with an element of tentativeness.

The press has done as much as any institution in this century to define what it means to be a citizen in the Chinese democratic order. But its service to the state has been limited by the fundamental paradox of propaganda—that once recognized as an attempt to control the perceptions of its audience, it puts its audience on guard. The democracy activists argued that only an independent press could break through the barriers of suspicion to arouse and persuade the public in a way that it had not done since the late Qing. Together with competitive elections, an independent press was one of two reforms that the more radical among the activists considered essential to the democratization of Chinese politics. The confrontation of the party and the democrats showed that this was a reform the party could not accept. The party's tolerance for electoral competition was to be tested in the people's congress elections of 1980.

10

THE 1980 ELECTIONS

The final conflict between the democrats and the reformers came in 1980, when the party implemented the centerpiece of its Gengshen Reforms, competitive elections for seats in local people's congresses. This was the only one of the reforms that mobilized the entire population for a common act of political participation. By reviving the congressional election system, which had been in abeyance since the Cultural Revolution, the leaders hoped to restore the public's sense of identification with government. Moreover, these elections—more open and competitive than any in PRC history—were intended symbolically to renew the party's claim to rule in the public interest and with public consent. What the leaders did not foresee was that the democrats would view the election as an opportunity to try to put their own ideas of democracy into effect.

People's congresses, or soviets, symbolize popular sovereignty in all socialist systems. They embody the ideal of the Paris Commune, which Marx had identified as the embryonic form of the eventual communist state. Socialist countries have all established people's congress systems in attempts to fulfill his prediction. Recognizing the congresses as sovereign, socialist constitutions provide for no separation of powers nor for any authority higher than the Supreme Soviet (in Russia) or the National People's Congress (in China). The national congress appoints, empowers, and reviews the work of all branches of government including the judiciary, and itself interprets the constitutionality of the laws it passes. As explained by Chinese political scientists, people's congresses

> concentrate the people's will and interests and constitute the organ by which the people exercise state power. They represent the people in giving consent in important matters of state. They bear responsibility to the people and subject themselves to supervision by the people. . . . All the

other organs of state come into being through the decision of the people's congresses, are responsible to them, and make work reports to them.

In Western eyes the popular sovereignty so described appears more nominal than real. Even under the 1982 constitution the National People's Congress needs to meet only once a year. The constitution contains a number of provisions designed to enable the congress and especially its Standing Committee to play a greater role than in the past. But the day-to-day work of government is still managed by the state bureaucracy under the direction of the Communist Party. No legislation or policy ever really originates with the congress. Nonetheless, the very existence of the congress system signifies to Chinese communist theorists that "the people of the whole country . . . enjoy the supreme power to manage the state." Because the people elect the congresses and the congresses give their approval to important matters of state, the congresses transmit the people's assent.

The national congress, elected for a five-year term, is the highest of four levels of congresses that correspond to the four-level structure of Chinese administration. At the bottom are the congresses of some 50,000 townships (formerly communes), elected every two years according to the provisions of the 1979 Organic Law for Local People's Congresses and Local People's Governments. Second are the 2,757 congresses of the county level, elected for a three-year term. This level includes not only counties, but also the administrative districts into which the largest cities are divided; smaller cities that are not divided into districts; and the so-called autonomous counties and prefectures where substantial populations of national minorities live. At the third level, elected for five-year terms, are the congresses of China's 29 provinces, autonomous regions, or major cities with provincial-level administrative status. All three lower levels are described as "local," with the lowest level also referred to as "basic."

People's congress elections are festive public rituals in all socialist states. Huge numbers of people are involved. In the Soviet Union, for example, about one of every hundred voting-age citizens serves as a candidate in each election, and 50 percent of the candidates are rotated each time. One in twenty participates in electoral commissions. About one in three attends election meetings. Millions serve as agitators who attempt to visit every citizen in his or her home. Because elections at different levels are on different cycles, elections occur three years out of four, and each election takes about two months, leading one scholar to estimate that "the Soviet voter is experiencing state elections for one-eighth of his existence."

Election day in the Soviet Union is always a Sunday. The polling places are decorated with red bunting and pictures of Lenin and Central Committee members. At some polls refreshments are available and brass bands play. At any time between 6:00 A.M. and midnight voters can pick up their ballots (one for each level of soviet being elected) and deposit them in the urn without even having to look at them. A few people manage to miss the election despite extensive provisions for voting while traveling, in the hospital, and even at home. And it is possible to cast a negative vote by entering a separate booth or room provided and crossing the single candidate's name off the ballot. The combined number of absentees and negative voters in a series of elections in the 1950s and 1960s ranged from 0.2 percent in one region to a little over 1 percent in another. Only about one candidate in ten thousand was defeated. That dissenting votes are permitted and that massive efforts are made to discourage them shows how seriously the elections are viewed by the ruling party of the USSR. The 99-percent triumph of the official slate caps an intense period of political education that ritually renews the bond of unity between the people and the government. The regime seeks much more than compliance from voters in these campaigns; it seeks active assent.

Elections more or less on the Soviet model were held in communist-ruled areas in China beginning in the late 1920s. Local soviets, congresses, or people's conferences were elected wherever and whenever possible in the long course of the civil war and in the first years after liberation. The 1953 election law and 1954 constitution established the regular four-level hierarchy. But only the lowest-level congresses were directly elected, a departure from Soviet practice. Drawing from the traditional idea that political leaders should educate the people, the communist leaders argued that the people's lack of political experience made it premature to hold direct elections for congresses at the county level and above. These would be chosen indirectly, by vote of the congresses at the level below. The 1953 law provided, Soviet-style, for one candidate per seat and, because many voters were illiterate, for voting by a show of hands instead of by secret ballot at the option of the local election committee.

Six basic-level elections were held under this system from 1953 to 1966 and three National People's Congresses were chosen, meeting an average of once a year for two or three weeks at a time. Then the work of the congresses was interrupted by the Cultural Revolution. The fourth and fifth national congresses, which met in 1975 and 1978, were chosen by "democratic consultation." Not much is known about this process, but a letter to the editor of the *People's Daily* in early 1979 complained that the county congress then about to meet had simply been appointed by the party leaders and approved with a show of hands after ten minutes' discussion at meetings called ostensibly to "seek the masses' opinions." This process of selection could hardly renew the popular mandate. The new electoral system designed as part of the Gengshen Reforms aimed to do this more effectively.

The key innovation of the 1979 Electoral Law of the People's Republic of China for the National People's Congress and the Local People's Congresses of All Levels (a measure complementary to the Organic Law for

Local People's Congresses discussed above) was that it provided for direct election of people's congresses not only at the township level but also at the county level. The elections would thus be not only the first nationwide direct elections for people's congresses in thirteen years, but also the first nationwide elections based on universal suffrage for offices above the lowest level since China had become a republic in 1912. Elections in the early republic had been based on limited suffrage; county-level elections called for in the 1931 Tutelage Constitution were never held; National Assembly and Legislative Yuan (national legislature) elections of the late 1940s were not held nationwide because of the civil war; direct congress elections since 1953 had been limited to the commune/township level; and no basic-level elections had been held on a national scale since 1966.

The 1979 law adopted some provisions from Eastern European systems not found in the Soviet-style 1953 election law. The provisions varied slightly depending upon the level of the election. On the county level, which concerns us here, the committee running the election was to insure that the number of candidates in each precinct was one and a half to two times the number of delegates to be elected rather than, as in the past, the same number. Electoral precincts were to be established mainly in factories, schools, and offices where people worked together and knew one another well, and only citizens without a place of work would be registered in residence-based precincts, which had formerly been the only type. Citizens and groups that nominated candidates had the legal right to disseminate propaganda on their behalf, a right not afforded in the past. Where necessary, an excessive number of candidates could be reduced to the mandated number by a primary election, rather than by the election committee itself as in the 1953 law. All voting was to be by secret ballot, never by show of hands. Election meetings, the sole format permitted under the old law, could be replaced where preferred by polling stations.

The party put great care into election preparations. Twenty million local cadres, especially assigned to election work, attended training classes to study the significance of the campaign and the procedural regulations. The Masses' Publishing House issued a handbook for local officials, called *Questions and Answers on the Election System*, which detailed how the electoral law would be applied and what goals officials should seek to achieve. Numerous detailed directives and media stories about model units repeated the same points.

The elections, officials were told, were intended to educate the masses in the concepts of socialist democracy and law, subject local cadres to popular scrutiny, encourage them to cultivate closer relations with the people, and promote a sense of unity among the citizenry. Responsibility for achieving all this was placed on local party officials. As the *Questions and Answers* handbook pointed out:

> Democratic centralism is the fundamental organizational principle of our party and state. To carry it out in our work requires us to uphold the line and method of coming from the masses and going to the masses, of centralism on the basis of democracy and democracy under the leadership of centralism.

In other words, the task of conducting the election was placed in the hands of county and unit party secretaries.

The election procedures were designed to combine this party control with a high level of mass involvement. Somewhat over thirty days before the election date chosen by it, the existing county people's congress standing committee was to formally appoint an election commission, consisting of members of the local Communist Party organization, the authorized minor parties, the recognized mass organizations (youth league, women's federation, trade union federation), local army units, and national minorities located in the county. The commission would ordinarily be led by the county first party secretary, who usually also chaired the standing committee that appointed the commission. The commission's staff would consist of cadres seconded from other jobs in the county. Election guidelines emphasized that public security personnel and those from the procuratorial organs and the courts must be included on the staff so they could help maintain vigilance against subversion, while also assuring that landlords, rich peasants, counter-revolutionaries, and others discriminated against in the past, who had reformed and been rehabilitated, were not excluded from voter registration. All costs of the election were to be borne by these local commissions and reimbursed by the national treasury.

The first task of the commission, and the second stage of the election, was to draw precinct lines and assign to each precinct a number of seats to be filled. Counties ranged in population from 150,000 to a million or more, and their congresses had an average of about 300 delegates. The precincts ranged in size from 2,000 to 20,000 persons, each electing one to four delegates. The average deputy represented some 1,200 people; although in keeping with the Marxist principle that the proletariat is more progressive than the peasantry, the election law mandated that urban populations be represented by four times as many delegates as equivalent rural populations. So rural precincts were larger, consisting of several production brigades or an entire commune, while urban precincts were smaller, consisting of factories, schools, and offices, or of several factories or offices combined with others in the same line of work. Housewives and retirees who did not work were grouped in precincts consisting of one or more neighborhood committees or a neighborhood committee and nearby offices, schools, or factories. Once the precinct boundaries were drawn, the county election commission was to appoint election management committees or offices in each commune, township, or other major administrative unit. The voters in each precinct were divided in turn into "voters' small groups" to discuss campaign propaganda and to participate in nominating and weeding out candidates.

Voter registration was the third stage of the election, a task the question-and-answer handbook called "of important political significance." This was a chance for the election staff to make contact with all citizens, review their qualifications to vote, and begin to mobilize their enthusiasm for the coming events. At this time public-security and political personnel serving on the election staff reviewed the household registers maintained in police stations, traced missing persons, and updated political dossiers. For example, in a county attached to Tianjin municipality, forty-two "bad elements" appeared in police records, nineteen of whom were in hiding or had fled the county. Careful checking cleared the twenty-three at home; then the missing nineteen were tracked down and seventeen of them rehabilitated. The other two were brought back to the county and put to labor under supervision.

For people cleared of political or criminal stigmas during the registration process, the election meant a chance to claim jobs, housing, or other restitution. Those not granted registration had the right to appeal. In the end, over 99.9 percent of the voting-age population proved eligible to vote and run for office. The complementary task of the registration officials was to see that the remaining fraction—unreformed landlords and rich peasants, criminal elements judicially deprived of political rights, and the like—were not registered.

The posting of voter registration lists and issuing of registration certificates thirty days before the election was an important civic event, one that had not occurred anywhere in the country in at least thirteen years. The election handbook said:

The broad masses are greatly concerned with the distribution of voters' certificates. Some regard them as identity cards, the warrant that the holder is a good person, a master of the state. Some localities have adopted solemn ceremonies for the distribution of the certificates, such as special mass meetings or personal visits of the local leaders to deliver them to voters' homes. . . . After the masses receive the certificates there is a strong response. Some say, "The old traditions of the Communist Party have returned, they are letting us masses be the masters again!" Even more deeply moved are the minority who have just been rehabilitated and who receive their certificates for the first time. Some wrap the certificates in fresh paper and place them in boxes for preservation; some say, "Now that I have my voter's registration my burden is gone. Chairman Hua's policy is a good one. From now on I will make even greater efforts for production." Some say, "When I was living in the 'cowshed' [makeshift prison of the Cultural Revolution] I never even dreamed of having the right to vote. Today when the party has given me a second life, I will certainly devote the rest of it to the Four Modernizations."

The issuance of voters' certificates was intended to be an episode of "broad and deep political education."

Nomination was the fourth stage of the election, and it in turn consisted of three steps: initial nomination twenty days before the election, weeding out of excess candidates through a process called "fermentation," and publication of the final list of nominees five days before the election. The initial names were put forth by the local party organization, the minor parties, the trade union, the women's federation, the youth league, and other recognized organizations. Also, any four voters could join together to nominate a candidate. Any registered voter could be nominated. Any number of candidates could be put forward in the first round, and press reports indicate that at least in model counties almost every voters' small group put forward at least one candidate. Six to ten thousand candidates might be named for a few hundred congressional seats.

But the election law required that no candidate be elected without the votes of more than half of the electorate. Without this rule the election could not fulfill its function of creating a sense of unity; it could not establish the conviction of having chosen candidates who represented the unit as a whole, rather than just some factions within it. To bring such majorities within reach, the nomination lists were required to be pared before the final election to one and a half to two candidates per seat.

Many cadres in charge of elections seemed to feel it would be better to follow the old custom and pare the candidates to one per seat. That would guarantee truly satisfying majorities for each candidate. With competition for seats, it might be hard to assure overwhelming majorities. Besides, there would be losers, and if the losers were cadres, authority would suffer. Election propaganda conceded that multicandidate elections were demanding to administer. But they were a good way to engage the masses' interest and give them a feeling of being "masters of the state." True, the election would pit cadres against competition, but this "will be helpful in cleaning up the remnant poisons of Lin Biao and the 'Gang of Four' "—i.e., in defeating cadres of the left who still had popular support in certain units. Moreover, cadres undergoing scrutiny by the masses should take the opportunity to recognize their own strengths and flaws.

As for the problems of possible conflict or the wrong candidates winning, everything depended on how well the fermentation process was managed. If democratic centralism was properly employed, by the time of the final election opinions would be "concentrated" and the right candidates would be approved with strong majorities. The election committee had the duty of steering the voters toward a mix of final candidates both "advanced" and "broad."

> "Advanced" means that the nominees must be advanced personalities who support the leadership of the Chinese Communist Party, who are going the socialist road, and who are keen to serve the popular masses. . . . "Broad" means that we must pay attention to [getting] excellent persons from diverse sectors and obtain a ratio among the deputies of intellectuals, overseas Chinese, patriotic personages, nonparty masses, youth, women, and members of national minorities.

But the process by which this mix was to be achieved was not very clear in the law. According to a speech by a national official in charge of the elections, there were actually three steps involved. First, the original nominations came "from the masses." Then the election committee in each precinct would go "to the masses" by giving each voters' small group the list of first-round candidates and short biographies of them. The voters' opinions expressed in the small groups would be reported back up to a meeting of voters'-group leaders called by the committee. This meeting, led by the committee head, would pare down the list, keeping in mind the need for a balance of candidates of different ages, sexes, occupations, nationalities and political affiliations. The new list would go back to the small groups for discussion. These discussions would be reported back to a second meeting of group leaders. It would pare the list again to the final required number of candidates and hand the final list back to the masses five days before the election. There was plenty of room in this system to combine involvement by the voters with control by the party-dominated election committee.

The law recognized that sometimes voters' small groups would insist that their candidates were too well qualified to be withdrawn. In such cases the election committee could, "as a supplementary technique," call a primary election. Election guidelines emphasized that this was a last resort, by no means a substitute for the time-consuming process of fermentation. The outcome of a primary should not be left to chance; the voters should be protected from manipulation by superficially plausible candidates who did not deserve to win. Should a primary be necessary to help persuade less worthy candidates to withdraw, the law left maximum leeway for the election committee to control the outcome. It neither specified the exact procedures to be followed nor stated that primary results would be binding.

Publication of the final list of candidates marked the start of a five-day campaign period. The election committee was to post and distribute the candidate biographies submitted at the time of nomination. These were typically brief accounts of the candidates' work experience and political character. For example:

Wu Jianqing, 24, works in a coal-mining machinery plant. His technical innovations enabled him to do 15 months of work in 12 in 1978. In the first half of 1979, he completed a 13-month production quota. He was cited as a young shock worker of the new Long March towards the nation's socialist modernization.

Candidates might also visit voters in their homes, go to their workplaces and join in collective labor, speak at meetings, or broadcast talks over unit-run radio or TV stations. Besides talking about their own background, "candidates should express their political attitudes toward the affairs of state, explain their views on matters of concern to the masses, and indicate how they intend to serve the people if they should be elected." Candidates were expected not to appeal to factional or family loyalties or to class or regional grievances. The elections were not intended to serve as a means of competition among interest groups but as a way to help the community rise above such clashes. Thus there need be none of the exotic salesmanship, the tearing down of others, the "slippery, cheating" words of bourgeois elections. "Ours is a proletarian state under the unified leadership of the Communist Party," stated the election handbook. "There is no question of a power struggle over the distribution of seats among political parties during the campaign. We propagandize the candidates in order to enable the voters to make the best possible choice and to enable the candidates who are elected to serve the people better."

Besides informational activities under the auspices of the election committee, the law contained a provision for campaign propaganda by groups of candidates' backers. Specifically, article 30 read:

The parties, organizations, and voters may use various forms to propagandize the candidates. But this propaganda must cease on the day of the election.

There were ambiguities in this article. Could propaganda begin with the first round of nominations? Since all election expenses were to be borne by the state treasury, was it illegal to spend one's own money on posters or flyers? Could one call a meeting other than those the election committee convened? Such questions remained to be answered in practice.

Campaigning culminated in the final vote. The day varied from county to county, but all precincts in a county must vote on the same day. Each precinct election committee could choose whether to hold an election meeting or set up one or more polling stations. As in the Soviet Union, these places were to be gaily decorated with red banners and slogans. There might be gongs, firecrackers, recorded music. The voter was handed a ballot and his or her name was checked off the registration list. The ballot was set up in one of two ways: by the number of pen-strokes needed to write the candidates' family names or by order of their finish in the primary election, if there had been one.

Voters could vote for the full number of candidates to be chosen from the precinct (usually two or three), or for any smaller number. They could even register dissatisfaction with all the candidates by crossing out all their names. In place of names crossed out they could write in names, if they wished. All these options would produce valid ballots. The voter could also spoil the ballot by placing it in the box unmarked, or discard it without casting it. Such acts would indicate dissatisfaction with the slate of candidates or with the way the election had been run, but they were also ways of affecting the outcome, since electoral victory required not just a majority of votes cast but the votes of a majority of all registered voters. Spoiled and discarded ballots were thus votes against the candidates in the lead.

Since almost a quarter of the adult population was still illiterate or semi-literate, the law provided that these people as well as blind or ill voters or those unavoidably absent from the district could designate friends or relatives to cast their ballots. Sick people could also arrange for a circulating ballot box to be brought to them. Since the elections were only on the county level and were held at different times in different counties, the Chinese could not emulate the Soviet practice of providing ballot boxes in trains and airports, but they did everything else to assure high turnouts. The first nationwide people's congress elections in 1953 had achieved a turnout of 85.88 percent. The model precincts publicized in the press in 1979 and 1980 expected turnouts of 98 or 99 percent or higher; by the end of the elections in 1981, the average for the country came to 96.56 percent.

After the vote, the ballot boxes were to be opened by persons assigned to count the vote, in the presence of the precinct election committee and observers chosen from among the voters. If the number of votes cast was greater than the number of voters, the election was invalid and would have to be repeated. If there was a tie vote, the voters had to choose again between the tied candidates. If fewer than the needed number of candidates had won the support of over 50 percent of the registered voters, the election committee must call a supplementary election to fill the remaining seats. For this purpose a wholly or partly new slate of candidates might be formed if the committee believed that none of the existing candidates could win the confidence of a majority. If even this second election failed to produce enough winners, the committee might have to go back to the voters a third time. The framers of the law knew that in some precincts long-standing factional enmities could make it difficult to achieve majority consensus on any candidate. It was their intent not just to pry one or two delegates out of such communities, but to force the communities to generate a majority vote in favor of the deputies they sent to the county congresses.

Finally, certificates of election were issued to the winning candidates. The county congress would meet only once a year, and the new deputies would continue to make a living doing whatever they had been doing before. Still, the three-year term carried honor and obligations—to serve as a model in implementing the constitution and laws, to help promote and publicize state policy, and to "maintain close links with the masses" by receiving citizens at home or going out to meet them individually or in groups. At the county congress to which they traveled on a state allowance, the deputies would hear reports of the administrative, procuratorial, and judicial organs, would vote on matters before the congress, and would have the legal right to suggest legislation and to address inquiries to the local organs of government, which were supposed to answer before the expiration of the session. The law also stated that no people's congress deputy could be arrested or tried without the approval of the standing committee of the congress.

Over the years the Chinese Communist Party has developed a technique of trying out mass mobilization campaigns in a limited number of units before conducting them nationwide. The same was done with the county-level elections. Experimental polls were conducted in sixty-six county-level units in the second half of 1979, even before the new election law had officially taken effect. In December of that year the Ministry of Civil Affairs convened a meeting in Peking for officials from the provinces to learn about problems that had cropped up during precinct construction, voter registration, and polling. The provinces followed the national symposium with meetings of the local officials who were to conduct a larger set of pilot elections in the first half of 1980.

The man in charge of the elections nationwide was the minister of civil affairs, Cheng Zihua. Aged seventy-six and a communist since 1926, Cheng had been a member of the central election commission that ran the 1953–54 people's congress elections. Now he headed the national office managing the county-level elections. Cheng reported to the NPC Standing Committee in February 1980 that the experimental elections had been generally successful. He received authorization to proceed with pilot elections in another 486 county-level units in the first half of 1980, and announced the following August that the elections would proceed on a countrywide basis.

In the two pilot stages, Cheng revealed in a radio address over the central people's broadcasting station, the elections had "met with much resistance" from cadres who were afraid of the democratic provisions of the new law. Some county heads refused to allow more than one nomination per seat, and others allowed competition in form only without letting the masses actually decide the outcome. If the county party secretaries balked the elections could hardly achieve their goals. Cheng argued that mobilizing mass interest and allowing multicandidate competition could actually help hard-pressed local officials maintain social order and raise agricultural and industrial production. The *People's Daily* pointed out:

> We should recognize that China has a long history of feudal society and that the ideological influence of autocracy and patriarchal work style still exist. This is the biggest obstacle to our current work of bringing democracy into play and doing a good job of promoting election work.

"Some of our comrades," chimed in *Red Flag*, "have a very faint conception of democracy."

With the extension of the election campaign to all counties in the nation, however, the concern of Cheng and the national press turned from cadre resistance to instances of disruption from below. *Red Flag* noted in September 1980 that

> a tiny number of people have indulged in extreme democracy and have approached the elections with a bourgeois stand, viewpoint, and method. Some have tried to seduce the voters with bourgeois democratic programs and "election campaigns." Some have pushed anarchism, describing orderly and well-led democratic elections as undemocratic, resisting and opposing them. Some commit factionalism, forming gangs and cliques to contest the election. All these harm socialist democracy.

In March 1981 Cheng denounced "ultraindividualists" who would "abandon the party's leadership, ignore the socialist legal system, oppose the four basic principles, and undermine stability and unity with a desire to stir up trouble everywhere." He was referring to the activities of members of the democracy movement, who had entered election campaigns in a number of university- and factory-based precincts.

The government had been restricting the democrats' other activities. The sentencing of Wei Jingsheng, the removal of Democracy Walls in Peking and other cities to inconvenient locations, the deletion of the "four great freedoms" from the constitution, and the local harassment of activists' publications seemed to suggest that boundaries were being drawn around what the democrats would be allowed to do. Yet 1980 was the year of the Gengshen Reforms, and the party was encouraging participation from below. The new draft party constitution contained fresh attacks on bureaucratism. The media drummed on the problem of cadres' feudal-mindedness, privilege-seeking, and autocracy. The open press reported with careful objectivity the news of Polish Solidarity, whose influence was then at its height. Students and workers in a number of places ventured to conduct demonstrations or strikes against local bureaucrats over issues like housing and campus security. In a few factories workers even demanded independent trade unions. Unsure of the attitude of the center, local cadres dealt hesitantly with these expressions of social unrest.

To some democrats these events were proof that real democratic reform was still possible in the socialist state. The election provisions for open nomination, fermentation among competing candidates, and multicandidate competition seemed to be an invitation by the party reformers for the people to exert pressure from below, while the reformers worked from above, to give the people some means of control over the party dictatorship. Already, in one of the pilot elections at Fudan University in Shanghai, according to the Canton democratic periodical *People's Road*, a number of candidates had come forth from among the Fudan students and organized their own propaganda groups, posted pictures and biographies, held meetings with voters, and given speeches. The school authorities encouraged these activities. In the end three students were elected from the university to the county congress. The election was praised in inner-party documents, and observers came from other campuses to study the Fudan experience.

"Our country is democratizing, there can be no doubt," wrote the Shanghai worker and democracy activist Fu Shenqi. "Equally beyond question is that no matter what shape and concrete form the process of democratization takes, its essence will be the historical advance from no elections to elections, and from empty elections to authentic elections." Independent candidates who dared to speak out might be suppressed at first, wrote another democrat, but "no matter what opposition or resistance the election process now meets, it will not lose its vitality, but on the contrary will gain greater vitality from each winning or losing clash. You can count on it: all over the country there will be more and more workers and students participating in election campaigns. The election movement is just beginning to grow."

In this view the elections represented not just a chance to speak out but a chance to alter the structure of state power through the congresses. As Fu Shenqi observed, "The democracy movement is based on the laws, but it also ceaselessly demands new laws. These ceaseless demands for new laws will be satisfied precisely as the election system is perfected." As a case in point, Fu cited the people's periodicals, hitherto the movement's main means of action, but now under pressure. He advocated linking the election and periodicals aspects of the movement, with the candidates fighting for better laws to protect the periodicals and the periodicals publicizing the programs of the candidates.

At Peking University, one of the candidates produced a draft publications law that was widely circulated and supported by activists nationwide. The draft would have allowed groups and individuals to publish journals free of party supervision, overseen only by a body established by the National People's Congress, and it would have required the government to provide paper, printing, and other facilities to groups who wanted to publish. *Responsibil-*

ity, the newly established journal of the National People's Periodicals Association which Fu edited, published this draft law and other news of the election movement. At Wuhan University students founded *University Students' Bulletin* for nationwide exchange of election-related news and views. In a number of universities and factories new mimeographed periodicals were produced in connection with local campaigns.

At their boldest, the optimists envisioned that they could gain control of a series of county congresses over the course of several elections and eventually elect their own candidates from the county level to the provincial and national congresses. As the powers of the people's congresses grew, they would become what the Solidarity trade union was trying to be in Poland— what, indeed, people's congresses had always been described as being in Marxist theory—a direct expression of the people's will, independent of the Communist Party and supervising the state.

A more pessimistic view was expressed by Xu Wenli, editor of *April Fifth Forum,* who argued that the election law still gave the crucial control over the short list of final nominees to the party-dominated local election committees. The Chinese people were too cowed and cautious to challenge their unit party secretaries unless they were given absolute protection from above. If the party reformers wanted to use the elections as a first step in transferring real power to the people, Xu said, they would have to pass a more effectively democratic election law. To Hu Ping, a candidate at Peking University, the potential of the election law would have to be tested in practice:

> History will show whether we can preserve competitive elections beyond this one time and whether we can develop and expand them. This is the key that will determine whether this movement has any real value. The powers of a county-level deputy are small and the period in office is brief. If we don't seize the immediate opportunity to put the election firmly on its feet, if it doesn't take root and start to grow, then no matter how much noise and show we can make today, any cold breeze that comes along can blow the whole thing away.

At Peking University Hu Ping's view seemed fairly typical. Of over 500 students questioned about the significance of the election in a student-run poll, 53 percent saw it as the first step toward the realization of socialist democracy, 38 percent said it might have some positive effects but was of no great significance, and 9 percent said it was just a formality.

The most promising precincts for the democrats were factories and colleges. One effect of the new election law had been to create virtual youth precincts by registering workers and students not in their places of residence but in their factories and schools. Because China's population was young and the industrial work force had quintupled since 1949, some 60 percent of the factory labor force were "youth" by the Chinese definition—under thirty-five. "The young workers have become the main body of the Chinese working class and this is an important fact," noted *Red Flag*, adding nervously, "Having traversed a tortuous path [during the Cultural Revolution], these young workers have a more complicated ideology, world outlook, and view of life [than older workers]." The campuses, of course, were also dominated by young people. There were 1.14 million students enrolled in 675 colleges in 1980. And special circumstances gave the 1980 student body a unique complexion. The seniors and juniors were products of the first two nationwide college entrance examinations following the Cultural Revolution, those of 1977 and 1978. As a special concession to the tens of millions who had not had a chance to attend college during the Cultural Revolution, these exams were opened to candidates up to the age of thirty, instead of the usual limit of twenty-one. In 1977, 5.7 million hopefuls sat for 278,000 college places; in 1978, 6 million candidates applied for 300,000 slots. Political criteria, while not ignored, were made secondary to exam scores. Students with "bad class backgrounds," former Red Guards, and activists of the Tiananmen Square incident were among those admitted. Although some 80 percent of college students were party or youth league members, they had complicated personal histories and strong political views.

Democracy activists dominated the election at Peking University, China's preeminent liberal arts university. The campaign began there in November 1980 to elect two student deputies to the congress of Haidian District, part of Peking Municipality. (The university was divided into two precincts, one composed of students, the other of faculty and staff and their families.) Among the eighteen candidates who emerged from the earlier stages of fermentation were Hu Ping, Wang Juntao, and Fang Zhiyuan. Hu Ping was a thirty-two-year-old graduate student in European philosophy specializing in Hobbes, Locke, and Hume, the author of a long essay defending the social utility of freedom of speech, and a contributor to the people's periodical *Fertile Earth*. To be admitted to Peking University he had ranked first in Sichuan Province (China's largest) among humanities students in the exam of 1978 and had overcome family black marks of "overseas relationships" and "historical problems." Wang Juntao was twenty-one, the son of a military officer, a youth league member, and a student in the department of technological physics. He had been jailed in 1976 for participating in the Tiananmen Square incident and was among those lionized by the party when the verdict on the incident was reversed. He was a vice-editor of *Peking Spring* and the youngest on its staff. Fang Zhiyuan was a member of the exam class of 1978 in the department of international politics, and Peking liaison for the Canton democracy periodical *People's Voice*. He was the chief author of the draft publications law discussed earlier.

Conscious of the prominence of their school, the Peking University students put on a lively show. There were posters and handbills all over the campus. Candidates held regular reception hours to answer questions. Several groups of students published periodicals to carry news of the election. A series of opinion polls was conducted. All the campaign documents, tape recordings, and other information were gathered into an archive by a volunteer group from the history and Chinese departments. Candidates worked out careful campaign positions in consultation with groups of advisors.

In a series of forums and question-and-answer sessions that brought crowds to the dining hall and lecture rooms, students made all the candidates express their opinions on the turning points in PRC history, such as the Anti-Rightist campaign of 1957, the Great Leap Forward, and the split with the Soviet Union. Wang Juntao created a boiling controversy by evaluating Mao as "a revolutionary enlightened by Marxism but not a Marxist" and claiming that the Cultural Revolution was not Mao's fault but was a genuine mass movement, if a misguided one, reflecting the actual problems of bureaucratism and privilege. Candidate Xia Shen propounded "socialist humanism" and the rotation of political parties in power. Fang Zhiyuan argued that China was not yet a socialist society because it lacked democracy, which he said ranked with collective ownership as a criterion of socialism. Someone raised the question of Wei Jingsheng. While nobody defended Wei, all the candidates criticized the trial, either on procedural grounds or because the fifteen-year sentence was too harsh. One of two female candidates was booed at meetings and attacked on wall posters for running on the slogan "Oriental Beauty"—meaning that Chinese women should both be independent and take care of their families—which many students felt was not an important enough issue for the campaign.

One of the major topics of debate was the prospects and strategy for democratic reform, which almost all the students favored. Some candidates said that political reform would spring naturally from economic change; others emphasized "liberation of thinking" and still others stabilization of the legal system. Such ideas differed little from the party reformers' program, but more radical suggestions were also made: for a separation of powers in government, for an independent press (Fang Zhiyuan's draft press law), for a breakup of the concentration of power in the party center. In one of the campus polls, 37 percent of the students questioned said they preferred to elect a radical social reformist, 20 percent a moderate socialist reformist, 19 percent a status quo type, and 10 percent a person without strong political coloration; the remainder gave other preferences. But however strong their views on democracy, most students agreed that nothing should be done to alarm the authorities. They expressed their ideas with caution, hoping that this would be only the first in a series of election campaigns.

The scope of the debates, however, did offend the municipal party authorities, who according to more than one source issued a judgment that the campaign was treading on "bourgeois" ground. But the school party committee refused to intervene. It allowed the campaign to proceed to its conclusion. On December 11, Hu Ping was elected with the votes of 57 percent of the registered voters. Neither Wang Juntao, in second place, nor student union chairman Zhang Wei, in third, managed to get the required fifty-percent-plus vote in either the first round of balloting or the runoff. Although the election law required that more runoffs be held until the second seat was filled, the university did not arrange one. Nor did the school allow Hu Ping to take up his post as a deputy. Hu, in fact, had made himself so notorious in the campaign that the university could not find him a job after he completed his graduate degree. He was kept on for at least a year as a special student, in what people called "cold storage."

While a direct clash between students and administration had been avoided at Peking University, a spectacular one occurred at Hunan Teachers College in the provincial capital of Changsha. Hunan is the province of Mao Zedong's birth, and its people are considered restless and stubborn. Changsha lies on the east side of the Xiang River. On the west bank is a complex of campuses on wooded hills. Besides the teachers college, the district includes Hunan University, South China Mining Academy, Hunan Finance and Trade Academy, and other educational institutions. At the time of the election, the province was in conservative hands: the first party secretary was Mao Zhiyong, considered a supporter of Hua Guofeng, who had been his predecessor as Hunan's chief. The teachers college constituted the Seventy-sixth Precinct of West District. Its 5,830 voters were supposed to elect four deputies. Because the president of the college was away in Peking, the man in charge of the election was Vice-President Su Ming, aged about seventy, a veteran party member and educator.

In any Chinese college the Chinese department is one of the most politically active units. Many of its students are preparing for careers as fiction, poetry, or script writers, newspaper reporters, or teachers—vanguard service on the "literary and art front" or the "education front." The Chinese Department at Hunan Teachers College, one of the largest on campus, had about six hundred students. Among them were a number of older students with established literary careers and strong political views. Several had been active in a writers' group called the April Fifth Literary Society; one was nationally known for his short stories. This society had put up wall posters at the provincial party committee offices in 1978 criticizing First Party Secretary Mao for slowness in implementing Deng Xiaoping's reforms. They had been investigated and held up to campus criticism for that action. Now two of them decided to run for people's deputy.

Another forceful figure in the Chinese Department was Tao Sen, aged thirty-one. According to Tao's campaign biography, as a teenager he had been attacked and sent down to the countryside because of the links of his father, a deceased party veteran, with high-ranking targets of the Cultural Revolution. After years in the countryside, in 1973 young Tao passed a local college entrance examination but was denied admission because of his father's past. Meanwhile he had already begun a series of personal assaults on bureaucratism. In 1970 he exposed what he termed "criminal problems" in a fertilizer factory where he worked. In 1975 he traveled to Peking and managed to use his party connections to get a high central official, Wang Zhen, to clear his father's name. Returning to Hunan, Tao had his father's bones transferred to the martyrs' cemetery in his hometown. In 1977 Tao sold his bicycle to finance a second trip to Peking, this time submitting to Wang Zhen an unsolicited report on the management failures of a machinery plant where he was now working. In 1978, Tao, now in college, sold his sewing machine and furniture to raise money to return several more times to Peking to seek the rehabilitation of three elderly cadres who must have been comrades of his father. He contributed several hundred yuan to help these men get back on their feet. He also played a leading role in a student disturbance protesting a decision by the college administration to reduce the length of schooling from four years to three. The following year he publicly defended the April Fifth Literary Society members against the campus criticism campaign confronting them for their poster attack the previous year on the provincial first party secretary.

In putting his name forward in 1980 for the county people's congress, Tao Sen articulated a ten-point platform: support for Marxism; support for CCP leadership combined with recognition of the sovereignty of the people's congresses; thorough democratic reform of the bureaucracy; exposure of party members to criticism from the masses; collective and rotating party leadership; rigorous enforcement of the law against errant cadres; streamlining of administration; recognition of appropriate independence for literary workers in their task of serving socialism; improved conditions for intellectuals, including freedom to select one's own profession; and improved conditions for peasants and teachers. Tao called his program "a great socialist reform." Tao's campaign biography similarly reflected a self-confident personality:

Comrade Tao Sen is concerned with affairs of state. He has strong political sensitivity. He has a knowledge and understanding of cadres at the higher, middle, and lower levels. He dares to struggle against cadres who disobey the law. He likes to help people. He has helped any member of the masses who is in trouble, regardless of whether they share his views or not. He is upright, candid, and unselfish. He has no slavish character and dares to speak out, dares to take responsibility, dares to struggle to the end. His personal history is clean. He has never committed a political error.

A fourth candidate in the Chinese Department was Liang Heng, a tall, energetic twenty-seven-year-old who was married to an American. (Liang subsequently came to the United States and has described his early life in a book, *Son of the Revolution*.) Like Tao, Liang was the son of a cadre, a deputy editor of the official *Hunan Daily News*. Liang's mother had been labeled a rightist in 1957 and was divorced by her husband; during the Cultural Revolution the father was attacked and sent down, first to a cadre school and then to the countryside. Liang roamed China as one of the youngest Red Guards. He ended up camping out in his parents' deserted apartment, where he witnessed an armed battle around the newspaper's office and apartment building. He was reunited with his father and sisters in the countryside for several years, then recruited by a shale-oil factory in Changsha for its basketball team. Hoping to become a writer, he sat for the 1977 examinations and gained admission to the Chinese Department at the teachers college. There he met and married a visiting teacher of English, Judith Shapiro.

At the regular Tuesday small-group study sessions on September 16, students were told that the election campaign was starting, with the final election scheduled for October 14. The election committee, it was announced, consisted of the school vice-president, Su Ming, together with the head of the college's Propaganda Department, the secretary of the campus Communist Youth League, the chairman of the student association (himself a student in the Chinese Department), and the head of each department's party cell (in most cases the department chair). Students were invited to stand up one by one and voice enthusiasm for the campaign—a standard practice in political study sessions.

On the next political study day, Friday, all the study groups in each department met together for nominations. In the Chinese Department Tao Sen was ready to run, but reluctant to move first. Liang Heng stood up, apparently on impulse, and said he would run, with the goal of trying to reform the job assignment system. Middle-school and college graduates in China are assigned to their lifetime jobs by small committees of party and school officials who try to fulfill personnel quotas set by higher levels. Little is done to take student preferences into account or to see that spouses are assigned together; instead, the system is often used to reward or punish students for their behavior during the years of schooling. Reform of the system was an issue at Peking University and in other campus precincts. Liang went on to present his other basic views and reasons for becoming a candidate. First, he wanted to see whether the new election system would be truly democratic. Second, he supported the reform policies of the government. Third, the essential nature of socialism should be a subject for inquiry; he did not believe in taking Marxism-Leninism on faith.

It was this last remark that lit the fuse. Even if Liang had said he disbelieved (*bu xiangxin*) Marxism, it might logically have seemed permissible since he was not, after all, a party or youth league member. What he had said was even less than this: merely that he did not take Marxism on faith (*bu xinyang*). Yet as word spread, this innocuous remark turned out to be wickedly titillating in the staid political atmosphere of Hunan. At a series of political rallies, such colloquies as the following took place:

> QUESTION FROM THE AUDIENCE: Is the Marxism that you don't believe in false or true Marxism?
>
> LIANG HENG: What I don't believe is the kind of Marxism-Leninism propagandized and taught all through China. I don't know which is true and which is false Marxism because I have not had a chance to study Marxism independently. I do not know enough about what Marxism is.
>
> Q: Then, how about the "ism" of the Three People's Principles [of Sun Yat-sen]? (Laughter from the audience.)
>
> LH: I think it had a positive function in history. But since I don't fully understand the Three People's Principles, I don't take them on faith either.
>
> Q: Would you believe Marxism-Leninism if you knew it was correct?
>
> LH: In my lifetime I will never know that. (Laughter.)
>
> Q: But what if it *were* true?
>
> LH: "Practice is the sole criterion of truth" [Deng Xiaoping's reform slogan]. At present there is no national or social structure in the world that proves the truth of Marxism-Leninism in practice. The proofs are all in textbooks. (Laughter.)
>
> Q: How many "isms" do you believe in? Don't you think you should understand several before running for election? (Laughter.)
>
> LH: Do you think a person has to understand several ideologies in order to run for office?
>
> Q: Liang Heng, what will you do if the police detain and investigate you? (Nervous laughter.)

Hundreds of students and citizens from the surrounding neighborhood came before the regular Saturday-evening campus movie to hear Tao, Liang, and their friends make campaign speeches. The candidates had organized and publicized this forum themselves, without the blessing of the college election committee.

On Tuesday afternoon, September 23, Su Ming and the Propaganda Department head appeared at the Chinese Department and called Tao Sen into the chairman's office. The conversation that followed was secretly tape-recorded by Tao. An abridgment follows:

CHINESE DEPARTMENT CHAIR: Tao Sen, I'm concerned about you. You should firm up your political standpoint. Don't go along with Liang Heng's mistakes. He has said that he doesn't believe in Marxism-Leninism.

PROPAGANDA DEPARTMENT HEAD: We are worried about you. Liang Heng's speech the other night was bourgeois. By giving a speech at the same time, you are making yourself an associate of his.

SU MING: Your speech at the movie Saturday night was a political error, a Western, bourgeois election method. A speech like that is an example of the "four great freedoms" that were abolished by the National People's Congress. Your action certainly has nothing to do with the right of propaganda under the election law. That is limited to propaganda by the school election committee on behalf of the candidates, to introduce all of them equally. It is against the law for any individual to conduct election propaganda. All the candidates have to do what the election committee says unless there is a contrary instruction from the center. Your individual propaganda is interfering with our planned election propaganda.

CHINESE DEPARTMENT CHAIR: You and Liang Heng, are you a faction? You both referred to "a bureaucratic class" and used the phrase "don't be slaves" in your talks. These two phrases sound a lot like talk from the Cultural Revolution. If every student talked like that, it would be as if Democracy Wall and Wei Jingsheng had come back. Don't let Liang Heng get you into trouble.

Instead of isolating Liang Heng, the authorities' intervention hardened Tao's attitude. He posted a transcript of the interview all over the campus.

Liang composed in response a series of three declarations which he both posted and circulated in mimeographed form. One read:

A nation's people have sunk into servitude, no different from slavery. Alas! Who can say this condition of slavery started only during the ten years' catastrophe [the Cultural Revolution]? In fact it has existed for several thousand years. . . . How can we speak of a nation of citizens, when both people and officials are like this? And how can we speak of enriching the people and strengthening the state? . . . That is why I say: slaves have no rights; citizens have rights. Slaves have no responsibility; citizens have responsibility. Slaves like to be controlled; citizens love freedom. Slaves bow and scrape; citizens talk about equality. Slaves like to follow; citizens prefer independence.

The cadenced semiclassical style was none other than Liang Qichao's new-style prose, still ready to hand eighty years later for the discussion of large political issues. The argument, too, echoed what Liang Qichao had said in the 1890s: that a state whose people have no rights is a state without rights. A central issue in Chinese politics had persisted for nearly a century.

But it was over procedural rather than substantive issues that the election controversy boiled up into a major incident. After Tao Sen's interview with Su Ming and Liang Heng's reply, scores of students got involved in the campaign, resentful of Su Ming's interference. The walls dripped with posters. Although the school refused to lend candidates electric megaphones, many held meetings. Sympathetic staff in a few departments furtively allowed access to mimeograph machines. Tao Sen's group produced a journal called *Heart's Light*. In the midst of all this the school election committee conducted the three cycles of "weeding out" that the election procedures required. Unwisely, they chose to use primary elections, which made it difficult to control the results. The six names the voters chose as finalists for four seats included Tao Sen in first place and Liang Heng in third. The number-two candidate was a physics lecturer, number four an elderly nonparty personage, number five the chairwoman of the Education Department, and number six a school custodian who was a model worker. There were still three days before the final candidate list had to be posted, and the election committee desperately held two extra rounds of primary elections, presumably trying to get rid of Liang in particular. Despite what must have been vigorous lobbying by party members and activists, the same six candidates continued to come out on top.

About nine o'clock on the evening of October 8 the school loudspeakers crackled with an announcement. After consultation with the broad masses of voters and having obtained their approval, it said, the election committee announced the final list of nominees. But instead of the six candidates the voters had approved, the list had seven names. The added name was that of Fan Xiaoxin, chairman of the college student association, vice-chairman of the Hunan provincial student association, and a member himself of the college election committee. Although the names on the list should have been arranged by order of finish in the primaries, they were given instead in order of the number of pen-strokes in the Chinese character of each candidate's family name. This procedure put Tao Sen's name sixth and Liang Heng's last. For students in the fever of their first experience with competitive democracy, the election committee seemed to be stretching its prerogatives to the breaking point in the effort to discourage Tao's and Liang's election.

The bedtime loudspeaker announcement brought the students pouring out of their dormitories in a rage. They marched on Su Ming's office. He ordered them to stop what he called a Red Guard–style action and said he was going home to bed. The students regrouped and perhaps two thousand of them marched on the provincial party headquarters—a hike of several miles from West District across the bridge to the eastern outskirts of town. As in demonstrations ever since the May Fourth movement, the students linked arms in chains of eight abreast. Marshals emerged from the ranks to lead in singing the "Internationale" and shouting slogans: "Down with bureaucratism," "We want democracy." At the party headquarters sixteen delegates were elected, headed by Tao Sen, to present a set of demands to the officials inside. The first was that the students be allowed to come indoors, since it was now early in the cold morning of October 9, and some demonstrators were still wearing whatever they had thrown on when the loudspeaker announcement was made the night before. This was refused. The second and third demands were that the province send an investigation group to the university and that it declare the present demonstration legal and its participants innocent of any wrongdoing. The party officials agreed to these demands, and the students marched back to the campus to celebrate.

A day later three or four men came from the province election office to investigate Su Ming's conduct of the election. After less than a day, spent mainly with administrators and department chairpersons, the commission announced that the college had not broken the law. With this, the school authorities went on the offensive, calling on party and youth league members among the students (many of whom had participated in the October 9 demonstration) to "firm up their political stand" and work for "stability and unity" or suffer the consequences. Now the way seemed clear to an election four days later that the administration could control.

But at a mass meeting on October 12, Tao Sen, Liang Heng, and the second most popular candidate, the Physics Department lecturer, announced the withdrawal of their candidacies and urged the students to boycott the election. If there were only four candidates for four posts, the election would arguably be illegal. And if enough voters stayed away, no candidate could win the requisite number of votes—those of more than half of the registered voters. Tao Sen told the rally that the important thing was not to complete the election but to fight for principle. He demanded the resignation of the college election committee, and revealed that he had sent telegrams to several central party officials protesting the suppression of voters' democratic rights by both the school and the provincial authorities.

The election committee, however, refused to honor the three candidates' withdrawals. "Three thousand voters supported your nomination," Tao Sen was told, "and you are not allowed to resign on your own initiative." On October 13, when a student delegation waited on Su Ming to protest, he refused to see them and announced through his secretary that the election would go forward the next day. Again the students formed ranks of eight and marched through the city shouting slogans. Several thousand arrived at the gates of the provincial party committee near midnight on October 13. The party officials refused to talk. Sitting on the muddy ground before the gate of the party compound, fifty-odd students began a hunger strike around two-thirty in the morning of October 14. The number of hunger strikers soon reached eighty-seven.

Other students went back to the campus to strike classes. Still others turned out a mimeographed "Letter to the People of the City" that explained their grievances and asked for support. Copies were handed out at railway stations in order to reach other cities. To a gathering crowd of students and citizens the hunger strikers made a series of speeches through a megaphone. Tired, hungry, and cold, many wept as they spoke. From the crowd came vows of support from other schools in West District and shouted slogans against bureaucratism. Senior literary figures who happened to be attending a conference at a nearby hotel made appearances, emotionally comparing the students to revolutionaries of earlier generations. Tao Sen lectured hoarsely, encouraging his troops. As October 14 wore on, a number of students collapsed from the cold and had to be taken away to the hospital. On the fifteenth the weather turned hot and more students fainted in the sun.

Although not a word of this appeared in the Chinese media, reporters who were present sent "internal" bulletins to the central government. In addition, Liang Heng's wife placed a call to the *New York Times* correspondent in Peking, Fox Butterfield; his story and those of other foreign reporters were broadcast back to China by the Voice of America. The students sent telegrams to all the top party and government officials and also to universities throughout China. No doubt the provincial authorities were also reporting to Peking.

First Party Secretary Mao Zhiyong finally received Tao Sen as the students' chief delegate, but they could not find a compromise. The two sides waited for intervention from above. When the call came, it was from Tao Sen's old contact, Wang Zhen. Wang was a Politburo member and a vice-premier. Although mainly concerned with agricultural policy, he had also been involved in the problems of sent-down youth, and in that capacity had helped solve the Shanghai youth troubles of February 1979. He was a native of Tao Sen's hometown in Hunan and apparently an old commander of Tao's father. Since Tao had played on this connection to clear his father, now Wang was playing on it to solve the Changsha crisis. Instead of speaking to Mao Zhiyong, Vice-Premier Wang asked for Tao Sen to be called to the phone. He urged Tao to "take stability and unity as the key link, end your hunger strike and go back to school. The center will send an investigating team to look into the whole incident."

Wang's request brought into the open a split among the students. Some had believed from the start that Tao Sen was making a mistake when he tried to solve the problem "through the back door" by sending personal telegrams to Wang Zhen; by trying to bring outside influence to bear on Mao Zhiyong,

Tao was also opening himself to pressure to compromise. By contrast, Liang Heng and others wanted a solution in principle, one that was a test of the ability of the law to assure democracy for everybody, not just for those with access to influential patrons. During the October 9 demonstration, in fact, Liang had advocated suing the college election committee in court rather than accepting the offer of an inspection team from the province. Now Liang urged that Tao refuse Wang Zhen's phone call. Tao did refuse Wang's first call, but took a second several hours later. That done, Liang felt there was no choice but to accept Wang Zhen's offer of a central investigating team, because the stamina of the students was exhausted. Tao, who may have felt outfoxed, now wanted to continue the strike to the death. But after a bitter debate, Tao lost, and on the morning of the sixteenth the strikers marched back through a violent rainstorm to the campus, again claiming victory. Calling the Liang group "capitulationists, rightists, and splittists," Tao wrote later:

> I was the last to leave. Facing the workers who had come to shout their support, the students from the other schools, and the reporters on the scene, I cried bitter tears. The flame of the great socialist reform against bureaucratism and for democracy had been snuffed out. Intellectuals are so weak!

The central investigating group, three men from Cheng Zihua's national election management office, arrived in Changsha the same day that the students returned to campus. But Tao Sen refused to cooperate with them. He and about twenty followers resumed the sit-in at the provincial party offices. When the sit-in failed to gain support, Tao decided to take his case to Peking. He and his group arrived by train on October 28 and were received the next day at the letters and visits office of the State Council by Cheng Zihua himself.

Tao presented his version of events and asked that the college officials who had violated the election law be punished. He demanded that Mao Zhiyong be reprimanded for his bureaucratic attitude toward the hunger strikers. He charged that the Hunan authorities had lied to the center about the students' activities. Tao was also upset about the Voice of America broadcasts on the hunger strike, which apparently left the impression that the issue was not Su Ming's tampering with the candidate list but Liang Heng's lack of faith in Marxism. Tao demanded that Cheng Zihua use the official news media to issue a correction about the goals of the strike. Finally, Tao wanted to be received by the top party officials to make his own report. To all these demands Cheng Zihua was unyielding. The students must go home, he said, and await the center's decision based on the investigating group's report. Tao spent the next week or so meeting with Peking University students and other democracy movement figures in Peking. The Peking University elections were scheduled for the following month, and by some accounts both the candidates and the school administration were interested in learning from the Changsha experience what mistakes to avoid.

Back in Changsha, classes had resumed while the three investigators went about their work, interviewing students and faculty, taking notes on wall posters, and meeting with the administration. After about two weeks they returned to Peking, and on November 9 Cheng Zihua's national election office issued its opinion. Tao Sen was allowed to carry it back to Changsha, and it was read to students in a large meeting November 15. It was also circulated nationally as ideological study material, although never officially published.

The opinion noted that despite the hunger strike the school administration had held the scheduled election meeting on October 14. About 3,500 voters showed up, only 59 percent of the registered voters in the precinct. Of these, 607 discarded their ballots or cast blank ballots in protest. Tao, Liang, and the third candidate who had withdrawn came in last in the voting, not surprisingly since they had asked their supporters to stay away. But the highest tally for any candidate was only 36 percent of the registered vote, far short of the 50 percent–plus required to win. The opinion stated that the election was invalid. Su Ming had committed an "error" in holding it, as well as two other errors: enlarging the candidate list to seven without proper consultation with the masses, and refusing to talk with the students when they came to his office to protest this decision. Since errors are inevitable in unfamiliar work, the opinion continued, Su Ming should make a public self-examination so as to reunite the people of the precinct, and Teachers College should conduct a new election. Once this was completed, the New China News Agency would issue a report to correct all domestic rumors and foreign distortions. The opinion refused either to endorse or to criticize the actions of the students except to note that what went on up until the tampering with the candidate list had been "democratic" and "correct," a backhanded note of support for the students' criticism of what went on afterwards. But the opinion said that it was not within the purview of the national election office to decide whether the subsequent sit-in and hunger strike were legal actions.

Su Ming issued the written self-criticism required by the national election office, but when school met again for the spring term of 1981, he canceled the first three days of classes for intensive small-group study of the tough speech Deng Xiaoping had given on December 25 against "bourgeois liberalization." Students were required to cite examples of how Tao Sen and Liang Heng had violated the "four upholds." The students were told that Liang had absorbed bourgeois ideas, presumably from his foreign wife, and that his claim that Chinese citizens were free not to believe in Marxism did not apply to college students, who were receiving education from the state and should be held to stricter ideological standards than ordinary citizens. Tao Sen was criticized for "antiparty and antisocialist thought," for managing an illegal periodical, for "usurping the name of a central party leader [Wang Zhen] to carry out wrecking activities," and for "bad morals"—at age thirty-two, unmarried, he had had several girlfriends. The criticism campaign went on every Tuesday and Friday all semester, and spread to colleges throughout the province. In June 1981, several months before he would have graduated, Tao was expelled from college, arrested by two public-security men, and sentenced to three years' labor education, to be served, according to one source, hauling rocks at a labor camp in the Hunan countryside. The next month, Liang Heng left China for graduate studies in the United States. The remedial election was never held.

Democrats were active in factory precincts as well. Perhaps the best-known was Fu Shenqi, a repairman in the Shanghai Generator Factory, editor of *Voice of Democracy*, leader in the National People's Periodicals Association and editor of its journal, *Responsibility*. At the time of the elections Fu was twenty-six, a Shanghai native from a worker family who had had one year of college in 1977–78. Writing under his own name and under the pen name Xin Hua, he was one of the democracy movement's most optimistic strategists. Fu believed that democracy required multiple independent parties, a free press, and parliamentary rule, and that a country like China that already had state ownership of the means of production could be impelled the rest of the way to full democratic socialism by a people's movement that would force the creation of democratic institutions and eventually take over the state. Fu saw the elections in his factory as a good opportunity to advance this process. On April 29, 1980, the day after the voter registration list was posted, Fu distributed a handbill announcing his desire to serve as a people's deputy.

Although nominally a youth league member, Fu was distrusted by his factory leadership for his democracy movement activities of the previous year and a half. The evening of his declaration his workshop party branch secretary and two members of the factory election small group called him into the workshop office for a talk. They said it was illegal to distribute a campaign handbill without being recognized as a candidate by the election small group and getting its permission. A few days later Fu had a visit from the factory youth league secretary, who suggested it would be better for him not to run. Each workshop director began talking with those of his workers known to sympathize with Fu, explaining that Fu's tactics were illegal, that he would be expelled from the youth league, and that anyone who stood with him would earn a black mark. The rumor went around that Fu's past activities were "antiparty and antisocialist" and, moreover, that Fu was not right in the head. But still he was listed among the first-stage nominees, since he had more than the required four signatures.

Fu fought back with additional flyers on May 6 and 12. He defended the legality of his first handbill on the grounds of both article 45 of the constitution (freedom of speech) and article 30 of the election law (right of propaganda). He quoted a study of the election system by the Shanghai Academy of Social Sciences as saying that the propaganda privilege of article 30 was not limited to the five days before the election but covered the whole period "both before and after the list of final candidates." Fu charged that the people who called his *Voice of Democracy* antisocialist did not know what socialism was. If he was antiparty and antisocialist he should by law have been deprived of the right to vote, but his name had been listed among the registered voters, so he must have done nothing wrong. Those who were interfering with his campaign were the ones violating the election law.

The factory leaders continued to exert pressure on the voters, and, according to Fu's later charges, tried to get the local public security office to arrest him. Meanwhile a closed meeting of the election committee and the voters' small-group leaders produced a list of three final candidates for the factory's two posts. Fu Shenqi was not among them. Yet on the day of the election, June 1, Fu garnered 636 write-in votes, 43 percent of the number of registered voters, and came in second. The candidate ahead of him was elected, but neither Fu nor the two candidates behind him won the required majority vote. Two months later, no runoff election had yet been held for the second post. Fu protested to the district election office, but was told that that office had already wrapped up its work.

Besides the cases of Peking University, Hunan Teachers College, and the Shanghai Generator Factory, I have information on nine other instances in which democracy activists participated in elections. They are Qinghua University (in the same Haidian District as Peking), Guizhou University, Shandong Teachers College, and Zhejiang University; factories in Shaoguan (Guangdong Province), Qingdao (Shandong Province), Zhaoyang District (part of Peking), and Qingyuan County (Hebei Province); and a neighborhood in the West District of Peking. There are also several other reports of unusual election activity in which I cannot be sure whether established democrats were involved: at Wuhan University, at People's University in Peking, and in a rural county of Shanghai Municipality. The fact that the known cases include so many examples from Peking suggests that other tumultuous contests may have occurred in places where there were no foreign observers and simply went unreported. In September 1981 Cheng Zihua reported that there were still 210 counties where elections were not complete but should be finished by the end of the year. So far as I know he never announced the end of the campaigns in these counties. There may have been places where elections were never completed, either because of cadre resistance or because of "anarchism" or "factionalism" among the masses.

Election disruptions clearly contributed to the leaders' decision to launch a final crackdown on the democracy movement. In his December 25, 1980, speech at a party work conference in which he attacked "bourgeois liberalization," Deng Xiaoping specified among the targets of concern "illegal organizations and illegal magazines," which he said were publishing antiparty and antisocialist ideas and agitating for support. In April 1981 the center issued its Document No. 9, which instructed provincial authorities to conduct investigations in all units, arrest participants in illegal groups, expel party members who supported them, and conduct a mass campaign of education against them. Deng's speech and the new central instruction amounted to the long-awaited judgment on the democrats' election activities as well as on their publications. As party ideologist Hu Qiaomu explained, "A small number of people have abandoned the basic principles of Marxism and spread the prejudices and cherished illusions of bourgeois democracy. They advocate the so-called natural rights favored by bourgeois ideologists and try to practice bourgeois multipartyism and the election contest system in socialist China."

In April 1981 several democracy activists, Fu Shenqi among them, were arrested in Peking after holding a ceremony in Tiananmen Square in observance of the fifth anniversary of the Tiananmen Square incident. In the next few months, fifty or so leaders of the movement were arrested nationwide (others may have been arrested with no publicity abroad). Those detained had been editors and authors of people's periodicals, and candidates in factory and campus elections. They included Xu Wenli, Wang Xizhe, Chen Erjin (author of "On the Proletarian Democratic Revolution"), Sun Feng (editor of the Qingdao publication *Sea Spray*), He Qiu (editor of the Canton publication *People's Road*), and Lu Lin (successor to Wei Jingsheng as editor of *Explorations*). The government announced few trials, leading to the supposition that most of the detainees were sentenced without trial to labor reeducation, which is usually for a three-year term and is subject to renewal in the event the prisoner fails to reform.

In late 1981, the graduating members of the college class that had been recruited by the examination of 1977 were given their permanent work assignments by committees of administrators and teachers at their schools. Nationwide, according to the official press, in this particular year "relatively large numbers of graduates are urgently needed in remote border areas, areas where people of minority nationalities reside, areas where economic and cultural developments are slow, and departments where technology is poor." Students who refused the assignments would forfeit the right to state-assigned jobs for five years. According to interviews, the students of this class, along with the class recruited in 1978—arguably the most intellectually promising classes in thirty or more years—were scattered to jobs primarily in remote locations. Beginning with the class recruited in 1979, the Ministry of Education required each applicant's home unit to conduct a "political screening." The screening was given increasing weight in college admissions from 1980 on.

"There are serious shortcomings in our propaganda work," stated Deng Xiaoping in his speech of December 1890. "The main one is that we have not . . . forcefully and convincingly publicized the four basic principles, and have failed to wage effective struggle against gravely erroneous ideas opposed to them." In February 1981 *People's Daily* reported on its front page the successful conduct of a study campaign by the party authorities at Qinghua University in Peking to clear up confusion caused during the elections by some students who "openly voiced doubts" about the four basic principles and party leadership. At Peking University, according to one report, several students were charged with being Trotskyites and others were put on warning. At Canton's Zhongshan University the authorities closed *Red Bean*, the last student periodical still in operation. Universities and research institutes were required to submit for review lists of the foreign periodicals they subscribed to. At Peking Teachers College and elsewhere, a program was adopted of annual appraisal of each student's moral and ideological standing. In factories fresh emphasis was placed on "ideological and political work." Study groups tightened up their twice-a-week schedule of regular meetings. The Chinese youth league and trade union federation, together with related organizations, launched the campaign in February 1981 called the "Five Stresses and Four Beauties," emphasizing public deportment and civic virtue. March became "Socialist Ethics Month," an annual occasion from 1981 on for strict enforcement of traffic laws and sanitation regulations and propaganda on public discipline in cities throughout China.

On September 3, 1981, Cheng Zihua made his final report on the elections to the Standing Committee of the National People's Congress. Elections had been completed in 2,546 counties. The average turnout was 96.56 percent. Well over half a million deputies had been chosen. They showed the targeted mix of characteristics. About 67 percent were Communist Party members; 22 percent women; 48 percent peasants; 26 percent cadres; 11 percent workers; and 8 percent intellectuals. In many counties the congresses had already met to perform their chief task of electing local government officials. In the next three years the deputies would have few official duties. They would meet once a year to approve official resignations and appointments and hear reports on the work of the county governments.

The Standing Committee approved Cheng's suggestion that the terms of all the county congresses elected since 1979 start as from 1981, thus scheduling the next round of elections for 1984. To assure better management of future elections, the National People's Congress in 1982 adopted several amendments to the election law. To avoid repeated runoffs in cases where the voters refused to give the required 50 percent–plus of the registered vote to a sufficient number of candidates, the congress lowered the requirement for winning a runoff to "one-third of the votes cast." This not only reduced the absolute number of votes needed to win, but also meant that anyone boycotting a meeting or spoiling a ballot could not affect the outcome of a runoff. The congress also cleared up the ambiguities of article 30, which candidates had used to defend their right to conduct election propaganda. The new language deleted this right:

> The election committee shall brief voters on the candidates for deputy. Parties, organizations, and voters who have nominated candidates for deputy may brief voters on their candidates at the meetings of the voter small groups.

The election-law revisions of 1982 made clear once again the official view of what the limits of Chinese democracy should be. The voters needed to know only which candidates had a good labor history and a commitment to socialism. They could learn who best embodied these qualities at officially sponsored meetings in the few days just before an election. Democracy did not require the hurly-burly of rallies, wall posters, and question-and-answer forums: elections should not be seen as occasions for contests of ideas. As intended, the 1984 county congress elections were carried on throughout China without a single reported incident of dissent or disruption.

CONCLUSION:
CHINESE DEMOCRACY
AND WESTERN VALUES

In the charter speech of the Gengshen Reforms, given to his Politburo colleagues on August 18, 1980, Deng Xiaoping presented an eloquent statement of the benefits of democracy. It would, he said, help pool collective wisdom for economic development, assure a smooth leadership succession, recruit new and more able cadres into local posts, restrict overcentralization of power and consequent bureaucratic immobility, and prevent the making of "hasty decisions" by cadres. It would discourage corruption and prevent the reemergence of one-man dictatorship. It would "promote the smooth development of our modernization drive."

Such arguments show that despite differences over whether democracy is an end or a means, many in China and the West share the belief that democracy has functional benefits. First, democracy regulates conflict. It allows social and ideological clashes to be carried out peacefully and encourages groups to press their interests through legal processes rather than corruption and violence. It protects government from control by any single social force and so enhances its ability to make decisions in the public interest. And it gives the leaders information that allows them to adjust in response to the attitudes of the public and the effects policies have on people's lives. Second, democracy makes government more legitimate. People who feel they have been consulted are readier to accept decisions once they have been made. Groups that have witnessed the strength of their opponents know that government may not be able to give them all that they want. Policy issues are partially resolved through compromise and platform-building in the public arena before they are brought to the government for resolution. Third, democracy improves the quality of government. It provides the best means for supervising the great bureaucracies of the modern state and also helps prevent government leaders from abusing their powers. The leaders think through more carefully policies that they have to defend in public. Democracy can recruit political leaders from a larger pool of contestants than autocracies, so bringing abler people and more diverse viewpoints into government. Finally, democracy encourages stability. The struggle for office is conducted through peaceful means at regular intervals. Politicians do not need to use violence to get office or keep it. Policies, too, are less liable to sudden change since they are the product of protracted bargaining among interest groups.

As recently as the 1960s democracy's benefits were not widely accepted in developing countries. It was fashionable to say that democracy was a luxury of rich countries. When national survival and development required ruthless action, democracy meant endless debate and stalemate. One justification given for the Maoist "dictatorship of the proletariat" was precisely that the regime could not afford to relax its vigilance because it needed to carry out rapid development while repulsing enemies' attacks at home and abroad. But the 1970s brought fresh disillusionment with authoritarian regimes around the world. They were ineffective in managing social conflict: antagonisms and resentments broke out violently whenever the government's repression weakened. They failed to win the consent of their people. Corruption grew as the only way for excluded social forces to influence public decisions. Leaders who operated without public oversight or criticism made foolish, wasteful decisions, while falling prey to the delusion of infallibility. Worst of all, such regimes often failed to deliver the one benefit that was their excuse for being, political stability. Their politics were violent and unpredictable. These were some of the points in the Chinese indictment of the Maoist regime. The Gengshen Reforms thus were part of a worldwide trend towards liberalizing reform.

The democracy activists agreed with the reformers in regarding democracy as an effective means to the end of national development. But the more radical among them insisted that democracy could not perform its functions unless it involved the exercise of real power by the people. Participation without power, they argued, could neither arouse popular energies nor help check the abuse of power. For the people to exercise real influence required two minimal conditions: competition for office and an independent press (the right to organize, which is logically linked to these conditions, received less of their attention). The competition for office might be limited to Marxists and might even take place, in the view of some democrats, within a single ruling party. The press might be held to strict national secrecy laws. But authentic electoral competition of some sort and a truly independent press were necessary if the people were to be able to supervise government. The significance of the democracy movement in modern Chinese history was thus that it denied the facile identification of the people's interests with the state's, an identification that had dominated the Chinese vision of democracy since Liang Qichao. The democrats challenged party dictatorship in the name of popular power.

What makes the movement significant from the standpoint of Western values is the fact that, without knowing it, the democrats had arrived at the same thesis about the minimal requisites of democracy that is central to contemporary democratic theory in the West. As formulated by Joseph A. Schumpeter in his influential book *Capitalism, Socialism, and Democracy* (1942), the "theory of the competition of elites" defines "the democratic method [as] that institutional arrangement for arriving at political decisions in which individuals acquire the power to decide by means of a competitive struggle for the people's vote." Democracy defined in this way is a technique, one to be adopted for whatever benefits might flow from the accountability of government to the people. But Schumpeter insisted that in order to assure this accountability, the democratic technique must include a free vote and a degree of freedom of the press and of association sufficient to guarantee that the competition for office is truly open.

Schumpeter's reasoning here was essentially the same as that of the Chinese democrats. It is by providing a measure of popular control of government that democracy fulfills its promise of regulating conflict, legitimating government, supervising officialdom, and providing stability. In turn, only open competition for office can guarantee that government is placed under popular control. As the English political scientist John Plamenatz puts it,

> There is democracy where rulers are politically responsible to their subjects. And there is political responsibility where two conditions hold: where citizens are free to criticize their rulers and to come together to make demands on them and to win support for the policies they favor and the beliefs they hold; and where the supreme makers of law and policy are elected to their offices at free and periodic elections.

This "pluralist" conception of democracy, as it has been called, has been criticized both in the West and in the socialist world for defining democracy in terms of procedures instead of substance. As the Chinese press argued in 1979–80, the abstract conditions of free speech and free political competition are not equally congenial to everyone's interests. Western political scientists have argued that ideas for radical change may be ignored, languishing in the status of "non-issues." Unless there is some compensating force at work, such as a political party that mobilizes the lower classes, the well-off and better-educated are usually better served in a pluralist system. Moreover, many citizens in pluralist systems are apathetic. They may have a theoretical right to influence government, but the political system is so complicated and biased that they give up trying.

Proponents of pluralist democracy by and large concede these points, but they argue that by subjecting the leaders to the periodic discipline of elections, competitive democracy does at least, in the words of Plamenatz, "make it in the interest of rulers to take account of the interests of their subjects." As an American student of democracy, Robert A. Dahl, puts it, "elections and political competition do not make for government by majorities in any very significant way, but they vastly increase the size, number, and variety of minorities whose preferences must be taken into account by leaders in making policy choices." Pluralist democracy does not necessarily realize a transcendent common good, if such a thing even exists, but it is the only form of government that can assure that rulers will be regularly responsive to the public.

Can the Chinese experience teach us anything about the West's—and the Chinese democrats'—identification of democracy with pluralism? Chinese citizens today, as they have for thirty years, perform their political roles through a network of organizations that the government has designed for society. Life is organized in the countryside through production teams (or villages) and townships and in the cities through neighborhood offices, schools, and work units. Each unit has extensive control over the lives and prospects of those who belong to it. Citizens sit in on weekly study sessions, go once every few days to the unit reading room, vote periodically in unit, township, and county-level elections, participate in Socialist Ethics Month and other campaigns. They may try to qualify for the youth league or the party. Those who are workers, students, or bureaucrats know that party officials are keeping a record of their political attitudes. Chinese citizens are well informed about policy; are asked for their concurrence with it; discuss its application in their units; and make their sentiments about it known to the higher leaders through the reports of unit officials. They are politically involved—more so than the average Westerner.

But they have no influence over the selection of officials above the level of their own units and the local county congresses. They cannot contribute time or money to lobbies or pressure groups that influence government policy. They can—although few do—send their opinions about policies or specific officials to government representatives or the official press, taking some risk of retaliation, but they have no legitimate means to influence the response. Chinese citizens have occasionally used illegal methods—bribery, demonstrations, work slowdowns, and strikes—to try to influence government, but at great risk and, so far as is known, with little success. Instead of enabling the citizen to influence government, the entire web of participatory organizations is designed to, and does, render the citizen more susceptible to control from the party center in Peking. Chinese democracy involves participation without influence.

The difference between the party and democrats, however, and also between the dominant Western and Chinese theories of democracy, does not concern whether the Chinese public influences its government—the party does not claim that it does—but whether despite the lack of public influence the system is able to perform the functions that both Chinese and Westerners wish democracy to perform. As we have seen, the party holds that a regime is democratic not when it is open to influence by the people but when it serves their higher interests. Government accountability, in this view, is not only unnecessary but harmful, since it subjects the state to manipulation by narrow interests with one-sided views. The party acknowledges that its record in making correct decisions on behalf of the people was poor for the last two decades of Mao's life, but claims that it altered its own course without having to be forced to do so by the people. This argument of the leaders is at once classically Leninist and rooted in the long-held Chinese belief that the people and the rulers have a fundamental harmony of interests.

On this assumption of ultimate harmony, indeed, most of the democracy activists agreed with the party. But the more radical democrats rejected the view that a tragedy on the scale of the Cultural Revolution could have been caused by the mistakes of one man and the corruption of a few around him. They insisted that abuse of power was inherent, at least as a potentiality, in a system of overcentralized power, and that such a system can never be consistently fair, legitimate, or stable. Even if power is held by good leaders for the time being, as most of the democrats believed was the case under Deng, what remains so long as control of government rests outside the hands of the people is the possibility of "A Tragedy That Might Happen in the Year 2000"—a reversion from benevolent dictatorship to tyranny.

What we know of the limited effectiveness of the Gengshen political reforms tends to support these arguments. The reforms represented a model of democracy in which responsive government in the sense defined by pluralist theory was not the goal. Rather, the reforms aimed to change China from a terror-based, totalitarian dictatorship to a "mature," administered dictatorship of the post-Stalinist Soviet or Eastern European type. They tried to do this by increasing procedural regularity in the exercise of power, fostering consultation among decision-makers, specialists, and bureaucratic interest groups, and allowing nonparty managers and intellectuals more discretion in their jobs. Reinvigoration of the citizen's relationship with the state was only meant to contribute to a more consultative and predictable form of party dictatorship.

Democratization under the Gengshen Reforms involved changes in four sets of institutions. First, the reforms revitalized the appeal system—"letters and visits work"—so that citizens who felt wronged by bureaucrats could carry their complaints to higher-level offices or to the newspapers. The appeal system is designed to alert the central leaders to abuses of power in the bureaucracy below, to assure the people of the fundamental justice of the system, and to separate the party from the unpopular acts that are sometimes committed in its name.

Second, the reforms expanded the use of unit-level elections—elections of production-team or village cadres in the countryside and of workers' and staff congresses and some managerial cadres in state-owned factories. Unit elections are designed to work in conjunction with other administrative changes to reduce the work load of party officials and buttress the authority of nonparty managers in the enterprise. They are intended to involve workers and peasants in enterprise affairs and, like the appeal system, to facilitate popular supervision of unit officials.

Third, the reforms attempted to restore the effectiveness of the propaganda system, expanding the number and variety of the mass media and diversifying and enlivening their content. The job of the media is to make sure that citizens know what government policy is and to enlist their consent and cooperation. The interview results reported in this book suggest that the reforms have succeeded in increasing both the drawing power and to some degree the credibility of the media. The media, of course, remain under the control of the Propaganda Department of the Central Committee. They criticize individual officials for violating government policy; they do not dissent from policy itself.

The final aim of the Gengshen Reforms was to restore and extend the system of people's congresses and congress elections. The four levels of congresses in which sovereignty is constitutionally vested meet more often, function more vigorously, and have more substantial standing organs and committee structures than in the previous history of the People's Republic. The two lower levels of congresses, township and county, are now directly elected in competitive elections. Although the elections remain under the easy control of local party secretaries, they serve as a civic ritual and an information-gathering mechanism.

The reforms have made the Chinese political system more pluralist only in a special, narrow sense—the same sense in which the post-Stalin Soviet and Eastern European regimes are pluralist, because they invite bureaucratic interest groups and specialists to contribute to the making of complex decisions. And the system has become more participatory in a special sense—it cultivates a greater flow of information and sentiment between citizens and the state. As a consequence the present regime seems better able to manage social conflict, gather information from the people, gain their support, and combat bureaucratic abuse than was the regime of the later years of Mao's rule. But the effectiveness of the political reforms has fallen short of the reformers' expressed goals. The people are still wary; much information is blocked; bureaucratic abuse is difficult to expose; the stability of the regime after Deng remains uncertain. While the regime appears to have prospered economically by tapping the dynamism of the people, it has not succeeded in introducing much vigor to the political realm. Both pluralist theory and the arguments of the democrats suggest that this is because the average citizen is still far more the object of control than the exerciser of influence.

The most eloquent evidence for the democrats' thesis that power will continue to be abused so long as it remains uncontrolled has been the treatment of those who propounded it: the democracy movement has been effectively crushed within China. In 1981, Fu Yuehua, leader of the Peking petitioners' demonstrations, was released from prison but transferred to a labor camp. Liu Qing, the editor of *April Fifth Forum* who had been sent for three years of labor reeducation for distributing the transcript of Wei Jingsheng's trial, was sentenced in 1982 to another seven years after he smuggled out a camp diary that was published in the West. His brother and a colleague were arrested for assisting him. Xu Wenli, another editor of *April Fifth Forum* and a strong backer of Deng Xiaoping among the democrats, was sentenced to fifteen years' imprisonment; Wang Xizhe, the independent Marxist theorist of Canton, to fourteen years; and He Qiu, former editor of *People's Road*, to ten years, all for counterrevolutionary propaganda or incitement. Late one night in August 1983, teams of police and militiamen appeared on the streets of Shanghai and other cities, carrying lists and knocking on doors. An estimated 100,000 suspected criminals were arrested nationwide in this and a second sweep in October. Most were sentenced to labor reeducation in border areas, their urban residence permits revoked so that they would have to stay in the borderlands after their sentences had expired. According to interviews, a number of former activists were swept into the net. By 1984, Wei Jingsheng had served the first five years of his fifteen-year sentence in solitary confinement in a prison near Peking; according to Amnesty International, his mental health had seriously deteriorated.

Ren Wanding, the founder of the China Human Rights League, was freed from prison in 1983. His term had been extended to four years because of his failure to make a satisfactory self-criticism. Other activists, especially those who were given labor reeducation terms, must also have been released, although reliable word of this has seldom reached the outside world. All have remained silent.

Chinese advocates of democracy today face a difficult prospect. At one time many activists believed that the advance of legal codification and the people's congress system would permit their movement to prosper. But these activists obviously overestimated the tolerance of the reformers whose support they thought they had. Other democrats dreamed that Deng's economic reforms would fail, thereby bringing about a Polish-style workers' rebellion which would force the regime to permit some form of political pluralism (a possibility that apparently also worried some of the leaders for a time). But the success of the economic reforms to date has made this scenario appear increasingly unlikely. Some activists (and foreigners) now hope that the development of the economy will cause a kind of natural political evolution—that the government will loosen its control of the economy, accommodate more and more ideas from the West, and yield to the demands for freedom of a rising technical and managerial class. Judging from the experience of the developed socialist economies of Europe, such economically induced change may include greater legal protection for individuals, enhanced intellectual and cultural tolerance, and a consultative style of decision-making—the types of evolution that are in fact occurring in Deng's China. But there is little prospect that the party will adopt, voluntarily or under pressure, either of the two conditions that the radical democrats identified as essential for authentic democracy: free elections and an independent press. (The government may adopt a law permitting privately owned publications, but if so these would certainly be kept under effective government supervision.)

The democracy movement persists in the open only overseas. A government-funded Chinese student, Wang Bingzhang, after completing a combined M.D.-Ph.D. program at McGill University, announced in New York in November 1982 that he was staying in the West to continue the movement that had been suppressed at home. Together with a number of other Chinese in the U.S. and Canada, he launched a magazine called *China Spring*, which analyzes events in China and publishes theoretical discussions of democracy and reform, some of them purportedly sent by contributors living in China. The magazine's platform includes political pluralism and an independent press. In December 1983, the group held its "first international representative conference" in New York, attended by fifty-three delegates from around the world. Adopting the name "Chinese Alliance for Democracy," the organization claimed chapters in Hong Kong, Japan, Australia, France, West Germany, Holland, Belgium, and Mauritius, as well as in thirteen U.S. and Canadian cities, and an underground network in China.

Nonetheless, support for pluralist democracy among Chinese both at home and abroad seems if anything weaker today than when the democracy movement emerged. Even those who agree with the democrats' analysis that overconcentration of power is at the root of China's political problems fear the disorder they believe would flow from any weakening of party control. Most intellectuals appear to accept the party's claim that political order in their country requires leaders with strong authority. They hold to the old view that, because of China's feudal tradition and peasant backwardness, institutional change is useless until the culture is reformed. Many who speak this way seem unaware of how their words echo back through history: to the judgment of Liang Qichao that China was fit only for enlightened despotism; to the political passivity and cultural reformism of dispirited liberals of the 1920s and 1930s; to the tutelage theory of the Guomindang.

Never seriously addressed in the course of the democracy controversy was the feasibility, as distinct from the desirability, of pluralist democracy in

China. Proponents might have pointed to the relative success of pluralism in other countries with approximately China's level of development, such as India; or to the apparent compatibility of robust political rights and freedoms with political stability and economic growth in other settings with Confucian cultural traditions, such as twentieth-century Japan and even, to some extent, contemporary Taiwan. They might have argued that even though China is still backward, conditions for pluralism are much more promising now than during the abortive experiment of the early republic, because there is a strong government to guarantee political order and a better-educated population that is also becoming better off economically.

Like the early Liang Qichao and other reformers in China's tradition of Confucian optimism, however, the democrats seemed to see institutional change as needing only to be ordained to be successful. Confucius once said, "Is virtue a thing remote? If I desire to be virtuous, virtue will be at hand." To the democrats, pluralist reform was similarly a matter of making up one's mind as to its desirability, and so they concentrated on demonstrating the benefits of their proposed reforms, as if this were all that was needed to make the case for adopting them. By default, they left the task of evaluating their ideas' practicality to those who feared, in the pessimistic tradition of the later Liang and other conservatives, that society was still too backward to allow the people to hold real power. In the end, the democrats may have had the better of the theoretical argument that democracy cannot perform its functions without competitive elections and an independent press. But so far, China's century-long obsession with political order and national strength has made it impossible for most other Chinese, even non-Marxists, to share their vision of change.

APPENDIX

SOURCE NOTES

INDEX

APPENDIX:
THE INTERVIEWS

Interviews with Chinese émigrés and travelers provided information for this book that could not have come from any other source. The official press is devoted to propagandizing good and bad models of behavior relevant to current policy, and seldom explains everyday life in a way that makes things clear to an outsider. Field research is limited to topics that are acceptable to the Chinese government. Emigré interviewing has been an important tool of research since the 1950s and remains an indispensable technique of China study today.

Many Chinese come abroad as students and scholars or members of delegations. I interviewed twenty or so such persons for this book, on such subjects as the appeal process, the internal organization of newspapers, the activities of the democracy movement, the county-level elections, and so on. Some of these conversations were brief and some extended over several meetings. Since I promised most of the informants anonymity, I cite them in the notes only as "interview." These people were well placed to know what they told me and they gave me information that was consistent with what I learned from other sources.

This Appendix describes sixty-nine additional interviews conducted during 1979–82 that followed a fixed procedure and a structured questionnaire, and that provided most of the information on media use, political participation, and attitudes towards propaganda that I report in Chapters 8 and 9. The Appendix explains why and to what extent statistical information gathered in this way can be used to draw valid conclusions. It also provides added details of the findings.

It was easy to find recent émigrés from China in New York and Washington, D.C., where forty of the interviews were done, and in Hong Kong, where twenty-nine persons were interviewed. Over four hundred thousand Chinese moved from China to Hong Kong from 1977 to 1981, some legally and some surreptitiously. Eight to ten thousand PRC immigrants came to live in the United States each year during the same period. Thousands more came temporarily to study or visit. When my research assistants and I conducted the interviews, our respondents had been out of China for an average of twenty-four months. One had been away from home for nine years, but many had left very recently, seventeen of them no more than six months before we spoke with them.

Before I could start the interviews I had to get approval for my procedures from my university's Human Subjects Review Committee. Federal regulations require universities that accept federal grants to establish such committees to oversee not only government-funded projects but also those that are privately funded, as mine was. The committee is mandated to assure that subjects' participation is voluntary and based on "informed consent," that subjects' anonymity is protected, and that subjects do not undergo undue risk.

In the United States I recruited most of my respondents by distributing circulars through institutions that provide services to recent immigrants and visitors. (I also met some subjects through introductions or chance encounters.) One such circular, for example, read as follows, with texts in both English and Chinese:

> I am a professor at Columbia's East Asian Institute who teaches courses about China. At present, I am conducting a study of China's mass media. I have interviewed a number of people from China about their personal experiences with the mass media, and I would like to interview some of you as well.
>
> The interview will take place in my office, and will require three to four hours. The questionnaire has five sections: personal background, experiences in a particular work unit, media use habits, knowledge of certain news items, and finally a few of your general opinions. The interview is conducted in Chinese. You are not obligated to answer any questions that you do not wish to answer, and you are free to withdraw from the interview at any time. You will receive an honorarium of $25 for your participation.
>
> Your answers to the questionnaire will be combined with other people's answers to provide statistical information. We will not publish people's names or personal information about individuals.

The other circulars were similar. When I called to make an appointment for the interview I spoke in Chinese and repeated that the respondent would not have to answer all questions and could break off the interview at any time.

In New York, most of the interviews were conducted in my office. I started by giving the respondent my name card, on which were printed my name, title, and home and office addresses and phone numbers in both English and Chinese. After some small talk, I picked up the questionnaire and read aloud the following paragraph in Chinese:

> This is a research project on mass communication in the People's Republic of China, undertaken by the East Asian Institute of Columbia University. Your answers to this questionnaire will be combined with other people's answers to provide statistical information. We will not publish people's names or personal information about individuals.

Some respondents asked to see the questionnaire, which was written in both English and Chinese, and I showed it to them. I answered any other questions, repeated for the third time that the person was not required to answer all questions or to complete the interview, and finally said, "Shall we begin?" All these steps were designed to secure "informed consent." The Human Subjects Review Committee agreed not to require me to ask for a signed consent form, which I believed might seem to conflict with my assurances of anonymity and might scare off respondents who were illegal immigrants. (As it happened, none of my U.S. respondents turned out to be an illegal immigrant.)

The questionnaire was "semistructured." That is, some questions had fixed answers that could be checked off (e.g., "Married?": yes, no). Others were open-ended ("How satisfied were you with your job?"). We conversed in Chinese and I took notes in English on the questionnaire form. When an answer seemed incomplete, I probed for more information as neutrally as possible ("What else?" or "Please tell me more"). If I did not understand what was said, I asked the respondent to write the Chinese characters for a term or explain its meaning. Some respondents had had such complicated lives that I spent over an hour on the part of the questionnaire concerning their personal backgrounds and had to skip some of the last part, which is one reason why some of the tables below are based on fewer than sixty-nine cases. At the end of each interview I thanked the respondent for his or her help and, in keeping with Chinese custom, pressed him to accept an envelope containing the cash honorarium as "a small token of thanks from our project."

In Hong Kong, respondents were mostly recruited through classified ads in a popular Chinese-language newspaper. The most effective wording of several tried was the following:

> Temporary part-time work. Assist American professor to do research. Prefer person who was worker or peasant in China. Time at your convenience. Reply by letter to Box 41.

A research assistant telephoned those who responded to make an appointment and explain the ground rules: that this was a half-day interview, that
anonymity would be preserved, that participation could be broken off at any
time, and that participants would be paid HK$75 (then worth about
U.S.$15). Once the respondent appeared I followed the same procedures as
in New York. I held the Hong Kong meetings in an office at the Universities
Service Centre, an academic research facility supported by American universities and foundations.

To make good my guarantee of anonymity, I did not write the respondent's name on the questionnaire. Instead, I coded each questionnaire and
kept the name on a separate card. Someone looking at the questionnaires
or the notes of my book would have no way of knowing who had given me
what information. I could not, it is true, prevent an observer from noting
who was coming to see me either in New York or in Hong Kong. But I did
not believe that there was a serious risk of reprisal simply for meeting with
me.

On this point, however, not all the Chinese I met agreed. One or two refused to go through with the interview after seeing the questionnaire. "These
questions about my participation in political movements and my attitudes towards propaganda might seem innocuous to you," one told me, "but Hong
Kong is full of eyes and ears. I could get into trouble for discussing these
subjects." I dismissed a couple of respondents who were willing to talk but
who wanted a stronger guarantee of security than I could provide. Several respondents emphasized over and over during the interview that I should not
identify them in my book even by circumstantial reference. As one said, "If
you mention my unit's type and location, people there will know I was your
source because no one else has left there to come to America."

But most seemed unworried about talking to me. They were participating
in the interview mainly to earn money. Many seemed even to enjoy reflecting
on their lives in a way that they probably did not do among friends. Many
recognized the name of Columbia University, and a few even refused pay-
ment. As one put it, "It is my duty as a Chinese to help a foreign scholar understand our society better."

Was the information I collected any less reliable than that collected in
most surveys, given the fact that my respondents were émigrés (or visitors)
from, rather than current residents of, the political system I was asking
about? The section where I asked about news items dating from the early and
mid-1970s presented special problems of recall, which I will discuss below.
On other sections, some false information must have crept in when respondents misunderstood me or I them, or when I made a mistake in taking down
answers or reading my notes afterwards. These problems are found in any
survey, particularly where a foreign language and open-ended questions are
involved. The real question in émigré interviewing is whether respondents lie

about what they experienced or thought in their home country, when they are interviewed about it after they have left.

One reason for doubting that fabrication was a serious problem is that my major questions created no motive to lie. There was no reason to tell anything but the truth about the media facilities of one's unit or one's daily habits of media use. Some of my supplementary questions were more sensitive, such as whether the respondent had left China legally or illegally. The answers to these questions should be treated more skeptically, and I report them only as background information in this Appendix, rather than as part of the central argument of the book.

A second reason for believing the interviews is that I was able to compare what each respondent said to what I knew from other sources and to what the same respondent said during the rest of the interview. In the interview's face-to-face, open format I could follow up whenever a respondent said something unusual or apparently contradictory. If the answers did not seem believable I could always discard the interview—as I did with Part IV of one interview, not because the respondent seemed to be lying but because he seemed confused. Cross-checked both internally and against other data, the interview results may even be more trustworthy than data obtained in large surveys where there are many interviewers, who are under pressure to finish in a fixed time and who are not allowed to ask follow-up questions except when designed as part of the questionnaire.

My data may also be more reliable than some material gathered during field research in China. We know that in at least some fieldwork studies, informants were secretly assigned to work with the researcher and drilled beforehand about what to say. Even when this is not the case, Chinese interviewed in China are constrained by guidelines, both published and unpublished, about how to speak with foreigners. A five-point guideline for intercourse with foreigners published in 1982, for example, tells the citizen to defend national policies firmly against criticism and to watch out for foreigners who seek to discover political, military, economic, or cultural secrets. My respondents, by contrast, came to the interviews as voluntary, private participants and dealt with me without official guidance.

If my respondents did tell the truth as they saw it, were their views nonetheless distorted by antigovernment bias? Again, concrete, objective information on media facilities or time spent per day reading newspapers probably would not be affected by bias. But resentment towards the regime could certainly have made them untypical in their levels of political interest and participation and attitudes towards the believability of the press. In order to estimate how biased the interview group might have been compared to the general population, I included in the questionnaire a number of items designed to reveal potential sources of antiregime sentiment. The results are displayed in Table 1.

TABLE 1

Indicators of Potential Political Bias Among Respondents

Class background	Good	Middling	Bad	NA	Total
	19	31	16	3	69
Emigration status	Legal	Illegal			
	55	11		3	69
Self-described political activism	High	Average	Low		
compared to others	11	36	20	2	69

Notes

NA means "not asked," "not answered," or "answer not clear."

"Class background" refers to the classification officially given to oneself or one's father in the years just before or after liberation. "Good" class backgrounds in this table are worker, cadre, poor peasant, and lower-middle peasant. "Middling" backgrounds are white-collar employee, intellectual, teacher, professional, and middle peasant. "Bad" backgrounds are national capitalist, Guomindang bureaucrat, merchant, petty capitalist, and landlord.

"Emigration status" refers to whether the person left China on valid traveling documents or not. All but eight of the respondents said they had relatives living overseas before their own departures from China, which helps explain why they were able to get passports to leave.

"Political activism" is a Chinese term referring to the individual's level of participation in unit political activities. The question read: "Comparing yourself to others in your working group, was your political activism . . . high? average? low?"

These data themselves may not be completely reliable. A person might be embarrassed to admit coming from a bad class background or afraid to confess to being an illegal emigrant. Even if the figures are correct, I have no way to compare them to the general population since I do not know what proportion of China's population have bad class backgrounds, display low-to-average political activism, or would leave China if they could. At least Table 1 shows that the interview group was not composed predominantly of victimized people or illegal refugees. But since the level of political bias is unmeasurable, it is safest not to regard the distribution of politically influenced attitudes among the respondent group as representative of the general Chinese population.

In any case potential bias is only one kind of unrepresentativeness encountered in émigré interviewing, and, depending on the questions asked, not necessarily the most serious kind. People who emigrate are different in many ways. In China's case, so far as we know, they tend to be younger, more educated, more often from coastal areas, and more often male. Table 2 shows some of the ways in which my respondent group differed from the Chinese population as a whole along dimensions that must specifically have affected their experiences of and attitudes towards the media.

Of course, in the study of closed societies unrepresentativeness of human sources is not a problem unique to émigré interviewing. It affects even more

TABLE 2

Respondents Compared to the Chinese Population

	Respondents		*Population*
Sex			
Male	58.0%	(40)	51.3%
Female	42.0%	(29)	48.7%
Education			
None	0.0%	(0)	39.6%
Some primary	1.4%	(1)	35.3%
Some secondary	40.6%	(28)	24.4%
Some tertiary	56.5%	(39)	0.6%
Some graduate	1.4%	(1)	
Illiteracy	0.0%	(0)	23.5%
Place of residence			
Urban	61.0%	(42)	13.9%
Rural	39.0%	(27)	86.1%
Annual income (workers and staff)	686 yuan		614 yuan

Notes

Numbers in parentheses represent the number of respondents in each category.

Population data for sex are from 1981; for education and illiteracy from 1982; for place of residence from 1981; for income from 1978.

For respondents, place of residence was the unit they were living in during the time covered by Part II of the questionnaire—the same unit for which I collected information on media facilities. My classification of type of place of residence may not be the same as the one used by Chinese administrators. Mine is based on distance from the nearest city and type of unit rather than on the administrative status of the place of residence, which is information I do not have. I classified communes near cities as rural but other suburban units (e.g., factories and schools) as urban.

For respondents, the income figure is the average annual income for 38 respondents who appear comparable to the "workers and staff" category used by Chinese statisticians for their population-wide income data—that is, factory and commercial enterprise employees. It excludes 10 respondents on whom I lack income data, 7 students or others without income, 13 peasants or state farm workers, and one "worker-student" who would not be considered "workers and staff." The 38 respondents include some professionals, temporary workers, and persons in other categories who might also not be classified as "workers and staff," but since the term is so broad in PRC usage it is hard to be sure. I chose 1978 as the comparison date because it is the date for which official data and my data most closely intersect. Among my 38 cases, the income data are for a time period that includes the year 1978 in 22 cases, for a period prior to that year in 11 cases, and for a period later than that year in 5 cases. Although the PRC has released peasant income data, I have too few peasants to make comparison meaningful.

Sources for population data

Sex, place of residence, income: *Statistical Yearbook of China 1981*, English ed., State Statistical Bureau, comp. (Hong Kong: Economic Information and Agency [*sic*], 1982), pp. 89, 429.

Education: BR 40 (1983): 27.

Illiteracy: BR 45 (1982): 20.

seriously news reporting and field research done inside such societies. The people who choose or are allowed to talk with foreign journalists and scholars are doubtless even less representative of the general population than are émigrés, although perhaps in different ways. To get a truly representative group of informants one must interview a scientific sample of the entire population. Soviet and East European scholars have done some modern surveys of this type, but only on innocuous subjects so far as we know. Chinese social scientists have shown an interest in the techniques involved, and have published the results of some local surveys of household income, living standards, and the like. But so far as I know, no communist country has allowed a foreign scholar to do a study based on a sample survey of its population.

I might have gotten a less unrepresentative group of respondents if I had used a technique called "quota sampling." This entails hunting for respondents with certain predetermined characteristics in order to build up a respondent pool with roughly the same demographic makeup as the population at large. For example, I could have made special efforts to interview illiterates and peasants. But such persons are rarer among Chinese émigrés than they are at home, and they are particularly difficult to contact through such means as circulars and newspaper ads. The approach also requires a larger sample in order to provide enough respondents in each demographic category to make comparisons across categories meaningful; otherwise the whole procedure is not worthwhile. Even after making the effort, the respondent pool would still be unrepresentative in terms of characteristics other than those controlled in the sampling, so the results still could not be generalized with confidence to the population as a whole.

In short, one important kind of conclusion was precluded by the nature of my respondent group. I could not make statistical inferences about the distribution of an attribute among the general population on the basis of its distribution among my respondents. For example, I cannot say that Chinese in general are as well informed about the names of their political leaders as my respondents were, or that they have as little interest in politics. This kind of inference is valid only if the sample is randomly drawn and is large enough to reduce to a small size the variation attributable to accident.

But my sixty-nine respondents still provided an adequate basis for four kinds of conclusions which I present in Chapters 8 and 9. First, any attitudes and experiences found among the respondents must be found in the parent population. For example, the decipherer syndrome described in Chapter 9 must exist in China, even if one cannot say whether it is as widespread among all Chinese as it was among my respondents. Likewise, the pattern of defensive curiosity described in Chapter 8 may not be as common among the general population as it was among my interviewees, but it must exist. Emigré interviews thus establish the existence in the general population of characteristics that are not known from other sources.

Second, by the same logic, if the experiences of the respondent pool are diverse in certain ways, at least the same range of diversity must exist in the parent population. For example, unit reading facilities in China must be of at least as many different kinds as those described by my respondents.

Third, interviews can provide strong reasons for believing that a certain pattern of experiences or attitudes is common in the parent population. For example, all but one of my respondents reported that their units had some kind of public reading facility. They came from a wide variety of units, and there is no reason to think that their experiences in this respect were atypical even though the respondents were in some ways atypical as individuals. Since the finding is consistent with information from other sources, it can be taken in combination with them to support the generalization that unit reading facilities are common, even though it cannot establish the precise percentage of units that have such facilities.

Finally, if subgroups within the émigré group differ in their experiences or attitudes, it is reasonable to conclude that subgroups in the parent population differ in the same direction, although not necessarily with the same magnitude. For example, decipherers among my respondents were usually people who came from units with rich media resources, while accepters came from media-poor units. It is likely that the same correlation exists in the population as a whole. We can draw this conclusion even without knowing exactly what proportion of units are media-rich or -poor or what proportion of citizens are decipherers or accepters.

Since these are the kinds of generalizations to be drawn from a nonrepresentative sample, it follows that the conclusions are strongest when they come from the most diverse possible respondent group. But most of the people who answered my circulars and ads were males, with at least secondary educations, from urban backgrounds. I faced a shortage of people from remote provinces, from rural units, and with little education. To correct this, I made two trips to Hong Kong, where it is easier to find persons of humble backgrounds than among Chinese in the U.S., and specified in my Hong Kong newspaper ad, "prefer person who was worker or peasant in China." In New York and Washington, D.C., I employed two female research assistants, both young Americans who spoke Chinese, who were better able than I to contact and interview young female Chinese, who are often shy about talking with an American male professor. These assistants did twenty-five of the interviews. They followed the same procedures as I did to assure that respondents gave informed consent and to protect their anonymity.

These efforts did produce a fairly diverse set of respondents. Twenty-four had been born in Guangdong (the south China province bordering on Hong Kong), but there were also twelve from Shanghai, five each from the provinces of Zhejiang and Fujian, and four from Peking. All told, I was able to interview respondents who had been born in twenty-one different provinces as well as some born outside China who had returned there to live. At the time of the interviews the respondents ranged in age from nineteen to fifty-five, with almost half of the group in their twenties. Table 2 shows the sex and educational makeup of the group.

The respondents' professions and the nature of the units they worked in were also quite diverse. Part II of the questionnaire was headed "Experience in the Work Unit." Having reviewed the respondent's life history in Part I, I selected the unit where he or she had most recently spent a considerable period of time. If the time span was very long I specified a subperiod within it, such as the period after Mao's death. "Now let's discuss the situation that existed during (specified span of time)," I said. "For the time being, we won't be discussing the situation in other units you were in." Table 3 displays the kind of work the respondents were doing in the units, some characteristics of the units, and the time spans involved. The location of the units on an urban-rural dimension was shown in Table 2. The diversity of the respondents and their units provides the best reason for believing in the validity of my findings.

One part of the questionnaire presented special problems of reliability. This was Part IV, "Information from the Mass Media," where I asked each respondent to remember how and when he or she had heard about thirteen news items that had occurred a decade or so before the time of the interview. The problem was that after the lapse of so much time respondents might have forgotten hearing about an item which they knew at the time, or might think they had heard about it when they actually learned of it later, or might confuse the item I was quoting with a similar one heard earlier or later. I could have reduced the severity of this problem by asking each respondent about news items that occurred immediately before his or her departure. But then the items would have been different for each respondent. They would have been of varying importance, circulated in different ways, and perceived by the public differently because of the different propaganda strategies in effect at the time they occurred. This would have prevented me from comparing how well known different items were. More important, it would have made it impossible to analyze the range of attitudes towards the press at a particular point in time. For this, I needed a fixed list. I chose items from the early to mid-1970s in order to accommodate the largest possible number of potential respondents. As it turned out, I could have selected somewhat later items, since fifty-four of my respondents left China in 1978 or afterwards. Even so, I had to exclude six questionnaires from some of the analysis of Part IV because the respondents left China before all the events occurred (see the table in Chapter 8, p. 167).

Having decided to use a fixed set of items, I tried to minimize potential unreliability by counting respondents as knowing an item only if they could recall something concrete about the circumstances under which they heard it

TABLE 3

Work and Work Units Covered in Part II of the Questionnaire

Respondent's Occupation

Farm work (peasant/state farm)	23
Industrial work/Construction/Driver	16
Professional	10
Manager/Technician/Engineer	7
Teacher	7
Student	3
Not working	3
Total	69

Type of Unit

Commune or state farm	23
State factory, mine, or enterprise	15
School	11
Professional office (hospital, institute, etc.)	9
Neighborhood factory or enterprise	4
Street committee	4
Government office	3
Total	69

Location of Unit

Guangdong	25
Shanghai	11
Zhejiang	7
Peking	5
14 other provinces	21
Total	69

Time Span

Longest stay in unit	16.0 years
Shortest	0.3
Average	5.3
Earliest assignment to unit	1962
Latest departure from unit	1980
Assignment ends in 1976 or earlier	21 persons
Assignment begins in 1977 or later	7
Assignment spans the two periods	41

and could remember more about its content than was given in the question (for examples, see Chapter 8). This meant that people who actually knew the items at the time they occurred might not remember enough about them ten years later to convince me that they had known them. But if any errors of this sort were introduced, they were less damaging to my main conclusions than systematic upward errors would have been, since I ended by arguing that the level of news knowledge among my respondents was remarkably high. Nonetheless, the findings should be treated with caution. The table in Chapter 8 reports the results of this part of the questionnaire in terms of the percentage of respondents able to identify each item. Table 4 below shows how many respondents could identify how many items. And Table 5 describes respondents' performance on a related question, naming incumbents of certain party and government offices at the time the respondent left China. The figures in Table 5 are also discussed in Chapter 8, page 168.

Another subject discussed in Chapter 8 is respondents' level of political participation. I measured this in two ways: in terms of membership in political or politically related organizations, and in terms of the frequency with which the respondent said he or she had engaged in any of nine specified political or quasi-political acts while in the work unit discussed in the questionnaire's Part II. The texts of these two questions and the results are given in

TABLE 4

Number of News Items Identified

Number Correct	Number of Respondents
13	13
12	4
11	13
10	11
9	5
8	5
7	8
6	3
5	1
0–4	0
Total	63

Notes

The thirteen items are listed in the table in Chapter 8, p. 167.

Six questionnaires were not used because the respondents had left China before all the events happened.

This table as well as the one in Chapter 8 includes four respondents who were interviewed according to a trial version of the questionnaire that had fifteen news items. For the purposes of comparability the two items that were not given to all respondents are excluded from the statistics.

TABLE 5

Number of Officials Named

Number Named	Number of Respondents	Total Officials Named
10 or more	13	163
9	2	18
8	9	72
7	3	21
6	12	72
5	9	45
4	5	20
3	4	12
2	2	4
1	4	4
0	3	0
Totals	66	431

Average number of officials named: 6.5

Notes

The question was, "At the time you left China, that is (date), can you tell me who were the members of the CCP Politburo? Who was the chairman of the Standing Committee of the National People's Congress? Who was minister of foreign affairs?"

Only correct answers were counted.

Three respondents were not asked this question.

Tables 6 and 7. I regret that I did not also ask, "How often did you participate in elections of unit leaders?" When I drew up the questionnaire I assumed that unit leaders were virtually never elected. This was probably true until the recent reforms, which occurred too late to be reflected in most of my questionnaires. On the other hand, regulations dating from 1962 did provide for regular election of production-team cadres in the countryside, and research by John Burns shows that such elections were held in some places, although not nearly as frequently as the regulations required.

As discussed in Chapter 8, the questionnaire also attempted to probe respondents' attitudes of trust in the responsiveness of the political system. To do this, I asked four questions adapted from *The Civic Culture* by Gabriel A. Almond and Sidney Verba, a landmark study of the political cultures of five nations done in 1959–60 and published in 1963. The questions and the results are listed in Table 8. To measure what Almond and Verba called "citizen competence"—"the degree to which citizens believe they can influence the course of governmental decisions"—they asked, among other things, "Suppose a regulation were being considered by (most local governmental unit) that you considered very unjust or harmful. What do you think you could do?" Fifty-one percent of Italians questioned said they thought they

TABLE 6

"Were You a Member of . . ."

	Number
Chinese Communist Party	0
Communist Youth League	15
Militia	30
Trade union	24
Poor and lower-middle peasants' association	5
Women's association	4
Art ensemble, propaganda group, or the like (within the unit)	22
Work team (temporary group sent to another unit to conduct a campaign)	12
Other membership group or organization	6
None	18

TABLE 7

"How Often Did You . . ."

	Often, Regularly	Occasionally, Rarely, Seldom	Never or Virtually Never	NA
Speak in meetings	29	21	18	1
Write wall posters	3	37	29	0
Write letters to the editor	0	4	64	1
Bring personal problems up to the leadership	17	30	22	0
Make criticisms to the leadership	16	20	33	0
Write to higher levels	2	6	60	1
Discuss politics with other members of the unit	35	14	20	0
Use complaint box	2	1	65	1
Have interview with reporters	1	9	58	1

Note
    NA means "not asked" or "not answered."

TABLE 8

Responses to Questions on Citizen and Subject Competence

	Number	Percentage of Those Answering

1 "Suppose the (production team, neighborhood committee) was considering a decision that you felt was very unjust or harmful. Would you have done something about this?"

	Number	Percentage
Yes	18	39
No	28	61
NA	23	—
Total	69	

2 "We'd like to find out how decisions were made on your job. Did you have any influence on these decisions?"

	Number	Percentage
Had influence	30	44
None, or only through personal favoritism of leaders	38	56
NA	1	—
Total	69	

3 "If a decision were made affecting your own work that you disagreed with strongly, would you have done something about it?"

	Number	Percentage
Yes	28	47
No	32	53
NA	9	—
Total	69	

4 "Suppose there were some personal question that you had to take to a government office at the (county or urban-district) level—for example, a question of housing or job assignment. How do you think you would be treated?"

	Number	Percentage
Expected at least fair treatment	19	31
Expected unfair treatment or no results	43	69
NA	7	—
Total	69	

Note

NA means "not asked" or "not answered."

Answers were open-ended.

Answers were coded according to the predominant attitude expressed.

could do something about such a regulation; the figure for Mexico was 52 percent, for Germany 62 percent, for the United States 77 percent, and for Great Britain 78 percent. For China, I changed the question to ask about the production team or neighborhood committee, depending on whether the respondent lived in the countryside or the city, and about "decisions" rather than regulations. Almond and Verba also asked whether respondents were consulted when decisions were made on their jobs. Depending on the country, from 59 to 80 percent of the respondents said that they sometimes or often were. Given the quasi-governmental character of the work unit in China, this question can also be used to measure citizen competence there. I asked, "We'd like to find out how decisions were made on your job. Did you have any influence on these decisions?"

Almond and Verba also explored "subject competence," defined as the perception that government officials are responsive to citizens' appeals. Their question concerned tax and housing problems. I changed the question to ask about housing and job assignments, the problems Chinese citizens are most likely to bring to government offices outside their units. From 42 to 83 percent of respondents in the five Almond and Verba nations expected "equal treatment" and from 14 percent (in Mexico) to 59 percent (in England) expected "serious consideration for their point of view." Among my respondents, 31 percent indicated that they expected fair and equal treatment.

The fact that my respondents as a group had lower levels of citizen and subject competence than the Almond and Verba samples does not enable us to conclude that Chinese have less trust in their government than do Americans, Britons, Germans, Italians, or Mexicans. Not only were the two studies done at different times, but, as already argued, my findings cannot be generalized to the parent population the way that the Almond and Verba findings can. One can of course speculate, as I do in Chapter 8, about how typical my respondents' attitudes were.

The real purpose of probing citizen and subject competence was to see whether competence as a variable could be related to other variables looked at in the study. Table 9 shows that people who had a lower sense of political competence also tended to be less active in political participation. The table divides the respondents into two groups of nearly equal size according to the number of participatory acts they reported engaging in "often" or "occasionally." The resulting figures suggest that those with stronger feelings of competence were more likely to report higher participation, and those with weaker feelings of competence were more likely to report lower participation. Because of the small number of cases, this finding can only be tentative. This is true also because the measure of competence used in the table is a weak one compared to the ten questions used by Almond and Verba to measure citizen and subject competence, plus their additional questions used to probe attitudes towards participation in the home, school, and workplace.

TABLE 9

Relationship Between Competence and Participation

Participation (%)

Competence	High		Low		Total	
High	67	(14)	33	(7)	100	(21)
Low	38	(14)	62	(23)	100	(37)
Total	48	(28)	52	(30)	100	(58)

Notes

Numbers in parentheses represent the number of respondents in each category.

Competence was defined in terms of positive or negative answers to the four questions listed in Table 8. High competence was defined as giving two or more positive answers; low competence as giving two or more negative answers. Seven cases were excluded from the analysis because they gave two positive and two negative answers, and four cases were excluded because they gave one positive and one negative answer and were not asked or did not answer the other two questions in the series.

Participation is defined in terms of the nine acts listed in Table 7. High participation is defined as participating "often" or "occasionally" in four or more acts; low participation as participating "often" or "occasionally" in three or fewer acts. This definition divides the respondents as nearly as possible into two equal groups.

The positive relationship between competence and participation is consistent with common sense. We expect people who have more faith in the responsiveness of government to participate more, and participation in turn should reinforce the sense of being able to affect government. But the table also suggests that quite a few Chinese who had a weak sense of confidence in the responsiveness of the political system could still be mobilized by their unit cadres to speak in meetings, write wall posters, and engage in similar approved forms of participation. One can speculate that people in the high-participation, low-competence category were going through the motions of participation with little expectation of exerting influence.

A less easily anticipated pattern emerges when one explores the effect that political participation and feelings of competence together have upon media use. Table 10 shows that most of the respondents made significant use of the media no matter what their habits of political participation were and no matter how much or how little trust they had in the responsiveness of government. In this respect they differed from citizens of most other countries. Usually those who pay more attention to the media are also those who participate more and who have a stronger sense of political competence. These findings, too, must be treated with caution because of the low number of cases, but I suggested in Chapter 8 that the Chinese pattern might reflect an attitude of defensive curiosity.

A final attempt to explore the interactions of several variables appears in Chapter 9. There I classify respondents as accepters, skeptics, or decipherers

TABLE 10

Relationship Between Political Participation, Competence, and Media Use

	Media Use (%)		
	Significant	Less Than Significant	Total
High participation and high competence	86 (12)	14 (2)	100 (14)
High participation and low competence	100 (12)	0 (0)	100 (12)
Low participation and high competence	83 (5)	17 (1)	100 (6)
Low participation and low competence	91 (20)	9 (2)	100 (22)
Total	91 (49)	9 (5)	100 (54)

Notes

Numbers in parentheses represent the number of respondents in each category. The table excludes eleven cases who could not be scored for competence and four cases who could not be scored for media use.

Participation and competence are defined in the same way as in Table 9.

"Significant" media use is defined as at least one-half hour per day spent reading newspapers (including *Reference News*) or one-half hour per day listening to the radio and/or loudspeaker.

depending upon their attitudes towards the press, and try to see how these three kinds of audience members differ from one another. Few respondents displayed the same attitude toward the media throughout the interview. They might say they believed twelve of thirteen news items but doubted one; or that they were skeptical about several but tried to decipher one or two. As I observe in Chapter 9, some who were skeptical in the early 1970s became more trusting after the press reforms of the late 1970s, and some may even have moved into a fourth category not reflected in the questionnaires, that of believers.

Nonetheless, respondents had to be placed in exclusive categories in order to see whether there were systematic differences in background and media access among people who displayed different patterns of attitudes. I established the following operational definitions:

ACCEPTER: accepted all thirteen news items in Part IV of the questionnaire at face value and said nothing during Part III (the section on media-use habits) to indicate that he or she did not take the media at face value.

SKEPTIC: expressed disbelief or two or more items in Part IV; or made a clear statement of general disbelief during Part III. May or may not have offered some speculation about the story behind the news, but if he or she did, was uninformed.

DECIPHERER: offered informed speculation on two or more items and/or stated in Part III that his or her general approach was to try to figure out the truth by collating diverse sources of information.

The definitions were scaled in such a way that persons who displayed any significant tendency to decipher the news were classified as decipherers even if they were also sometimes skeptical and sometimes accepting, and persons who were skeptical on two or more items were classified as skeptics even if they were usually accepting. To be classified an accepter, a respondent had to show a consistently accepting attitude throughout Parts III and IV of the questionnaire. Thus only the accepter is a pure type, while the skeptic may be part accepter and the decipherer may be part skeptic and part accepter.

The differences among the three types in terms of personal and unit characteristics are summarized and explained in Chapter 9. Table 11 provides the data on which those explanations are based. Once again, because of the small number of cases, the conclusions drawn can only be tentative. Among other possible problems, the fact that a larger proportion of females than males were accepters may have been an artifact of my sampling procedure, since I had purposely sought respondents who were both female and young in order to diversify my group on two dimensions at once.

TABLE 11

Characteristics of Accepters, Skeptics, and Decipherers

	Accepters (%)		Skeptics (%)		Decipherers (%)		Total (%)	
1 Unit media facilities								
Very poor	30	(6)	10	(2)	18	(2)	20	(10)
Poor	25	(5)	55	(11)	27	(3)	37	(19)
Average	25	(5)	15	(3)	18	(2)	20	(10)
Above average	20	(4)	20	(4)	36	(4)	24	(12)
Total	100	(20)	100	(20)	99	(11)	101	(51)
2 Unit type								
Rural or suburban agricul-								
tural	60	(12)	35	(7)	18	(2)	41	(21)
Urban "collective" unit	10	(2)	15	(3)	0	(0)	10	(5)
Urban state-owned unit or								
professional institution	30	(6)	50	(10)	82	(9)	49	(25)
Total	100	(20)	100	(20)	100	(11)	100	(51)
3 Age in 1971								
16–20	45	(9)	25	(5)	27	(3)	33	(17)
21–30	45	(9)	40	(8)	18	(2)	37	(19)
31+	10	(2)	35	(7)	55	(6)	29	(15)
Total	100	(20)	100	(20)	100	(11)	99	(51)
4 Sex								
Male	40	(8)	75	(15)	91	(10)	65	(33)
Female	60	(12)	25	(5)	9	(1)	35	(18)
Total	100	(20)	100	(20)	100	(11)	100	(51)
5 Class								
Bad	30	(6)	20	(4)	45	(5)	29	(15)
Middling	55	(11)	50	(10)	18	(2)	45	(23)
Good	10	(2)	30	(6)	36	(4)	24	(12)
NA	5	(1)	0	(0)	0	(0)	2	(1)
Total	100	(20)	100	(20)	99	(11)	100	(51)

	Accepters (%)		Skeptics (%)		Decipherers (%)		Total (%)	
6 Negative political experiences								
0	15	(3)	30	(6)	45	(5)	27	(14)
1	25	(5)	20	(4)	0	(0)	18	(9)
2	25	(5)	30	(6)	18	(2)	25	(13)
3+	35	(7)	20	(4)	36	(4)	29	(15)
Total	100	(20)	100	(20)	99	(11)	99	(51)
7 Political interest								
None, low, slight	75	(15)	55	(11)	18	(2)	55	(28)
High	15	(3)	35	(7)	82	(9)	37	(19)
NA	10	(2)	10	(2)	0	(0)	8	(4)
Total	100	(20)	100	(20)	100	(11)	100	(51)

Notes

Numbers in parentheses represent the number of respondents in each category.

NA means "not asked" or "not answered."

Six cases were excluded because the respondents were sixteen or younger in 1971, too young to have meaningful attitudes towards the press at the time covered by Part IV of the questionnaire. One case was excluded because the respondent left China too early to answer Part IV, and one because the respondent seemed confused on that section of the questionnaire.

For definitions of the terms "accepter," "skeptic," and "decipherer," see pages 252–53.

The unit media facilities tallied in the table were those the respondent described during Part II of the questionnaire. They were not necessarily those of the unit where the respondent was located in 1969–74, the period covered by Part IV. The categories of facilities were defined as follows: *very poor:* substantially fewer resources than poor units; *poor:* 1–2 national newspapers, 1–2 local papers, and 2–3 magazines; *average:* roughly 10–20 periodical subscriptions; *above average:* substantially more than 20 subscriptions.

Age in 1971 was chosen as a measure of age because Part IV covers the period 1969–74.

Class categories are the same as those used in Table 1.

"Negative political experiences" were discrete episodes in which the respondent or family members were subjected to "struggle" or "criticism" or were otherwise punished during political campaigns; or were discriminated against because of bad class backgrounds, preliberation political affiliations, or "overseas connections."

Political interest score is based on the question, "Do you think politics are interesting?"

SOURCE NOTES

To keep these notes as short as possible, I generally give only the information necessary to trace a citation. So in the case of newspaper articles I cite the newspaper, date, and page, but not the article's author or title. In citing non-scholarly Hong Kong Chinese-language magazines I list the magazine's title, number and year (or date, if there is no number), and page, but not the author or title of the item. Similarly, in citing works from the people's periodicals I indicate only the periodical, issue number (or date, if there is no number), and page. Further practices are explained in the list of abbreviations and conventions.

An exception to the general rule is full citation of books and scholarly articles. No source is given for well-known events like party congresses, on which information is easily available in *Beijing Review* or the "Quarterly Chronicle and Documentation" section of *The China Quarterly*. When I cite a source for an event I generally cite only one, although usually many more could be listed.

The writings of the democracy activists are available in a variety of forms. As copies of their magazines trickled out of China, some came into the hands of Hong Kong newspapers and magazines and were reprinted in Chinese; some were obtained by the U.S. government and published in English translation in the *China Report* series of the Joint Publications Research Service. To simplify matters I cite a JPRS text if one is available. When no English text is available I cite a single Chinese source, even if several exist. There are a number of published or archival collections and sets of translations of democracy movement materials. The major archive is that of Claude Widor in Paris. There are also holdings at the Hoover Institution, in the Bodleian Library, in other libraries, and in private hands. The largest reprinting project in Chinese is *Dalu dixia kanwu huibian* (Taipei: Zhonggong yanjiu zazhi she, 1980–   ), 18 volumes so far. A second major reprinting project is Hua Da (Claude Widor), ed., *Zhongguo minban kanwu huibian* (Hong Kong: Guanchajia chubanshe, 1981–   ), 2 volumes so far; this work is also available from the Éditions de l'École des Hautes Études en Sciences Sociales, and carries the French title *Documents sur le mouvement démocratique chinois, 1978–1980*. Substantial translations from the people's periodicals have been published in English in James D. Seymour, ed., *The Fifth Modernization: China's Human Rights Movement, 1978–1979* (Stanfordville, N.Y.: Human Rights Publishing Group, 1980); David S. G. Goodman, ed., *Beijing Street Voices: The Poetry and Politics of China's Democracy Movement* (London: Marion Boyars, 1981); Gregor Benton, ed., *Wild Lilies, Poisonous Weeds: Dissident Voices from People's China* (London: Pluto Press, 1982); and James Tong, ed., "Underground Journals in China," in *Chinese Law and Government* XIII:3–4 (Fall–Winter 1980–81) and XIV:3 (Fall 1981).

Articles from official Chinese publications, too, are often available in both Chinese and English. For the convenience of readers, I cite an English version whenever one is easily available, especially in the JPRS and FBIS series; full citation of the original Chinese source is available in the English source. But I have taken the liberty of making minor alterations in direct quotations from these and other sources without specific annotation to that effect, in order to correct or improve translations or to bring terminology and spelling into consistency with the rest of the book.

In citing interviews, I give the code number of the respondent except when the subject matter is sensitive; then I use the annotation "interview." See the Appendix for details on the coding of interviews and the reasons for protecting the respondents' anonymity.

Abbreviations and Conventions Used in the Notes

AFP Agence France Presse. See further under FBIS.

BR *Beijing Review* (through 1978, *Peking Review*). I provide the issue number, year, and page.

CNA *China News Analysis* (Hong Kong). I give the issue number and page; the year is not needed since issues are numbered consecutively.

DXF *Dongxifang* (Hong Kong). I provide the issue number and page because, as with CNA, issues are numbered consecutively.

DXKW *Dixia kanwu*. A magazinelike item published in Hong Kong sometime in 1979. No second issue has been published.

FBIS Foreign Broadcast Information Service, *Daily Report: China* (before April 1, 1981, *Daily Report: People's Republic of China*). I cite the date and page of the item. If the source is a foreign news agency, I note this (e.g., AFP means Agence France Presse, Kyodo is a Japanese agency. Tanjug a Yugoslav agency); likewise if the source is a Hong Kong magazine or newspaper. If I do not list such information, the source is an official PRC magazine, newspaper, news agency release, or radio or TV broadcast.

GMRB *Guangming ribao* (*Enlightenment Daily*). The citation 1980.9.23.3 means September 23, 1980, p. 3.

JPRS Any of several publications on China of the Joint Publications Research Service, such as *China Report: Political, Sociological and Military Affairs* or *China Report: Red Flag*. Since all JPRS publications are consecutively numbered, I identify the JPRS item by that number only, which suffices to locate it in a library or to order it from the National Technical Information Service. In indicating the source from which the article is translated, I give the title of the periodical and either the date or the issue number and year, not the author or title of the specific article. Where the source is one of the people's periodicals or a well-known official periodical, I give its title in English, using the English translation that I have made standard in this book. Otherwise I follow the JPRS citation form, but correct errors in romanization.

LRGNP Ding Wenjiang, *Liang Rengong xiansheng nianpu changbian chugao*, 2 vols. (Taipei: Shijie shuju, 1962).

NYT *The New York Times*. I use the same citation form as for GMRB.

QCD "Quarterly Chronicle and Documentation" section of *The China Quarterly*. I give the number of the *China Quarterly* issue (since these are consecutive, the year is not needed) and the page.

RMRB *Renmin ribao*, the *People's Daily*. I use the same citation form as for GMRB.

WHB *Wen hui bao*, a Shanghai newspaper. I use the same citation form as for GMRB.

XMS Liang Qichao, *Xinmin shuo* (Taipei: Zhonghua shuju, 1956).

XWZX *Xinwen zhanxian* (*News Front*). In the citation 1978.6.2, 1978 is the year, 6 the issue number, and 2 the page.

YBSWJ Liang Qichao, *Yinbing shi wenji*, 16 vols. (Taipei: Zhonghua shuju, 1960). In the citations, the roman numeral stands for the volume, the next number for the *juan* or chapter, and the numbers after the colon for the pages.

CHAPTER 1

3 location of posters: Roger Garside, *Coming Alive: China After Mao* (New York: McGraw-Hill, 1981), 210, 286.

–quotations from *Enlightenment* No. 1: JPRS 73215: 3, 6, 9, 11.

4 Huang Xiang's place of work: *Enlightenment Series* No. 4, in JPRS 73922: 98.

–sent-down youth: DXKW: 3; NYT 1978.11.27.A3.

–candles: *Enlightenment* No. 1 in JPRS 73215: 1.

–Mao, "stood up": *Selected Works of Mao Tsetung* (Peking: Foreign Languages Press, 1961–77), V: 15.

–housing statistic: BR 48 (1979): 18.

5 quotes from Marx's *Civil War*: Robert C. Tucker, ed., *The Marx-Engels Reader*, 2d ed. (New York: W. W. Norton, 1978), 632–33.

–democracy "always linked": *Enlightenment* No. 3 in JPRS 73215: 51.

6 "fire will enable": *Enlightenment* No. 2 in JPRS 73215: 36.

–events of 1977–81: see appropriate issues of QCD.

–1978 constitution: BR 11 (1978): 13 (Article 45).

7 Hu Yaobang's role in rehabilitation campaign: BR 44 (1981): 24.

–twenty million labeled: RMRB 1984.11.2.4; cf. BR 3 (1980): 14; FBIS 1 November 1982, K7; CNA 1152.

–rightists and antisocialist elements: Liao Gailong, "Historical Experiences and Our Road of Development," *Issues and Studies* XVII: 10 (October 1981): 81.

–three million cadres: FBIS 22 July 1983, K2.

–wrongly convicted: FBIS 9 June 1983, K8.

–100 million affected: Tanjug in FBIS 23 June 1980, L1.

–personal appeals appear in Tiananmen Square: interviews.

–geography and history of Peking: *Nagel's Encyclopedia-Guide: China* (Geneva: Nagel Publishers, 1973), 420–536; L. C. Arlington and William Lewisohn, *In Search of Old Peking* (Peking: Henri Vetch, The French Bookstore, 1935), 25–61, 94–104; BR 32 (1979): 9–23; BR 47 (1980): 12; Zhou Shachen, *Gujin Beijing* (Hong Kong: Sanlian shudian, 1980), 13–22; P. J. M. Geelan and D. C. Twitchett, eds., *The Times Atlas of China* (New York: Quadrangle/The New York Times Book Co., 1974), 124–25.

9 central work conference: Garside, *Coming Alive*, 202–3; FBIS 22 July 1981, K4.

–quotation praising Deng: *Enlightenment* No. 3 in JPRS 73215: 43.

–"if anyone interferes": *Enlightenment* No. 2 in JPRS 73215: 20.

10 rechecking of Tiananmen cases: BR 47 (1978): 6.

–events of November 15–30: *April Fifth Forum* No. 14 in JPRS 75147: 18–20; also see John Fraser, *The Chinese: Portrait of a People* (New York: Summit Books, 1980), 203–71; Victor Sidane, *Le Printemps de Pékin* (Paris: Editions Gallimard/Juilliard, 1980), 21–25.

12 Wu De's unusual status: interview.

–attacks on Wu De, Kang Sheng, Wang Dongxing: *Peking Spring* Nos. 1, 2 in JPRS 73728: 31–33, 62; *Beijing zhi chun* No. 3: 7, 13, 37.

–Wu subordinate's suicide: *Peking Spring* No. 1 in JPRS 73728: 33; QCD 77: 174.

13 other posters: *April Fifth Forum*

No. 14 in JPRS 75147: 7, 8, 15, 28, 30, 38, 45.

14 premarital sex: Kyodo in FBIS 5 January 1979, E22.

–appeals to Carter: *Enlightenment* No. 3 in JPRS 73215: 45–57; "A Communication from Citizens to the President of the USA, Jimmy Carter," mimeo copy of English translation of a wall poster signed December 7, 1978, "The Human Rights Group."

–nineteen points: *China Human Rights*, February 1979 in JPRS 73421: 67–70.

–Vietnam: AFP in FBIS 26 February 1979, E5–6.

–"Fifth Modernization": *Explorations* No. 1 in JPRS 73756: 7.

15 apology: *Beijing zhi chun* No. 3: 12.

–approached printers: *Peking Spring* No. 2 in JPRS 73728: 51–52.

–attempt to borrow a typewriter: "Unofficial Transcript of the Trial of Wei Jingsheng," Amnesty International document ASA 17/01/80, mimeo (June 1980), 7.

–typewriter-cut stencils: *Jintian* No. 3.

–mimeo equipment: interviews O-3, GB-3; *Peking Spring* No. 2 in JPRS 73728: 51–52.

–*April Fifth Forum* profit: AFP in JPRS 74099: 41–42.

–attempt to pay taxes: *Siwu luntan* No. 5: 14; *April Fifth Forum* No. 14 in JPRS 75442: 12.

16 copies of *April Fifth Forum* to officials and libraries: *Zhongguoren* 5 (1979): 16.

–appeals to register: *Zhongguoren* 5 (1979): 13, 16.

–November 1979 announcement: BR 49 (1979): 3.

–1952 publication regulations: G. Raymond Nunn, *Publishing in Mainland China* (Cambridge, Mass.: The M.I.T. Press, 1966), 60–63.

–attempts to register and closing: *Guanchajia* 31 (1980): 15.

–*Enlightenment* publication history: Nos. 1, 2, 3 in JPRS 73215: 1–75; quote on 19.

17 Thaw society: "newborn organization" in DXKW: 45; manifesto in JPRS 73922: 6–8.

–*April Fifth Forum* background: No. 4 in JPRS 75442: 6; *Le Monde* in JPRS 75255: 8; NYT 1980.2.12.A2. Quotation from Helmut Opletal, "In Search of a Better Tomorrow," *Far Eastern Economic Review* (September 7, 1979): 29.

–reformers and conservatives: *Siwu luntan* No. 4 in *Zhongguoren* 8 (1979): 16; *April Fifth Forum* No. 8 in JPRS 73987: 3; *April Fifth Forum* No. 14 in JPRS 75442: 3; *April Fifth Forum* No. 8 in JPRS 73987: 44–45.

18 constructive suggestions: *April Fifth Forum* special New Year issue in JPRS 73787: 16; *Siwu luntan* No. 5: 4.

–Gang of Four trial: *Siwu luntan* No. 5: 10.

–Yu Luoke: *April Fifth Forum* No. 8 in JPRS 73987: 17–20; cf. treatment in RMRB 1980.7.25.4.

–Western culture and democracy: *April Fifth Forum* No. 14 in JPRS 75442: 10–11; *April Fifth Forum* No. 9 in JPRS 73731: 8–13.

–anti-bell-bottom trousers: *April Fifth Forum* No. 8 in JPRS 73987: 29.

–Chen Erjin's essay: *Siwu luntan* No. 10; his background: Robin Munro, trans., *China: Crossroads Socialism: An Unofficial Manifesto for Proletarian Democracy* (Lon-

don: Verso Editions, 1984), 5.
18 *April Fifth*'s previous argument:
e.g., No. 7 in JPRS 73922: 16.
–*Peking Spring:* No. 1 in JPRS
73728: 1; date follows Claude
Widor, *Documents sur le mouvement démocratique chinois,
1978–1980,* Vol. II (Paris: Éditions
de l'École des Hautes Études en
Sciences Sociales, 1985), "Background."
19 publication priorities: *Beijing zhi
chun* No. 3: 24.
–flavor of insiderism: examples taken
from *Peking Spring* Nos. 1–5.
20 *The Second Handshake:* E. Perry
Link, Jr., *Mandarin Ducks and
Butterflies: Popular Fiction in
Early Twentieth-Century Chinese
Cities* (Berkeley, Calif.: University
of California Press, 1981), 236–38.
–Zhang Zhixin: *Peking Spring* No. 8
in JPRS 74764: 106–23 and JPRS
74909: 9–19.
–*Peking Spring* editors: Peter Chan,
"Popular Publications in China: A
Look at *The Spring of Peking,*"
Contemporary China III:4 (Winter
1979): 103–11; *Zhengming* 19
(1979) in JPRS 73474: 23; DXKW: 2;
Widor, *Documents,* II, "Back-
ground."
–Quotation on Wu De: *Peking
Spring* No. 2 in JPRS 73728: 62.
–"Trampled": *Peking Spring* No. 2
in JPRS 73728: 69–74.
–Ma Danian threat: *Peking Spring*
No. 1 in JPRS 73728: 9.
–search of staff's house: *Explorations*
9 September 1979 in JPRS 74764:
12.
–"Destitute": *Peking Spring* No. 1
in JPRS 73728: 8.
–"Year 2000": *Peking Spring* No. 8
in JPRS 74970: 17–32.
21 *Today:* No. 1 in JPRS 74909:
20–21.

–production of *Today:* interview.
–campus literary magazines: Chiang
Chen-ch'ang, "Democratic Aspira-
tions of Mainland China College
Students," *Issues and Studies*
XVII: 9 (September 1981): 61–64.
–sold at Democracy Wall: e.g., see
Hongdou No. 3: 55.
–*This Generation: Zheyidai* No. 1;
information on its organization in
the typeset foreword and in mimeographed material at the beginning
and end of the issue.
22 *Explorations* registration and taxes:
Zhongguoren 5 (1979): 13.
–publication statement: *Explorations*
No. 1 in JPRS 73756: 6.
–questions on Deng interview: *Explorations* No. 1 in JPRS 73756: 24.
–Wei's background: "Unofficial transcript" (Amnesty), *passim*; James
D. Seymour, ed., *The Fifth Modernization: China's Human Rights
Movement, 1978–1979* (Stanfordville, N.Y.: Human Rights Publishing Group, 1980), 15–16; Wei
Jingsheng, "A Dissenter's Odyssey
Through Mao's China," *New York
Times Magazine* (November 16,
1980), 134–43; *Explorations* 9 September 1979 in JPRS 74764: 32–33;
Explorations No. 5 in JPRS 74970:
120–21.
–unable to break with Marxism: *Explorations* No. 5 in JPRS 74970:
120.
–meeting and decision to publish:
Explorations 9 September 1979 in
JPRS 74764: 2–3.
–members: *Explorations* 9 September 1979 in JPRS 74764: 34–35;
"Unofficial Transcript" (Amnesty),
20–22; NYT 1979.10.7.3; DXF 17:
26–27.
23 Amnesty report: *Political Imprisonment in the People's Republic of
China: An Amnesty International*

Report (London: Amnesty International Publications, 1978).

23 at least 55 people's periodicals published in Peking: This figure and the figures given below for the number of cities and titles outside Peking are based on a collation of four lists of titles, supplemented by a few additional references. The lists collated are: "Checklist of the C. Widor Collection of Chinese Democratic Movement Material," photocopy of a typescript, 22 pp., undated; "List of Chinese Unofficial Publications of the 'Democracy Movement,' 1978–1980," [collection presented by Dr. David Goodman to the] Bodleian Library, Oxford, photocopy of a typescript, unpaged, undated; Chen Ruoxi, *Democracy Wall and the Unofficial Journals,* Studies in Chinese Terminology No. 20 (Berkeley: Center for Chinese Studies, University of California, 1982), 106–112; *Monthly Bulletin on the Chinese Democratic Movement* (Hong Kong) I:1 (January 1981), 3, 9–11. A few additional titles were found in the following sources: DXF, throughout; *The Asian Messenger* III:3–IV:1 (Winter 1978–Spring 1979), 30; *Guanchajia* Nos. 37 (1980): 21, and 44 (1981): 30; *Dongxiang* No. 7 (1979) in JPRS 73381: 28; *Zeren* No. 3, 68. Finally, I have included the title *Zheyidai* (photocopy in my possession). Despite the variety of sources consulted, this cannot be considered a complete enumeration of democracy movement publications.
   –stance of *Voice of the People: Renmin zhi sheng* No. 3.
   –events in Shanghai: Ann McLaren, "The Educated Youth Return: The Poster Campaign in Shanghai from November 1978 to March 1979," *Australian Journal of Chinese Affairs* No. 2 (July 1979): 1–20; interview; quotations from W. Zafanolli, "Shanghai, Place du Peuple," *Esprit* No. 6 (June 1979): 23–25.

24 26 other cities, 127 titles: same sources cited for 55 periodicals in Peking, above.
   –at least 45 campus periodicals: Chen Ruoxi, *Democracy Wall,* 113–115.
   –each publication's larger circle: interviews.
   –rejection of "dissident": e.g., *Guanchajia* 36 (1980): 14.
   –Qu Yuan: Laurence A. Schneider, *A Madman of Ch'u: The Chinese Myth of Loyalty and Dissent* (Berkeley: University of California Press, 1980), 28.
   –Censorate: Charles C. Hucker, "Confucianism and the Chinese Censorial System," in David S. Nivison and Arthur F. Wright, eds., *Confucianism in Action* (Stanford, Calif.: Stanford University Press, 1959), 182–208; Mencius quote, 195.

25 quotations from Mao: Stuart Schram, ed., *Chairman Mao Talks to the People: Talks and Letters, 1956–1971* (New York: Pantheon Books, 1974), 187; *Mao Zedong sixiang wansui* (April 1967), reprint ed. ([Taipei]: n.p., n.d.), 7. The "five fear-nots" come from a speech of Wang Hongwen at the Tenth Party Congress, in BR 35/36 (1973): 31.
   –Changchun factory worker: GMRB 1980.4.19.3; *Gongren ribao* 1980.4.23.2.
   –repairman: FBIS 7 October 1980, L11–L15.

25 husband and wife: GMRB 1980.
   11.4.1.
   –Zhang Zhixin: *Peking Spring* No. 8
   in JPRS 74764: 106–23 and JPRS
   74909: 9–19.
26 Guo Weibin: GMRB 1980.9.4.1 and
   1980.9.9.2; *Gongren ribao* 1980.
   9.27.4.
   –Hangzhou demonstrations: FBIS 12
   February 1979, G1.
   –Xi'an demonstrations: AFP in FBIS 5
   January 1979, M1.
   –Shanghai sent-down youth:
   Thomas P. Bernstein, *Up to the
   Mountains and Down to the Villages: The Transfer of Youth from
   Urban to Rural China* (New
   Haven: Yale University Press,
   1977), 29.
27 National Work Conference, Shanghai demonstrations: Suzanne Pep-
   per, "Chinese Education After
   Mao: Two Steps Forward: Two
   Steps Back and Begin Again?"
   China Quarterly 81: 49–53.
   –600,000 job seekers: *Dongxiang* 12
   (1979) in JPRS 74714: 51.
   –disruption of rail service: FBIS 12
   February 1979, G1–G3.
   –Peking petitioners' cases: *Explorations* No. 5 in JPRS 74970: 107–10.
28 "Blue Sky" poem: no. 17 in a series of photos taken at Democracy
   Wall.
   –petitioners' living conditions: AFP
   in FBIS 25 January 1979, E2–E3;
   Explorations No. 2 in JPRS 73787:
   58: *Peking Spring* No. 1 in JPRS
   73728: 10.
   –January 8 demonstration: *Qun-
   zhong cankao xiaoxi* No. 3: 6; also
   reported by AFP in FBIS 9 January
   1979, E1.
29 subsequent demonstrations: AFP in
   FBIS 15 January 1979, E1, 22 January 1979, E1, 23 January 1979,
   E2, and 30 January 1979, E9.

–petitioner statistics: BR 25 (1982):
   24.
–petitioner's complaint: *Explorations*
   No. 5 in JPRS 74970: 101–12.
30 *Peking Daily* editorial: FBIS 27 February 1979, E2.
   –"Virtue Forest": *Explorations* No.
   3 in JPRS 73421: 37–40.

CHAPTER 2

31 Deng to American reporter: John
   Fraser, *The Chinese: Portrait of a
   People* (New York: Summit Books,
   1980), 245.
   –Deng's interview with Japanese:
   NYT 1978.11.27.A1.
   –editorials and statements: NYT
   1979.1.4.A1.
   –Third Plenum communiqué: BR 52
   (1978): 7, 13–14.
   –Li Yizhe release: BR 9 (1979):
   15–16.
   –November 30 events: Fraser, *The
   Chinese*, 266–69.
   –End of forums: *Los Angeles Times*
   1978.12.12.10.
   –"Spirit of the Peking Municipal
   Committee": no text is available,
   but it is described by Roger Garside, *Coming Alive: China after
   Mao* (New York: McGraw-Hill,
   1981), 244, and in various places in
   the people's periodicals, e.g., *Explorations* No. 2 in JPRS 73421:
   23–25; *China Human Rights*, February 1979 in JPRS 73421: 64–66;
   Enlightenment No. 1 in JPRS
   73787: 20–21.
32 police: there is a great deal of information on their behavior in the
   people's periodicals; examples include *Peking Spring* No. 1 in JPRS
   73421: 8 and JPRS 73728: 9–10;
   Explorations 9 September 1979 in
   JPRS 74764: 9–13. Also see Fraser,
   The Chinese, 318–33.

32 joint statement: JPRS 73421: 26–27.
–individual periodicals' statements: *Siwu luntan* No. 5: 2; *April Fifth Forum* No. 9 in JPRS 73731: 14; *China Human Rights Paper* in *Zhongguoren* 5 (1979): 30; *Explorations* No. 2 in JPRS 73421: 25.
–arrest of Fu Yuehua: FBIS 26 December 1979, L1.
–protests about Fu Yuehua's arrest: *Explorations* No. 3 in JPRS 73421: 35–36; *China Human Rights* (undated, [No. 2]) in JPRS 73922: 55–63; *Huang he* 6 (1979): 19; DXKW: 36.
–Deng's political troubles: Daniel Tretiak, "China's Vietnam War and Its Consequences," *China Quarterly* 80: 740–67; also see FBIS 14 April 1982, K2.
–Deng's March 16 speech: NYT 1979.3.23.A7; AFP in FBIS 21 March 1979, L1–L2.
–Deng's March 30 speech: *Deng Xiaoping wenxuan* (Peking: Renmin chubanshe, 1983), 144–70.
33 Peking March 29 notice: FBIS 2 April 1979, R1–R2.
–removal of other posters: NYT 1979.4.2.A11; AFP in FBIS 2 April 1979, L1.
–similar notices elsewhere: RMRB 1979.3.26.1; throughout FBIS, March–April 1979; *Peking Spring* No. 6 in JPRS 74591: 6–10.
–Wei poster: *Explorations* Extra in JPRS 73421: 28–30.
–arrests of Ren Wanding, Chen Lü, and others: AFP in FBIS 4 April 1979, L1–L3.
–arrests elsewhere: *Issues and Studies* XVI: 11 (November 1980): 10.
–Huang Xiang's arrest: Garside, *Coming Alive*, p. 298; compare *Peking Spring* No. 8 in JPRS 75147: 72.
–*People's Daily* editorial: BR 15 (1979): 9–13.

–Tiananmen Square scene: AFP in FBIS 5 April 1979, L7; FBIS 6 April 1979, L3–L4; *Dongxiang* 7 (1979) in JPRS 73381: 8–10.
34 *Peking Daily* editorial: FBIS 10 April 1979, R1–R3.
–*Workers' Daily* editorial: FBIS 19 March 1979, L7–L8.
–criminal law: FBIS, Vol. 1, No. 146, Supplement 019 (27 July 1979), 47 (Article 90).
–Wei trial: "Unofficial Transcript of the Trial of Wei Jingsheng," Amnesty International document ASA 17/01/80, mimeo (June 1980).
–Fu trial: FBIS 6 December 1979, L1–L2.
–November 29 announcement: BR 49 (1979): 3.
1951 counterrevolutionaries act: Jerome Alan Cohen, *The Criminal Process in the People's Republic of China, 1949–1963: An Introduction* (Cambridge, Mass.: Harvard University Press, 1968), 299–302.
–1957 punishment act and council decision: Cohen, *Criminal Process*, 200–295; 1957 Decision Concerning Offenders Ordered to Be Reeducated Through Labor republished, see BR 15 (1980): 5; Supplementary Regulations on Reeducation Through Labor, FBIS 30 November 1979, L3.
35 1951 state secrets regulations: reprinted, FBIS 14 April 1980, L7–L11.
–"shopping window": *Explorations* No. 5 in JPRS 74970: 116.
–Standing Committee attack on Democracy Wall: FBIS 28 November 1979, L1–L2.
–city administration notice: FBIS 7 December 1979, L1; RMRB 1979.12.7.1.
–billboards: AFP in FBIS 9 May 1980, L19.

35 arrangements at Moon Altar Park:
Los Angeles Times 1979.12.9, I:
14, 1979.12.16, VI: 2; AFP in FBIS
10 December 1979, L2–L3.
–arrangements elsewhere: FBIS
throughout, e.g., Hangzhou in FBIS
12 December 1979, O5–O6.
–*Peking Daily* comment: FBIS 18
December 1979, R1–R2.

36 Deng speech: *Zhengming* 29
(1980) in FBIS supplement 11
March 1980, 1–27.
–abolition of "four greats": FBIS 10
September 1980, L30.
–spoiled ballot: RMRB 1980.9.17.1.
–subsequent press campaigns:
throughout FBIS early 1981.

37 articles on U.S. outnumber those
on other countries: my impression,
confirmed for 1981 by content
analysis reported in Susan Wang,
"Chinese Press Looks at the
United States: A Research of the
People's Daily 1981," seminar
paper, Columbia University, May
5, 1982.
–admiring American technology:
e.g., GMRB 1980.9.23.3; RMRB
1980.11.5.7; WHB 1981.7.7.4; WHB
1981.1.10.4.
–skyscrapers and shadows: e.g., WHB
1982.12.18.3; RMRB 1979.10.17.6;
RMRB 1981.3.16.7; GMRB 1982.
10.2.4.
–super-rich: GMRB 1981.11.2.4.
–problems of the middle class: Shi
Zhisheng and Shen Yongxing,
Minzhu de lishi yanbian (Peking:
Beijing chubanshe, 1982), 124.
–religious cults: FBIS 2 December
1981, B1–B2.
–average New York City office
worker: *People's Daily*, 28 April
1980, in JPRS 75878: 66–78.
–college professor's salary: *China
Youth News*, 7 July 1980, in JPRS
76002: 10–14.

38 pamper dogs: RMRB 1981.4.20.7.
–racial discrimination: e.g., *People's
Daily*, 20 July 1979, in JPRS 74012:
1–4; RMRB 1981.1.9.7; RMRB
1981.6.6.8.
–"six great illusions": RMRB
1982.1.14.4.
–"one-party system under the
guise": FBIS 5 March 1980, B1–B2.
–specialized campaign techniques:
FBIS 26 March 1981, B3–B6.
–"How many top figures?": Shi and
Shen, *Minzhu*, 123.
–"lively atmosphere": FBIS 21 March
1980, B2–B4.
–no news of minor parties: FBIS 30
October 1980, B1–B2.
–"If criticizing the government":
FBIS 4 May 1981, B5–B6.
–Mao on relaxing and restricting:
e.g., *Selected Works of Mao
Tsetung* (Peking: Foreign Languages Press, 1961–77), IV: 244,
V: 432.

39 meaning of democracy: FBIS 19 January 1981, L6; RMRB 1980.11.24.5
and 1980.11.25.5.
–*Peking Spring* closing: AFP in FBIS
29 February 1980, L16–L17.
–*April Fifth Forum*: *Guanchajia* 33
(1980): 8–10; AFP in FBIS 2 April
1980, L1.

40 *Voice*: *Guanchajia* 31 (1980): 15;
DXF 18: 10–11.
–Liu Qing's arrest and subsequent
events: NYT 1979.11.12.A7; NYT
1979.11.13.A5; AFP in FBIS 21 May
1980, L16; *Guanchajia* 33 (1980):
11; DXF 22: 4–9, 13–14; DXF 23:
30–31.
–*Responsibility*: AFP in FBIS 28 September 1980, L4–L5; *Guanchajia*
37 (1980): 22–27; *Zeren* Nos.
1–5.
–"regional congresses": Fu Po-shek,
"The 'Unknown Phase' of the Chinese Democratic Movement,

1980–1981," seminar paper, Stanford University, fall term 1981, 19.

40 new periodicals, number: "Checklist of the C. Widor Collection of Chinese Democratic Movement Material," photocopy of a typescript, 22 pp., undated.

–new periodicals, nature and circulation: Fu, " 'Unknown Phase,' " 7–9; *Guanchajia* 37 (1980): 19–22.

–responses to poster: *Dongxiang* 7 (1979) in JPRS 73381: 6.

–anti-Wei propaganda: e.g., RMRB 1979.10.17.4, RMRB 1979.10.23.4.

41 identification of democrats with Gang of Four: FBIS 19 January 1981, L8–L11; AFP in FBIS 15 January 1981, L7.

–popular attitudes and level of information: NYT 1980.2.12.A2; interviews O-1, O-5, GB-3.

–1980 disorders, Solidarity: e.g., AFP in FBIS 3 March 1981, R1; AFP in FBIS 20 March 1981, L1–L2; *Qishi niandai* 135 (1981) in FBIS 16 April 1981, W1–W10. Also see Chapter 10.

–terrorist and espionage organizations: e.g., Hu Qiaomu in *News Front* 4 (1980) in JPRS 76971: 25–26.

–Deng, "soft-handed": *Zhengming* 29 (1980) in FBIS supplement, 11 March 1980, 12.

42 sympathizers within the party: among other indications, see Hu Qiaomu speech of August 8, 1981, in *Red Flag* 23 (1981) in JPRS 79936: 1; Hu Yaobang speech of August 3, 1981, in *Issues and Studies* XX:1 (January 1984): 115.

–Deng, January 1980 speech: *Zhengming* 29 (1980), in FBIS Supplement, 11 March 1980, 12.

–Hu Qiaomu warning: *News Front* 4 (1980) in JPRS 76971: 24.

–Hu Yaobang statement: quoted in

Zhengming 42 (1981) in FBIS, 10 April 1981, W5.

–Hu invitation: Liu Qing, "Prison Memoirs," in *Chinese Sociology and Anthropology* XV:1–2 (Fall–Winter 1982/83): 65.

–Academy of Social Sciences: see, e.g., Claude Widor, *Documents sur le mouvement démocratique chinois, 1978–1980* (Paris: Éditions de l'École des Hautes Études en Sciences Sociales, 1985), II: 73; interviews.

–Guangdong party secretary: Stanley Rosen, "Guangzhou's Democracy Movement in Cultural Revolution Perspective," unpublished paper, 1983, 32–33.

–youth league cadres: Rosen, "Guangzhou's Democracy Movement," 32–33, 40–44; Liu Qing, "Prison Memoirs," 86–89; *Qishi niandai* 125 (1980): 54–56; *Dongxiang* 7 (1979) in JPRS 73381: 28–29.

43 contacts with journalists: Liu Qing, "Prison Memoirs," 88–89.

–official magazines reprint: Widor, *Documents*, II: 74.

–Liu Qing and others offered jobs: "Prison Memoirs," 165.

–Wang Xizhe offered job: Rosen, "Guangzhou's Democracy Movement," 34.

–jobs to writers and artists: interviews.

–inside route: interviews. For the idea of sharper criticism within the party than outside, see Samuel P. Huntington, "Social and Institutional Dynamics of One-Party Systems," in Huntington and Clement H. Moore, eds., *Authoritarian Politics in Modern Society: The Dynamics of Established One-Party Systems* (New York: Basic Books, 1970), 44.

43 Xu Wenli quotation: *Qishi niandai* 133 (1981): 50–51; probably published originally in Xu's newsletter, *Xuexi tongxun.*

CHAPTER 3

An earlier version of this chapter was presented as "The Idea of Political Participation: Liang Ch'-i-ch'ao and Mao Tse-tung," prepared for the University Seminar on Modern East Asia—China, Columbia University, March 10, 1977.

My analysis of Liang's thought is influenced by Hao Chang, *Liang Ch'i-ch'ao and Intellectual Transition in China, 1890–1907* (Cambridge, Mass.: Harvard University Press, 1971). Other important intellectual biographies of Liang, on which I have also drawn, are Philip C. Huang, *Liang Ch'i-ch'ao and Modern Chinese Liberalism* (Seattle: University of Washington Press, 1972); Ji Bingfeng, *Qingmo geming yu junxian de lunzheng* (Nangang: Zhongyang yanjiu yuan jindai shi yanjiu suo, 1966); Joseph R. Levenson, *Liang Ch'i-ch'ao and the Mind of Modern China,* paperback ed. (Berkeley: University of California Press, 1970); Zhang Pengyuan, *Liang Qichao yu Qingji geming* (Nangang: Zhongyang yanjiu yuan jindai shi yanjiu suo, 1964); and Zhang Pengyuan, *Liang Qichao yu minguo zhengzhi* (Taipei: Shihuo chubanshe, 1978). A recent work placing Liang's thought in the context of Chinese social Darwinism is James Reeve Pusey, *China and Charles Darwin* (Cambridge, Mass.: Council on East Asian Studies, 1983).

45 events of 1895: Jung-pang Lo, ed. and trans., *K'ang Yu-wei: A Biography and a Symposium* (Tucson: University of Arizona Press, 1967), 64–65.
–eight thousand degree-holders: Chung-li Chang, *The Chinese Gentry: Studies in Their Role in Nineteenth-Century Chinese Society,* paperback ed. (Seattle: University of Washington Press, 1967), 126. Their age and status in life: 117, 125, 127.

46 historical student movements: Chow Tse-tsung, *The May Fourth Movement: Intellectual Revolution in Modern China,* paperback ed. (Stanford, Calif.: Stanford University Press, 1967), 11–12; Jonathan D. Spence, *Ts'ao Yin and the K'ang-hsi Emperor: Bondservant and Master* (New Haven: Yale University Press, 1966), 240–54.
–Kang on a constitution: Kung-chuan Hsiao, *A Modern China and a New World: K'ang Yu-wei, Reformer and Utopian, 1858–1927* (Seattle: University of Washington Press, 1975), 202.
–Hundred Days of Reform: Luke S. K. Kwong, *A Mosaic of the Hundred Days: Personalities, Politics, and Ideas of 1898* (Cambridge, Mass.: Council on East Asian Studies, 1984).
–Liang's reminiscences: "My Autobiographical Account at Thirty," *Chinese Studies in History* X: 3 (Spring 1977): 5, 6, 8, 15.

47 "Even Napoleon": L. T. Chen, trans., *History of Chinese Political Thought during the Early Tsin Period,* by Liang Chi-chao, reprint ed. (Taipei: Ch'eng-wen Publishing Co., 1968), 3.
–diplomat: Cheng Tianfang, *Cheng Tianfang zaonian huiyilu* (Taipei: Zhuanji wenxue chubanshe, 1968), 10.
–official: Shen Zonghan, *Shen Zonghan zishu* (Taipei: Zhuanji wenxue chubanshe, 1975), preface, 1.

48 college dean: Chiang Monlin,

Tides from the West (New Haven:
Yale University Press, 1947; reprint, Taipei: China Culture Publishing Foundation, 1957), 51.

48 historian (Gu Jiegang): Arthur W.
Hummel, trans. and ed., *The Auto-
biography of a Chinese Historian:
Being the Preface to a Symposium
on Ancient Chinese History (Ku
Shih Pien)* (Leyden: Late E. J.
Brill Ltd., 1931), 2.

–general: entry on Huang Fu in
Howard L. Boorman and Richard C. Howard, eds, *Biographical
Dictionary of Republican China*, 4
vols. (New York: Columbia University Press, 1967–71), II: 188.

–Buddhist leader: Yin Shun, *Taixu
dashi nianpu* (1950; republished,
Taizhong: Yin Shun, 1973), 33–34.

–literary critic: Cao Juren, *Wentan
wushinian, zhengbian* (Hong Kong:
Xin wenhua chubanshe, 1976), 77.

–Hu Shi: "An Autobiographical Account at Forty," Ch. II, William A. Wycoff, trans., *Chinese
Studies in History* XI: 4 (Fall
1978): 86.

–other examples of Liang Qichao's
influence: see Lai Guanglin, *Liang
Qichao yu jindai baoyeh* (Taipei:
Shangwu yinshuguan, 1968), 123–
25.

–Liang on revolution: XMS, 60, 64.

–"too few convictions": Liang Ch'i-
ch'ao, *Intellectual Trends in the
Ch'ing Period*, Immanuel C. Y.
Hsü, trans. (Cambridge, Mass.:
Harvard University Press, 1959),
106.

–Confucianism of 1870s and 1880s:
Chang, *Liang*, 31–33; Lloyd E.
Eastman, "Political Reformism in
China before the Sino-Japanese
War," *Journal of Asian Studies*
XXVII: 4 (August 1968): 695–710.

–Lin Shu: Boorman and Howard,

Biographical Dictionary, II: 383.
On the dating of his first translation, see Ah Ying, *Ah Ying wenji*
(Peking: Sanlian shudian, 1981),
806.

–Yan Fu: Benjamin Schwartz, *In
Search of Wealth and Power: Yen
Fu and the West* (Cambridge,
Mass.: Harvard University Press,
1964).

49 Japanese studies of Western theory:
Joseph Pittau, *Political Thought in
Early Meiji Japan, 1868–1889*
(Cambridge, Mass.: Harvard Uni-
versity Press, 1967); Frank O.
Miller, *Minobe Tatsukichi: Inter-
preter of Constitutionalism in
Japan* (Berkeley: University of Cali-
fornia Press, 1965).

–first Chinese mention of Marx:
Maurice Meisner, *Li Ta-chao and
the Origins of Chinese Marxism*
(Cambridge, Mass.: Harvard University Press, 1967), 52; BR 11
(1983): 20.

–study societies: YBSWJ I.1: 31–34.

–Liang on a state: YBSWJ II.2: 64.

50 Hunan memorial: YBSWJ II.3:
40–48.

–Hunan independence suggestion:
LRGNP I: 46.

–rights (two quotations): YBSWJ I.1:
99.

51 rights as a substance: cf. Chang,
Liang, 193.

–the role of citizen: YBSWJ I.1: 80.

–participation unleashes energies:
YBSWJ I.1: 5–6, 15–16, 60, and
elsewhere in the serial article
"Bianfa tongyi."

–merchant community in Japan,
chamber of commerce: YBSWJ II.3:
65–77; YBSWJ II.4: 1–7, 7–11,
11–18.

–racial conflict and the threat to
China: YBSWJ II.4: 56–58.

52 cooperate without concern for

profit: YBSWJ II.4: 7–11.
52 East India Company analogy:
   YBSWJ II.4: 7.
   –bees: YBSWJ II.4: 2.
   –reform and patriotism: YBSWJ II.3:
   65–77.
   –"Study Notes on Hobbes": YBSWJ
   III.6: 89–94.
53 Quotation from *Leviathan:* Chapter 17.
   –"Study Notes on Rousseau": YBSWJ
   III.6: 103.
   –Quotation from *The Social Contract:* Book I, Ch. 7.
54 Bentham: YBSWJ V.13: 37–38.
   –"Sources of China's Weakness":
   YBSWJ II:5: 12–42.
   –virtues of a constitution: YBSWJ
   II.5: 3–4.
55 "Dialectical Unity": YBSWJ II. 5:
   42–51.
   –letter to Kang: LRGNP I: 125–28.
   –circulation and readership of *The
   New Citizen:* see Chapter 7.
   –race and language statistics: XMS,
   7–9.
   –anecdote of the Englishman: XMS,
   33–34.
56 yieldingness, rights, and foreign
   aggression in China: XMS, 34, 35,
   36, 39.
   –freedom: XMS, 40, 41, 46.
   –self-rule: XMS, 50–54.
57 struggle for survival occurs among
   groups: e.g., YBSWJ V.12: 78–96.
58 optimistic versus pessimistic reformers: cf. Thomas A. Metzger,
   *Escape from Predicament: Neo-
   Confucianism and China's Evolving Political Culture* (New York:
   Columbia University Press, 1977),
   155–58, 188–90.
58ff Liang's American trip: Liang Qichao, *Xin dalu youji jielu* (Taipei:
   Zhonghua shuju, 1957), 42, 65,
   94, 122–23; Jerome B. Grieder, *Intellectuals and the State in Mod-*

ern China: A Narrative History
(New York: The Free Press, 1981),
167. For dates, I follow Levenson,
Liang, 69–76.
60 Liang's depression, the photo:
   Zhang, *Liang . . . Qingji,* 177–81.
61 Bluntschli and Bornhak: YBSWJ
   V.13: 69, 85, 86.
   –enlightened despotism: YBSWJ VI.
   17: 15, 21.
62 "a state with rights": XMS, 39.
63 "bourgeois democrats": *Selected
   Works of Mao Tsetung* (Peking:
   Foreign Languages Press,
   1961–77), IV: 414.
   –progressive for his time: e.g., Geng
   Yunzhi, "The Movement for a Parliament in the Last Years of the
   Qing Dynasty," *Social Sciences
   in China* No. 3 (1980): 115–54;
   Li Zehou, "Liang Qichao
   Wang Guowei jianlun," *Lishi
   yanjiu* No. 7 (July 15, 1979):
   28–37.
   –young Mao reads *New Citizen:* Li
   Jui, *The Early Revolutionary Activ-
   ities of Comrade Mao Tse-tung,*
   Anthony W. Sariti, trans.,
   James C. Hsiung, ed. (White
   Plains, N.Y.: M. E. Sharpe, Inc.,
   1977), 4.
   –Mao "worshipped" Kang and
   Liang: Edgar Snow, *Red Star Over
   China,* paperback ed. (New York:
   Grove, 1961), 133.
   –Mao's marginalia: BR 18 (1984):
   24.
   –Liang on Mao in 1921: LRGNP II:
   604–6.
   –Liang rejects Marxism: Levenson,
   Liang, 211.
64 Mao on class and contradictions:
   Richard Curt Kraus, *Class Conflict
   in Chinese Socialism* (New York:
   Columbia University Press, 1981);
   John Bryan Starr, *Continuing the
   Revolution: The Political Thought*

of Mao (Princeton, N.J.: Princeton
University Press, 1979).

64 Mao's reading notes: *Miscellany of
Mao Tse-tung Thought* (1949–
1968), Part II, in JPRS 61269-2:
290.

65 Enlightenment Society quotation:
Enlightenment No. 2 in JPRS
73215: 34.
–*Red Flag* quotation: No. 18 (1980)
in JPRS 76966: 3–4.
–*Four Modernizations Forum:* No.
1 in JPRS 74532: 28.

CHAPTER 4

67 corrupt officials: e.g., YBSWJ II.5:
12–42.
–Huang Zongxi quotation: Wm.
Theodore de Bary, Wing-tsit Chan,
and Burton Watson, comps.,
Sources of Chinese Tradition (New
York: Columbia University Press,
1960), 587–88; quotation slightly
altered.

68 Huang's critique: Wm. Theodore
de Bary, "A Plan for the Prince:
The *Ming-i tai-fang lu* of Huang
Tsung-hsi Translated and Ex-
plained," Ph.D. diss., Columbia
University, 1953, esp. 208–11.
–Liang and colleagues circulate
Huang: Liang Ch'i-ch'ao, *Intellec-
tual Trends in the Ch'ing Period,*
Immanuel C. Y. Hsü, trans. (Cam-
bridge, Mass.: Harvard University
Press, 1959), 36.
–"Young China": YBSWJ II.5:
10–11.

69 people supervise officialdom: YBSWJ
II.5: 3.
–late Qing bureaucracy: Chung-li
Chang, *The Chinese Gentry: Stud-
ies in Their Role in Nineteenth-
Century Chinese Society,* paper-
back ed. (Seattle: University of
Washington Press, 1967), 116.

–clerks and runners: T'ung-tsu Ch'ü,
*Local Government in China under
the Ch'ing* (Cambridge, Mass.:
Harvard University Press, 1962),
38–41, 57–60.
–Ming bureaucracy: Ray Huang,
*1587, A Year of No Significance:
The Ming Dynasty in Decline*
(New Haven: Yale University
Press, 1981), 53.
–28 million state bureaucrats: calculated from World Bank figures in
China Business Review (September–October 1981): 46; cf. BR 31
(1981): 3. Figure for nonadministrative workers on the state payroll
also estimated from these figures.
–commune and cooperative officials:
my rough estimate; cf. *Red Flag*
No. 8 (1983) in JPRS 83808: 41.
–armed forces: John L. Scherer, ed.,
*China Facts and Figures Annual,
Volume 1, 1978* (Gulf Breeze,
Fla.: Academic International Press,
1978), 76.
–35 million party members: BR 36
(1977): 36.
–regularization: Ezra F. Vogel,
"From Revolutionary to Semi-Bu-
reaucrat: The 'Regularisation' of
Cadres," *China Quarterly* 29:
36–60.
–ranks and grades: Ch'en Po-wen,
"Rising Prices and Wages in Mainland China: An Analysis," *Issues
and Studies* XVI:2 (February
1980): 42–45.

70 paperwork and meetings: Michel
Oksenberg, "Methods of Communication within the Chinese Bureaucracy," *China Quarterly* 57:
1–39.
–peasant and worker legal status: Su-
lamith Heins Potter, "The Position
of Peasants in Modern China's Social Order," *Modern China* 9:4
(October 1983): 465–99.

70 controls on movement, housing,
and careers: Lynn T. White III,
*Careers in Shanghai: The Social
Guidance of Personal Energies in a
Developing Chinese City,*
1949–1966 (Berkeley: University of
California Press, 1978).
–college enrollment statistics: BR 20
(1981): 18.
–planned birth system: Pi-chao
Chen, *Population and Health Policy in the People's Republic of
China* (Washington, D.C.: Smith-
sonian Institution, 1976), 78–90.
–campaigns: Charles P. Cell, *Revolution at Work: Mobilization Campaigns in China* (New York:
Academic Press, 1977); Frederick C. Teiwes, *Politics and
Purges in China: Rectification and
the Decline of Party Norms,
1950–1965* (White Plains, N.Y.:
M. E. Sharpe, Inc., 1979), 30–57.

71 techniques of control: see, e.g.,
Harry Harding, *Organizing China:
The Problem of Bureaucracy,
1949–1976* (Stanford, Calif.: Stanford University Press, 1981).

72 "tottered": *Selected Works of Mao
Tsetung* (Peking: Foreign Lan-
guages Press, 1961–1977), V: 184.
–Mao 1956 speech: *Selected Works,*
IV: 344–345.
–Mao's campaigns against bureau-
cracy: John Bryan Starr, *Continu-
ing the Revolution: The Political
Thought of Mao* (Princeton, N.J.:
Princeton University Press, 1979),
158–65, 194–201; Roderick Mac-
Farquhar, *The Origins of the Cul-
tural Revolution,* 2 vols. (New
York: Columbia University Press,
1974, 1983).

73 "newly engendered bourgeois ele-
ments": BR 10 (1975): 5–10; Peer
Moller Christensen and Jorgen
Delman, "A Theory of Transitional

Society: Mao Zedong and the
Shanghai School," in *China from
Mao to Deng: The Politics and Ec-
onomics of Socialist Development,*
Bulletin of Concerned Asian Schol-
ars, ed., paperback ed. (Armonk,
N.Y.: M. E. Sharpe, 1983), 9–20.
–Mao 1965 directive: *Mao Zedong
sixiang wansui* (April 1967), reprint
ed. ([Taipei]: n.p., n.d.), 31.
–Mao on Djilas and Trotsky: Starr,
Continuing, 97–128.

74 "There must be a party": *Miscellany of Mao Tse-tung Thought*
(1949–1968), Part II, in JPRS
61269-2: 453.
–"masses more progressive": cited in
Starr, *Continuing,* 196.
–confused Red Guard leader: *Miscellany,* II, in JPRS 61269-2: 496.
–1968 Red Guard document: Klaus
Mehnert, *Peking and the New
Left: At Home and Abroad* (Berkeley, Calif.: Center for Chinese
Studies, 1969), 97.
–Li Yizhe poster: *Issues and Studies*
XII:1 (January 1976): 145.
–"two-line struggle": BR 10 (1975):
6.

75 Zhao, "low efficiency": BR 51
(1981): 35.
–39 approvals: *People's Daily* 11
December 1981 in JPRS 79913: 29.
–120 pounds of documents: RMRB
1983.3.7.1.
–"twelve stations": RMRB 1981.
5.12.8.
–Deng complaint: *Ching pao [Jing
bao]* No. 10 (1980) in FBIS 21 October 1980, U2.
–Deng charter speech: BR 40 (1983):
15, 18, 21.

80 Liao Gailong on the reforms: *Qishi
niandai* 134 (1981) in FBIS 16
March 1981, U14.
–letters and visits work: BR 25
(1982): 23–28; interviews.

81 "They must read": *Red Flag* 4
(1982) in JPRS 80713: 66–67.
–discipline inspection commission
statistics: RMRB 1983.10.3.1.
–press praises officials: e.g., FBIS 11
September 1979, P1; FBIS 25 September 1979, P2; FBIS 27 September 1979, O1; FBIS 11 October
1979, L1; RMRB 1980.8.18.1.
–"letters travel up and down": FBIS
7 October 1983, K1.
–"you cannot create a disturbance":
RMRB 1979.11.22.1.
–"habitual troublemakers": e.g.,
RMRB 1979.12.11.4; FBIS 15 January 1980, O2–O3; WIIB
1981.9.4.4; RMRB 1981.9.23.3.
–1981 regulations for workers' congresses: FBIS 23 July 1981, K3–K7.
82 101,000 enterprises: *Red Flag* 2
(1982) in JPRS 82391: 60.
–election of managerial cadres: BR
35 (1980): 24–26; BR 52 (1981): 5.
–neighborhood committee election
regulations: FBIS 16 January 1980,
L1–L2.
–rural election regulations: "Regulations on the Work in the Rural
People's Communes (Draft for
Trial Use)," *Issues and Studies*
XV: 8 (August 1979): 103.
–mediation committee election regulations: FBIS 24 January 1980,
L6–L7.
–1983 trade union constitution:
RMRB 1983.10.24.3.
–Deng adviser on media reform:
Qishi niandai 134 (1981) in FBIS
16 March 1981, U12.
–history of soviets and congresses in
China: see notes to Chapter 10.
83 "rubber stamp": *Qishi niandai* 134
(1981) in FBIS 16 March 1981, U8.
–September 1980 NPC session: e.g.,
RMRB 1980.9.5.4; FBIS 10 September 1980, L30–L31; FBIS 15 September 1980, L7–L9.

–1982 constitution: BR 52 (1982):
20–21, 26 (Articles 67, 70, 104).
–*Red Flag* on democracy: No. 18 in
JPRS 76966: 3–4.
84 democracy like basketball: FBIS 11
April 1979, O8.
–Li Jiahua on democracy: *Enlightenment* No. 2 in JPRS 73215: 34, 36.
–Lu Mang: *Enlightenment* No. 3 in
JPRS 73215: 67.
–antibureaucratism: throughout the
democracy movement's periodicals;
e.g., the writings of Cui Quanhong
in *Four Modernizations Forum*
No. 1 in JPRS 74970: 67–100; Hui
Jun in *Seek the Truth Journal*
(March 1979) in JPRS 74591:
26–40; Long Ren in *Beijing zhi
chun* No. 5: 1–4; Lü Min in *Peking Spring* Nos. 1, 2 in JPRS
73421: 1–6, 15–19, and *Beijing zhi
chun* No. 3: 25–27.
85 "feudalism . . . deep-rooted": *Red
Flag* 24 (1980) in JPRS 77436: 53.
–feudal culture's manifestations:
WIIB 1980.7.10.3.
–Liu Shaoqi article: *Red Flag* 14
(1980) in JPRS 76503: 7.
–bureaucratism "not inherent":
China Youth News, 7 February
1981, in JPRS 77844: 25.
86 *People's Daily* attack on democrats:
FBIS 9 February 1981, L7.

CHAPTER 5

87 "Tragedy in the Year 2000": *Peking Spring* No. 5, reprinted in No.
8, in JPRS 74970: 17–32.
89 Duke Zhao and Prince Wei: *Peking Spring* No. 6 in JPRS 74591:
17.
–Chen Erjin, "On the Proletarian
Democratic Revolution": *Siwu luntan* No. 10: 1, 13, 17, 48–52,
56–69, "proletariat cannot allow"
quoted from p. 60; trans. by Robin

Munro, *China: Crossroads Social-
ism: An Unofficial Manifesto for
Proletarian Democracy* (London:
Verso Editions, 1984).

90 Fu Shenqi, "Democracy and So-
cialism": in *Xueyou tongxun* 5
(1980), reprinted in *Xin shehui*
(Hong Kong) (October 1980): 151.
–*Sea Spray* article: No. 1 in JPRS
74764: 101, 102.
–publicity in China about the Paris
Commune: John Bryan Starr,
"Revolution in Retrospect: The
Paris Commune through Chinese
Eyes," *China Quarterly* 49:
106–25.
–Marx on the Paris Commune:
"The Civil War in France," in
Robert C. Tucker, ed., *The Marx-
Engels Reader*, 2d ed. (New York:
W. W. Norton Co., 1978),
618–52.
–Lenin on the Paris Commune:
V. I. Lenin, *State and Revolution*
(New York: International Publish-
ers, 1943), 37.
–"system of elections": Klaus Meh-
nert, *Peking and the New Left: At
Home and Abroad* (Berkeley,
Calif.: Center for Chinese Studies,
1969), 101.

91 Lü Min on Paris Commune: *Peking Spring* Nos. 1, 2 in JPRS
73421: 1–6.
–Lü's additional article: *Peking
Spring* No. 2 in JPRS 73421: 15–19;
more on the same lines in *Beijing
zhi chun* No. 3: 25–28.
–Wang Xizhe, "Strive for Proletarian Class Dictatorship" reprinted
in *Qishi niandai* 116 (1979): 27.
–Wang private essay: printed in
*Zhongguo minzhu yundong
tongxun* (Hong Kong) II:2 (June
1982): 6–9; partial translation in
Freedom at Issue No. 69 (November–December 1982): 28–31.

92 Canton handbill on Mao: DXKW: 7.
–*China Human Rights Paper* on
Mao: *Zhongguoren* 5 (1979): 27.
–Wang Xizhe on Mao: *Qishi nian-
dai* 133 (1981): 34–35.
–Huang Xiang poem on idols: *En-
lightenment* No. 1 in JPRS 73215:
5.

93 Mao "alone with the masses":
André Malraux, *Anti-Memoirs*,
Terence Kilmartin, trans. (New
York: Holt, Rinehart and Winston,
1968), 388.
–Huang's colleague on idols: *En-
lightenment* No. 2 in JPRS 73215:
30, 34.

94 Qin Shi Huang's totalitarianism:
Enlightenment No. 2 in JPRS
73215: 32.
–Stalin on 1936 constitution: Samuel Hendel, ed., *The Soviet Cruci-
ble: The Soviet System in Theory
and Practice*, 5th ed. (North Sci-
tuate, Mass.: Duxbury Press,
1980), 183.
–Marxists' views on democracy: Leszek Kolakowski, *Main Currents of
Marxism*, P. S. Falla, trans., paperback ed., 3 vols. (Oxford: Oxford
University Press, 1981), II: 49 and
throughout.

95 Luxemburg quotation: Rosa Luxemburg, *The Russian Revolution
and Leninism or Marxism?*, paperback ed. (Ann Arbor: University of
Michigan Press, 1961), 71.
–Trotsky quotation: Leon Trotsky,
*The Revolution Betrayed: What Is
the Soviet Union and Where Is It
Going?*, 5th ed., paperback ed.
(New York: Pathfinder Press,
1972), 252.
–proposals after Stalin's death: see,
e.g., Kolakowski, *Main Currents*,
III: 456–69; Roy A. Medvedev, *On
Socialist Democracy*, Ellen deKadt,
trans. and ed. (New York: Al-

fred A. Knopf, 1975).

95 Chinese specialists' access to non-Leninist Marxist works: Cheng Hsueh-chia, "The 'Thoughts of Marx' Disturb Maoists," *Inside China Mainland* (Taipei), Supplement (June 1983): 3.

–*Philosophical Research* on "privileged class": No. 2 (1979) in JPRS 73710: 11. Wang Xizhe cited this article approvingly in his essay "Strive for Proletarian Class Dictatorship," reprinted in *Qishi niandai* 116 (1979): 28.

96 *Historical Research* on seventeenth century: No. 1 (1980) in JPRS 76664: 40.

–*Historical Research* on Thomas Jefferson: *Lishi yanjiu* No. 4 (1980): 149–64.

–social science journal: *Social Science* No. 4 (1980) in JPRS 76858: 28. The same point was argued in *Philosophical Research* No. 12 (1980) in JPRS 77613: 19–31.

–*Bitter Love:* FBIS 21 May 1981, K11, K13.

–local Guangxi party journal: *Ideological Liberation* No. 1 (1980) in JPRS 75962: 67.

–*People's Daily* on "democracy under centralized guidance": RMRB 1980.10.30.5; also see RMRB 1981.1.19.5, CNA 1195: 6.

–"contributing commentator": FBIS 22 September 1980, L23.

–Hu Qiaomu on "bourgeois liberalization": *Red Flag* 23 (1981) in JPRS 79936: 1, 3.

97 academic and ideological debates: sources too numerous to cite, but see *Renxing, rendaozhuyi wenti taolunji,* Zhongguo shehui kexue yuan zhexue yanjiu suo "guonei zhexue dongtai" bianjibu, comp. (Peking: Renmin chubanshe, 1983), esp. p. 35 (linkage of topics

of humanism, goal of production, view of life, and bureaucratism), and pp. 505–20.

98 alienation in Marx: Tucker, ed., *Reader,* 66–125; Kolakowski, *Main Currents,* I: 138–41.

–600 articles: RMRB 1983.11.5.5.

–Wang Ruoshui's June 1980 talk: XWZX 1980.8.8–13.

–Wang's Shanghai article: FBIS 22 October 1980, L8–L11.

99 Wang to visiting Americans: Jerome Ch'en, comp., "Ideology and History: Report on the Visit of the North American Delegation on Socialism and Revolution to the People's Republic of China, June–July 1980," photocopy of a typescript, 25 August 1980, 33.

–Wang, "self-criticism is good medicine": *New Era* 8 (1981) in JPRS 79407: 46.

–Wang Zhen October 1983 speech: RMRB 1983.10.25.1.

100 *New China Daily: Xinhua ribao* 27 September 1981 in JPRS 79473: 16.

–prominent philosopher's attack: FBIS 7 November 1983, K9.

–Hu Qiaomu accusation: FBIS 7 February 1984, K12.

–Deng Liqun accusation: FBIS 16 January 1984, K5.

–Wang Ruoshui loses his post: see, e.g., *Zhengming* 78 (1984): 6.

–intellectuals' opinions of democracy movement: interviews.

101 Hu Qiaomu speech: *News Front* 4 (1980) in JPRS 76971: 31.

–fear of disorder in Chinese politics: Richard H. Solomon, *Mao's Revolution and the Chinese Political Culture* (Berkeley: University of California Press, 1971).

–Deng's January 1980 speech: *Zhengming* 29 (1980) in FBIS 11 March 1980, supplement, 23.

–Deng's August 1980 speech: *Issues*

and Studies, XVII: 3 (March 1981): 102.

101 Deng's December 1980 speech: *Ming bao*, 2 May 1981, in FBIS 2 May 1981, W2.

102 no need for more than one party: Deng's January 1980 speech, *Zhengming* 29 (1980) in FBIS 11 March 1980, supplement, 23.

– CCP has no separate interest: FBIS 3 June 1981, K9–K17; BR 25 (1980): 17–20.

–no "blind faith" in masses: FBIS 3 June 1981, K14.

–no "bureaucratic class": FBIS 17 June 1981, K12–K20; *Red Flag* 5 (1981) in JPRS 77918: 17–26.

–"all have been corrected": BR 25 (1980): 18.

–"undermine the situation": FBIS 12 June 1981, K12.

–"anarchist thought": *Studies in Law* 3 (1980) in JPRS 76466: 63.

–"disciplined and orderly": *Red Flag* 6 in JPRS 75711: 56.

–Paris Commune imperfect: BR 15 (1981): 17.

–"we did it 31 years ago": FBIS 17 June 1981, K16.

–"spoil the prospect": FBIS 23 April 1981, K9.

–"If people are swayed": *Ming bao*, 3 May 1981, in FBIS 4 May 1981, W8.

–party resolution on Mao: BR 27 (1981): 10–39.

103 Deng on bourgeois liberalization: BR 36 (1981): 13.

–Hu Qiaomu at "forum on problems": *Red Flag* 23 (1981) in JPRS 79936: 3.

–importance of ideology in legitimizing communist power: cf. Kolakowski, *Main Currents*, III: 90–91.

104 "autocratic rulers," "society composed of individuals": *Explorations* No. 1 in JPRS 73756: 17.

–"heaven-given human rights": *Explorations* No. 3 in JPRS 73421: 31.

–"masters of our own destiny": *Explorations* No. 1 in JPRS 73756: 12.

–socialism inclined to democracy, undermined by "blind faith": *Explorations* No. 1 in JPRS 73756: 21.

105 pictures of cake and plum: *Explorations* No. 1 in JPRS 73756: 8.

–"fight for survival," "right to fight": *Explorations* No. 3 in JPRS 73421: 32–33.

–"human rights are limited": *Explorations* No. 3 in JPRS 73421: 31.

106 *China Human Rights*: excerpts in JPRS 73421 and in *Zhongguoren* 5 (1979).

–*China Human Rights Paper*: excerpts in JPRS 73922 and in *Zhongguoren* 5 (1979).

–two other articles asserting primacy of rights: *Sea Spray* No. 1 in JPRS 74764: 86–105; *Future* No. 1 in *Issues and Studies* XVI:12 (December 1980): 84–88.

–*April Fifth Forum* on Wei trial, "Marxism": e.g., issue of 20 October 1979 in JPRS 74764: 54–60.

–rights not absolute: *April Fifth Forum* No. 7 in JPRS 73922: 13–14.

–democracy a means: *April Fifth Forum* No. 8 in JPRS 73987: 10.

–Xu Wenli on Human Rights League: *April Fifth Forum* No. 14 in JPRS 75442: 9–10.

–Wei prosecutor statements: "Unofficial Transcript of the Trial of Wei Jingsheng," Amnesty International document ASA 17/01/80, mimeo (June 1980), 49.

CHAPTER 6

A longer and more fully documented version of this chapter appears in R. Randle Edwards, Louis Henkin, and Andrew J. Nathan, *Human Rights in*

Contemporary China (New York: Columbia University Press, 1986).

The constitutional texts from 1908 through 1954 may be found in Zhang Jinfan and Zeng Xianyi, *Zhongguo xianfa shilue* (Peking: Beijing chubanshe, 1979), Appendix 2. The 1975 and 1978 constitutions may be found in Chen Hefu, ed., *Zhongguo xianfa leibian* (Peking: Zhongguo shehui kexue chubanshe, 1980), 1–18, 333–43. The 1982 constitution is in RMRB 1982. 12.5.1–3.

113 Confucian and Legalist views of law: see, e.g., Roger T. Ames, *The Art of Rulership: A Study in Ancient Chinese Political Thought* (Honolulu: University of Hawaii Press, 1983); Derk Bodde and Clarence Morris, *Law in China, Exemplified by 190 Ch'ing Dynasty Cases . . .* (Cambridge, Mass.: Harvard University Press, 1967), 1–51.

114 de Bary, "moral restraints": W. T. de Bary, "Chinese Despotism and the Confucian Ideal: A Seventeenth-Century View," in John K. Fairbank, ed., *Chinese Thought and Institutions*, paperback ed. (Chicago: University of Chicago Press, 1967), 195.

–developments in Western legal theory: see, e.g., Edward Allen Kent, ed., *Law and Philosophy: Readings in Legal Philosophy* (Englewood Cliffs, N.J.: Prentice-Hall, 1970); J. Roland Pennock, "Rights, Natural Rights, and Human Rights—A General View," in Pennock and John W. Chapman, eds., *Human Rights*, Nomos XXIII (New York: New York University Press, 1981), 1–28.

115 drafting of Principles: Norbert Meienberger, *The Emergence of*

Constitutional Government in China (1905–1908) (Bern: Peter Lang, 1980), 84–85.

–Guomindang scholar quotation: W. Y. Tsao, *The Constitutional Structure of Modern China* (Carlton, Victoria, Australia: Melbourne University Press, 1947), 57.

–"In a class society": *Red Flag* 3 (1984) in JPRS-CRF-84-006: 11.

–"not heaven-given": *Hongqi* 7 (1982): 35.

116 "the content of civil rights": FBIS 20 June 1979, L8.

–*Workers' Daily* quotation: FBIS 30 March 1981, L14.

–John Wu quotation: Wu Jingxiong, *Falü zhexue yanjiu*, 2d printing (Shanghai: Huiwentang shuju, 1937), 45.

–"state has right to intervene": FBIS 21 October 1981, K6.

117 legal official to journalist: Gerd Ruge, "An Interview with Chinese Legal Officials," *China Quarterly* 61: 119.

–verdicts in camera: Hungdah Chiu, "Socialist Legalism: Reform and Continuity in Post-Mao Communist China," *Issues and Studies* XVII:11 (November 1981): 45–57.

–Peng Zhen quotation: RMRB 1984.4.8.1.

–judges to be guided by party policy: see, e.g., *Legal Research* 2 (1980) in JPRS 76527: 1–5; RMRB 1983.3.28.5.

–"the party's policies": FBIS 14 November 1979, L1.

–1981 text: Chen Shouyi and Zhang Hongsheng, chief eds., *Faxue jichu lilun* (Peking: Beijing daxue chubanshe, 1981), 231.

118 Taiwan state of siege: Ming-min Peng, "Political Offenses in Taiwan: Laws and Problems," *China Quarterly* 47: 471–93.

118 trial of the "Gang of Four": Chiu,
    "Socialist Legalism," 69–72.
    –definition of counterrevolutionary
    offenses: e.g., *Faxue yanjiu* 2
    (1982): 13–17; FBIS 1 September
    1983, K13–K15.
119 *Red Flag* quotation: FBIS 27 April
    1981, K19.
    –"Speech takes place": FBIS 12 June
    1981, K11.
    –freedom in diaries: RMRB 1979.
    8.4.6.
    –diary entries used as evidence: e.g.,
    FBIS 26 September 1983, O3–O4.
    –treatment of demonstrations: e.g.,
    FBIS 17 September 1979, O7–O8;
    FBIS 6 February 1980, O1–O2.
    –punishment of appeals: e.g., RMRB
    1979.11.22.1; RMRB 1979.12.11.4;
    WHB 1981.9.4.4; RMRB 1981.
    9.23.3.
    –"counterrevolutionaries . . .":
    Jerome Alan Cohen, *The Criminal
    Process in the People's Republic of
    China, 1949–1963: An Introduc-
    tion* (Cambridge, Mass.: Harvard
    University Press, 1968), 249.
120 Confucian view of selfish behavior:
    Donald J. Munro, *The Concept of
    Man in Contemporary China* (Ann
    Arbor: University of Michigan
    Press, 1977), 162.
    –Liang, "that which is appropriate":
    YBSWJ I.1: 99.
    –Liang, "The individual . . .": YBSWJ
    II.5: 49.
121 Liu Shipei: quoted by Michael
    Gasster, *Chinese Intellectuals and
    the Revolution of 1911: The Birth
    of Modern Chinese Radicalism*
    (Seattle: University of Washington
    Press, 1969), 177.
    –Hu Shi: quoted by Jerome B.
    Grieder, *Hu Shih and the Chinese
    Renaissance: Liberalism in the Chi-
    nese Revolution, 1917–1937* (Cam-
    bridge, Mass.: Harvard University

Press, 1970), 95.
–Chen Duxiu: translated in Ssu-yü
Teng and John K. Fairbank,
*China's Response to the West: A
Documentary Survey, 1839–1923*
(Cambridge, Mass.: Harvard Uni-
versity Press, 1961), 241–42.
–Guo Moruo, "ego": Leo Ou-fan
Lee, *The Romantic Generation of
Modern Chinese Writers* (Cam-
bridge, Mass.: Harvard University
Press, 1973), 190.
–Guo, "the minority": *Moruo wenji*
(Peking: Renmin wenxue chu-
banshe, 1959), Vol. X, "Wenyi
lunji xu," 3.
122 Mao, "individual element of collec-
tive": *Miscellany of Mao Tse-tung
Thought (1949–1968)*, Part II, in
JPRS 61269-2: 250.
–Chinese philosopher quotation:
Philosophical Research 5 (1979) in
JPRS 74625:32.
–*Red Flag* quotation: No. 10 (1980)
in JPRS 76076: 20.
–"legitimate individual interests":
People's Daily 20 April 1979 in
JPRS 73881: 30.
–"spirit of selflessness": *Changjiang
ribao* 3 March 1979 in JPRS 78120:
23–24.
–"when inconsistent": Ibid., 25.
123 *Legal Research* quotation: *Faxue
yanjiu* 2 (1981): 7.
–"legal" versus "legitimate" individ-
ual interest: GMRB 1980.11.15.3.
–*Workers' Daily* quotation: 16
March 1981 in JPRS 78083: 29.
–"freedoms can exist only when":
Beijing ribao 28 December 1981 in
JPRS 80211: 3.
124 commentary on 1982 constitution:
FBIS 28 May 1982, K10.
–Mao, "I don't trust": *Mao Zedong
sixiang wansui* (1969), reprint ed.
([Taipei]: n.p., n.d.), 667.
–"may not appear as colorful": *Red

Flag 4 (1979) in JPRS 73650: 28.
125 "Is it not freedom?": *Hongqi* 22
(1981): 19.
–"people are the basis": the discussion is based chiefly on Jin Yaoji,
*Zhongguo minben sixiang zhi shi
di fazhan* (Taipei: Jiaxin shuini
gongsi wenhua jijinhui, 1964);
Wang Erhmin, *Wan Qing
zhengzhi sixiang shilun* (Taipei:
Huashi chubanshe, 1969), Ch. 9;
Wei Zhengtong, *Chuantong yu
xiandaihua* (Taipei: Shuiniu chubanshe, 1968), 111–42; Zhou
Daoqi, "Woguo minben sixiang de
fenxi yu jiantao," in Zhongyang
yanjiu yuan, comp., *Guoji Hanxue
huiyi lunwenji, Sixiang yu zhexue
zu* (Taipei: Zhongyang yanjiu yuan,
1981), II: 951–94.
–Mencius: The quotations are, in
order, from the following books,
parts, and chapters of Mencius: I.I.
13, I.II.10, I.II.7, I.II.8, and
VII.II.14. The translations are
adapted from Arthur Waley, *Three
Ways of Thought in Ancient
China* (Garden City, N.Y.: Doubleday Anchor Books, n.d.), and
James Legge, *The Chinese Classics
with a Translation, Critical and Exegetical Notes, Prologomena, and
Copious Indexes*, 5 vols. (Hong
Kong University Press, 1960), Vol.
II.
126 "statecraft school": Philip A.
Kuhn, "Local Self-Government
Under the Republic: Problems of
Control, Autonomy, and Mobilization," in Frederic Wakeman, Jr.,
and Carolyn Grant, eds., *Conflict
and Control in Late Imperial
China* (Berkeley: University of California Press, 1975), 261–75; Judith
Anne Whitbeck, "Averting Dynastic Decline: Political Ethics in
Kung Tzu-chen's Reform

Thought," paper presented to the
Modern China Seminar, Columbia
University, October 9, 1980.
–reformers' arguments: from Wang,
Wan Qing, 236–38.
127 Kang Youwei 1898 memorial: Jian
Bozan et al., comps., *Wuxu bianfa*
(Shanghai: Renmin chubanshe,
1961), II: 236.
–Liang, "ten thousand eyes": Hao
Chang, *Liang Ch'i-ch'ao and Intellectual Transition in China,
1890–1907* (Cambridge, Mass.:
Harvard University Press, 1971),
100.
–Sun Yat-sen, "steamship": Sun Yatsen, *San Min Chu I, The Three
Principles of the People*, Frank W.
Price, trans., L. T. Chen, ed., reprint ed. (New York: Da Capo
Press, 1975), 342–43.
128 Mao, "atomic energy": *Chinese
Law and Government* IX:3 (Fall
1976): 84.
–Hua Guofeng, 1979: BR 27 (1979):
22.
129 Liang on Bentham: YBSWJ V.13:
32.
–Schwartz on Yan Fu: Benjamin
Schwartz, *In Search of Wealth and
Power: Yen Fu and the West*
(Cambridge, Mass.: Harvard University Press, 1964), 141.
–Luo, "On Human Rights": Luo
Longji, "Lun renquan," in Liang
Shiqiu, Hu Shi, and Luo Longji,
eds., *Renquan lunji* (Shanghai:
Xinyue shudian, 1930), 37, 42–43,
59–73.
130 Sun, "Europeans rebelled": *San
Min*, 210.
–Qian Duansheng: quoted in Lloyd
Eastman, *The Abortive Revolution:
China under Nationalist Rule,
1927–1937* (Cambridge, Mass.:
Harvard University Press, 1974),
149.

130 Hu Shi, "kindergarten": Grieder,
    Hu Shih, 266–68.
131 "All political rights": FBIS 30
    March 1981, L13.
    –*Red Flag* quotation: No. 6 (1979)
    in JPRS 73956: 83–84.
    –Xinhua quotation: FBIS 22 January
    1980, L7.
    –Shanghai radio quotation: FBIS 11
    April 1979, O8.
    –Hu Qiaomu quotation: XWZX
    1980.4.8.
    –Chiang on tutelary rule: Chiang,
    *China's Destiny and Chinese Eco-
    nomic Theory* (New York: Roy
    Publishers, 1947), 183–213.
    –Deng echoes Sun: *Zhengming* 29
    (1980) in FBIS 11 March 1980, sup-
    plement, 23.
    –"We have been building social-
    ism": FBIS 22 October 1980, L12.
132 "Proletarian democracy history's
    highest form": RMRB 1979.6.9.2.
    –rural reconstructionists: Charles W.
    Hayford, *To the People: Y. C.
    James Yen and Rural Reconstruc-
    tion in China*, book manuscript;
    Guy S. Alitto, *The Last Confu-
    cian: Liang Shu-ming and the Chi-
    nese Dilemma of Modernity*
    (Berkeley: University of California
    Press, 1979), 192–225.

CHAPTER 7

Portions of Chapter 7 were presented
before in the following forms: "Liang
Ch'i-ch'ao's 'New-Style Writing' and
Late Ch'ing Propaganda," paper pre-
sented to the 29th annual meeting of
the Association for Asian Studies, New
York City, March 25–27, 1977; "The
Late Ch'ing Press: Role, Audience and
Impact," *Proceedings of the Interna-
tional Conference on Sinology: Section
on History and Archeology* (Taipei:
Zhongyang yanjiu yuan, 1981), III:

1281–1308; and (with Leo Ou-fan Lee),
"The Beginnings of Mass Culture: Journalism and Fiction in the Late Ch'ing
and Beyond," in David Johnson, Andrew J. Nathan, and Evelyn Sakakida
Rawski, eds., *Popular Culture in Late
Imperial China: Diversity and Integration* (Berkeley: University of California
Press, 1985), 362–97.

133 Liang, "constitutional govern-
    ment," newspapers: YBSWJ IX. 25a:
    19–23.
134 "From Heaven the people receive":
    Wm. Theodore de Bary, Wing-tsit
    Chan, and Burton Watson, comps.,
    Sources of Chinese Tradition (New
    York: Columbia University Press,
    1960), 183.
    –*Sacred Edict*, popular culture: see
    the essays in Johnson, Nathan, and
    Rawski, eds., *Popular Culture*.
    –traditional Chinese periodicals:
    Roswell S. Britton, *The Chinese
    Periodical Press, 1800–1912*
    (Shanghai: Kelly and Walsh, 1933;
    reprint ed., Taipei: Ch'eng-wen,
    1966), 1–15; Zeng Xubai, *Zhong-
    guo xinwen shi* (Taipei: Guoli
    zhengzhi daxue xinwen yanjiu suo,
    1966), 94–100.
135 Milne: quoted in Britton, *Periodi-
    cal*, 18–19.
    –missionary periodicals: Britton, *Pe-
    riodical*, 16–29; Zeng, *Xinwen*,
    125–39.
    –Hong Rengan's proposal: Zeng,
    Xinwen, 101–2.
    –court rejects gazette: Zeng, *Xin-
    wen*, 104.
    –foreign affairs agency's journals:
    Zeng, *Xinwen*, 104.
    –1901 gazette preface: Zeng, *Xin-
    wen*, 106–7.
136 other gazettes: Zeng, *Xinwen*,
    113–18; quotation from *Political
    Gazette*, 118.

136 early foreign and Chinese-language papers: Britton, *Periodical*, 16–85; Zeng, *Xinwen*, 125–90.

–*New Paper* inaugural statement: Zeng, *Xinwen*, 142.

137 press's new techniques: Zeng, *Xinwen*, 140–51, 362–67.

–Liang, "When you open one": YBSWJ III.6: 52.

138 Shanghai *News* circulation: Zeng, *Xinwen*, 153.

–Bao Tianxiao: Bao, *Chuanying lou huiyilu* (Hong Kong: DaHua chubanshe, 1971), 135, 145.

–*Chinese and Foreign News*: Britton, *Periodical*, 90–91; Zhang Pengyuan, *Liang Qichao yu Qingji geming* (Nangang: Zhongyang yanjiu yuan jindai shi yanjiu suo, 1964), 254–56; Zeng, *Xinwen*, 106.

–Kang Youwei's reform petition: Luke S. K. Kwong, *A Mosaic of the Hundred Days: Personalities, Politics, and Ideas of 1898* (Cambridge, Mass.: Council on East Asian Studies, 1984), 130.

139 historian of journalism: Ge Gongzhen, *Zhongguo baoxue shi* (Shanghai: Shangwu yinshuguan, 1927; reprint ed., Taipei: Xuesheng shuju, 1964), pp. 145–50.

–Liang's statistics: quoted in Zeng, *Xinwen*, 192.

–record-breaking circulations: Zeng, *Xinwen*, 107, 205.

–Liang's 1896 view: YBSWJ I.1: 100–103.

–"Preface and Regulations": YBSWJ II.3: 29–31.

–hundredth issue of *China Discussion*: YBSWJ III.6: 47–57.

–press as supervisor: YBSWJ IV.11: 37–38.

140 Tongcheng style: Wang Qizhong, "Tongcheng pai zai Zhongguo wenxue shi shang de diwei he zuoyong," reprinted from *Anhui lishi xuebao* (1957) in *Tongcheng pai yanjiu lunwenji* (Hefei: Anhui renmin chubanshe, 1963), 1–25; David E. Pollard, *A Chinese Look at Literature: The Literary Values of Chou Tso-jen in Relation to the Tradition* (Berkeley: University of California Press, 1973), Appendix A.

–Liang studied Tongcheng: Liang Ch'i-ch'ao, "My Autobiographical Account at Thirty," *Chinese Studies in History* X:3 (Spring 1977): 6.

–Chen Duxiu on Liang's style: quoted in translator's introduction to Liang Ch'i-ch'ao, *Intellectual Trends in the Ch'ing Period*, trans. Immanuel C. Y. Hsü (Cambridge, Mass.: Harvard University Press, 1959), 2.

–Japanese terms: Gao Mingkai and Liu Zhengtan, *Xiandai Hanyu wailaici yanjiu* (Peking: Wenzi gaige chubanshe, 1958).

–changes in Liang's style: my analysis, but cf. Hu Shi, "Zhongguo xin wenxue yundong xiaoshi" (1935), reprinted in *Hu Shi xuanji: lishi* (Taipei: Wenxing shudian, 1966), 60–63.

141 Qu Qiubai on the "new classical style": *Qu Qiubai wenji* (Peking: Renmin wenxue chubanshe, 1953), III: 887.

–"eight-legged essays": *Selected Works of Mao Tsetung* (Peking: Foreign Languages Press, 1961–77), III: 53.

–Liang on his own style: *Intellectual Trends*, 102.

–Huang Zunxian on Liang's style: LRGNP I: 150.

–Hu Shi on Liang's style: Hu Shi, "Zhongguo xin wenxue," 62.

142 proposals for using vernacular: Tan Bi'an, *Wan Qing de baihuawen yundong* (Wuhan: Hubei renmin chubanshe, 1956).

142 Liang's proposal: YBSWJ I.1: 48–54.
   –Liang's criticism of Yan Fu: quoted
   in Benjamin I. Schwartz, *In Search
   of Wealth and Power: Yen Fu and
   the West* (Cambridge, Mass.: Harvard University Press, 1964),
   93–94.
   –reform of primers: YBSWJ I.1:
   50–53.
   –"Talks on Poetry": Liang Qichao,
   Yinbingshi shihua (Shanghai:
   Zhonghua tushuguan, 1909).
   –Liang's three unfinished operas:
   Helmut Martin, "A Transitional
   Concept of Chinese Literature
   1897–1917: Liang Ch'i-ch'ao on
   Poetry-Reform, Historical Drama
   and the Political Novel," *Oriens
   Extremus* X:2 (December 1973):
   189–94.
143 Liang on fiction, 1896: YBSWJ I.1:
   54.
   –Liang on fiction, 1897: YBSWJ II.2:
   56.
   –Liang on fiction, 1898: YBSWJ II.3:
   34–35.
   –"On the Relationship between Fiction and Democracy": YBSWJ
   III.10: 6–10.
   –*New Fiction, Future of New
   China*: Philip C. Huang, *Liang
   Ch'i-ch'ao and Modern Chinese
   Liberalism* (Seattle: University
   of Washington Press, 1972),
   84–89.
   –later-developing countries: see especially Daniel Lerner, *The Passing
   of Traditional Society: Modernizing the Middle East*, paperback
   ed. (New York: The Free·Press,
   1964).
144 Bao, "explosion": *Huiyilu*, 150.
   –Cao, *New Citizen*: Cao Juren,
   Wentan wushinian, zhengbian
   (Hong Kong: Xin wenhua chubanshe, 1976), 32.
   –Huang to Liang: cited in Zhang

Pengyuan, "Huang Zunxian
de zhengzhi sixiang ji qi dui Liang
Qichao de yingxiang," *Jindai shi
yanjiu suo jikan* No. 1 (August
1969): 225.
   –printing presses and paper: He
   Shengding, "Sanshiwu nian lai
   Zhongguo zhi yinshuashu" (1931),
   reprinted in Zhang Jinglu, *Zhongguo jindai chuban shiliao* (Shanghai: Shanghai chubanshe,
   1953–54), I: 257–85.
   –police authority over press: Lee-hsia
   Hsu Ting, *Government Control of
   the Press in Modern China,
   1900–1949* (Cambridge, Mass.:
   East Asian Research Center, 1974),
   33–43.
   –Liang magazines' sales agencies:
   Zhang Pengyuan, *Liang Qichao yu
   Qingji geming* (Nangang: Zhongyang yanjiu yuan jindai shi yanjiu
   suo, 1964), 320.
   –Bao and general stores: Bao,
   Huiyilu, 169.
145 customs commissioner's comment:
   Report of Commissioner F. Hirth,
   Decennial Reports, 1882–1891
   (Shanghai: Inspectorate General
   of Customs, 1893), 315, cited in
   Ying-wan Cheng, *Postal Com-
   munication in China and Its Modernization, 1860–1896* (Cambridge,
   Mass.: East Asian Research
   Center, 1970), 49; quotation corrected to conform to original
   source.
   –Zou Lu quotation: Zou Lu, *Huigu
   lu*, reprint ed. (Taipei: Duli chubanshe, 1951), I: 11.
   –Hu Shi's recollection: Hu Shih,
   "An Autobiographical Account at
   Forty," Ch. IV, William A. Wycoff, trans., *Chinese Studies in History* XII:2 (Winter 1978–79): 27.
   –estimate of periodical publication:
   see citations in Nathan, "Late

Ch'ing Press," 1297–98.

145 postal statistics, 1908: China, Imperial Maritime Customs, *Report on the Working of the Imperial Post Office, 34th Year of Kuang Hsü (1908)* (Shanghai: Inspectorate General of Customs, 1909), 21–22.
–ratio of the 1920s: Jiaotong bu, comp., *Zhongguo youzheng tongji zhuankan* (Nanking: Jiaotong bu, 1931), 96–97.
–delivery boys and vendors: see citations in Nathan, "Late Ch'ing Press," 1301–2.

146 newspapers resold until "ragged": J. W. Sanger, *Advertising Methods in Japan, China, and the Philippines*, Department of Commerce, Special Agents Series No. 209 (Washington, D. C.: Government Printing Office, 1921), 61.
–Zhu De: Agnes Smedley, *The Great Road: The Life and Times of Chu Teh* (New York: Monthly Review Press, 1956), 72–73.
–Bao gets journal at school: Bao, *Huiyilu*, 299–300.
–American observer: Charles Frederick Hancock, "Introduction and Influence of Modern Machinery in China," M.A. thesis, University of Texas, 1926, 82. Citation courtesy of Thomas Rawski.
–specialist estimate: Zhang, *Liang*, 320.
–1893 population and urban percentage: G. William Skinner, "Regional Urbanization in Nineteenth-Century China," in Skinner, ed., *The City in Late Imperial China* (Stanford, Calif.: Stanford University Press, 1977), 225–26.

147 age and sex ratios, literacy: Evelyn Sakakida Rawski, *Education and Popular Literacy in Ch'ing China*

(Ann Arbor: University of Michigan Press, 1979), 183 and throughout.
–Zhang Zhongli's analysis of the gentry: Chung-li Chang, *The Chinese Gentry: Studies on Their Role in Nineteenth-Century Chinese Society*, paperback ed. (Seattle: University of Washington Press, 1967), 10, 92, 111, 165.
–elementary and middle-school enrollments: see citations in Lee and Nathan, "Beginnings of Mass Culture," 376–77.
–Shanghai *Upright*: Bao Tianxiao, *Chuanying lou huiyilu, xubian* (Hong Kong: DaHua chubanshe, 1973), 39.

148 mosquito papers: Ōtsuka Reizō, "Shanhai no shōhō ni kansuru ichikōsatsu," *Mantetsu Shina gesshi* VI:3 (December 15, 1929), 63–73.
–Lang study: Olga Lang, *Chinese Family and Society* (1946), reprint ed. (n.p.: Archon Books, 1968), 85.
–mid-1930s: Lin Yutang, *A History of the Press and Public Opinion in China*, reprint ed. (New York: Greenwood Press, 1968), 144, 152–53.
–circulations: Zeng, *Xinwen*, 117, 215, 355.
–postal statistics: *Youzheng tongji huiji* (Taipei: Jiaotongbu youzheng zongju, 1966), 120–21.
–20 to 30 million: Lin, *History*, 149.
–Lin Yutang on 1930s: Lin, *History*, 165–66.
–"Once a journalist," theory of "shock": YBSWJ IV.11: 38–39.

149 Liang on freedom of the press: see Lai Guanglin, *Liang Qichao yu jindai baoyeh* (Taipei: Shangwu yinshuguan, 1968), 80–86.
–"change the world": YBSWJ IV.11: 47.

149 professionalization: Cao Juren,
Wentan wushi nian, xubian (Hong
Kong: Xin wenhua chubanshe,
1973), 77–82.
–obstacles to professionalization:
Bao, Chuanying lou . . . xubian,
320–22, 415; Zeng, Xinwen, 289.
150 laws relating to journalism: Ting,
Government Control, 8–13.
–Japanese support to 15 newspapers:
revealed in a typescript document
in the Japanese Gaimushō archives:
Gaimushō jōhōbu, "Kankei
shimbun chōsa," carbon of a typescript, 83 pp., dated July 1929, un-
catalogued.
–newspaper setups: Zhao Xiaoyi,
Baotan fuchen sishiwu nian (Taipei: Zhuanji wenxue chubanshe,
1972), 26.
151 traditional de facto press freedom:
Zhu Chuanyu, Zhongguo minyi yu
xinwen ziyou fazhan shi (Taipei:
Zhongzheng shuju, 1974), 40–53.
–legal regulation, late Qing on:
Ting, Government Control, 9–10,
13, 18.
–Lin, "official": Lin, History, 136,
quotation condensed.
–Chinese experience of political history: see, for example, Cai Dong-
fan, Minguo tongsu yanyi, 8 vols.
(Shanghai: Huiwen tang xinji
shuju, 1936).

CHAPTER 8

152 book publishing and selling: Tao-
Tai Hsia and Kathryn Haun,
"Communist Chinese Legislation
on Publications and Libraries,"
The Quarterly Journal of the Library of Congress XXVII: 1 (January 1970): 20–33.
–distribution assigned to post office:
Ma Hong, genl. ed., Zhongguo
jingji shidian (Peking: Zhongguo

shehui kexue chubanshe, 1982),
281–83.
–four Central Committee departments: Banyue tan bianji bu,
comp., Shishi ciliao shouce (1982
nianban) (Peking: Xinhua chubanshe, 1983), 13.
–role of Propaganda Department:
Alan P. L. Liu, Communications
and National Integration in Communist China (Berkeley: University
of California Press, 1971), 34–47.
153 party control of press in general:
Lu Keng, "The Chinese Communist Press as I See It," The Asian
Messenger IV:2, 3 (Autumn
1979–Spring 1980): 44–53; Roderick MacFarquhar, "A Visit to the
Chinese Press," China Quarterly
53: 144–52; CNA 104; interview O-
5; XWZX 1982.10.14–15.
–Zhou "read every word": CNA
1070: 2.
–State Council regulations:
Guowuyuan gongbao No. 345
(1980 No. 18): 583–85, and No.
347 (1980 No. 20): 659–61.
–party secretary's supervision: see,
e.g., XWZX 1984.3.2.
–spare-time correspondents: XWZX
1982.6.2–6.
–literary and art organizations: BR 52
(1979): 15; interview O-5; Red
Flag 24 (1980) in JPRS 77436:
59–64.
154 1982 pact: FBIS 28 June 1982, K10.
–Hu speech: Red Flag 20 (1981) in
JPRS 79712: 8–35.
–Mao 1948 speech: Selected Works
of Mao Tsetung (Peking: Foreign
Languages Press, 1961–77), IV:
241.
–Mao, 90 percent of work: XWZX
1983.12.14.
–1958 note: Mao Zedong sixiang
wansui (April 1967), reprinted
([Taipei]: n.p., n.d.), III:19.

154 Liu 1948 speech: XWZX 1982.1.
2–3.
155 Liu quotations: XWZX 1980.5.9 and
1982.1.5–6.
156 1950 resolution: XWZX 1979.6.2–3.
–journalists' rights of investigation:
interviews.
–Liu, "criticize," "tempering":
XWZX 1982.1.3–4.
–most letters to the editor critical:
XWZX 1982.11.11.
–"mass work sections": interview
with three WHB editors, New York,
September 1, 1983; interview with
three GMRB editors, Peking, March
15, 1984; May Lipton, press release
dated 9/19/79 (based on a visit to
the *People's Daily*) in the visitors'
report file, Starr East Asian Library, Columbia University.
157 card file, internal publication, content analysis: XWZX 1982.12.14–15;
XWZX 1983.11.17.
–estimated 1946 circulation: Zeng
Xubai, *Zhongguo xinwen shi* (Taipei: Guoli zhengzhi daxue xinwen
yanjiu suo, 1966), 452–53.
–1953, 1965, 1967 statistics: State
Statistical Bureau, comp., *Statistical Yearbook of China 1981*
(*English Edition*) (Hong Kong:
Economic Information and Agency
[*sic*], 1982), 446–67.
–1973 post office catalogue: *Union
Research Service*, LXXVIII:8–10
(February 4, 1975), 123–27.
–rehabilitations of periodicals: e.g.,
FBIS 6 February 1979, E18–E19;
FBIS 7 February 1979, K2; RMRB
1980.2.8.3; FBIS 16 February 1979,
L4–L5.
–155 social science journals: contained in list, "Quanguo gaodeng
yuanxiao shehui kexue xuebao
1980 nian zong mulu shoulu de
gaoxiao xuebao xiaoming, kanming,
tongxun dizhi," in possession of

Starr East Asian Library, Columbia
University.
–200 literary magazines: FBIS 13
March 1981, L16.
–900 science and technology magazines: BR 47 (1979): 31.
–soccer magazine: XWZX 1980.2.35.
–abacus magazine: BR 50 (1980):
28.
–nature magazine: FBIS 17 September 1980, L34.
–family-planning journal: FBIS 9 November 1981, K4.
–fashion quarterly: FBIS 26 October
1981, K19.
–*UFO Exploration:* FBIS 5 December 1980, L13.
–complaint about expansion: RMRB
1981.9.3.4.
–paper shortage: see, e.g., XWZX
1980.12.23–24; *China Business Review* (July–August 1981): 43–44;
E. Perry Link, Jr., *Mandarin Ducks
and Butterflies: Popular Fiction in
Early Twentieth-Century Chinese
Cities* (Berkeley: University of California Press, 1981), 242; CNA 1126:
3–4.
158 *China Youth News* circulation:
Beijing wanbao 1982.5.29.1; RMRB
1981.6.15.1.
–*Reference News* circulation: BR 5
(1980): 30 and BR 20 (1981): 24.
–*Popular Cinema* circulation: *Chinese Literature* 6 (1981): 130.
–*People's Daily* circulation: BR 1
(1980): 7 and BR 20 (1981): 23.
–intended increase: FBIS 21 April
1980, L12.
–private periodical peddlers: e.g.,
RMRB 1984.5.9.1.
–carriers deliver six times as many
periodicals: BR 25 (1982): 6.
–subscription procedures: *1982
niandu quanguo baozhi zazhi
jianming mulu* (n.p.: Yunnan
sheng youdian guanliju, 1981);

RMRB 1979.11.24.3; RMRB
1981.11.25.4.

158 1981 postal service: BR 40 (1981):
22.
–commune mobilizes students:
RMRB 1982.11.27.5.
–quotas: Yunnan list, cited above.
–complaints about quotas: RMRB
1981.9.3.4; GMRB 1980.7.23.2;
RMRB 1979.10.8.3.
–ending of quotas: FBIS 29 October
1980, L17.
–U.S.-China comparison: Magazine
Publishers Association, *Magazine:
Newsletter of Research*, No. 39
(July 1982): 3; *Statistical Yearbook
1981*, 466–67.

159 prices of periodicals: *1979 baokan
mulu* ([Peking]: Beijing shi you-
zhengju, 1979).
–peasant expenditure: BR 43 (1983):
22–23.
–household subscriptions: XWZX
1984.2.2.
–rural postmaster report: RMRB
1979.8.17.4.
–magazine rental: RMRB 1981.4.16.7;
Link, *Mandarin Ducks*, 241–42.
–technician: interview GB-4.
–medical equipment factory: interview GR-7.
–petrochemical plant: interview
GB-6.
–cultural stations: BR 5 (1982): 20;
BR 11 (1982): 21, 25; photo in
RMRB 1982.12.26.3.

160 Hainan state farm: interview
QN-8.
–army farm: interview QN-6.
–farmer: interview NM-1.
–road construction brigade: interview GR-2.
–construction worker: interview
GR-9.
–harbor barge: interview GR-10.
–sheep tender: interview QN-10.
–Peking prison: FBIS 22 October

1981, K7.
–electrician: interview GR-6.
–farmworker: interview QN-17.
–rural resident: interview QN-9.
–90 percent subscribe: BR 5 (1980):
30; *Jiefang ribao* 14 December
1979 in JPRS 75104: 56.
–many teams do not: FBIS 28 October 1981, T4.
–American study: William L. Parish,
"Communication and Changing
Rural Life," in Godwin C. Chu
and Francis L. K. Hsu, eds., *Moving a Mountain: Cultural Change
in China* (Honolulu: University
Press of Hawaii, 1979), 365.

161 1982 census results on literacy: BR
45 (1982): 20.
–literacy standards: BR 14 (1984):
22; however, this is contradicted by
John S. Aird, "The Preliminary Results of China's 1982 Census,"
China Quarterly 96 (December
1983), 620.
–9-6-3 system: BR 4 (1983): 25; FBIS
6 March 1981, K12.
–Central Committee investigation:
Red Flag 4 (1981) in JPRS 77881:
48.
–newspapers used to paper walls:
RMRB 1979.8.17.4; see also RMRB
1982.5.15.1.
–former commune resident: interview NM-4.

162 county-level papers: see, e.g., XWZX
1981.5.42–43 and the same column in later issues.
–peasant editions: e.g., FBIS 20 May
1980, P2–P3.
–comic books: BR 10 (1981): 29; on
content, John C. Hwang, "*Lien
Huan Hua*: Revolutionary Serial
Pictures," in Godwin C. Chu, ed.,
*Popular Media in China: Shaping
New Cultural Patterns* (Honolulu:
University Press of Hawaii, 1978),
51–72.

162 reading to peasants: e.g., interview
QN-13.

  –1980 magazine: *Gushi hui*, reported in WHB 1980.7.13.1.

  –political study groups: Martin King Whyte, *Small Groups and Political Rituals in China* (Berkeley: University of California Press, 1974).

  –respondents on study groups: interviews GB-5, GR-2, and QN-6.

  –Hiniker research: Paul James Hiniker, "The Effects of Mass Communication in Communist China: The Organization and Distribution of Exposure," Ph.D. diss., Massachusetts Institute of Technology, 1966, esp. 152, 162, 166, 206.

  –American multiple readership: Magazine Publishers Association, *Magazine: Newsletter of Research*, No. 39 (July 1982): 3.

163 radio and cinema before 1949: Chu Chia-hua, *China's Postal and Other Communications Services* (London: Kegan Paul, Trench, Trubner and Co., 1937), 192–94; Rudolf Löwenthal, "Public Communications in China Before July, 1937," *The Chinese Social and Political Science Review*, XII:1 (April–June, 1938): 47–48, 56–57; Zeng, *Xinwen*, 601–21.

  –electronics production: Philip D. Reichers, "The Electronics Industry of China," in Joint Economic Committee of the U.S. Congress, comp., *People's Republic of China: An Economic Assessment* (Washington, D.C.: U.S. Government Printing Office, 1972), 105.

  –wired loudspeakers: Jack Craig, "China: Domestic and International Telecommunications, 1949–1974," in Joint Economic Committee of the U.S. Congress, comp., *China: A Reassessment of the Economy* (Washington, D.C.: U.S. Government Printing Office, 1975), 291, 293–95, 307. For smaller figures concerning the distribution of loudspeakers see BR 27 (1979): 41 and FBIS 20 May 1982, K19.

  –broadcasting had larger audience: BR 8 (1982): 19.

  –loudspeakers run by tractor: interview QN-12.

  –local unit broadcasting facilities: for example, see the picture in Peggy Printz and Paul Steinle, *Commune: Life in Rural China* (New York: Dodd, Mead, and Co., 1977), 172.

164 shift from tubes to transistors: Craig, "Telecommunications," 105; interview O-13.

  –cost of radios and loudspeakers: interviews; *Statistical Yearbook 1981*, 427.

  –1982 number of stations: BR 19 (1983): x.

  –poor reception: FBIS 7 September 1984, K20; cf. Craig, "Telecommunications," 307.

  –radio output: Craig, "Telecommunications," 304; BR 20 (1982): 17; BR 19 (1983): iv.

  –urban radio ownership: William C. Parish, "Egalitarianism in Chinese Society," *Problems of Communism* XXX:1 (January–February, 1981): 44; BR 8 (1982): 19.

  –survey on radio ownership: BR 20 (1983): 8.

  –film production: e.g., for 1982, BR 19 (1983): x.

  –nationwide projection facilities: BR 19 (1983): x. Different figures are given in BR 5 (1982): 20 and BR 20 (1983): 8.

  –film audience: BR 9 (1982): 27; contradictory figures in FBIS 28 September 1979, L18; NYT

1980.6.15. Sec. 2:1; BR 8 (1981):
30; BR 5 (1982): 20; Carol S. Gold-
smith, "China's Wide-Screen
Comeback," *China Business Review* (November–December 1981):
36.
164 senior official: RMRB 1981.4.15.5.
165 television history: Craig, "Telecommunications," 293, 305–6; CNA 630.
 —major investment: BR 10 (1981):
21, 26.
 —1978, 1983 outputs: BR 35 (1982):
15; BR 8 (1984): 15.
 —end-of-century goal: *U.S.-China Relations: Notes from the National
Committee* X:1 (Spring 1980): 3.
 —size of network: BR 19 (1983): x.
 —programming: BR 10 (1981): 21–27.
 —landlines and relay stations: BR 19
(1983): x; BR 10 (1981): 21; FBIS 1
April 1983, K12; *U.S.-China Relations: Notes from the National
Committee,* XI: 1–2 (Spring–Summer 1981): 2.
 —*TV Weekly*: BR 10 (1981): 27.
 —poor reception: FBIS 4 January
1980, L12.
 —satellite: FBIS 1 April 1983, K11.
 —rationing of TV sets: interviews.
 —TV prices: *Shichang* 1980.9.25.4;
FBIS 24 October 1980, O9.
 —urban worker income: BR 25
(1983): 15.
 —quality of domestic sets: e.g., BR 10
(1981): 26; BR 45 (1980): 4–5; FBIS
28 November 1979, L16; RMRB
1979.6.8.2.
 —customs duty: *China Business Review* (November–December 1981):
4.
 —black market: interview.
 —Peking TV ownership: BR 29
(1980): 25; BR 10 (1981): 21.
 —100 or more viewers: Craig, "Telecommunications," 306.
 —30-million audience: BR 29 (1980):
25; BR 2 (1981): 30.

166 200-million audience: *U.S.-China
Relations: Notes from the National
Committee* XI:1–2 (Spring–Summer
1981): 1; *China Daily* 1984.8.9.3.
168 Americans' knowledge of politics,
advertising: examples taken from
W. Lance Bennett, *Public Opinion
in American Politics* (New York:
Harcourt Brace Jovanovich, 1980),
44.

CHAPTER 9

Although they are not cited in any specific place, the following works influenced my analysis in this chapter:
Jacques Ellul, *Propaganda: The Formation of Men's Attitudes* (New York:
Alfred A. Knopf, 1965); Czeslaw Mi-
losz, *The Captive Mind*, Jane Zielonko,
trans. (New York: Alfred A. Knopf,
1953); Ithiel de Sola Pool, "Communication in Totalitarian Societies," in
Pool, Frederick W. Frey, Wilbur
Schramm, Nathan Maccoby, and
Edwin B. Parker, eds., *Handbook of
Communication* (Chicago: Rand
McNally, 1973), 462–511.

An earlier version of this paper was
presented as "Propaganda and Alienation in the People's Republic of
China," paper presented at the Annual
Meeting of the Association for Asian
Studies, Washington, D.C., March
23–25, 1984.

In the first part of the chapter, I use
quotations from my interviews to illustrate the attitudes of accepters, skeptics,
and decipherers. As explained in the
Appendix, respondents' attitudes were
rarely of a pure type. Those who were
consistently accepting were classified as
accepters; those who were sometimes
accepting and sometimes skeptical were
classified as skeptics; and those who displayed a mix of all three attitudes were
classified as decipherers. Because the attitudes were mixed, the quotations

I use here to illustrate them do not always come from respondents classified in the category being illustrated.

173 state farm worker: interview QN-5.
–middle-school student: QN-14.
–another student: XS-4.
–student, "big wind": QN-3.
–"we did not pay": QN-4.
–"internal" media system: Harald Richter, *Publishing in the People's Republic of China: Personal Observations by a Foreign Student* (Hamburg: Institut für Asienkunde, 1978), 38–47; NYT 1980.12.31.A3; interviews.

174 punishment for listening to foreign radio, and jamming: interviews.
–skeptical student: XS-3.
–farm worker: QN-6.
–state farm worker: QN-6.
–student who met tourists: XS-3.
–peasant from model brigade: NM-3.

175 importance of rumor: Miriam London and Ivan D. London, "China's 'Byroad' News Leaks: A New People's Channel," *Freedom at Issue*, No. 47 (September–October 1978): 9–12; Alan P. L. Liu, "Public Opinion in Communist China," paper prepared for Conference on Communication and Societal Integration in China, East-West Communication Institute, East-West Center, Honolulu, January 1–7, 1979, 24–35.
–"shall we shoot him down" story: GR-7.
–"transfer commanders" story: NM-4.

176 jokes: NM-4, GR-1, and other interviews.
–*Comrade Chiang Ch'ing:* Boston: Little, Brown; rumor: GR-7.
–Wang recruits women, "Little Zhang," and related stories: inter-

views; DXF 14: 16–17; DXF 15: 79; DXF 17: 69–71.

177 underground literature in general: Ding Wangyi, "Zhongguo dalu de dixia wenxue," *Huang He* Nos. 3, 4, 5 (April 25, 1977, September 1977, March 1978).
–*The Second Handshake:* E. Perry Link, Jr., *Mandarin Ducks and Butterflies: Popular Fiction in Early Twentieth-Century Chinese Cities* (Berkeley: University of California Press, 1981), 236–38.
–internal books: interviews; Miriam London and Mu Yang-jen, "What Are They Reading in China?" *Saturday Review* (September 30, 1978): 42–43.

178 Mao on *Reference News: Selected Works of Mao Tsetung* (Peking: Foreign Languages Press, 1961–77), V: 369.

179 warehouse worker: GR-8.
–interpretation of Japanese militarism: ZS-3.
–middle-school teacher on Zhou: ZS-4.

180 antiwar demonstrations: ZS-5, GR-7.
–worker on satellite: GR-1.
–sent-down youth: QN-10.
–Gang of Four and the media, in general: Central Document No. 37 of 1977 in *Issues and Studies* XIV: 9 (September 1978): 78–101.

181 Yao ruled *People's Daily:* RMRB 1978.1.12.2; 1978.3.21.2.
–"black should be red": *Chinese Literature* 10 (1978): 38.
–"China's Goebbels": RMRB 1976.11.20.3.
–evening papers: XWZX 1982.2.4.
–pretty girls: GMRB 1982.4.21.1.
–increased diversity of media content: W. J. F. Jenner, "1979: A New Start for Literature in

China," *China Quarterly* 86:
274–303; Marián Gálik, "Foreign
Literature in the People's Republic
of China Between 1970–1979,"
Asian and African Studies XIX
(1983): 55–95; Lee Yuet-lin,
"Changing Faces of China's
Press," *Asian Messenger* V:3 (Winter 1981): 32–35; Leonard Chu,
"Changing Faces of China's TV,"
Asian Messenger V:1–2 (Winter
1980–Spring 1981): 34–36.
181 *Futureworld*: NYT 1979.1.7.42.
   –music: David Holm, "The Difficulty of 'Walking on Two Legs':
Music Censorship in China,"
Index on Censorship XII:1 (February 1983): 34–37; *Enlightenment
Daily* 31 December 1981 in JPRS
80149: 105–6; BR 29 (1981): 28;
FBIS 19 November 1980, L17; *Red
Flag* 8 (1981) in JPRS 78358:
63–68.
   –science fiction: *Los Angeles Times*,
1982.2.19. Part I.1: 16–17.
   –*News Front* quotation: XWZX
1984.2.8.
182 Liu complaint: XWZX 1980.5.3.
   –Liu orders: XWZX 1980.5.9–10.
   –Cultural Revolution denunciation of Liu: Ding Wang, ed., *Zhongguo
dalu xinwenjie wenhua dageming
ciliao huibian* (Hong Kong: Zhong-
wen daxue, 1973), esp. 26–39 and
40–45.
   –142-year-old man: XWZX 1981.2.
12–13.
   –Bloomingdale's: XWZX 1982.5.3–5.
   –water control, drought: XWZX
1980.8.5.
   –statistics not necessarily true: WXZX
1981.3.21.
183 stories from officials inaccurate:
XWZX 1982.8.16–17.
   –"few isolated cases": XWZX 1980.
8.5.

   –*People's Daily* on some reporters:
FBIS 31 July 1979, L13.
   –journalism education: "Journalism
Education in China's Universities
since 1978," *Asian Messenger* VI:1
(Spring 1982): 61–68; James Aron-
son, "By Your Pupils You'll Be
Taught," *Columbia Journalism Review* (January 1980): 44–48.
   –"not naturalistic recording": XWZX
1983.10.6.
   –criticisms of stories: XWZX 1981.
9.31;1983.5.26–27; XWZX 1984.
2.32–33.
   –"reason propaganda can play a
role": RMRB 1980.1.4.5.
   –"rat droppings in soup": FBIS 26
November 1979, O11.
   –mass work departments: *People's
Daily* described by May Lipton,
press release dated 9/19/79, based
on a visit there, in visitors' reports
file, Starr East Asian Library, Columbia University; GMRB from an
interview with three of its editors,
Peking, March 15, 1984.
   –tens of thousands of letters: XWZX
1982.11.11; BR 20 (1981): 25.
   –popularity of investigation findings:
GMRB interview.
184 reporters harassed: e.g., RMRB
1979.12.1.3; RMRB 1980.4.13.4;
XWZX 1980.9.2–3; RMRB 1983.
3.23.8.
   –"Proper Rights of Correspondents": XWZX 1980.9.2.
   –photographer complains: GRMB
1982.10.17.4.
   –cadres used welfare fund: FBIS 26
February 1980, O7.
   –party official: FBIS 10 October
1979, L11–L12.
   –land sold off: RMRB 1981.3.17.1.
   –accountant harassed: GMRB
1981.11.2.1.
   –wood on bus: RMRB 1981.8.12.4;
XWZX 1981.9.11–13.

184 plea to end "paying special visits":
    RMRB 1984.3.31.5.
    –Hu appointed: FBIS 14 November
    1983, K1.
    –Hu speech: XWZX 1979.6.11,
    13–14.
185 *People's Daily* exposures of 1980:
    summarized in *Dongxiang* 24
    (1980): 17–18.
    –Ren Zhongyi statement: XWZX
    1981.1.8.
    –*People's Daily* defense: FBIS 17 No-
    vember 1980, L18.
186 last 1980 issue of *News Front*:
    XWZX 1980.12.11.
    –Document No. 7: never published,
    but can be partly reconstructed
    from a number of sources: *Dong-
    xiang* 30 (1981) in FBIS 19 March
    1981, U1–U3; interview ZS-2; *Red
    Flag* 23 (1981) in JPRS 79936:
    9–11; FBIS 13 February 1981,
    L8–L10; FBIS 23 October 1981,
    T1–T2.
    –Ren's criteria: XWZX 1984.4.5.
    –Mao's earlier statements: XWZX
    1983.12.2, 5, 6.
    –*People's Daily* editor: XWZX
    1983.9.12.
187 letter on goods in transit: FBIS 24
    May 1981, K14–K17.
    –returned intellectuals: RMRB
    1983.1.31.1; RMRB 1983.2.16.3;
    RMRB 1983.3.31.3.
    –pressure on Hunan University: FBIS
    17 May 1983, P3–P7.
    –criticism of Guangxi: FBIS 10 June
    1983, P3–P7.
    –*Mao's Harvest*: New York: Oxford
    University Press, 1983.
    –*Stubborn Weeds*: Bloomington: In-
    diana University Press, 1983.
    –Fourth National Congress: Howard
    Goldblatt, ed., *Chinese Literature
    for the 1980s: The Fourth Con-
    gress of Writers and Artists*

    (Armonk, N.Y.: M. E. Sharpe,
    Inc., 1982).
188 quotations from Document No. 7:
    Red Flag 23 (1981) in JPRS 79936:
    29–30.
    –Mao, Yanan Forum: *Selected
    Works*, III: 70.
    –"depicting reality": *Red Flag* 6
    (1981) in JPRS 77984: 51.
    –"sense of responsibility": FBIS 13
    July 1981, K9.
    –Zhou Yang on conscience: FBIS 5
    May 1981, K18.
    –*Fairytales in Spring*: among others,
    Guangzhou ribao 21 May 1982 in
    JPRS 81380: 80–83; FBIS 25 May
    1982, K7–K16; FBIS 26 May 1982,
    K1–K3.
    –"what is truthfulness?": FBIS 14
    January 1981, L11.
    –"facts are not literature": *Red Flag*
    4 (1980) in JPRS 75525: 69.
189 "truthfulness of typification": FBIS
    13 July 1981, K7.
    –inner essence: *Red Flag* 12 (1980)
    in FBIS 3 July 1980, L10–L11.
190 propaganda themes for festival:
    GMRB 1982.1.12.1.
    –five stresses found favor: FBIS 12
    January 1983, K4.
    –"Learn from Lei Feng Groups": BR
    14 (1982): 6.
    –"village pacts": RMRB 1982.3.29.1;
    RMRB 1982.4.7.1.; RMRB 1983.4.
    7.5.
    –diary: RMRB 1983.3.30.4.
    –Wangxi brigade: RMRB 1982.1.2.1.
191 rags to riches: RMRB 1981.7.3.1.
    –Fengyang: *China Daily* 1983.9.
    24.1.
    –Dazhai: FBIS 14 June 1983, K2–K3.
    –1982 reader survey: XWZX 1983.
    9.11; FBIS 31 January 1983,
    K13–K14; cf. XWZX 1984.9.13–14.
    –reader survey in Tianjin: XWZX
    1981.12.3.

191 *News Front* critique: XWZX
     1984.3.8–9.

CHAPTER 10

193 "concentrate the people's will": Xu
     Chongde and Pi Chunxie, *Xuanju
     zhidu wenda* (Peking: Qunzhong
     chubanshe, 1980), 168–69.
194 "people enjoy supreme power":
     Hongqi 17 (1980): 9.
     –numbers of administrative units: BR
     20 (1978): 22–23; number of
     county-level congresses is given in
     many press reports of the elections,
     e.g., RMRB 1981.1.13.1.
     –Organic Law: FBIS 27 July 1979,
     Supplement 019, 1–12.
     –Soviet participation statistics: based
     on Everett M. Jacobs, "Soviet
     Local Elections: What They Are,
     and What They Are Not," *Soviet
     Studies* XXII:1 (July 1970): 62, 68.
     –"one-eighth of his existence": Ron-
     ald J. Hill, "The CPSU in a Soviet
     Election Campaign," *Soviet Stud-
     ies* XXVIII:4 (October 1976): 590.
     –election-day atmosphere: Max E.
     Mote, *Soviet Local and Republic
     Elections: A Description of the
     1963 Elections in Leningrad Based
     on Official Documents, Press Ac-
     counts, and Private Interviews*
     (Stanford, Calif.: Hoover Institu-
     tion, 1965).
195 absentees and negative voters:
     Jerome M. Gilison, "Soviet Elec-
     tions as a Measure of Dissent: The
     Missing One Percent," *American
     Political Science Review* LXII:3
     (September 1968): 820–22.
     –function of elections in communist
     states: Guy Hermet, Richard Rose,
     and Alain Rouquié, eds., *Elections
     Without Choice* (New York: John
     Wiley and Sons, 1978).
     –Soviet-style elections beginning
     late 1920s: James Pinckney Harri-

son, *The Long March to Power: A
     History of the Chinese Commu-
     nist Party, 1921–72* (New
     York: Praeger, 1972), 203 and
     elsewhere.
     –1953 election law: Theodore H. E.
     Chen, ed., *The Chinese Commu-
     nist Regime: Documents and Com-
     mentary* (New York: Frederick A.
     Praeger, 1967), 65–75.
     –congress elections to 1978: Xu and
     Pi, *Xuanju zhidu*, 16–34; James R.
     Townsend, *Political Participation
     in Communist China*, new ed.
     (Berkeley: University of California
     Press, 1969), 115.
     –meetings of NPC: John L. Scherer,
     ed., *China Facts and Figures An-
     nual, Volume I, 1978* (Gulf
     Breeze, Fla.: Academic Interna-
     tional Press, 1978), 19–20.
     –letter to editor: RMRB 1979.1.1.6.
     –electoral law: FBIS, 27 July 1979,
     Supplement 019, 12–19; Chinese
     text in Xu and Pi, *Xuanju zhidu*,
     174–82.
196 20 million cadres: this figure is ex-
     trapolated from Cheng Zihua's re-
     port of September 3, 1981, to the
     NPC Standing Committee, in FBIS
     14 September 1981, K3. Cheng
     says that over 10 million cadres
     were trained in 15 provincial-level
     units. China has twenty-nine such
     units.
     –*Questions and Answers*: Xu and Pi,
     Xuanju zhidu.
     –detailed directives: referred to, for
     example, in FBIS 4 March 1983,
     K5–K7.
     –elections will educate masses, etc.:
     Shanxi ribao 26 December 1981 in
     JPRS 80332: 43–53.
     –party officials responsible: Xu and
     Pi, *Xuanju zhidu*, 172.
197 "democratic centralism": Xu and
     Pi, *Xuanju zhidu*, 105.

197 election commission: Xu and Pi,
Xuanju zhidu, 75.

–roles of first party secretary: Xu
and Pi, *Xuanju zhidu*, 75; BR 8
(1980): 13, for an example.

–role of public security personnel:
Xu and Pi, *Xuanju zhidu*, 167.

–precinct drawing in general: Xu
and Pi, *Xuanju zhidu*, 77–78.

–county populations and congress
sizes: State Statistical Bureau,
comp., *Statistical Yearbook of
China*, 1981 (*English Edition*)
(Hong Kong: Economic Information and Agency [*sic*], 1982), 91;
FBIS 14 September 1981, K5.

–one deputy per 1,200 persons: FBIS
14 September 1981, K5.

–proletariat more progressive: Xu
and Pi, *Xuanju zhidu*, 64–65.

–election offices and voters' groups:
Xu and Pi, *Xuanju zhidu*, 75; BR 8
(1980): 14.

198 importance of voter registration:
Xu and Pi, *Xuanju zhidu*, 83.

–Tianjin county: *Tianjin ribao* 17
March 1980 in JPRS 75825: 68.

–99.9 percent registered: BR 50
(1982): 13.

–"The broad masses . . . ," "broad
and deep": Xu and Pi, *Xuanju
zhidu*, 88–89.

199 nomination process: Xu and Pi,
Xuanju zhidu, 89–91.

–press reports on numbers of candidates: FBIS 6 November 1980, R1;
FBIS 16 November 1979, R1; RMRB
1980.8.4.1; BR 8 (1980): 16.

–cadres resist competition: Xu and
Pi, *Xuanju zhidu*, 89–91, 103–5;
FBIS 9 September 1980, S5.

–defense of multicandidate system:
Xu and Pi, *Xuanju zhidu*, 90, 104.

200 "advanced" and "broad": Xu and
Pi, *Xuanju zhidu*, 96.

–three steps to achieve mix of candidates: FBIS 14 September 1981, K4.

–primary election: Xu and Pi,
Xuanju zhidu, 106–7.

201 Wu Jianqing biography: BR 8
(1980): 17.

–"candidates should express": Xu
and Pi, *Xuanju zhidu*, 112.

–comparison with bourgeois election: Xu and Pi, *Xuanju zhidu*,
114.

–polling places described: BR 8
(1980): 19; RMRB 1980.8.4.1.

–voting procedures: Xu and Pi,
Xuanju zhidu, 18–25.

202 illiteracy rate: BR 45 (1982): 20.

–1953 turnout: Xu and Pi, *Xuanju
zhidu*, 32.

–model turnouts: e.g., BR 8 (1980):
19; RMRB 1980.8.4.1.

–national turnout 1979–81: FBIS 14
September 1981, K6.

–determining outcome: Xu and Pi,
Xuanju zhidu, 126–32.

203 functions of deputies: Xu and Pi,
Xuanju zhidu, 137–45; for examples of deputies performing them,
see RMRB 1981.1.18.3; RMRB
1981.4.8.1; RMRB 1982.11.22.3; BR
5 (1982): 13–19, 21.

–phasing of the elections (sources
not separately cited below): FBIS 3
January 1980, L2–L3; FBIS 29 Jan-
uary 1980, P1; FBIS 5 March 1980,
L17–L18; FBIS 6 June 1980,
O2–O3, S1; FBIS 27 June 1980, L6;
FBIS 19 November 1980, O1,
R1–R2; FBIS 13 January 1981, L11;
BR 28 (1980): 4; BR 6 (1981): 7;
RMRB 1981.1.13.1; *Faxue yanjiu* 2
(1980) in JPRS 76527: 6–13; Zheng
Yushuo, "Zhongguo guojia jianshe
yu xuanju fa," Part 2, *Ming bao
yuekan* 192 (1981): 30–36.

–Cheng Zihua's background: Don-
ald W. Klein and Anne B. Clark,
*Biographic Dictionary of Chinese
Communism 1921–1965* (Cambridge, Mass.: Harvard University

Press, 1971), I: 155–58.
203 Cheng's August announcement:
RMRB 1980.8.4.1; FBIS 4 August
1980, L9–L12.
204 *People's Daily* in support: FBIS 26
August 1980, L13.
–*Red Flag*, "some comrades," disruption from below: *Hongqi* 17
(1980): 11, 4.
–Cheng on "ultraindividualists":
FBIS 10 March 1981, L6.
–student and worker unrest, Polish
influence, in 1980: FBIS 22 January
1981, U3; *Zhengming* 40 (1981) in
JPRS 77590: 5–7; AFP in FBIS 3
March 1981, R1; AFP in FBIS 4
March 1981, L8; AFP in FBIS 20
March 1981, L1–L2; *Qishi niandai*
135 (1981) in FBIS 16 April 1981,
W1–W10; *Shiyue pinglun* 11
(1982): 45–49.
205 *People's Road* reports on Fudan:
Guanchajia 33 (1980): 12.
–observers: interview O-8.
–Fu Shenqi quotation: *Minzhu zhi
sheng* No. 9 (1980): 7 (Xin Hua is
Fu Shenqi).
–another democrat quotation: *Zeren*
No. 3 (1981), in Hong Kong reprint edition of Nos. 1–3 issued by
Zhongguo minzhu yundong ziliao
zhongxin (1981), 67.
–Fu on laws, elections, periodicals:
Minzhu zhi sheng No. 9 (1980):
7–8.
–draft publications law: *Zeren* No.
3 (1981), Hong Kong edition,
54–57.
–circulation of draft: e.g., *Minzhu
zhuan* special number (1981.1.16)
in DXF 26: 25; *Zeren* No. 3 (1981),
Hong Kong edition, 67; *Monthly
Bulletin on the Chinese Democratic Movement* (Hong Kong) I: 3
(April 1981): 27, 30.
206 Wuhan University bulletin:
Monthly Bulletin on the Chinese

Democratic Movement I: 3 (April
1981): 26.
–boldest vision of optimists: interview.
–Xu view: *Qishi niandai* 133 (1981):
50–51.
–Hu Ping quotation: *Minzhu zhi
sheng* No. 9 (1980): 13.
–Peking University poll: *Guanchajia*
40 (1981): 21. A translation is in
JPRS 78012.
207 *Red Flag* quotation: No. 17 (1982)
in JPRS 82121: 47, 50.
–college enrollment in 1980: BR 20
(1981): 18.
–1977 and 1978 exam figures: BR 31
(1978): 4–5.
–80 percent party or youth league
members: this is as of 1981; FBIS
14 December 1981, K16.
–sources on Peking University elections: *Guanchajia* 40 (1981):
20–26; BR 18 (1983): 20; DXF 27:
18; *Qishi niandai* 133 (1981):
15–20; *Zhengming* 39 (1981):
42–43; *Le Monde* 6 December
1980 in JPRS 77288: 19–20; *Los
Angeles Times* 1980.12.15.1, 20;
Anita Rind, "To Be a Feminist in
Beijing," in Gregor Benton, ed.,
*Wild Lilies, Poisonous Weeds: Dis-
sident Voices from People's China*
(London: Pluto Press, 1982),
195–201; *Baixing* 5 (1981): 14–15;
Minzhu zhi sheng No. 9 (1980):
10–17; *Zeren* No. 3 (1981), Hong
Kong edition, 54–57, 61–63; *Zeren*
No. 5 (1981): 12; interviews.
209 Hunan Teacher's College election
(sources not separately cited
below): *Qishi niandai* 9 (1981) in
JPRS 79239: 60–64; *Guanchajia* 38
(1980): 16–18; *Minzhu zhi sheng*
No. 8 (1980): 18–21 and 9 (1980):
18–23; *Zeren* No. 2 (1980), Hong
Kong edition, 26; "The Student
Movement in Hunan," abridged

from *Minzhu zhi sheng* No. 6, in
Benton, ed., *Wild Lilies*, 106–11;
interviews.

209 Mao Zhiyong as Hua supporter:
Ming bao 23 February 1983 in FBIS
25 February 1983, W1–W2.

–nationally known for stories: see
Chinese Literature (January 1983):
5–6.

–Tao Sen's personal history, campaign statement, platform: drawn
from an untitled campaign document dated 1980.9.23, photocopy
in my possession.

211 *Son of the Revolution:* New York:
Alfred A. Knopf, 1983.

212 colloquies at political rallies: drawn
from tape recordings of forums that
occurred approximately September
24 and 25.

–Tao Sen's conversation with Su
Ming and others: interview.

213 Liang Heng's reply: "Gao xuanmin
shu," no date, approximately
1980.9.24, photocopy in my possession.

214 *Heart's Light:* photocopy, no date.

216 "Letter to the People of the City":
Shiyueh pinglun 49 (1981): 13.

–Butterfield story: NYT 1980.
10.15.A5; see also NYT 1980.
10.17.A9.

–Wang Zhen's background: "Wang
Chen—Member of the CCPCC
Politburo," *Issues and Studies* XV:
4 (April 1979): 92–98.

217 Tao Sen comment on end of hunger strike: *Zeren* 2 (1980), Hong
Kong edition, 26–27.

218 national election office opinion:
Zhongguo minzhu yundong I: 5
(May 1981): 8–9.

219 sources on Shanghai Generator
Factory election: DXF 20: 4–9 and
23: 37; *Guanchajia* 3 (1980):
13–14; *Baixing* 2 (1981): 53; Fu
Shenqi, "In Memory of Wang

Shenyou, Pioneer of the Democratic Movement, Teacher, Comrade," in Benton, ed., *Wild Lilies*,
122–27; interviews.

–Fu as Xin Hua: *Baixing* 3 (1981):
27; interview.

–Fu on role of people's movement:
Xueyou tongxun No. 5 (1980), reprinted in *Xin shehui* (October
1980): 144–54.

220 Qinghua University election: RMRB
1981.2.1.1.

–Guizhou University: *Gonghe bao*
No. 5 (1980): 1–2.

–Shandong Teachers College:
*Monthly Bulletin on the Chinese
Democratic Movement* I:3 (April
1981): 27.

–Zhejiang University: Ibid.

–Shaoguan factory: *Baixing* 2
(1980): 53; *Zeren* No. 3 (1981),
Hong Kong edition, 65.

–Qingdao: interview. The candidate
was Sun Feng, editor of *Sea Spray.*

–Zhaoyang: *Zeren* No. 3 (1981),
Hong Kong edition, 65. Also cf.
NYT 1979.11.7.A12.

–Qingyuan: *Zeren* No. 3 (1981),
Hong Kong edition, 65–67; also see
DXF 26: 22–24, 26.

–Peking West District: *Zeren* No. 3
(1981), Hong Kong edition, 69–72.

–Wuhan University unusual activity:
*Monthly Bulletin on the Chinese
Democratic Movement* I: 3 (April
1981): 26.

–People's University: NYT 1980.
11.29.2; *Los Angeles Times*
1980.12.15.1, 20.

–rural Shanghai: FBIS 2 June 1980,
O4.

–Cheng's September 1981 report:
FBIS 14 September 1981, K2.

221 Deng December 25 speech: *Ming
bao* 6 May 1981, in FBIS 6 May
1981, W2.

–Document No. 9: never published,

but described in, e.g., DXF 28: 65,
and many other Hong Kong publications.

221 Hu Qiaomu quotation: *Red Flag*
23 (1981) in JPRS 79936: 17.
–April 1981 arrests: FBIS 6 April
1981, K3; *Qishi niandai* 2 (1982)
in JPRS 80367: 41.
–fifty or so total arrests: U.S. Department of State, *Country Reports
on Human Rights Practices for
1981*, Report submitted to the
Committee on Foreign Affairs,
U.S. House of Representatives, and
the Committee on Foreign Relations, U.S. Senate (February 1982),
566.
–who was arrested and their fate: *Le
Monde* in FBIS 17 July 1981, K1;
DXF 29 (1981) in JPRS 79320:
49–51; *Shiyue pinglun* 64 (1982):
4–9; *Monthly Bulletin on the Chinese Democratic Movement* I: 6, 7
(July, August, 1981); Amnesty International, "List of Prisoners of
Conscience and Persons Reported
Held on Political Grounds," Appendix to the Memorandum submitted by Amnesty International to
the Government of the People's
Republic of China, January 1983,
17 pp.
–graduates needed in remote areas:
FBIS 1 October 1981, K12–K13;
also see FBIS 28 June 1982,
K16–K17.

222 political screening: e.g., FBIS 13
May 1980, L2–L5; FBIS 22
January 1981, L5; FBIS 12 April
1982, K11–K13; RMRB
1983.3.17.3.
–Deng on ideological and political
work: *Ming bao* 4 May 1981 in
FBIS 4 May 1981, W6–W7.
–study campaign at Qinghua: RMRB
1981.2.1.1.
–Peking University charges and

warnings: *Shiyue pinglun* 52/53
(1981): 87; NHK television in FBIS
23 March 1981, L20.
–closing of *Red Bean: Zhengming* 5
(1981) in JPRS 78312: 62.
–lists of foreign periodicals: DXF 27:
47.
–annual appraisal program: FBIS 6
April 1982, K4–K5.
–ideological and political work
stepped up: NYT 1981.2.3.A3; FBIS
21 January 1983, K1–K4.
–Five Stresses and Four Beauties
campaign: e.g., BR 15 (1981): 5.
–Cheng Zihua final report: FBIS 14
September 1981, K2–K10.
–Standing Committee approval: FBIS
14 September 1981, K2.
–revised election law: FBIS 17 December 1982, K14–K21; quotation
from article 30 corrected in accordance with Chinese text in RMRB
1982.12.16.3; explanation of revi-
sion: FBIS 21 December 1982, K8.
–1984 elections: see, e.g., RMRB
1984.5.14.1 and numerous reports
in FBIS throughout January–May,
1984.

CONCLUSION

224 Deng's August 18, 1980, speech:
BR 40 (1983): 14–22; BR 41 (1983):
18–22.

226 Western democratic theory: Joseph
A. Schumpeter, *Capitalism, Socialism, and Democracy*, 3d ed., paperback ed. (New York: Harper &
Row, 1962), 269; John Plamenatz,
*Democracy and Illusion: An Exam-
ination of Certain Aspects of Modern Democratic Theory*, paperback
ed. (London: Longman, 1977), 98,
184–85; Robert A. Dahl, *A Preface
to Democratic Theory*, paperback
ed. (Chicago: University of Chicago Press, 1963), 132.

226 pluralist democracy criticized: e.g.,
Carole Pateman, *Participation and
Democratic Theory*, paperback ed.
(Cambridge: Cambridge University
Press, 1970); Peter Bachrach, *The
Theory of Democratic Elitism: A
Critique*, paperback ed. (Boston:
Little, Brown and Company,
1967); Sidney Verba, Norman H.
Nie, and Jae-on Kim, *Participation
and Political Equality: A Seven-
Nation Comparison*, paperback ed.
(Cambridge: Cambridge University
Press, 1978).

227 distinction between participation
and influence: see, among others,
Andrew S. McFarland, *Power and
Leadership in Pluralist Systems*
(Stanford, Calif.: Stanford Univer-
sity Press, 1969); Joseph LaPalom-
bara, "Political Participation as an
Analytical Concept in Comparative
Politics," in Sidney Verba and Lu-
cian W. Pye, eds., *The Citizen and
Politics: A Comparative Perspec-
tive* (Stamford, Conn.: Greylock
Publishers, 1978), 167–94.

228 "mature" dictatorship, pluralism in
Soviet Union and Eastern Europe:
see, among others, Chalmers John-
son, ed., *Change in Communist
Systems*, paperback ed. (Stanford,
Calif.: Stanford University Press,
1970); H. Gordon Skilling and
Franklyn Griffiths, *Interest Groups
in Soviet Politics*, paperback ed.
(Princeton: Princeton University
Press, 1971).

230 Fu Yuehua: *China: Violations of
Human Rights: Prisoners of Con-
science and the Death Penalty in
the People's Republic of China*
(London: Amnesty International
Publications, 1984), 23.
–Liu Qing incident: "Prison Mem-
oirs," in *Chinese Sociology and
Anthropology* XV: 1–2

(Fall–Winter 1982–83); *Le Monde*
in FBIS 17 November 1982, K3;
Zhengming 9 (1982) in JPRS
82127: 37.
–sentences of Xu Wenli, Wang
Xizhe, He Qiu: *Shiyue pinglun* 71
(1982): 49–50; AFP in FBIS 11 June
1982, K2.
–1983 arrests: interviews; U.S. Department of State, *Country Reports
on Human Rights Practices for
1983*, report submitted to the
Committee on Foreign Affairs,
U.S. House of Representatives, and
Committee on Foreign Relations,
U.S. Senate (February 1984),
741–42. Those known by name are
listed in "List of Prisoners of Conscience and Persons Reported Held
on Political Grounds," Appendix
to the Memorandum Submitted by
Amnesty International to the Government of the People's Republic
of China, January 1983, 17 pp.
–Wei Jingsheng in solitary: Amnesty
International Urgent Action circular ASA 17/04/84, dated 1 June
1984.
–Ren Wanding freed: *Le Monde*,
1983.11.30.7.
–speculation on prospect of Polish-
style uprising: *Zhengming* 40
(1981) in JPRS 77590: 5–7;
Zhengming 9 (1982) in JPRS 82127:
43; interviews.
–hope for natural evolution: interviews; see also *Zhongguo zhi chun*
13 (June–July 1984): 3.

231 possible press law: FBIS 24 May
1984, K13.
–*China Spring* (*Zhongguo zhi
chun*): interviews with Dr. Wang
and other members of the movement; extensive coverage in New
York and Hong Kong Chinese-language press; and issues of *China
Spring*.

231 first international conference and
claims of movement's success:
No. 10 (February 1984).

232 Confucius, "virtue": *Analects*,
Book VII, Ch. 29.

APPENDIX

235 émigré interviewing as a tool of re-
search: see, among others,
Jerome Alan Cohen, "Interviewing
Chinese Refugees: Indispensable
Aid to Legal Research on China,"
in Cohen, ed., *Contemporary Chi-
nese Law: Research Problems and
Prospects* (Cambridge, Mass.: Har-
vard University Press, 1970),
84–117; William L. Parish and
Martin King Whyte, *Village and
Family in Contemporary China*
(Chicago: University of Chicago
Press, 1978), 339–51; Martin King
Whyte, *Small Groups and Political
Rituals in China* (Berkeley, Calif.:
University of California Press,
1974), 237–47.
–emigration figures: *Asia Yearbook
1982* (Hong Kong: Far Eastern
Economic Review, 1981), 148;
John L. Scherer, ed., *China Facts
and Figures Annual, Volume I,
1978* (Gulf Breeze, Fla.: Academic
International Press, 1978), 255–56;
U.S. Department of State, *Country
Reports on Human Rights Prac-
tices for 1982*, Report Submitted to
the Committee on Foreign Relations, U.S. Senate, and Committee

on Foreign Affairs, U.S. House of
Representatives (February 1983),
685.

239 informants secretly assigned: interviews; cf. Stephen Mosher, *Broken
Earth: The Rural Chinese* (New
York: The Free Press, 1983), 309.
–five-point guideline for intercourse
with foreigners: published in *Shishi
ziliao shouce* (1982 *nianbian*) (Peking: Xinhua chubanshe, 1983),
79.

242 polls in USSR and Eastern Europe:
see, e.g., Walter D. Connor and
Zvi Gitelman with Adaline
Huszczo and Robert Blumstock,
*Public Opinion in European So-
cialist Systems* (New York: Praeger,
1977); Ellen Propper Mickiewicz,
Media and the Russian Public
(New York: Praeger, 1981).
–generalizing from subgroups in interview population to subgroups in
parent population: see Alex Inkeles,
Raymond A. Bauer, et al., *The Soviet Citizen: Daily Life in a Totalitarian Society* (Cambridge, Mass.:
Harvard University Press, 1959),
21.

247 research by Burns on elections:
John P. Burns, *Political Participation in Rural China*, book manu-
script.
–*The Civic Culture*: Princeton, N.J.:
Princeton University Press, 1963;
abridged ed. (Boston: Little, Brown
and Company, 1965), 70, 72, 137,
141, 142, 169–70, 281.

INDEX